S0-GGO-043

The "Venerable Dean," Dr. Geo. W. Hubbard, of Meharry Medical College, now entering upon his 52d year of educational work among the colored people of the South.

AMERICAN CIVILIZATION AND THE NEGRO

THE AFRO-AMERICAN IN RELATION TO NATIONAL PROGRESS

BY

C. V. ROMAN, A.M., M.D., LL.D.

EDITOR OF THE JOURNAL OF THE NATIONAL MEDICAL ASSOCIATION; PROFESSOR OF DISEASES OF THE EYE, EAR, NOSE AND THROAT IN MEHARRY MEDICAL COLLEGE, NASHVILLE, TENN.; MEMBER OF THE AMERICAN ACADEMY OF POLITICAL AND SOCIAL SCIENCES; MEMBER OF SOUTHERN SOCIOLOGICAL CONGRESS; MEMBER TENNESSEE CONFERENCE OF CHARITIES AND CORRECTIONS; EX-PRESIDENT NATIONAL MEDICAL ASSOCIATION

"Slowly but surely we are coming together ... The pathetic melody of the Negro spirituals, the brave and rollicking strains of 'Dixie,' and the triumphant harmony of the 'Star Spangled Banner,' blend and interweave in the symphony of 'America.'"

GEO. S. MERRIAM, "The Negro and the Nation."

Illustrated with Half-tone Engravings.

PHILADELPHIA
F. A. DAVIS COMPANY, PUBLISHERS
1916

Philadelphia, Pa., U. S. A.
Press of F. A. Davis Company
1914-16 Cherry Street

TO THOSE TRUE FRIENDS OF HUMANITY WHO BELIEVE THAT ALL MEN HAVE AN EQUAL RIGHT TO LIFE, LIBERTY, AND THE PURSUIT OF HAPPINESS:

TO ALL WHO DREAM THE DREAM OF TRUE DEMOCRACY, AND LAST, BUT NOT LEAST:

TO MY MOTHER, WHOSE WISE SYMPATHY AND KINDLY ENCOURAGEMENT MADE POSSIBLE WHATEVER GOOD I MAY BE ABLE TO ACCOMPLISH IN THIS WORLD,

THIS VOLUME IS DEDICATED

BY

THE AUTHOR.

PREFACE.

If Job were an American Negro today he would have no occasion to voice the desire that his adversary should write a book; rather would he lament with the preacher, "Of making many books there is no end."

The problems herein presented have occupied my attention for many years. I have at various times written and spoken upon the different phases of the subject discussed in this book. Where this material represents my present views, I have drawn freely upon it.

This book is written without bitterness and without bias. The author aims to show that humanity is one in vices and virtues as well as blood; that the laws of evolution and progress apply equally to all; that there are no lethal diseases peculiar to the American Negro; that there are no debasing vices peculiar to the African; that there are no cardinal virtues peculiar to the European; that we are *all* sinners and have come short of the glories of civilization. Hence, one should be careful to hear all the available evidence before giving judgment, especially when that judgment involves the welfare of a people.

On behalf of the American people of African descent I ask, in the name of *justice,* for a full examination of the contents of this volume.

"He that answereth a matter before he heareth it, it is folly and shame unto him."

The value of a book, certainly its readable interest, may depend as much upon method as upon matter. It will assist the reader, then, if at the beginning he may gain an idea of both.

While presenting a continuous argument, the individual chapters are sufficiently complete in themselves to stand a separate reading. So with the Introduction and the different parts of the Appendix.

The method of treatment and the nature of the subject have entailed occasional repetition of facts and arguments, which it is hoped may prove a convenience to the reader.

The Introduction is a statement of general principles, forecasting the argument and evidence to follow.

Chapter I is devoted to a zoölogical examination of man as an inhabitant of this world—just as we might study the lion or elephant.

In Chapter II are discussed the forces with which man must struggle, and how he treats his fellow-man in that struggle.

Chapter III shows that without exception there is a great deal of difference in the separate individuals composing the different races of mankind.

Chapter IV is devoted to morals. The subject is continued from another angle in Chapter V; while some general principles of human development are discussed in Chapter VI.

Chapter VII reviews the question of Negro slavery in America.

In Chapter VIII we reach the crucial point in our study,—the presence of the colored man in the South and the effect of such presence.

Chapter IX is a frank statement of what the colored man expects of the white man, and Chapter X offers a practical solution of our ethnic puzzle.

Chapter XI shows the value of testimony is frequently dependent upon the character of the witness.

Chapter XII is an historical review of the political activity of the colored man and a forecast of his future intentions.

Chapter XIII is a scientific discussion of racial differences in form, function, and thought.

Chapter XIV shows that the colored man is reacting successfully to the American environment.

Chapter XV is a summary and conclusion.

The Appendix contains interesting and valuable evidential items not suitable for introduction into the body of the argument.

I am especially grateful to the many persons who so kindly responded to the requests for information or assistance in gathering data.

That this volume may increase *racial self-respect* and *diminish racial antagonism* is the sincere wish of

THE AUTHOR.

NASHVILLE, TENN.

Chapter IX is a frank statement of what the [illegible] and other [illegible] of the [illegible], and Chapter X gives a practical [illegible].

Chapter XI shows the [illegible] of [illegible] clearly demonstrates [illegible] the [illegible] of the [illegible] and [illegible].

Chapter XII is a [illegible].

[illegible] the American [illegible].

Chapter [illegible].

The Appendix [illegible] evidential [illegible] body of the [illegible].

[illegible]

[illegible]

CONTENTS.

LIST OF ILLUSTRATIONS.

"The Acid Test.—The Declaration of Independence furnishes an infallible test for every important public measure. However plausible the argument in its favor, no governmental policy can be right which is not strictly in accord with the doctrine that all men have equal rights to life, liberty, and the pursuit of happiness. That is the test which cannot be safely undergone by any of the laws or policies conferring privileges, limiting suffrage, or tending to interfere with the individual's right to freedom of action limited only by the equal rights of others."

Samuel Danziger.

The Public,
July 2, 1915.

INTRODUCTION.

ONE of the oldest and meanest of human follies is to blame one's short-comings upon others. The black man is not to blame for the white man's short-comings, nor is he a menace to the white man's civilization; neither is the white man to blame for all of the black man's woes, nor is he the only bar to the black man's progress. The most serious problem confronting each race now is the conquering of its own follies. Abusing each other only complicates the situation and helps nobody. The virulence of syphilis was not lessened by the English calling it French pox, and the French calling it Russian disease, and the Russians calling it English disease; or by the Germans saying it came from Italy, and the Italians saying it came from Spain, and the Spanish saying it came from the American Indians. All of this accusation contributed not one whit to the prevention or cure of that vile tax on human depravity. But vituperation ceased and effective remedies followed dispassionate and impartial investigation. So the vexed race question will disappear in the wider problems of human justice and human welfare.

Humanity is greater than race. It is said that Napoleon lost the Battle of Waterloo because he misunderstood the topography of the region over which his cavalry had to pass in their charge against the allied armies under Wellington. Ignoring a sunken road precipitated a series of reverses that ended ignominiously the martial career of the First Napoleon and eclipsed forever his star of world-wide conquest.

The careers of nations are typified in the careers of individuals. The Caucasian is the conquering war-lord among nations, and seems destined to rule the world. There is, however, a chasm in his path, whose depths and dangers he seems unable to appreciate. It is *color prejudice,*—the effort to substitute *race* for *merit* in measuring men.

Modern civilization will go the way of Sodom and Gomorrah unless justice and fraternity can obtain a firmer hold on the hearts and brains of men. No civilization can become world-wide and enduring if a white skin is the indispensable passport to justice and distinction. This would exclude from the fruits of civilization the majority of mankind.

The laboring white man is dwelling in a fool's paradise if he expects to find justice and fair play for himself while assisting in denying them to the laboring black man. Human experience and the laws of nature are both against his expectations.

Justice and liberty are for all or for none. Injustice cannot linger in a land that is really "bright with freedom's holy light."

No tyrant was ever free. No man is secure in his rights so long as any man is deprived of his rights. It is easier to be generous than to be just. Man's hope of justice has ever been an idle dream, and his quest for liberty a fool's errand; because he is not willing to be just, nor to meet the conditions of freedom.

As to the ultimate future of the races in this country, *no one knows what it will be;* and it is not profitable to speculate. Ultimate problems belong not to science, but to religion and philosophy. Common sense says: "Do right and be just in the present; this will prepare you for the future when it becomes the present."

The inhabitants of the South are geographically one people, but ethnically two races. All practical propositions for betterment must assume the permanency of this condition. It is wiser, therefore, that they respect each other and co-operate for the common good, marching in separate regiments, but solid phalanx, to the music of civilization. *Racial integrity and interracial confidence and respect are now the wise course.*

The writer of this volume believes that the differences in mankind are the differences between charcoal and diamond—difference of *condition* and not of *composition.* Quatrefages is right: there is but one species of man. St. Paul is right: men are of one blood. Religion and science agree in prescribing the same treatment for all—*intelligence, mercy,* and *justice.* All races of men are capable of the same virtues and susceptible to the same vices.

The opposition to this doctrine springs from hatred and error—the twin children of misinformation and inexperience, whose devotees not only dislike and mistrust their fellow-men, but dislike the very idea of justice and fair play. They not only claim that they are right, but wish to make everybody else conform to their views. They dislike people who hold dissenting opinions. Hence arise persecutions, which always spring from ignorance and hate, and not from love and knowledge as the persecutors claim.

The incompatibilities of races are psychological and not physiological; a conflict of cultural interests and beliefs rather than an antagonism of physical lineament and chemical content of blood. The great European War illustrates one phase of this proposition, and the numerous mixed progeny of the white man's contact with every race on earth illustrates the other.

It is with deepest regret that the author uncovers the cess-pools of human depravity exposed in some chapters of this work. It is only the "damnable iterations" of prejudice and injustice that make this unpleasant task necessary. The half-scientific rubbish and historical mendacity that seek to parade sexual excesses and moral delinquencies as peculiar racial vices are a travesty upon learning, a perversion of justice, and a degradation of human reason. There is nothing in the way of personal virtue that savage man is not capable of; and there is nothing in the way of viciousness that civilized man is not guilty of.

For filth, moral and physical; for cruelty, heartless and brutal; for venery, homosexual and heterosexual; for orgies, bestial and abandoned; for the degradation of women and the perversion of animal instinct; for all that is worst in the human animal; go not among the heathen denizens of darkest Africa, but among the civilized inhabitants of our city slums.

That men of scientific training and historic and social knowledge should be willing to pervert their talents and retard human progress by leading the superficial and thoughtless to believe that culture may be measured by *color* and morals limned by *race,* is a sad phase of "man's inhumanity to man," and a woeful example of the determination of some people to make a noise regardless of the canons of truth.

The variations in the different races are just about the same; that is, the difference between the lowest colored man and the highest colored man is just as great as from the lowest white man to the highest white man. Cettiwayo was as supreme over his command when he annihilated the British regiment as was Cæsar when he overcame the Nervii.

Someone has said that lies are of three kinds; plain lies, d——d lies, and statistics. The assertion that all colored people are alike in intellectuality and moral stamina partakes of all the elements of this triplicate form of mendacity. Even horses, cattle, and dogs vary in intelligence, affection, and appetite; as any observing farmer, dairyman, or dog fancier can tell you. The poet has said that

> "Error, wounded,
> Writhes in pain and dies amid her worshippers."

But here is an ethnological "error" that seemingly "age cannot wither, nor custom stale its infinite variety."

Though contrary alike to science, common sense, and daily experience, it is foisted upon the public as the pure gold of truth in the currency of argument on the race question.

In this work an effort will be made to administer a lethal dose of truth to this hoary old falsehood.

Judgments are either *problematic, assertory,* or *apodictic.* Problematic or contingent judgments are usually sufficiently obvious to be recognized at their true value, and hence give little trouble to the honest and intelligent thinker. But not so with the other two. The average person, while recognizing readily enough a *guess,* hopelessly confuses *facts* with *opinions.*

"Assertory judgments are true and certain subjectively but not objectively; that is, sure to him who holds them, but incapable of being enforced on the acceptance of others of a different moral disposition." In these judgments men of equal intelligence and honesty often differ. This, and not dishonesty or self-interest, is the usual explanation of the majority decisions of our higher courts. Misunderstanding rather than meanness makes men unjust.

"Apodictic or demonstrative judgments are subjectively and objectively sure and capable of being enforced upon all of sane mind, who can be made to understand them." In these judgments all sane people of equal intelligence and honesty reach the same conclusions.

Apodictic judgments are, therefore, proper subjects for exposition, illustration, or demonstration; depending for their acceptance upon intrinsic merit, the character of the witness presenting them being of no importance whatever. *They are facts.*

On the other hand, the accuracy of assertory judgments depends upon the mental processes of the individual rendering them. *They are opinions.* Here the character of the witness becomes of extremest importance. In this class of testimony, then, other things being equal, disinterested or altruistic witnesses are the most reliable, and self-interested or partisan witnesses are the least reliable.

The conclusions of ethnology are largely assertory; hence, to arrive at the truth, we eliminate the palpably false and self-serving witnesses and accept, what the lawyers call, the *preponderance of evidence.*

The facts of history and the preponderance of civilized opinion are on the side of the propositions which are amplified with proof in the succeeding chapters of this book.

In the interest of scientific impartiality, the author has introduced certain testimony in the exact language of the original sources.

This is not a statistical compilation of racial achievements and possessions, but an inquiry into racial traits, tendencies, and capabilities—an effort to examine basic facts, and not an attempt to compile details.

There is a tendency to obscure fundamental principles by accumulating a number of pleasant but incidental and uninteresting details. We deny to men the right of making a living and try to cover up the unpleasant matter by showing how often we have given a dinner to a hungry man. Thus, a visitor to any one of several large Southern cities, inquiring into the workings of the double-school system, would be told a great deal about what is being done for the colored people in an educational way,[1] and maybe shown some of the more creditable buildings, etc. It would take a great deal of skill and effort to extract from the city officials the following facts:—

1. White teachers are paid better salaries than colored teachers for the same work.

2. The colored teachers have, on the average, more children to teach.

3. On the whole, the buildings for the colored children are inferior to those for the white.

4. There are nearly twice as many grades in the white schools as in the colored.

5. The capacity of the white schools is sufficient to accommodate the white school population.

6. This is not true of the colored schools; for, inferior as they are, they will not begin to admit the colored children of school age.

7. The colored children are not given the same time in the grades nor the same equipment in the schools.

Now, all of these specific injustices and a thousand others grow out of one *basic principle,—denial of the Negro's manhood, womanhood, and citizenship rights.* Correct this one fundamental error, and all of these manifestations of injustice will disappear at once.

This is the condition of the race question today. We ignore fundamental principles in our interminable wrangling over details.

---

[1] See page 371 and Appendix G.

I think all the investigations that have been made up to the present time compel us to assume that the characteristics of the osseous, muscular, visceral, or circulatory system have practically no direct relation to the mental ability of man (Manouvrier).—Quoted with approval by Boas.

"A light that twinkles in a distant star,
A wave of ocean surging on the shore,
One substance with the sea; a wing to soar
Forever onward to the peaks afar,
A soul to love, a mind to learn God's plan,
A child of the eternal—such is man."

A. D. WATSON.

Negro warrior and statesman, Toussaint L'Overture (full-blood), the leader of the only successful slave rebellion in the history of the world.

CHAPTER I.

MAN.

MAN is so self-centered in his thinking that he views everything, even his fellow-man, in relation to himself. Nature he studies that he may dominate; God, he ponders that he may anticipate; Time is his instrument, and Eternity his hope. It is this autocentric attitude which has crystallized the conclusions of human experience into the sentiment that "the proper study of mankind is man."

One of the vivid recollections of my childhood days is the first circus parade I ever saw. I was 10 years old and imagination was active. For days groups of boys had stood before the circus bills and discussed with bated breath the coming sights. Could a man lead an elephant by the ear? Could anybody in our day and generation repeat the inimitable feat of Daniel —enter a den of lions?

With great excitement we took our places to watch for these wonderful sights upon that fateful day.

The half had not been told. All the daring feats of the handbills were being enacted before our very eyes. I was differently affected from my companions. They were carried away with admiration for the courage of the men. I was puzzled at the conduct of the animals. Why did the lithe and restless tiger hide in the corner and tremble when the keeper struck the bars of his cage? Why was the lion afraid of a man with a rawhide? Why did not the elephant strike back when the man struck him with a goad? Aye! Why? Why? And my head throbbed with excitement that night as I tossed upon a sleepless pillow. Ever and anon that vibrant interrogation echoes through the halls of memory; and while this work is the result of deep meditation upon the problems of today, it had its beginning in that awful puzzle of my youthful years.

I.

Man in his bodily makeup is an animal. All intelligent people who investigate the subject are forced to this conclusion. *Man in his bodily makeup is an animal,*—a blood-kinsman to the myriads of living things that move, struggle, and die upon the bosom of our common mother, *earth.*

"Linnæus, in his 'Systema Naturæ,' classified Man in the Animal Kingdom by designating the Order of Primates as composed of three groups—Half-apes, Apes, and Man (Lemur, Simia, and Homo).

"Later, Cuvier classified the animal world into Vertebrata, Articulata, Molluska, and Radiata. Gegenbaur proved man was a vertebrate. Our whole frame, both in its general plan and its detailed structure, presents the characteristic type of the vertebrate."

This is no longer seriously doubted by intelligent thinkers. Yet few thinkers are able to summarize the evidence. I therefore introduce here the masterly summing up of Ernst Haeckel, the great German philosopher and scientist, in his "Die Welträthsel" (The World-riddle). Whatever we may think of his philosophy, we cannot deny his facts.

Haeckel shows that even in the finest histological relations *man is a true mammal.* In his osseous system *man is a true vertebrate;* in Aristotle's classification of the higher warm-blooded animals, *man is a true tetrapod;* embryologically considered, *man is a true placental;* in the arrangement of his extremities *man is a true primate.* "In these and other important respects, particularly in the construction of the face and hands," he goes on to say, "man presents *all the anatomical marks of a true ape.*" These facts are set forth with a wealth of detail that is astonishing and a lucidity of expression that is charming. Space will permit only his closing words.

"Thus comparative anatomy proves to the satisfaction of every unprejudiced and critical student the significant fact that the body of man and of that of the anthropoid apes are not only peculiarly similar, but they are practically one and the same in every important respect. The same two hundred bones in the same order and structure, make up our inner skeleton; the same three hundred muscles effect our movements; the same hair clothes our skin; the same groups of ganglionic cells build up the marvelous structure of our brain; the same four-chambered heart is the central pulsimeter in our circulation; the same thirty-two teeth are set in the same order in our jaws; the same salivary, hepatic, and gastric glands compass our digestive process; the same reproductive organs insure the maintenance of our race.

"It is true that we find, on close examination, certain minor differences in point of size and shape in most of the organs of man and the ape; but we discover the same, or similar, differences among the different races of men, when we make a careful comparison—even, in fact, in a minute comparison of the various individuals of our own race. We find no two persons who have exactly the same size and form of nose, ears, eyes, and so forth. One has only to compare attentively these special features in many different persons in any large company to convince one's self of the astonishing diversity of their construction and the infinite variability of specific forms. Not infrequently even two sisters are so much unlike as to make their origin from the same parents almost incredible. Yet all these individual variations do not weaken the significance of the fundamental similarity of structure; they are traceable to certain minute differences in the growth of the individual features."

This is the truth beyond all cavil. In his bodily makeup, man is an animal. But this is not all; man's body is in many points inferior to that of his fellow-creatures. In strength he is outdone by many of the lower animals. It is a compliment to a man to call him a lion. The elephant will outlive several keepers. The average animal will easily live six times as long as it takes it to grow up. Man seldom or never does. No amount of training will render a man as agile as a cat or a tiger. Dogs have twice the hunger endurance of men. The animal world can, as a rule, see, hear, and smell better than man. Compare man's feeble orientation[1] with the wonderful development of that faculty in birds and insects. The accuracy of the insects' orientation is embalmed in the proverbs of our language. Everyone knows what it is to make "a bee-line" for a place. "A swallow, nesting in New England and wintering in Panama, can return to the rafter in the barn where its nest was last year." A homing pigeon will return safely over hundreds of miles. Every intelligent horseman knows the superiority of the horse over man in that particular. The cat's power in this line is both a proverb and a joke:—

"And the cat came back."

But why multiply examples? Man is not only a member of the animal kingdom by consanguinity, but in many ways an inferior member.

Nevertheless, man is the undisputed lord of this

[1] The ability to find one's way,—especially to locate points of the compass.

world. Neither the keenness of the eagle's eye nor the stretch of his mighty pinions has availed him to elude man's dominion. The lion is the king of the forest only so long as man is absent. The eagle's eye is keener than man's, but man sees farther than the eagle. The fox has a more delicate sense of smell, but man traps the fox. The elephant's massive strength does not enable him to resist man's puny hands.

> "From Greenland's icy mountain,"
> To "India's coral strand,"

from far-off Cathay to

> "Where rolls the lonely Oregon,
> Amid the sound of his own dashings,"

from the frozen haunts of the stunted Esquimaux,

> "Where the wolf and Northern fox
> Prowl among the lonely rocks,
> And tardy suns to desert drear,
> Give days and nights of half a year,"

from these cheerless regions to the ice-bound shores of remotely southern seas,—"from the rivers to the ends of the earth," so far as any other terrestrial inhabitant is concerned, *man is king*. He has sounded the chambers of the mighty deep and robbed the savage denizens of their terrors. With ingenious contrivances and intrepid daring he is treading the uncertain pathway of the wind.

Man is the soul of the world, the triumph of Nature, and the masterpiece of God's handiwork.

> "What a piece of work is man!
> How noble in reason!
> How infinite in faculty!
> In form and moving how express and admirable!
> In action how like an angel!
> In apprehension how like a God!"

"Glory to man in the highest,
For man is the maker of things."

He has climbed the heights of knowledge by slow and painful steps, and, standing upon the Himalaya of mundane achievements, proudly and truthfully declares,

"I am monarch of all I survey,
My right there is none to dispute,
From the center all round to the sea,
I am lord of the fowl and the brute."

There is but one menace to man's rule in this world now, and that is man. There is but one obstacle to man's earthly happiness, *man*.

But how did man obtain this pre-eminence over his animal kinsmen? The same answer occurs to every intelligent investigator. Reason, or the power to think, is the magic wand by means of which man has overridden obstacles in his upward march.

Whether we accept the soulless monism of Haeckel or the bodiless transcendentalism of Mrs. Eddy—whatever our beliefs as to the whys and wherefores of the universe, we are bound to admit that reason, or the power of logical, dynamic thought, forms the one impassable barrier between man and beast,—impassable in only one direction. It cannot be crossed by the beast, but it may be by man. A beast cannot become a man, but the converse of this proposition is not true. We have many examples of man's descent to the beast's estate.

Physically, man is as much bound to the earth and as dependent upon it as the meanest worm that crawls. Man is indeed of the earth, *earthy;* physiologically as well as anatomically.

We know nothing of life aside from its physical basis, the body; and all the mental and spiritual faculties of man spring from this source, as music from a harp. Yet the body is not *man* any more than the harp is music; but as we know not music aside from the instrument, so we know not man aside from the body. The better the harp, however, the better the music; and, other things being equal, the better the body the better the man.

Nature is neither charitable nor kind, but extremely selfish. She discriminates always in favor of her friends—the fit. She gives life only on her own terms. Physical stamina and longevity are the rewards of obedience—rewards that come whether the recipient is, or is not, conscious of their immanence. She values not intelligence that does not harmonize with her methods. She knows neither race nor color, nor fool nor philosopher—only the *fit* and the *unfit*—obedient and disobedient.

When the vital forces of the body, whether human or animal, harmoniously and successfully act and react with the environment, the result is health. When the reaction is inadequate or inharmonious, the result is disease. When the reaction ceases the result is death, and the body follows the elemental laws of matter.

There are three dominating traits that normally gain control of our lives, namely, digestive, sexual, intellectual. In other words, man's pleasurable physical activities to be healthful must be either nutritional, emotional, or intellectual; and it is the discrimination in regard to the proper sequence of these that differentiates man from his fellow-animals.

The digestive tract is rightly called prima via (first way). Man's first impulse after he draws the breath of life is to eat. He shares individually the common impulse of animated nature to cleave unto life. Having gained a foothold for himself, the next great impulse (stronger than the desire to live) is the perpetuity of the species by reproduction. These dominating passions are finally subjugated completely by the slowly evolving intellectual faculties; and man becomes the "moral and intellectual sensorium of nature."

There is no superiority of flesh and blood. In this respect "Man hath no pre-eminence above a beast," much less his fellow-man. *Intelligence* alone distinguishes man from beast, and forms the only basis for justice and fraternity among men.

II.

Waiving the question as to whether the difference between reason and instinct is one of kind or degree, and whether reason is an evolution or a special creation, let us notice certain distinctively human attributes:—

1. Man is the only animal adapted to an upright posture and locomotion, and whose brain literally crowns his body.

2. Man is the only animal that has developed a thumb—one digit that can oppose one or all of the other digits of the same hand. The hand of the ape approaches that of man in effectiveness no more closely than does the face of the orang-outang approach the beauty of the human countenance.

3. Man is the only animal that has the power of communicating directly his experiences to another member of his kind.

Warning each other at the approach of an enemy, calling to their mates and summoning their young; locating food for each other, etc., are habits of animals that simulate so strikingly human communication, that we may concede the point and let man's superiority rest upon degree and not upon kind. Language, indeed, may not be man's sole prerogative, yet, here voice has reached its culminating grandeur and importance. Written language is not only unknown to beasts, but to the less enlightened families of men. So evidently true is this, that a famous advocate of Negro inferiority was willing to put a knowledge of Greek as a bridge for the Negro to cross, if he could, into the realm of American citizenship.

Professor Boas very truly says: "The difference between the minds of animals and of man are so striking that little or no diversity of opinion exists. The two outer traits in which the distinction between the minds of animals and of man finds expression are the existence of organized articulate language in man, and the use of utensils of varied application. Both of these are common to the whole of mankind. No tribe has ever been found that does not possess a well-organized language; no community that does not know the use of instruments for baking, cutting, or drilling; the use of fire and weapons with which to defend themselves, and to obtain the means of living. Although means of communication by sound exist in animals, and although even lower animals seem to have means of bringing about co-operation between the different individuals, we do not know of any case of true articulate language from which the student can extract abstract principles of classification of ideas. It may also be that the higher apes employ now and then limbs of trees or stones for defense, but the use of complex utensils is not found in any representative of the animal series." ("Mind of Primitive Man.")

4. Man is the only animal that can make a fire, use a tool, or clothe himself. These factors alone have enabled him to make the entire world his dwelling-

place—disregarding alike climatic conditions and the opposition of nature's teeming millions. "In fact, man inhabits the whole earth from the icy regions of Greenland (in the neighborhood of the eightieth degree of north latitude) to the torrid zone, which stretches between the tropic of Cancer and the equator. He is found in countries situated at seventy-five or two hundred meters below the level of the sea (Caspian depression, depression of Louktchin in Eastern Turkestan), as well as on the table-lands at an elevation of more than five thousand meters,—Thibet." (Deniker.)

5. Man is the only animal that takes any cognizance of the future. Superficial observation might lead one to doubt this proposition. The thickening of the hairy coat of some animals; the preparation of their beds by others (hybernates); the storing of food supplies by ants, bees, squirrels, etc.; the long journeys of the migrating ones (birds and fishes) seem like intelligent preparation for future contingencies—a superior kind of foresight often wanting in man. Closer observation, however, will show that these habits are hereditary, tribal (phylogenetic[2]), and instinctive—a part of that evolutionary wisdom common to all living things; same as eating, drinking, walking, etc.; an adaptation to environment, without which life were impossible. Blind compliance with the necessary laws of their existence is not an evidence that animals have a care for the future, any more than acorns are an indication that an oak-tree has a care for the perpetuity of its species.

Beyond a doubt, man is the only creature who has any intelligent concern for the future. Mark, I do not say *knowledge* of the future. God alone has that.

An intelligent concern for the future distinguishes

[2] Belonging to a race.

man from the brute and furnishes the basis for civilization.

6. Man is the only consciously intelligent denizen of this world. (Huxley.)

Other animals make music, but man alone makes musical notation and musical instruments.

"We might almost define man as a being who ornaments himself; and certainly here is a difference separating him from the animals." (Quatrefages.)

"Man has his own attributes—faculties that belong exclusively to him—morality and religion. Well, these exclusively human faculties seem admirably to complete this exceptional being. It is these that ennoble him, and justify the incontestable empire that he claims over the globe; for it is these which, along with the sentiment of punishment, give birth to the idea of duty, the thought of responsibility.

"He is distinguished from all animals by these two fundamental characters which pertain only to him. He is the only one among organized and living beings who has the abstract sentiment of good and evil; in him alone, consequently, exists moral sense.

"Man everywhere, however savage he may be, shows some signs of morality and of religion that we never find among animals."

Man is always and everywhere the supreme occupant of his environment.

"The more we study, the better we know that all over the surface of the globe man surmounts every difficulty, so long as he wars against nature. If he is arrested, it is when he encounters man. In brief, man alone can arrest man."

Quatrefages, the great naturalist, after showing how the different varieties of turkeys arose from one stock and how the rabbit did also, says: "Now, man, who has progressed upon the earth a much longer time than the turkey or the rabbit, who has been upon the globe for thousands of years, living under the most diverse, the most opposite conditions, multiplying further the causes of modification by his manners, his habits, his kind of life, by the more or less care he takes of himself—man, I say, is certainly found in conditions of variation much more marked than those which have been encountered by the animals we have cited. It is not, then, surprising that men, from one group to another, present differences of which we here see the specimens. If there is anything in them to astonish us, it is that these differences are not more considerable."

There are, as we have said, *distinctively human traits* possessed by man and by man only. That all men, however low, possess these traits and no animals, however high, possess them, is proof positive of the *biological unity of man.*

All the facts of science support this proposition.

"We are accustomed to say that the essential characteristic of the mental processes of man is the power of reasoning. While animals as well as man may perform actions suited to an end, based on memory of results of previous actions, and suitable selection of actions fitting a certain purpose, we have no evidence whatever that would show that the abstract concepts accompanying the action can be isolated by animals, while all groups of men, from the most primitive to the most highly developed, possess this faculty."

The Negro possesses all of these traits and must, therefore, be human.

"Observation and experiment alone, applied to the animal and vegetable kingdom,—*science,* in a word,—leads us logically to this conclusion: *there exists but one species of man.*"[3]

[3] Quatrefages.

There is an impassable gulf between the lowest man and the highest ape. The missing link is an irridescent dream; and innate racial superiority is a baseless, egotistical fiction.

Science is the enemy of prejudice. Knowledge dispels superstition. The sunlight of investigation destroys the intellectual ghosts that walk in the night of ignorance.

Anatomy demolished the numerical superiority of woman's ribs, and physiology undermined the social prestige of "blue" blood. History shows civilization to be an evolution, and innate racial superiority an unjustifiable egotism common to the children of men. Ethnology and religion are alike in this, that those who hold to the partiality of nature or deity believe theirs the favored class. I never knew a foreordinationist in religion that did not count himself one of the elect; nor an advocate of racial superiority that did not think his the superior race. *Racial achievement means racial opportunity. Science knows no innately superior race.*

"Our lives are songs; God writes the words,
And we set them to music at pleasure.
The song grows glad or sweet or sad,
As we choose to fashion the measure."

"It is only the thorough application of the gospel of love and of common sense that can place each race in its proper attitude to the other."

"Those ministers who preached and labored regularly for the Negroes found it a blessed work, and they became deeply attached to their colored congregations."—REV. JAMES H. McNEILLY, D.D., "Religion and Slavery."

CHAPTER II.

DOMINATING FORCES.

WHAT we are physically, morally, and intellectually is the result of heredity and environment. These forces complement and overlap each other, but at times are quite antagonistic.

Heredity is that biological law by means of which living beings tend to repeat themselves in their descendants. Environment means literally that which environs or surrounds.

Heredity beginning before birth, continues with varying intensity during life. Environment also acts continuously throughout life; mediately before birth and immediately thereafter. While education may be regarded as a result of environment, it is not entirely so. Heredity plays a part. Cumulative or tribal education, *i.e.,* knowledge common to the species, is hereditary. "A beaver reared in captivity away from water dammed a stream of water running across a floor from a leaking bucket."

Education is a *drawing-out* rather than a *putting-in* process; as the Irish woman said, "I never yet saw a hen that could hatch out of an egg anything different from what was in it when it was laid." No amount of training will make a race horse out of a donkey.

Heredity is conservative: "Every tree bears fruit after its kind." "Like produces like." "The thing that hath been, it is that which shall be; and that which is done, is that which shall be done; and there is no new thing under the sun." "Is there anything whereof it may be said, See, this is new? It hath been already of old time, which was before." If heredity were unopposed, progress would be impossible.

Environment is educative, evolutionary, and progressive. The story of human development is repeated in the life of every individual adult, who has evolved from a single protoplasmic cell (monad) to the myriad-celled microcosm, *man.* 'Tis a wonderful story, the creation of man:—

> "Since God collected and resumed in man
> The firmaments, the strata, and the lights,
> Fish, fowl, and beasts, and insects,—all their trains
> Of varied life caught back upon His arm,
> Reorganized and constituted man,
> The microcosm,—the adding up of works."

'Tis not less wonderful because repeated in every child that is born. "There are animals representing all the phases of human evolution from cell to man. A hog, a fish, a man are scarcely distinguishable when a few days evolved from the egg." But environment unopposed would destroy all stability of form. As the union of the centripetal and centrifugal forces of gravity keeps the stars in their courses, so heredity and environment combine to keep humanity in the orb of progress. From the warp of heredity and the woof of environment the web of our lives is woven.

From a wide philosophical viewpoint, then, it is nonsense to speak of a self-made man. How can a man select his race, his parents, or his country, when and where he would be born? And upon what stage he would play his piece? Yet, notwithstanding the conditions are rigidly fixed, we are permitted *within these conditions* to fashion to our liking the play of life. It is this individual flavoring of life that gives us that intangible thing we call personality—that indescribable something that makes me, *me,* and you, *you.* It is an harmonious co-operative blending of individual personalities, fostered by heredity and favored by environment, that constitutes a race. Ontogeny is phylogeny in miniature. That is, the life-history of the individual is a repetition on a small scale of the life-history of the race. The distinctiveness of personality is a distinctiveness of thought rather than of appearance; of mind rather than of matter. Racial distinctions are psychical rather than physical. Common beliefs and experiences bind men more closely than blood. It is a well-known fact that the ties that bind comrades in arms, or through long and perilous association of any kind, are stronger than ties of blood. As with individuals, so with races; similarity of thought may bring unity of effort.

These are well-established scientific facts universally accepted by modern thinkers. The relative importance of heredity and environment is the only unsettled point. Around this point gather some of the most acrimonious phases of the Negro question. The favorite anti-Negro arguments are built up after the following manner:—

(*a*) A lurid description of the most degraded and backward portions of Africa.

(*b*) Historic argument to show these people have always been so.

(*c*) These man-eating savages were the ancestors of the American Negro.

(*d*) A people are like their ancestry, therefore the Afro-American of today is a savage. No savage is fit for citizenship in a republic, therefore "the war amendments to the Constitution were a huge blunder," etc.

They usually end by triumphantly quoting Jeremiah's famous question, "Can the Ethiopian change his skin, or the leopard his spots?" forgetting that this interrogation is but the vivid imagery of orientalism, and no more comprehends the alpha and omega of biology than the "everlasting hills" expresses the demonstrated principles of geology.

That anyone boasting of his knowledge of organic evolution[1], should reject the chronology of Usher, dismiss with a sneer the astronomy of Joshua, and accept as a finality the biology of Jeremiah, is a manifestation of the Jim-crow logic used by those who settle by their own word "ultimately and fundamentally"[2] the Negro question in America. *There is no ineffaceable differentiation between the African and Caucasian,* as will be fully demonstrated in a subsequent chapter.

"That civilization is but restrained savagery may perhaps be conceded; but if the restraint has grown to be the ever-dominant impulse, then has the savage been slain." Three well-established facts show the Afro-American has met these conditions and has become in reality a civilized man:—

1. Americo-Liberians have not returned to African savagery.

2. Afro-Americans resident in the United States of America have shown no desire to return to the association of their savage ancestry. This is a virtue and not a vice, as some anti-Negro writers[1] claim.

3. The Negro has never shown any desire to return to slavery.[3]

"Progress the Negro has made, unquestionably, in some directions; in some places; perhaps, even when we have regard to his whole race in the United States. He is no longer a slave, and his emancipation has uplifted him in heart and mind in some degree above the low plane of his former estate. Freedom has brought its responsibilities and cares and pains, but these he accepts without a murmur, in consideration of the blessed privilege of directing his own ways and calling no man 'Master.' He has justified his deliver-

[1] Shufeldt. [2] Archer. [3] See page 286.

ance even in the eyes of his former owner, by showing that he appreciates his liberty and loves it with all his soul.[4] There has been no sighing on his part for the fleshpots of slavery, even when he starved in sight of them. The husks that have been his portion but too often since he began, unaided, to provide for his own wants, are sweeter to the humblest, most ignorant of his race than all the dainties that fell to his lot from the kindest master's table.[5] Ask him, and he will tell you that he is not infrequently in sore straits, and knows not in the morning where his dinner, or eke his breakfast, will come from, if it shall come at all. But he feels that he is free—'free till he is fool,' is his own expressive language—and he would not change places with his former self for any price that

---

[4] This feeling is shown by the words of a Negro religious folk-song which was often sung in immediate post-bellum days with the solemnity of a Jewish Passover. Incidentally it throws a side-light upon the "humanity" of our late unlamented institution whose spirit and motives still survive under the name of "Segregation":—

"MANY THOUSAND GO.

No more peck o' corn for me,
No more, no more;
No more peck o' corn for me,
Many tousand go.

No more driver's lash for me,
No more, etc.

No more pint o' salt for me,
No more, etc.

No more hundred lash for me,
No more, etc.

No more mistress' call for me,
No more, etc.

No more auction-block for me,
No more, no more;
No more auction-block for me,
Many tousand go."

[5] Dr. B. T. Washington aptly illustrates this deep racial feeling by an amusing incident. A Northern white man visiting Alabama saw an old colored man seeking work. His clothing and general appearance gave every evidence of deepest poverty. The visitor was interested and began questioning the old man, who freely admitted that he was having a hard time. Following up this admission, the visitor asked him of slavery days. Again the old man was perfectly frank. He admitted having had an easy time in slavery. He had had a kind and indulgent master who cared well for his slaves, neither over-working them nor abusing them. The visitor, who was a disciple of racial inequality, saw his chance to gather some valuable testimony. "You were better off in slavery, then, than you are in freedom," he said, soothingly, to the old man. "No, sir! no, siree," came the quick and emphatic response,— "There is a looseness about dis freedom dat naturely makes a man happy," said the old man as he hobbled off.

could be offered him. And he is free, in so far as his intelligence enables him to assert his liberty. Free to come and go; to work or play; to live or die; as he pleases, or as may befall him."[6]

In the illiterate and the untrained the hereditary impulses readily predominate over environmental acquisitions. Training and environment combined can, however, not only reverse this, but can create new traits and tendencies that may become hereditary.[7] This is one of the basic facts in the civilization of man and the domestication of animals. In this principle lies the hope of the permanency of human progress.

The power of conservation can, and usually does, exist entirely independent of the faculty of creation or invention. Practically all the contrivances that bless and convenience our modern homes are the inventions of men; yet women are peculiarly adapted to their preservation. A man's right to a dinner and his capacity to enjoy it are in no wise necessarily connected with his ability to cook. Only an infinitesimal proportion of the people that ride on railroads or steamships know anything of their invention or construction. America was the discovery of but one European, and he was under a flag that has disappeared from the Western Hemisphere. Man's right to life does not rest upon his ability to create life, for no man has that ability. His right to life depends upon his ability to conserve, to serve, and to utilize it. So with the atmosphere. So with the telephone and all the blessings of civilization. Who invented them is of no moment in the adjudication.

The origin of civilization is no legitimate part of

---

[6] "An Appeal to Pharaoh."

[7] The experiments of Kammerer as well as those of Tower seem to have furnished proof that external conditions can cause hereditary changes in animals. (Loeb, "The Mechanistic Conception of Life," Jacques Loeb, M.D., Ph.D., Sc.D., University of Chicago Press, 1912.)

the Race question in America.[8] Neither is the relative culture attained by the European and African ancestry a proper factor in the discussion. Let us grant, for the sake of argument, the absurd and untenable anti-Negro contention that modern civilization is *the product of European genius* instead of the *attainment of mankind*—that it is the peculiar possession of the white man instead of the achievement of *whosoever can and will* among men.

Let us grant all this,—nay, more. Let us grant that the European has tried the experiment of democracy and that the African has scarcely dreamed of it; yet this fact remains,—the Afro-American's right to full citizenship in America depends not upon the state of culture of his African ancestry nor upon how long he has been removed from that state; but upon this fact: *Is he now prepared to exercise properly the functions of American citizenship?*

"The change from primitive to civilized society includes a lessening of the number of the emotional associations, and an improvement of the traditional material that enters into our habitual mental operations."[9] In other words, *the question is not what is the Negro's ancestry, but what are his acquirements.* Has the change in his emotional association and traditional material taken place?

Before answering this question, it may be profit-

---

[8] Even on this ground, the facts favor the colored man. One of the first great steps, if not the very first, in our civilization was the use of iron. This knowledge was born in Africa. "The African Negroes originated the art of smelting iron from the ore, and transmitted this art until it finally reached the ancestors of our civilization and made possible this age of steel, according to the theory of some of the greatest scientific students, among whom we may mention Professor von Luschau and Dr. Schweinfurth." "There can hardly be a question as to the negroid character of the Egyptians. Accordingly it must be conceded that the Negro race made important contributions—perhaps the most important of all—to early civilization. . . . The study of geometry, the chief basis of modern technology, came out of Egypt."—*The New Republic,* page 161, Sept. 11, 1915.

[9] Boas.

able to examine the methods of those who would exclude the Afro-American from the blessings of American civilization and modern democracy.

The tendency of even the most catholic and conservative men to "see red" on the Negro question is well illustrated in that excellent book, "The Present South," by Mr. E. G. Murphy, of Alabama. He says on page 271, "The possibility of racial fusion is not now repugnant to the instinct of the average Negro." This, with its context, is a restatement of the bugbear of social equality and miscegenation; though he is kind enough to admit, "A number of the wisest leaders of the Negro race are seeking to develop a deeper sense of race pride." That is to say, the bulk of the race is seeking to lose itself in the white race; albeit over the protest of "A number of the wisest leaders." That the facts do not warrant such a generalization, the following quotations from the later pages of the same work show very plainly. From a note at the bottom of page 276, I extract the following: "In the city of Boston, Massachusetts, for example, in a population of a half-million inhabitants, including twelve thousand Negroes, there is practically no intermarriage of the races. The instances that do occur are usually confined to the lower elements of both races and possess no serious social significance. Such couples are usually absorbed by the Negro race, although if they belong to the more educated classes they enter into natural relationship with neither race." And on page 331 the following: "The wisest men among the colored people of the Southern States of America do not desire the intermarriage of their race with the whites. They prefer to develop it as a separate people, on its own lines, though of course with the help of the whites. The Negro race in America is not wanting in intelligence. It is fond of learning. It has already made a considerable advance. It will cultivate self-respect better by standing on its own feet than by seeking blood-alliances with whites, who would usually be of the meaner sort."[10]

These words are not all the words of Mr. Murphy, but are quoted with approval by him to substantiate another proposition. On any other subject, a writer of the intelligence of Mr. Murphy would see that these citations contradict his previous assertions. A thing may be white at one time and black at another, but it cannot be white and black at the same time; neither can a statement be both true and false at the same time. It must be one or the other.

It is not often that so catholic and able a thinker as Mr. Murphy falls into such a grievous and mischievous error. Thoughtful Negroes are opposed to racial fusion because it would involve the degradation of colored women. While colored men might seek to *marry* white women, white men would seek to prostitute colored women. No race can reach respectability through the degradation of its women. The Negroes know this and the resentment of the colored people against Frederick Douglass ought to acquit the race of the charge Mr. Murphy prefers.

The fight of the colored people against segregation is not a fight against separation, but a fight against injustice. Segregation by law is a badge of inferiority. Segregation by choice is natural; "consciousness of kind" is just as strong in the colored people as among the whites. It is difficult to get evidence on this subject. The editor of the *Southern Workman* offers the following evidence and comment:—

"One interesting and significant bit of evidence is to be found in the public-school situation of Cincinnati. The State of Ohio prohibits by statute the compulsory

---

[10] Murphy, "The Present South."

separation of races in the public schools. Cincinnati has a colored population of nearly 20,000, and every colored child is as free as any white child to attend any public school in the city. There are, however, two colored schools which were established in response to the earnest request of the colored people themselves. These schools are full. Practically all the colored children who can do so attend them in preference to white schools, many even paying car-fare or walking long distances. It is clear that, at least in Cincinnati, the colored people prefer to have their children in colored schools, provided the schools are as good as those which the white children enjoy. In this city the equality of opportunity is complete. The Douglass School, for example, is a thoroughly modern, well-equipped building. It is even beautiful, and it suggests order and refinement in every part. The teachers, too, are well trained for their work, the majority of them having come up through the public schools and been graduated from the University.

"One other curious fact may be cited to show that the case of Cincinnati is not unique. Cincinnati has no separate colored high school. St. Louis, on the other hand, provides a separate high school for the colored people, in every way equal to the white high school, with the result that there are sixteen times as many colored students in the St. Louis high school in proportion to the population as there are in the mixed high schools of Cincinnati. The colored people of the latter city are awake to this situation and are looking forward to the time when the Board of Education shall provide a separate high school for their children.

"Without legislation there has been going on slowly but steadily for fifty years a residential segregation of races in this country. In country and city alike the two races are to be found in groups which are becoming more and more well defined. Whether this separation is wise or unwise, it seems inevitable, being due to some cause deep-seated in human nature. If it is inevitable, it is the height of unwisdom to attempt to hasten it by means that can only create in the hearts of those segregated feelings of resentment and bitterness. Segregation will not prove a cure for misunderstandings due to the proximity of unlike groups; it will at most only change the character of those misunderstandings, and it is by no means certain that the new problems will be any easier to solve than the old ones. Where individuals of different groups—whether the differences be racial, religious, or social—are in constant daily contact and are mutually dependent, misunderstandings are likely to adjust themselves; but where separation is more complete, suspicion has a rich soil in which to grow, and suspicion, when it has matured, produces a fruit of whose quality history affords too many unpleasant examples. The relations which shall exist between the blacks and the whites a generation hence are being determined today. It is unfortunate that these relations should become needlessly strained, simply because those who have the power are under the spell of that great political superstition which leads men to act as though legislation were the proper remedy for all ills of the social body.

"Fairness, patience, and good-will are more potent than statutes. A realization that we are all members of one body, and that if one member suffers all the members suffer with it, is the only sound basis from which race problems or any other social problems can proceed." (*Southern Workman.*)

Mr. Archer ("Through Afro-America") gives countenance, if not actual support, to the doctrine that the mixed bloods are inferior to both parent stocks, equalling neither the white nor the black. Yet he goes on to show that all the progress of the race in America has been made by and under the leadership of the mixed elements. I have shown in another chapter that Dr. Bean bases a sweeping generalization against the race upon a statement of facts which at best is less than 40 per cent. true. If preconception and prejudice can thus vitiate the reasoning of men of culture who are striving to be fair, what are we to expect from the ambitious, the interested, the hungerers after notoriety,—what, I say, are we to expect from this class upon whom the canons of truth lay little authority and to whom altruism is an unknown feeling? And yet, it is from such witnesses that most of the anti-Negro testimony comes.

Leaving the consideration of the character of the witnesses for another chapter, let us examine some of their methods and analyze some of their testimony.

I.

Mr. Edgar G. Murphy justly complains that so many people, in discussing national problems, assume that *the North is the nation;* yet, most white people approach the race question in just this spirit. They never include the Negro when they speak of "*the American people.*"[11] It is only such a biased mental attitude that could make a man like Mr. Wm. Archer put up such an argument as he does about the Negro being "ultimately and fundamentally" inferior to the white man, and therefore should not be permitted to occupy territories that "are fitted by their climate and resources to be not only a white man's land, but one

---

[11] So prevalent is this error that even colored men of culture are guilty. On page 50 of "Out of the House of Bondage," Prof. Kelly Miller says: "The Negro race in this country must become one with itself before it can become one with the American people."

of the greatest white men's lands in the world."[12] This is the "necessity" argument with a vengeance! No man has any right to anything that is suitable to my use; a buccaneering logic that would justify the meanest scoundrel that ever scuttled a ship or cut a throat. Many of the irreducible factors of our race problem are produced by that mental attitude that insists that nine-tenths of the people are the whole people. A part is not the whole. The idea behind segregation is that the Negro is not a part of the American people.

II.

Universal human frailties are paraded as peculiar Negro vices:—

"As a rule the youth of the American Negro are liars by nature. They are all predisposed to gambling and the majority of them will steal." This is true, but it is also true of nine-hundred and ninety-nine thousand, nine-hundred and ninety-nine of every million children born into the world of whatever color or race. Lying and stealing are common animal traits to which man is heir. You have to teach men to be honest and to tell the truth. They are all born liars. Lying is a phase of nature's deceptions which moral training eradicates from the conduct as cultivation removes weeds from the soil.

"The Negro has no conception of the monogamic régime." In this he is much like the white man, who certainly has very little knowledge of its practice. Prostitution or polygamy seems to obtain in every country and among all peoples. The sex relation is one of the unsolved problems of civilization.

A certain mendacity born of fanaticism seems to

[12] Archer, "Through Afro-America."

obsess many that essay to discuss the Negro question. They either deliberately falsify or arrange the truth in such a way as to deceive. I will give an example of each method: "The higher sentimental qualities of love are totally lacking in Negroes of both sexes in this country today." "A short and ugly word" of four letters is the only proper answer to such an assertion. I will, however, dignify it by a reply. I submit the following lines from a full-blooded American Negro as an answer:—

SONG.

"My heart to thy heart,
My hand to thine;
My lips to thy lips,
Kisses are wine
Brewed for the lover in sunshine and shade;
Let me drink deep, then, my African maid.

Lily to lily,
Rose unto rose;
My love to thy love
Tenderly grows.
Rend not the oak and the ivy in twain,
Nor the swart maid from her swarthier swain."

PAUL L. DUNBAR, "Lyrics of Lowly Life."

III.

A recent anti-Negro publication[13] illustrates the inferiority argument by a picture of a Negro lad between two monkeys. The pictures are so drawn as to accentuate the natural resemblances. The same thing could be done with a white boy of similar age. The white resembles the ape in features as much as the colored boy. While the colored boy's color is nearer the monkey's than the white boy's, the white boy's hair

[13] Shufeldt, "America's Greatest Problem."

is more like the monkey's than the colored boy's. As an anthropological argument for Negro inferiority the picture rates with the words quoted above. There is little difference in the features of children of different races, whatever the difference in adults. As far as features are concerned, the picture on the opposite page might be either Caucasian or Negro, while it is neither. Some years ago I knew a fine old Scotchman who had a terrier to which he was very much attached. They were often seen together. An artistic wag drew their pictures so that they looked much more alike than the boy and the monkeys above referred to.

IV.

They interpret facts in contradictory ways to make them apply against the Negro. Space will permit only a few illustrations:—

(*a*) In a comparative racial study, the white people are judged from the top and the Negro from the bottom.

(*b*) Punishment for adultery is usually cited as being one of the virtues of primitive people. Yet the following incident is elaborated to show Negro cruelty: "Our entrance interrupted a cruel execution. A 'sea-boy,' returning from a two years' absence, had found his wife living with another man. He had demanded a palaver and the man had been condemned. The 'sea-boy' was to do the job. It was the law of the bush. The cold chills chased one another up and down my spine when I saw the vindictive manner in which the injured husband went about his task. He crossed the culprit's ankles and tied them with rattan, drawing the knot until the rattan cut into the flesh; the hands were tied behind the back in the same way. Then he left the man on the ground, disappearing into his hut, and returning with an armful of tough withes and a rawhide whip. Not until then did we realize that the culprit was to be flogged to death."[14]

Compare that with the following about the Germans. Remember that the German customs are cited to show German devotion to female chastity and the Negro custom is introduced to show Negro cruelty. The unfairness of interpretation is evident:—

"But long before this time the Germans had visited severe punishment upon female delinquents, as they had upon those men who brought about the downfall of married women. Thus Tacitus in his 'Germania' writes of the punishment inflicted upon an adulterous woman: Naked and with her hair cut short, the unhappy creature, in the presence of her relatives, was driven from her home and flogged through the entire village by her angry husband.

"That the German continued after the time of Tacitus to preserve inviolate the honor of his women, is seen in the enactment of certain laws and the issuance of decrees. Thus, in the reign of one of the Frank Kings, Dagobert (638 A.D.), the law specified that the man who so much as touched the hand of a free woman was to be fined 600 denarii (a denarius is equivalent to about twenty cents), this fine to be doubled if he touched the arm, quadrupled if he took liberties with the woman's breast, and this law was rigorously enforced even to the extreme of cutting off the nose or ears of the prisoner unable to pay his fine."[15]

(*c*) Anatomical divergence from the animal type is usually interpreted to man's advantage. On this ground the Negro's lips go to his credit in the upward evolutionary process. Yet, I have noticed but one

[14] Edgar Allen Forbes, "The Land of the White Helmet."
[15] The Urologic and Cutaneous Review, June, 1915, page 354.

ethnologist (Boas) with the fairness to admit this. Again, development of the gluteal muscles is considered an anatomical peculiarity of man. In fact, it is a common anti-Negro argument to show the inferior development of the Negro woman in this region. The excessive development of this region in Hottentot women is used to reinforce the inferiority arguments against the Negro.

(*d*) In medicine, the Negro is alike blameworthy for anaphylaxis and immunity. If he is susceptible to disease (as tuberculosis), he is a weakling; if he is not susceptible (as hook-worm), he is a menace.

In morals, the Negro is guilty of his own frailties and the white man's short-comings.[16] If the Negro violates the commandments it is because he is "innately depraved or by nature non-moral." If the white man is guilty, it is because of "the degrading influence of contact with the Negro." In ethics, they abuse the Negro for lack of self-respect, if he be humble; if he is not humble, they abuse him for "bumptiousness." But the saddest and meanest phase of it is the persistent claim that all Negroes are practically alike. This is a fundamental and serious matter and needs to be examined in detail. (See following chapter.)

V.

They accept mere assumptions as demonstrated truths. It is a false assumption that the white man has charge of the earth, and must consider his advantage only when dealing with the other peoples. If

[16] Take U. S. Senator B. R. Tillman's explanation of South Carolina's Age of Consent law. "If you know anything about the Negroes, you know that very few of the women of that race have any idea of virtue at all, and that must be the reason why the 'age of consent' is so low. It is well understood that when the puberty arouses the passions in the sexes—and those passions are most virulent—Negro girls would take advantage inevitably of white men."

majority rules, then the earth belongs to the colored people. It is a false assumption that the American people are all white. The colored man is just as much the American people as the white man. And is not going back to Africa any more than the white man is going back to Europe. The Negro is not an alien in this country. He has been here as long as the white man has.

The fundamental error of most anti-Negro thinkers on the race problem is the unwarranted assumption that the white man is the *norm* of humanity; mentally, morally, and physically. Anti-Negro logic tries to fasten upon the American of African descent all the savagery of Africa and deny him all the past glories of the civilizations of that ancient and mysterious land, and at the same time claiming for the white man of European descent "the background of European culture." It is a mere assumption that the Negrophobe is the only one who has any knowledge of the subject or that he has no prejudice against the Negro. He always compares the worst Negroes with the best Caucasians, showing malevolence or ignorance in violating the well-known rules of comparison. The difference between the ignorant and vicious whites and the ignorant and vicious blacks is too inconsequential to carry his point. Ditto, the educated and upright. It is an unwarranted assumption that superior attainment means superior capacity or that attainment is always a measure of capacity.

Another fundamental error of the negrophobe is to assume that culture is foreign to the Negro and natural or innate to the Caucasian. But, enough! The most of this anti-Negro talk is, to quote Mr. Murphy, "A crude frenzy of the hustings which seldom has sincerity or validity." Finally, there is a conspiracy of silence in facts creditable to the race. Why

Malay boy of the Straits Settlement.

should items like the following be ignored or suppressed? Yet such is usually done[17]:—

CARRIERS HONOR VETERAN WORKER.

H. E. BURRIS, RECENTLY GIVEN SILVER STAR,

GUEST AT Y. M. C. A. BANQUET.

Henry E. Burris, first mail-carrier at the local postoffice to be tendered a banquet at the Y. M. C. A. Saturday evening by the mail-carriers.

Dinner was served at 7 o'clock. Christian Koch presided and presented Mr. Burris with a travelling bag, the gift of the carriers. The honored guest responded in a short talk extending his thanks to his fellow-workmen.

Assistant Postmaster Oliver P. Olsen made a talk concerning Mr. Burris's long career in the service and gave some figures relative to the mail he had handled in the past twenty-five years. It is estimated that over 13,000,000 pieces of mail were delivered by him.

The spirit of comradeship and co-operation exhibited among the men was commended in a few remarks made by the postmaster, H. P. Simpson. He spoke of the value of faithfulness in little as well as great things in life, and of those who adopt this course of conduct.

An original poem was read by Mr. Koch, in which Mr. Burris was lauded for the record he had made.—*Rock Island Argus,* Jan. 4, 1915.

The witty fling of *Life* is not without point. Referring to the inferiority of the Negro, *Life* says: "Our friends down South, being sure that the Negroes are inferior, deny them advantages and provide inferior schools for Negro children in order that they will continue to be inferior and thus prove the correctness of the contention of the scientist sentimen-

[17] A delegation of prominent colored men called upon the editor of an influential paper in a large Southern City to complain of the unfair treatment the race received from that paper. The editor frankly told these gentlemen: "It is the settled policy of this paper not to exploit the virtues of Negroes."

talists that the Negro is inferior. After all, there is nothing quite so satisfying as the feeling that you have got things fixed so that you will always have an inferior race in your midst."

The words of Mr. Murphy are pathetically true: "Of the destructive factors in Negro life the white community hears to the uttermost, hears through the press and the police court; of the constructive factors of Negro progress,—the Negro school, the saner Negro church, the Negro home,—the white community is in ignorance. Until it does know this aspect of our Negro problem it may know more or less accurately many things about the Negro; but it cannot know the Negro."[18]

I will close this discussion of testimony by a quotation from an address by a learned and fair-minded Southern white physician: "It is unsafe and unscientific to generalize from insufficient data. Especially does this apply to attempts at judging a whole race by a few individuals, or drawing conclusions from the experience of any one man. Many misstatements have been made concerning the prevalence of various diseases in the Negro. Some of these errors have remained unchallenged, because they were made with the stamp of authority upon them, and no one appeared with sufficient experience to offset them. A noted textbook on gynecology (Gilliam), in discussing cancer of the uterine cervix, says: 'The Negress is comparatively immune.' Tiffany, of Baltimore, has stated that 'carcinoma is very rare in the Negro.' This opinion was shared by Briggs, of Nashville, and Yandell, of Louisville. Later, Ballock, of Washington, held that epithelioma is almost never seen and carcinoma but rarely." All of these observers believed that sarcoma was very much more frequent in

[18] Murphy, *op. cit.*

the colored race than carcinoma. On the contrary, Michael, of Charleston, found about an equal number of uterine cancer among white and colored families, disproving Schröder's statement that carcinoma uteri, or any form of cancer, seldom affects Negro women. Richardson, in New Orleans, showed figures that indicated that cancer in the Negro was not so rare as believed by other surgeons. Corson, of Savannah, gives his experience as follows: "From all I can learn, however, cancer is more common now than before emancipation, when the vital equation of the race was better. The cases I meet are very rapid, especially of the cervix uteri." The question may be summed up in the words of Matas, of New Orleans, in whose opinion I concur: "In regard to the malignant neoplasms the Negro constitution has probably undergone some change under the conditions of the American civilization, since it cannot be doubted that cancer is rare in the native African, rare also in the original slave population of this country, and has only become a common disease in the American Negro of the last few generations. It is also probable that the conditions that are causing an increase in the prevalence of cancer among whites are also acting with the same effect upon the Negroes." That is to say, the temperate zone with its complex civilization is responsible for the fact that the colored race, as it comes to live more and more like the white race, will be subject to the same diseases.

In a similar way it was taught for years, in the Northern medical schools, that ovarian cysts practically did not occur in Negro women. This was the positive instruction that I received twenty years ago, and so surprised was I to find five cystomas of the ovary during my first year of surgical practice, that, following the lead of Dr. I. S. Stone, I presented a paper on this subject before the Tri-State Medical

Association in 1900. My contention was that, while these growths were not so common in the Negro as some other tumors, still they were by no means rare, and that, unless particular attention be called to them, mistakes might be made in the diagnosis of the doubtful abdominal enlargements. Up to the present time, I have had no reasons to change these views. The opinions of our distinguished teachers in respect to this matter are untenable. They are established on scanty observations.

Appendicitis has been looked upon as a rare affection in the Negro. I have no doubt but that it was and is now more uncommon in the Negro than in the white race. But, as is pointed out in an article by myself, it appears that this disease is becoming more frequent in the Negroes, and that, if they continue to live under conditions similar to the white people, we may expect them to have about the same number of inflamed appendices. The situation is almost identical with that of cancer, mentioned above. In his travels, Nicholas Senn found neither appendicitis nor cancer in Africa; nor did he observe either disease in Alaska at the most northern habitation of man. Civilization again! The chronic types of appendicitis, with kinks and membranes, do not seem to prevail in our series. Perhaps many of these escape a diagnosis in the midst of more pressing ailments. But, certainly for the past few years we have given very careful attention to these conditions, both before and during operations. Many of these cases, of course, never get to the hospital at all.

There are no surgical diseases which are peculiar to the colored race. It is true that some diseases occur frequently, while others are rare. For example, fibrous processes of all sorts are five times more common in the Negro than in the white; for the three diseases which, by common consent, prevail so largely as to be considered peculiar to the dark-skinned races, elephantiasis, keloid, and fibroma (or myofibroma) of the uterus. On the other hand, harelip and cleft palate and club-foot are noticeably infrequent. Those of us who have had the largest opportunities for observation are least likely to make positive assertions as to this affection being very prevalent in the Negro, or that affection being rarely or never seen. I have already pointed out the errors in reference to malignant disease, ovarian cyst, and appendicitis. You will surely overlook important questions in diagnosis, if you once begin to draw conclusions as to the rarity or frequency of various diseases. I feel very strongly with Professor Matas again, "*that absolutely specific diseases, ethnically speaking, have ceased to exist in the American Negro of today;* that absolute immunity from certain diseases does not exist; and that he differs from the white man simply in the relative predisposition to, or immunity from, the various diseases that prevail in this country. It is thus demonstrated that the *fundamental nature is the same in both races,* and that the study of the differences must be based upon the action of the common factors of disease upon the acquired constitution of the Negro, which, in America, must be regarded as the sum of his original race distinction, plus the modifications due to a new environment."[19]

[19] "A Review of the Operations at St. Agnes Hospital, with Remarks upon Surgery in the Negro," by H. A. Royster, A.B., M.D., F.A.C.S., Raleigh, N. C., Surgeon to Rex Hospital, Surgeon-in-Chief to St. Agnes Hospital. Read (by invitation) before the Nat. Med. Assn., at Raleigh, N. C., August 26, 1914.

"Only a few days ago I was discussing the Negro problem with a distinguished physician of one of our larger cities in Georgia, and I could not but take careful note of his remark that 'in our courts the Negro population never got justice.' Whether this is literally true or not, it is generally true. Since hearing that remark, I have been trying to think whether the Negro gets justice in any other line any more than he does in the courts of justice, and I am about to concede that the courts are no exception in the matter of justice."
—PROF. J. H. DE LOACH, PH.D., University of Georgia.

"What we have said before in regard to the overlapping of variations among different races and types, and the great range of variability in each type, may also be expressed by saying that *the differences between different types of man are, on the whole, small as compared to the range of variation in each type.*"—BOAS.

CHAPTER III.

SOME VITAL PHASES OF THE RACIAL SITUATION.

THE persistent effort to treat all colored people alike retards the healthful growth of class distinction among us and lessens the influence of the intelligent and virtuous over the ignorant and vicious. Segregation at the Capitol means degradation in the shrievalty. If a president condones discrimination the sheriff may practise unfairness. When the orderly (?) lynching of men guilty of certain crimes, "beyond the shadow of a doubt," is advocated or condoned by a supreme judge of the nation, the simple dwellers on the heath may gregariously murder *anybody, men, women, or children,* for *any offense,* real or imagined. The one is as legitimate as the other. The ability to gild vice with intellectual graces is not morality, and the race of the victim does not alter the crime.

Variation is one of the conditions of progress. Possibly the most frequent and useful form of its manifestation in racial life is the production of the exceptional individual man or woman. History[1] teems with the exceptional Negro from Ebedmelech who saved the prophet to Booker T. Washington who built Tuskegee. When the white man seeks to treat all colored people alike he is standing in his own light and barring the road of national progress; for he is endeavoring to rob these people of the only means of preserving racial integrity and establishing cultural self-sufficiency; namely, the development of exceptional individuals for racial leadership. Notwithstanding this handicap, Afro-Americans have pro-

[1] See page 295.

duced a surprisingly long list of men and women whose names are engraven in the annals of America.

The gulf between Linnæus, Humboldt, Huxley, Darwin, *et al.*, and the lowest whites is immensely greater than any difference between the lowest whites and lowest blacks. The distance between the highest colored man and the lowest colored man is just as great as between the lowest white man and the highest white man. Colored people are no more alike than white people.[2] This thought can best be illustrated diagrammatically:—

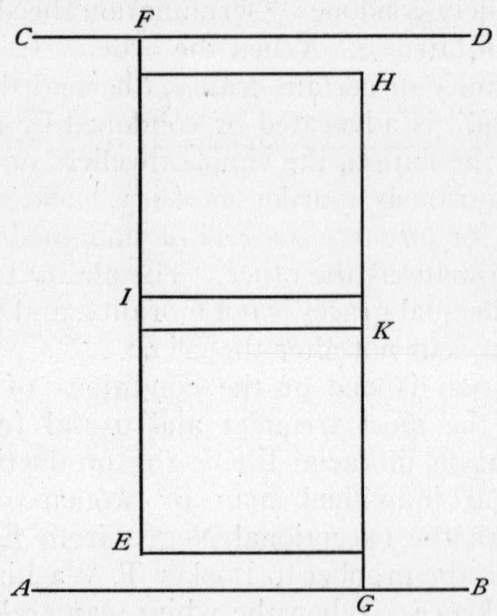

[2] That the contrary opinion is often held arises from the difficulty of discriminating among strange things. In a strange place it is difficult to tell directions. Streets running north and south in a city will remind the stranger of streets running east and west in his home town. He cannot get his bearings without assistance unless he can fix on some familiar object, as the sun. Chinamen all look alike to Englishmen and Englishmen all look alike to Chinamen. The "redskins" all looked alike to the white people and the "pale faces" all looked alike to the Indians. The "crackers" and "rednecks" look as much alike to the colored people, as the "niggahs" do to them.

Some years ago I was laughed at for saying in a medical discussion that the color of the skin was not always distinctive in scarlet fever. In reply, I invited my opponents to go with me. The invitation was

Afro-Americans with more than national reputation.

Let the line *A-B* represent the lowest state of human culture and capacity. Let the line *C-D* represent the highest state of human culture and capacity. The distance from *A-B* to *C-D* will represent the variations in human culture and capacity. The line *E-F* will represent the variations in the white and the line *G-H* that in the colored. These lines are of the same length; but *G* is below *E,* and *F* is above *H.* That is, the lowest state of culture and capacity among colored people is beneath the lowest state of culture and capacity among the whites; and the highest state of culture and capacity among whites is above the highest among the colored. The colored races possibly have not produced a Plato, an Aristotle, or a Bacon, or a Shakespeare. But the majority of whites are neither at *F* nor *E,* but *I; i.e.,* they are neither at the top nor bottom, but midway. The same is true of the colored. The majority is neither at *H* nor *G,* but at *K.*

Now study the diagram closely. It is not very far from *G* to *E,* nor from *K* to *I,* nor from *H* to *F;* but it is a long way from *G* to *F,* not much farther, however, than from *E* to *H.*

In the current discussion of the Negro question in America (U. S. A.) it is customary to dwell upon the distance from *G* to *F,* and to deny the distance from *E* to *H,* and ignore the spaces between *G* and *E, K* and *I,* and *H* and *F.* These writers invariably compare the highest whites with the lowest blacks and claim that each is typical. Why a recent anti-Negro writer illustrates his book with a vis-à-vis picture of Julius Cæsar and the lowest African savage he can find; im-

---

promptly accepted and in a few minutes we were at the bedside of a coal-black child. Not one of the half-dozen medical men had any trouble in recognizing the disease in this child, and yet he was not *scarlet* as a white child would have been, but the disease was just as distinctive. Discrimination is a matter of knowledge and observation.

plying, of course, that the average Euro-American is a Julius Cæsar and the average Afro-American is a savage. If it were only measurably true there would be no race question in the South. *White ignorance is the most serious menace in the race situation;* for this ignorance is in power and hopes to benefit itself, not by finding more light, but by increasing darkness. Hopes to *decrease* white ignorance by *increasing* black ignorance.

There has arisen in the South a type of politician that proposes to make the white people happy by making the Negroes unhappy. They propose to *better* the poor white man's condition relatively and negatively by *worsing* the black's condition. They would strangle the welfare of their country for power or pelf. Instead of striving to move forward themselves, they are striving to force the colored people back. It is a strange and weird delusion that seems to have completely obsessed the majority of some Southern States, and opened the door to political preferment. They expect to reach heaven for themselves by raising h——l for the Negroes. They hope by some political alchemy to put more rights in the Constitution for themselves by taking out any rights the Negro may have or thinks he has therein.

But, back to our diagram. All of the colored between *G* and *K* are below *I,* but only a small minority of them are below *E.* On the other hand, while all of the whites between *E* and *I* are above *G,* only a small minority is above *K.*

Finally, while all of the whites between *I* and *F* are above *K,* only a small minority of them are above *H* and only a minority of colored between *K* and *H* are below *I,* while all are below *F.*

This diagram will stand a second study. Observing the group between *G* and *K* we will notice that while its top is below *I* and its bottom below *E,* the major portion is above *E.* Taking the group between *K* and *H;* while its top is below *F* and its bottom below *I,* the major part is above *I.* Similarly studying the group between *E* and *I,* we notice that while the top is above *K* and the bottom above *G,* the major portion is below *K.* Take the group between *I* and *F;* while its top is above *H* and its bottom above *K,* its major portion is below *H.*

From these facts we reach the following conclusions:—

1. Taking averages, there is very little difference between the low type white man and the low type colored man. The same is true of both the medium grade and the highest grade in both races. *That difference, though, in each case is in favor of the white man.*

2. There is an almost immeasurable difference between the lowest colored man and the highest white one. *This difference is, of course, in favor of the white man.*

3. There is the same difference between the lowest colored man and the highest colored man that there is between the lowest white man and the highest white man. *This is equally to the credit of both races.*

4. There is not only a great difference between the lowest white man and the highest colored man, but a very great difference between the medium white man and the highest colored man. *In both of these instances the difference is in favor of the colored man.*

I.

These general ethnological truths based on world-wide facts are strictly applicable to the race situation in this country, and we can scarcely avoid questioning the sincerity or the sanity of those who essay to discuss this subject by ignoring the first conclusion, emphasizing the second, and denying the third and fourth.

These facts taken at their face value give at once racial predominance to the white and show at a glance the absurdity of the fatuous political slogan of "Negro Domination." Add to this the well-known tendency of racial units to co-operate in the presence of general danger, and it becomes self-evident that only through his own ignorance or venality can the white man's supremacy in this country be endangered.

Returning to our diagram, the true goal of the whites at *E* is *I;* and those at *I* should be headed for *F*. Those at *F* should study to maintain their own standing and lend all possible assistance to those at *E* and *I*. Similarly the colored people at *G* should head for *K* and those at *K* steer for *H* and those at *H* be circumspect to maintain their own standing and do all they can for *G* and *K*.

This constructive program means that the races will move on parallel lines to a higher civilization. Cross-firing at each other means, at the best, *delay,* and at the worst *retrogression* and *decay.* Two men can ride one horse successfully if the man in the front is a good rider and will devote his time to guiding the horse and picking the way—instead of trying to kick the hind man off. The white man has the front seat on the political horse in this country, and it will take all of his brains and energy to avoid the chasms wherein fell the "glory that was Greece and the grandeur that was Rome." Trying to kick the colored man off is a useless waste of energy, to say nothing of its injustice and its unfairness. Races, like individuals, to succeed must have either the brains to lead or the faith to follow. The colored man has the faith to follow. It is up to the white man to furnish the brains to lead. *Let us accept it as a fact, res adjudicata, that the Negro and the white man must survive or perish together in the South.*

II.

Grotesque is the array of the embattled line of prejudice.

"In England in the olden time, when a feudal lord fell behind in the collection of his man rent, and another baron, a hostile swashbuckler, roaring and strutting in feathers and iron, came to assault his castle, stone men, wooden men, and even sartorial ones, stuffed with sawdust and straw, were placed upon the battlements. The sawdust vassal did not put a hand to the springald; the cross-bow was not in his line; he had no stomach for pulling up the portcullis, and he poured down no cauldrons of boiling pitch upon the 'testudo' or the 'sow' that thundered away at the ballium gate. But, for all that, exalted upon the battlements, and with the proper distance lending enchantment to the view of him, the retainer of wood and the vassal of straw looked quite as formidable as would have done a Patroclus or a Black Agnes of Dunbar."[3]

Careful examination of "the army of facts" arrayed against the Negro, notwithstanding the great disturbance it is creating, will show it is composed mostly of the stuffed forms of old prejudices.

The wings of thought are heavy with the dust of centuries of injustice, and shadows from the gloom of the Dark Ages still lie athwart the path of modern man. Unfairness obstructs the way of progress.

There is a kind of gullible ignorance about the average man that makes him accept as absolute truth

[3] Saladin, "God and His Book."

anything bad about the other fellow, receive with satisfaction any amount of personal "taffy," and actually believe self-interested people when they promise something for nothing. Barnum said contemptuously, "The American people like to be humbugged;" and Jay Gould is reported to have said in disgust at this spirit, "The public be damned." It is this spirit that gives vitality and viciousness to the Negro question,—falsely so called. To put out of business the people who agitate the race question for power or pelf, we need in this country today an atmosphere of that intelligence and inquiry which is illumed by a critical skepticism.

In illustration of this contention take the following anecdote of a tramp;—

"No, I didn't lose that leg in the war," said the stranger, as he leaned up against the cold wall of the postoffice. "I used to claim that my leg was cut off at the battle of Antietam; but one day something happened to cure me of lying. I was stumping along the highway in Ohio, and stopped at a farmhouse to beg for dinner.

" 'Where did you lose that leg?' asked the woman.

" 'At Gettysburg.'

" 'Sit down till I call my husband.'

"He came in from the barn, and I was asked where my regiment was stationed in the battle.

" 'In the cemetery,' I replied.

" 'Oh! well, my son Bill was in the cemetery too. I'll call him in.'

"Bill soon came in, and he wanted to know what particular gravestone I took shelter behind. I said it was a Scotch granite monument.

" 'Oh!' grunted Bill. 'My brother Bob was behind just such a stone and I'll call him in.'

"Bob came in, and he swore a mighty oath that he

was there alone. He sort of pre-empted that monument, and remembered the inscription to a word. However, to give me the benefit of the doubt, I was asked my regiment and company.

" 'Company B, Fifth Ohio,' I promptly answered.

" 'Oh! Brother Jim was in that company; I'll call him in.'

"Jim came in, took a square look at me, and remarked: 'Stranger, our regiment wasn't within 200 miles of Gettysburg during the war.'

" 'I said Twenty-fifth. Of course, the Fifth wasn't there.'

" 'Oh! I'll call my brother Aaron; he was in the Twenty-fifth.'

"Aaron came in, called me a wooden-legged liar, and I was pitched over the fence into the road. They have got this war business down so fine that you can't go around playing tricks on the country no more, and the best way is to own the truth that you got drunk and got in the way of a locomotive."

From an ingenious and able monograph by Dr. Robert Bennett Bean, which, in the frank words of the author, is "an effort to show that there is a difference in the size and shape of the Caucasian and Negro brains," I quote the following:—

"The lot of brains includes a larger number from high-class Negroes than from high-class Caucasians, and a larger number from low-class Caucasians than from low-class Negroes, this being especially true in regard to the Negro males and the Caucasian females. This statement is based on the following facts:—

"1. There is a larger number of deaths resulting from acute illnesses and from accidents among the Negroes, giving a larger number of brains from normal individuals.

"2. That a larger number of Negro bodies are

regularly disposed of to anatomists indicates less respect for the dead among Negroes, and it follows that more of the better class of Negroes would be received, since the whites greatly outnumber the blacks in Baltimore.

"3. It is well known that only the lowest class of whites are unclaimed, especially among the women, who are apt to be prostitutes, or depraved, or the like, while among Negroes it is known that even the better class neglect their dead unless provision has been made for their care after death.

"4. It is a well-attested fact that the Negroes are at present roaming over the country without fixed abode in greater numbers than the whites, and this might result in many stray unclaimed bodies of the better class of Negroes being turned over to the anatomists; and, finally,

"5. Many mulattoes and mixed bloods are included among the Negroes."

Here are five statements of "facts" by a scholarly man who has had the liberalizing influence of a medical education. Surely, it is not unfair to take these "facts" as representative of all that is fairest and best in the anti-Negro propaganda!

The most casual reading of the statements show but one, the fifth, can be accepted as wholly true. Let us examine them seriatim. There is an error in the first proposition that is patent to the veriest tyro in medicine; namely, the assumption that the brains of people dying of acute diseases are normal. Would not acute yellow atrophy of the liver change the composition of the brain as well as other tissues of the body? Would not acute diarrhea reduce the brain weight in common with the general diminution of body weight? What organ of the body is left normal in the emaciated victim of typhoid fever? As a zero

An African Methodist Episcopal senior bishop and his predecessors.

factor neutralizes the multiplication product regardless of the value of other factors, so a false assumption vitiates a conclusion. Thus, statement number one disappears as a valid argument; being scientifically untrue, comparative data based thereon are worthless.

Number two, "That a large number of Negro bodies are regularly disposed of to anatomists indicates [*not*] less respect for the dead among Negroes," but that the whites are in control. Just as shabby school-buildings tell not of the colored man's lack of taste in public architecture, but of the white man's power and partiality in government. The rest of the sentence is a *false conclusion* and wholly irrelevant even if the first clause were true. The logic and syntax are equally bad, and the conclusions are unscientific. As a matter of fact, the truth is the opposite of the declaration in the first clause of this sentence. So strong is the colored man's orthodox faith and the fear of anatomization that it is only by subterfuge or accident that any but the poverty-stricken, friendless, or legally condemned ever reach the dissectors' tables.

The prosperity of the colored undertaker is strong evidence of the race's care for its dead. Any colored preacher could have given Dr. Bean better information.

To number three, as it relates to the Negro, I enter a general denial, and call as witnesses the officers, white and black, of industrial insurance companies doing business among the colored people.

A flat contradiction is the only answer to number four. It is *not* a fact that "the better class of Negroes are roaming around over the country without fixed abode."

This is the kind of literature that is poisoning the stream of our national life by increasing race prejudice.

The *doctrinaire ebullitions of the student often become slogans of war among the ignorant.* Newspaper and platform arguments about "white supremacy" often take the form of cruelty and oppression when interpreted by a street-car conductor, a ward policeman, or a workhouse guard. The extent of this oppression, I am sure, is entirely unknown to the majority of white citizens. It is an interesting if pathetic study, to see an artificial self-consciousness of racial superiority strangle the natural impulses of civilization. The other day I saw a good-looking, modest-appearing, well-dressed, but frail colored woman with a child in her arms attempt to board a street-car. She was about to fail. The conductor started to help her, then looked at the other passengers and desisted. His face was a study. Prejudice won; but it was a Pyrrhic victory. To prove a doctrine he damned a man. There is something wrong with a code of ethics that makes its votaries feel it is a humiliation to be kind to any sentient creature, much less a human being, however humble.

Chromatopsia (a perversion of the color sense) *yet may wreck the twentieth-century civilization.*

Conduct must be consistent or character will not be sound. An individual or people cannot long remain both Jekyll and Hyde; one character or the other will eventually triumph. No one can successfully change his character with his company. A race cannot be persistently unjust and dishonest to another race and be permanently either honest or just to itself. Kindness never degraded anyone, nor did rudeness ever vindicate anybody's claim to superiority. A virtuous man is an asset to his community, and a vicious man is a deficit, regardless of racial identity.

There is a mechanical principle called "superposition of small motions," which shows that the result of two forces acting simultaneously on a body is the sum or difference of these forces, according as they act in the same or in opposite directions. (Illustration: a cork in a still pond when two stones are thrown in.) This principle holds good in social and economic progress. Repressive measures against a part of the nation will retard the progress of the whole nation. Russia has been injured by her treatment of the Jew, and America by her treatment of the Negro. Strange that each nation can see the other's error, but not its own. Every white politician that has reached power and place by abusing the colored people has not only subtracted from the progress and prestige of the nation, but represents a positively retrogressive and deteriorating force in the civilization of the white man.

Science joins common sense, religion, and morals in warning the virtuous of both races to unite their efforts against the vicious of both races, if they would conserve the cultural integrity of their respective units and the political welfare of their common country.

The effort to substitute *race* for *fitness* in the qualifications for citizenship not only outrages morals and religion, but runs counter to the demonstrated truths of science.

"The differences between types of man are, on the whole, small as compared with the range of variations in each type." (Boas.) That is, there is more difference between an educated, moral white man and a vicious white man, than there is between a vicious black man and a vicious white man. The same is true of the colored people.

Cultural unities make races, and political unities make nations. The former may co-operate to form the latter without destroying or even endangering their own existence. The French of Quebec are still French in race after being British in nationality for more than a century. The Negro's difficulties are only human and natural; therefore, he must be patient, hopeful, and persistent. Others have won and so can he. God is just and Nature plays no favorities, though some fare worse than others. All humanity has a right to a place in the sun. There is room for all; therefore, the white man must be tolerant, considerate, and kind. The permanency of his racial primacy depends upon the general advancement of mankind. Civilization must finally rest upon the precepts of the Sermon on the Mount, or perish from the earth.

III.—Undesirable Variations.

The hard conditions of discrimination and repression under which Americans of African descent are forced to live have produced a class of individuals that have done untold harm to the race. Whether he has essayed to lead or has been taken as typical and has brought upon us the contempt of other races, the Negro ashamed of his blood or without faith in his race is a nuisance.

"The man without a country" has been held up as the verisimilitude of misery itself—at once the most pitiable and contemptible of mankind—but he is not comparable in meanness of spirit, in self-degradation and utter hopelessness of improvement with the man without a race. The football of heredity and the plaything of environment, he confuses all values and misinterprets all standards—with the heart of a traitor and the brains of a thief he destroys his own self-respect between the upper millstone of fruitless desire to be white and the nether millstone of senseless dread of being black. Without the respect of the white people, without either the respect or confidence of the black people, without self-esteem he enters the category of Dante's Neutrals:—

> "Souls
> To misery doomed who intellectual good
> Have lost. Fame of them the world hath none.
> *   *   *   *   *   *
> Speak not of them, but look and pass by."

Without apparent place in the socio-economic formula of the nation, this class has a catalytic value and deserves a careful examination.

It is a mental condition and not bodily characteristics that differentiates this group. They are usually of mixed blood, but not invariably.

W. B. T. Williams, a noted Negro educator, gives an apt and vivid description of this anomalous group:

"Out in Kentucky there lives an old colored man who has made a considerable little fortune out of his coal-yard. He is shrewd, economical, close. His wife is just like him. They delight in showing the less thrifty young colored people of today a cook-stove which they bought two years before the Civil War and have used constantly ever since. Although he keeps coal for sale, the old man takes pleasure in telling how he always manages to get discarded railroad ties to cut up and burn in the stove. 'Coal, you know,' he will tell you, 'just burns out stoves.' By such little economies the old couple have saved their money. They spend none that is possible to keep. Recently the city improved the street that passes the home of the old people. Their share of the expense amounted to several hundred dollars, which, of course, they had to pay. The old lady died from the shock. The old man made his will leaving his fortune to the son of his old master. No one has been able to induce him to leave his money to colored people or to any Negro institution. 'No,' he says, 'Niggers are no good. No use doing anything for Niggers.' Though he himself is a Negro who has done no little thing in the world in the face of many disadvantages, he is consumed with deadly, damning disbelief in the Negro. And there are others of his type, belated inheritors of a belief born of conditions that have happily passed away."

From charcoal to diamond is only a course in culture—a course that nature conducts easily and man imitates with partial success, only; but intellectual comprehension and physical execution are by no means synonymous. I saw a man throw an iron ring ten yards and hang it on a peg,—I understood at once, but five hundred trials did not enable me to do it. Had I tried it without seeing it done, I might have reached the conclusion that it could not be done. The difference between the despised ware of the charcoal vender and the sparkling joy of the jeweler's window is only a difference of experience, and not a difference of qualities or capacities.

Science, in its humbler aspects, consists in finding out the workings of nature—the secrets of her processes. Science in her nobler aspects, taking advantage of the knowledge gained in the humbler walks of observation, enters the region of experiment and speculation and seeks to measure the possible. From the certainty of *fact* she essays the uncertainty of *prediction.* Observation warrants prediction so long as the former is done with care and the latter with modesty. It is a proper exercise of the intellect to widen the mental horizon by extending the frontiers of knowledge over the borders of actual experience. Speculation upon the *possible* is legitimate so long as it does no violence to the *actual.* In speaking of the actual we must not confuse *facts* with *opinion.* This error has at times extinguished the torch of reason.

If we read the past aright, we may, in the light of the present, forecast the future. With nature and man it is the same.

Science and history agree in holding facts as the only just basis for prediction. The more extended and accurate the knowledge of facts the more modest and limited the field of prediction. A knowledge of the facts of physical sciences will temper our zeal in the speculative ones. Demonstration is more exacting than prophecy. Physics and physiology are more potent than ethnology and politics. We can accept the theories of the latter only when they do not conflict with the proven facts of the former.

The geographical study of the earth and the historical study of the activities of man both point to the North American Continent as the theater of the coming Golden Age of human civilization. The fate of the United States will determine the fate of the continent and *the Race Question with its economical ramifications is the crucial point in the civil and political life of this nation.* The higher the state of civilization the more complicated and diverse may be the co-operating elements. As the simplest animal bodies are homogeneous throughout, with no differentiation of tissue or function, so the simplest civilizations and states admit but single cultural unities or races. As animal bodies increase in beauty and effectiveness they increase in complications and differentiations until the climax is reached in man, the most complicated mechanism of terrestrial existence,—"the moral and intellectual sensorium of the world." Just so with civilization; as it increases in effectiveness it increases in comprehensiveness. First the family, then the tribe, then the vicinage, then the nations, and finally *man* without limitation, either geographical or consanguineous. The great European War was possible only because civilization had not passed beyond the stage of nationality. Before man can pass that point, a nationality must arise that can and will give all races a place in the sun. This means not only increasing complications, but increasing effectiveness, if harmony of action can be maintained.

More than a generation ago Guyot truly said: "The progress, we say, is diversification—it is variety of organs and of functions. What, then, is the condition of a greater amount of life, or a richer life, or a completer growth for the animal? Is it not the multiplicity and the variety of the special organs, which are so many different means whereby the individual may place himself in relation with the external world, may receive the most varied impressions from it, and, so to speak, may taste it in all its forms, and may act upon it in turn? What an immense distance between the life of the polyp, which is only a digestive tube, and that of the superior animals; above all, of man, endowed with so many exquisite senses, for whom the world of nature, as well as the world of ideas, is open on all sides, awakening and drawing forth, in a thousand various ways, all the living forces wherewith God has endowed him!

"And what we here say of organic individuals, is it not true of societies of individuals, and particularly of human societies? Is it not evident that the same law of development is applicable to them? Here, again, homogeneousness, uniformity, is the elementary state, the savage state. Diversity, variety of elements, which call for and multiply exchanges; the almost infinite specialization of the functions corresponding to the various talents bestowed on every man by providence. . . .

"All life is mutual, is exchange. In individuals, as well as in societies, that which excites life, that which is the condition of life, is *difference*. The progress of development is diversity; the end is ***harmonious unity*** allowing all differences, all individualities to exist, but co-ordinating and subjecting them to a superior aim.

"Every being, every individual, necessarily forms a part of a greater organism than itself, out of which we cannot conceive its existence, and in which it has a special part to act. By performing these functions, it arises to the highest degree of perfection its own nature is capable of attaining. Unhappy he who isolates himself, and refuses to enter into those relations of intercourse with others which assure to him a superior life. He deprives himself voluntarily of the nutritive sap intended to give him vigor, and, like a branch torn from the vine, dries up and perishes in his egoism."[4]

That political nationality does not necessarily coincide with cultural unity is neither illusory nor deplorable. The American colored man and the American white man can develop distinctive cultural unities and preserve an identical political nationality. The objective, mechanical, impersonal side of civilization has been tending toward unity. The *body politic,* the framework of government, judiciary, executive, legislative, is a very different thing from the *soul politic,* the traditions and ideals of the citizenry. The diatribes against the danger of Negro citizenship are not more harrowing than those against educating women (see French argument against admitting women to High School), or the licensing of railroads (see English speeches against the dangers of 12 miles an hour).

The Amphictyonic Council failed among the Greeks and the Heptarchy failed among the Saxons, but the Union in America endured the shock of civil

[4] Arnold Guyot, "Earth and Man."

war and still stands. The Greeks were all white and so were the Saxons, but the Americans were of different colors—heterogeneous in race, but homogeneous in nationality. So they were, so they are, and so they will remain. Advancing civilization will strengthen alike individual cultural unities and a common *national patriotism.*

Patriotism is no longer a brutal instinct of blood, but a high expression of community of ideals and of moral as well as material interests.

They make fun of the Negroes' religion. There be those that make fun of all religion, but if justice ever dwells among men and humanity ever knows the joy of freedom, these blessings will come through religion.

The history of the world has been called, aptly enough, the martyrdom of man. Civilization, or human progress, seems to have risen by slow increments, generation being superimposed upon generation, like the coral isles of the sea—one dies to make a foundation for the other's life. Contemplation of this phase of human life always leads to sadness and sometimes to pessimism.

"What is man that Thou art mindful of him?" asks the Psalmist. "Man has no pre-eminence over a beast," says the preacher. "Oh, why should the spirit of mortal be proud!" exclaims one poet.

"This world is but a fleeting show
To man's illusion given,"

laments another—and so on and on throughout all literature. There is not one cheerful word from anyone contemplating this phase of existence. History is a continuous funeral procession and the earth one vast graveyard.

"The hills,
Rock-ribbed and ancient as the sun; the vales,
Stretching in pensive quietness between;
The venerable woods, rivers that move
In majesty, and the complaining brooks
That make the meadows green; and poured round all
Old ocean's gray and melancholy waste,
Are but the solemn decorations all
Of the great tomb of man. The golden sun,
The planets, all the infinite hosts of heaven
Are shining on the sad abodes of death,
Through the still lapse of ages.
All that tread
The globe, are but a handful to the tribes
That slumber in its bosom."

But there is another phase of human existence; and the struggles of mankind shall find fruition in a life free from pain. Religion and philosophy unite in looking forward to a golden age. The struggle of man with his appetite is indicative of this and the approach of the one can be told by the progress of the other. Ancient Israel struggling against the idolatrous excesses of the people and modern America fighting color prejudice are but phases of this evolutionary battle of man for civilization—for a life guided by reason and actuated by love. This view of life is inspiring, and those who look upon it believe in the ultimate triumph of right and the final glory of mankind.

Bayard Taylor's vision of America will some day be true:—

" 'Twas glory once, to be a Roman;
She makes it glory, now, to be a *man*."

The truly cultivated mind will not regard disagreement as sufficient cause for enmity. Only two classes of people can agree on all points—the densely ignorant and the profoundly wise. People that can see nothing can always agree on what they see, and people who see everything clearly and accurately can do the same thing. We that belong to neither of these classes must be charitable, which is the goal of ethics; and try to understand and help each other, which is the hoped-for fruition of all science. In other words, among cultivated individuals, differences of opinion become subjects of converse; as a diversity of products promotes commerce among nations.

"A certain resemblance is found in any two opposite regions of the sky, no matter where we may choose them." So with human conduct, "Learn what is true," says Science. "Do what is right," says Ethics. Either road leads to the desired goal; for when men seek the *true* they will also find the *right;* and when they seek the *right* they will also find the *true.*

SCIENCE AND CHRISTIAN ETHICS.

CHAPTER IV.

SOME BASIC PROBLEMS.

An old principle of ethics is that they that seek justice must do justice. They that come into the court of equity must come with clean hands. "Let him without sin cast the first stone."

The moral sins of the colored people are great and deserving of condemnation; but what race is without similar sin? The slum proposition and prostitution and immorality are just as urgent in large cities where they are all Caucasians as in the cities where there are Negroes. Since it is so often asserted that the colored man has neither morals nor moral sense, it is well to consider this subject somewhat in detail.

"To surround one's life with a confused mass of spiritual horrors; to believe in ghosts, or in vampires, in demons, in magic, in witchcraft, and in hostile gods of all sorts; to tangle up one's daily activities in a net of superstitious customs; to waste time in elaborate incantations; to live in fantastic terrors of an unseen world; to be terrified by taboos of all kinds, so that numerous sorts of useful deeds are surreptitiously forbidden; to narrate impossible stories and believe in them; to live in filth; to persecute; to resist light; to fight against progress; to be mentally slothful, dull, sensuous, cruel; to be the prey of endless foolishness; to be treacherous; to be destructive—well, these are the mental traits of no one or two races of men."[1]

---

[1] Josiah Royce, "Race Questions and Other American Problems."

I.

Kant says that an action to have moral worth must be done from a sense of duty, and adds, "That an action done from duty derives its moral worth, *not from the purpose* which is to be attained by it, but from the maxim by which it is determined, and therefore does not depend on the realization of the object of the action, but merely on the *principle of volition* by which the action has taken place, without regard to any object or desire. . . . The purposes which we may have in view in our actions, or their effects regarded as ends and springs of the will, cannot give to actions any unconditional or moral worth. In what, then, can their worth lie, if it is not to consist in the will and in reference to its expected effect? It cannot lie anywhere but in the *principle of the will* without regard to the ends which can be attained by the action. For the will stands between its *à priori* principle, which is formal, and its *à posteriori* spring, which is material, as between two roads; and as it must be determined by something, it follows that it must be determined by the formal principle of volition when an action is done from duty, in which case every material principle has been withdrawn from it.

"Duty is the necessity of acting from respect for the law."[1] That is, *moral conduct* is *conduct controlled by intellect.*

Animals have no morals (or very feeble moral sense) because of the state of their intellectual development. We then have no morals only when no reason enters into our actions. Huxley said he never had found a fool—that is, a man with no reason for

[1] Kant, "Fundamental Principles of Morals."

his actions. He had come across what appeared at first sight splendid specimens, but closer examination always revealed some reason in the position *from that man's viewpoint*. As there are no men without language and reason, so there *are no men without morals*. In the face of these fundamental facts those who persist in asserting the Negro has no moral sense are either innocently ignorant, willfully mendacious, or theory-mad beyond redemption.

It is as difficult to comprehend the morals of a people as it is the motives of an individual. To do either correctly we must think their thoughts and have their experiences. Since this is impossible, human experience says *judge not,*—"With what measure ye mete, it shall be measured to you again." That is just what has happened in the race situation in this country. The races have been pulled apart until they are suspicious of each other. Misunderstanding has made them both mean.

All men have reason, but all men do not reason equally well. When a man correctly forecasts the consequences of his deeds, his reasoning is sound. To reason thus soundly one must have full knowledge of all the factors in a situation. Hence the soundness of the conclusions reached by reason depends upon the accuracy and fullness of the data upon which it is working. Failure to recognize this obvious fact, is one of the tragedies of human history. A strictly logical mind of limited intelligence is one of the most dangerous forces of civilization. Logic without knowledge is force without direction. A man with such a mind is like a ship with a strong engine, but weak steering apparatus and a defective chart; the stronger the engine, the more disastrous the inevitable wreck.

As we have all kinds of reasoning, so we have all grades of morals—good, bad, and indifferent. The ignorant are always prejudiced and the prejudiced are always ignorant. The ignorance of the prejudiced is incurable because they obstinately refuse the only remedy—*knowledge*. Race prejudice is the meanest of prejudices and race pride the most fatuous of follies. They are complementary inanities. The white man that is proud of his white skin and the black man that is ashamed of his black skin are both sinners in the sacred courts of civilization; for they have missed their high calling to be men. Why should a man be proud or ashamed of that for which he is justly due neither praise nor blame? No man is responsible for his *color,* but he is responsible for his *character*.

This has nothing to do with social preferences and consciousness of kind. Man, like other animals, instinctively prefers to associate with his own kind. "Pares cum paribus, facillime congregantur, vetero proverbio,"[2] wrote Cicero two thousand years ago. There is a difference between my preferring to associate with black people because I am black, and my wanting to injure white people because they are white.

How curious is the world-wide infirmity of human reason shown in the attitude of the average individual toward new facts, especially if they seem to run counter to his present conclusions. The more overwhelming the evidence, the more obstinate the opposition. This attitude has been likened to the pupil of the eye: the more light you throw into it, the smaller it gets.

Some years ago I was present at the meeting of a society devoted to scientific research. The question of spiritualism came up. Sentiment was divided. There were various phases of belief. Some believed, some disbelieved, and some were non-committal. The

---

[2] Might be freely translated "According to the old proverb, birds of a feather flock together."

disbelievers got the best of the argument by producing incontrovertible evidence that a popular medium then operating in the city was a fraud. The situation was relieved by an intelligent, refined, and educated man taking the position that the spurious was only an evidence that the genuine existed. The president innocently asked if this gentleman could tell the genuine from the spurious. Upon receiving an affirmative answer the subject was dropped.

Several months after this incident, a notice appeared in the local papers that a prominent spiritualist had secured the services of a great medium to vindicate spiritualism before the Society. His identity was not disclosed for prudential reasons. The night came and so did the crowd. The meeting was enthusiastic, the vindication a success, and the spiritualists were jubilant. There was but one regret: the president and secretary, both hard-headed disbelievers, were unfortunately absent, having been called away from the city some days previous. Speeches were made, appropriate resolutions were adopted, and then the presiding vice-president pulled aside a curtain, exposing the president and secretary, as the world-famous medium and materializing ghost.

It would seem that the antis had won, at least to the extent of proving that the elect could be deceived. Result? The spiritualists, led by the proposer of the test, left the society in a body, excitedly declaring they had been imposed upon. They were simply angered by evidence.

Well has it been said that the greatest gift of wisdom is to *liberalize* (set free) the mind. Ignorance enslaves as surely as the truth frees.

Another trait of human reason is to measure everything by itself. If we do not know the other man's motives, we judge him by ours. That is, if we do not know why an individual does a certain thing, we say he did it for the reasons we would do it under the circumstances as we see them. This process is often unconscious, but it is unvarying with the average individual. This fact has been crystallized in the proverbial wisdom of mankind:—

> "To the pure all things are pure."
> "Evil be to him who evil thinks."

It is not the wisest of mankind that claims all other people are ignorant. Neither is it the most virtuous in any race that deny all virtue in other races. The wisest and best of mankind have ever been the most philanthropic and most universal in their sympathies. The history of the world furnishes no example of a benefactor of mankind being a misanthrope, or of a misanthrope being an intentional benefactor. The very best of mankind have always believed in *justice* for *all.* The American colored man is quite willing to rest his case with the civilized white man.

Sex and food are probably the first perplexities of human relationship, and, notwithstanding their primary nature, are still unsolved problems of civilization. Among all peoples, morality falls lowest and reason seems weakest on these subjects.

Monogamy is only an ideal, not even professed, much less sought or understood, by the majority of mankind. Fair play is but a dream of culture, which readily enough gives way in an emergency to the so-called law of necessity. Only insincerity, insanity, or ignorance will claim that these problems are peculiar to any race or the exceptional phenomena of interracial friction. The honest and patriotic people (and there are some) who claim that the presence of the colored people created these problems for America are lacking in knowledge of the empirical facts of the situation, or deficient in that historical perspective and philosophic insight necessary to the application of these facts to the principles of human development.

To understand complex fractions one must know simple fractions; to solve quadratic equations one must understand the simple equations. The more thoroughly he is grounded in the simpler operations, the more readily will he grasp the difficulties of the more complicated ones. So with all the problems of life—anthropology, ethnology, sociology, and economics form no exception. To understand the relationship of the men and women of one race to the men and women of another race, one must have a knowledge of the simpler, but more fundamental problem of intraracial sexual relation. One cannot understand the economic and moral relationship of cultural units to each other unless he have knowledge of the intraracial habits of the different cultural units and the simpler individual relationships.

An honest but unsophisticated black man is cheated by a white man. He concludes rascality is one of the attributes of a white skin. An honest but inexperienced white man has his chickens stolen by a black man and he reaches an unwarranted generalization about colored people and chickens. Wider knowledge would correct these false conclusions. An experience or two with a black confidence man will change the black man's mind on the subject of a white skin and rascality. Similarly, the white man would be taught by wider experience that the black man was not the only one likely to rob hen-roosts. Unless this further enlightenment comes, these experiences will make these men partizan, prejudiced, and bitter.

That is what is happening in the South.

The races know and believe in the vices of each other, but do not know or believe in the virtues of each other. The average white Christian believes that the colored man neither understands nor practises the true principles of Christianity, and the colored man knows that the white man so believes. But the colored man believes identically the same thing of the white man, and this the white man does not know. Yet neither doubts the other's vices. Further, the average colored man believes it impolitic to be manly, and dangerous to be frank with white people. May it not be possible that each race has given the other more evidence of its vices than it has of its virtues? Each has demonstrated, to the full satisfaction of the other, its guilt of falsehood, theft, and immorality; but each has failed to impress upon the other its love of truth, honesty, and virtue.

Before passing judgment upon the black man's effect on the men, women, and morals of the white man, it is but fair to study these relations in general, and particularly in the white man where the colored man is not present.

Around the sexual relation gather nine-tenths of all that men desire or dread. The most intense and pervading appetite, animal or human, is the sexual feeling. The keenest physical pleasure and the most poignant physical pain find alike their origin here; yea, man's mental gifts and spiritual aspirations also center here. Religion itself is closely akin if not identical with this passion. Certainly they are interchangeable; as anyone can prove to his own satisfaction by observing people given to extremes of each feeling. Many of our artistic and sculptural forms find here their first pattern, and phallic worship was possibly the first religious ceremony. "The fall of man" was a perversion of this passion, and the "loss of Eden" resulted from the effort of man to enjoy sexual pleasure without entailing procreative responsibility. Sexual indulgence without the object or possibility of parenthood is at once the bane and abomination of civilization. Man has pitted his free-will against the designs of the Creator, and, by open rebellion against the laws of his being, created for himself the hell of venereal disease.

"Our earliest acquaintance with the human race discloses some sort of society established. It also reveals the existence of a marriage tie, varying in stringency and incidental effects according to climate, morals, religion, or accident, but everywhere essentially subversive of a system of promiscuous intercourse. No nation, it is believed, has ever been reported by a trustworthy traveller, on sufficient evidence, to have held its women generally in common. Still there appears to have been in every age men who did not avail themselves of the marriage covenant, or who could not be bound by its stipulations, and their appetites created a demand for illegitimate pleasures which female weakness supplied. This may be assumed to be the real origin of prostitution throughout the world, though in particular localities this first cause has been assisted by female avarice or passion, religious superstition or a mistaken sense of hospitality.

"Accordingly prostitution is coeval with society. It stains the earliest mythological records. It is constantly assumed as an existing fact in Biblical history. We can trace it from the earliest twilight in which history dawns to the clear daylight of today, without a pause or a moment of obscurity."[3]

The sexual problem is a human problem. In the

---

[3] Sanger, "History of Prostitution."

sexual life it is hard for man to get away from the beast. Read the annals of the Jewish people, one of the oldest and certainly one of the noblest, cultural units of history; remember that the idol worship they so frequently preferred to the worship of Jehovah was accompanied by sexual orgies.

The popular belief is that sexual feeling, especially in women, is a manifestation of puberty only. On the contrary, it is deeply rooted in our being, and is probably congenital.

Havelock Ellis quotes approvingly from the experienced gynecologist, Braxton Hicks:—

"I venture to think," Braxton Hicks says, "that those of my hearers who have much attended to children will agree with me in saying that, almost from the cradle, a difference can be seen in manner, habits of mind, and in illness, requiring variations in their treatment. The change is certainly hastened and intensified at the time of puberty; but there is, even to an average observer, a clear difference between the sexes from early infancy, gradually becoming more marked up to puberty. That sexual feelings exist (it would be better to say 'may exist') from earliest infancy is well known, and therefore this function does not depend upon puberty, though intensified by it. Hence, may we not conclude that the progress toward development is not so abrupt as has been generally supposed? . . . The changes of puberty are all of them dependent on the primordial force, which, gradually gathering power, culminates in the perfection both of form and of sexual system, primary and secondary."[4]

That the extramarital and premarital sexual relation may be a cult or a custom is well illustrated by

---

[4] Ellis, "Psychology of Sex.

the following: "On the opposite side of the Baltic, in the Königsberg district, the same observation has been made. Intercourse before marriage is the rule in most villages of this agricultural district, among the working classes, with or without intention of subsequent marriage. 'The girls are often the seducing parties, or at least very willing; they seek to bind their lovers to them and compel them to marriage.' In the Köslin district of Pomerania, where the intercourse between the girls and youths is common, the girls come to the youths' rooms even more frequently than the youths to the girls. In some of the Dantzig districts the girls give themselves to the youths, and even seduce them, sometimes, but not always, with a view to marriage."[5]

In some places in Europe "Christians worshipped in a state of nudity, and accompanied prayers with promiscuous intercourse." St. Crysostum complains that in places he designates, "women were baptized in a state of nature, without even being permitted to veil their sex."

"It is unquestionable, however, that the author of the Massacre of St. Bartholomew lived in incestuous intercourse with his sister Margaret, and there seems no reason to doubt the truth of the story that Catherine more than once entertained the king and court at a banquet at which nude females served as waiters."

"Perhaps the best idea of the morals of the time can be obtained from the adventures of the Margaret just mentioned, who married Henry IV, King of Navarre, and afterward King of France. It is said that at the age of 11 she had two lovers, both of whom claimed to have robbed her of her virtue. . . .

[5] *Ibid.*

"He (the king) changed his mistress once a month at least." (Sanger.)

"Again turning to the pages of Fiducin, we find that, 'in all the great towns of the German Empire, the public protection of women of pleasure (*lust dirnen*) seems to have been a regular thing,' in proof of which he says: 'Did a creditor, in taking proceedings against a debtor, find it necessary to put up at an inn, one of the allowed items of his expenditure was a reasonable sum for the company of a woman during his stay (*frugen geld*).' This was a question of State Etiquette in Berlin in 1410, a sum having been officially expended in that year to retain some handsome woman to grace a public festival and banquet given to a distinguished guest, Diedrich von Quitzow, whose good-will the citizens desired to cultivate."[6]

As an evidence that the presence of the Negro is not the cause of sexual excesses and bacchanalian orgies, I quote from the work called "Berlin," by Dr. Sass, a description of the Tans Wirthschaften (dancing-houses):—

"The dance is carried to its wildest excess, to ear-splitting music in a pestilential atmosphere. The poor are extravagant; drunkenness and profligacy abound. Servants of both sexes, soldiers and journeymen, workwomen and prostitutes make up the public. Here, on the most frivolous pretenses, concubinage and marriage are arranged, and from this scene of folly and vice the family is ushered into the world. The wet-nurse is met here, 'the type of country-girl simplicity,' who after a night of tumult and uproar with her lover will go in the morning to nurse the child whose mother neglects her parental duties at the dictates of fashion. The working classes have their

[6] Sanger, "History of Prostitution."

representatives, who drown their cares in drink, while boys and girls make up the motley party. In these assemblies there is a difference. Some are attended by the citizens of the humbler classes, by working men and women; others by criminals and their paramours. In these latter resorts the excesses are of a more frightful character than in those where a show of decency restrains the grosser exhibitions; youth of both sexes are among the well-known criminals, who are habituated to drinking, smoking, and the wildest orgies, long before their frames have attained proper development. Physiognomies which might have sprung from the most hideous fancy of poet or painter may be met with."

Again quoting from Dr. Sass's work we get the following description of private life in Berlin:—

"Let us enter the house. The first floor is inhabited by a family of distinction; husband and wife have been separated for years; he lives on one side, she on the other; both go out in public together; the proprieties are kept in view, but servants will chatter. On the second floor lives an assessor with his kept woman. When he is out of town, as the house is well aware, a doctor pays her a visit. On the other side of the staircase lives a carrier with his wife and child. The wife had not mentioned that this child was born before marriage; he found it out; of course, they quarreled, and now he takes his revenge in drunkenness, blows, and abuse. We ascend to the third floor. On the right of the stairs is a teacher who has had a child by his wife's sister; the wife grieves sorely over the same. With him lodges a house-painter who ran away from his wife and three children, and now lives, with his concubine and one child, in a wretched little cupboard. On the left is a letter-carrier's family. His pay is fifteen thalers (twelve dollars) a month, but the people seem very comfortable. Their daughter has a very nice front room, well furnised, and is kept by a very wealthy merchant, a married man. Exactly opposite there is a house of accommodation, and close by there is a midwife, whose sign board announces 'an institute for ladies of condition where they can go through their confinement in retirement.' I can assure the reader that in this sketch of sexual and family life in Berlin, I have nothing extenuated, nor set down aught in malice."

This is a clean, modern, moral city, one of the very best that European civilization affords, and all Caucasians, too.

Dr. Sanger says: "In London this system of close lodging was carried to a fearful pitch. In some places from five to thirteen persons slept in a single bed, while in the country the evil was nearly as bad; although, from the slight restraint imposed by family ties, the actual evil is positively less, though the moral contamination is of nearly the same extent, and paves the way for other relations out of doors. The facts which justify these conclusions are to be found in a variety of shapes—parliamentary reports, statistical tables, appeals from clergymen, addresses from philanthropic associations, etc."

He also quotes from the Honorable and Reverend S. O. Osborne, the description of country life in England:—

"From infancy to puberty the laborer's children sleep in the room with his wife and himself; and whatever attempts at decency may be made, and I have seen many ingenious and praiseworthy attempts, still there is the fact of the old and the young, married and unmarried, of both sexes, all herded together in one and the same sleeping-apartment. . . . I do not choose to put on paper the disgusting scenes that I have known to occur from the promiscuous crowding of the sexes together. Seeing, however, to what the mind of the young female is exposed from her very childhood, I have long ceased to wonder at the otherwise seeming precocious licentiousness of conversation which may be heard in every field where many of the young are at work together."

In Europe under the feudal system, "the king claimed the disposal of the hands and fortunes of heiresses; the barons claimed a still greater privilege from their tenants. In some localities the feudal lord insisted upon enjoying the person of one of the daughters of each tenant who happened to be blessed with a plurality of them. He returned her to her parents within a given time." (Sanger.)

"Every Babylonian female was obliged by law to prostitute herself once in her life in the temple of the Chaldean Venus, whose name was Mylitta.

"The Mylitta of Chaldea became Astarte in Phœnicia, at Carthage, and in Syria. Nothing was changed but the name; the voluptuous rites were identical."

The Negroes of Africa were not the only ones who had sexual initiation for women. Among the Athenians, "The legal principle with regard to the dicteriades appears to have been that they should conceal nothing; no doubt in contrast to the regular prostitutes. . . . There was no rule, however, forbidding the wearing of garments in the dicterion, but the common practice appears to have been to dispense with them, or to wear a light scarf thrown over the person. . . . There appears to have been attached to these dicteria, schools of prostitution, where young women were initiated into the most disgusting practices by females who had themselves acquired them in the same manner."

"In most of the nations prostitutes figured as pariahs; in Greece they were an aristocracy, exercising a palpable influence over the national policy and social life, and mingling conspicuously in the great march of the Greek intellect. No less than eleven authors of repute have employed their talents as historiographers of courtesans at Athens. Their works have not reached us entire, having fallen victims to the chaste scruples of the clergy of the Middle Ages; but enough remains in the quotations of Athæneus, Alciphron's Letters, Lucian, Diogenes, Lætius, Aristophanes, Aristænetus, and others to enable us to form a far more accurate idea of the Athenian hetairæ than we can obtain of the prostitution of the last generation.

"Into the arts practised by the graduates of the Corinthian Academies it is hardly possible to enter, at least in a modern tongue. . . . One may form an idea of the shocking depravity of the reigning tastes from the sneers which were lavished upon Phryne and Bacchus, who steadily adhered to natural pleasures." . . .

"To judge from the Etruscan paintings, the morals of the indigenous Italians must have been disgustingly depraved." . . .

"Floralian Games. . . . It is certain the chief attraction of these infamous celebrations was the appearance of prostitutes on the stage in a state of nudity, and their lascivious dances in the presence of the people." . . .

"Cato cohabited with a female slave."

"Clodius, the all-powerful tribune, is accused by Cicero of having seduced his three sisters."

"One is appalled at the great variety of classes into which by the Roman law prostibulæ, or unregistered prostitutes, were divided. Such were the *Delicatæ,* corresponding to the kept woman, or the French lorettes, whose charms enabled them to exact large sums from their visitors; the *Famosæ,* who belonged to respectable families and took to evil courses through their lust or avarice; the *Doris,* who were remarkable for their beauty of form, and disdained the use of clothing; the *Lupæ,* or she wolves, who haunted the groves and commons, and were distinguished by a peculiar cry in imitation of the wolf; the *Ælicariæ,* or bakers' girls, who sold small cakes for sacrifice to Venus and Priapus, in the form of the male and female organs of generation; the *Bustuariæ,* whose home was the burial ground and who occasionally officiated as mourners at funerals; the *Copæ,* servant-girls at inns and taverns, who were invariably prostitutes; the *Noctiluæ,* or night walkers; the *Blitidæ,* a very low class of women, who derived the name from *blitum,* a cheap and unwholesome beverage drunk in the lowest holes; the *Diobolares,* wretched outcasts, whose price was two oboli (say two cents); the *Forariæ,* country girls who lurked about country roads; the *Gallinæ,* who were thieves as well as prostitutes; the *Quadrantariæ,* seemingly the lowest class of all, whose fee was less than any copper coin now current. In contradistinction to these, the meretrices assumed an air of respectability, and were often called *bonæ meretrices.*"

Though the Roman law regulated the dress of prostitutes, "nudity appears to have been quite common, if not the rule. . . . Others, however, preferred the silk and gauze dresses of the East, which, according to the expression of a classical writer, 'seemed invented to exhibit more conspicuously what they were intended to hide.' "

"Add to these causes of immorality the baths, and a fair case in the support of Juvenal will be already made out. A young Roman girl with warm southern blood in her veins, who could gaze on the unveiled pictures of the loves of Venus, read the shameful epigrams of Martial, or the burning love-songs of Catullus, go to the baths and see the nudity of scores of men and women, be touched herself by a hundred lewd hands, as well as those of the bathers who rubbed her dry and kneaded her limbs—a young girl who could withstand such experiences and remain virtuous would need, indeed, to be a miracle of principle and strength of mind." . . .

Once a year, at the Lupercalia, she saw young men running naked through the streets, armed with thongs with which they struck every woman they saw; and she noticed that the matrons courted this flagellation as a means of becoming prolific."

"The author does not seem to admit the possibility of virtue's existence; all his men and women are equally vicious and shameless." . . .

"The Egyptian and Ionian dancing girls stripped themselves, or donned the nebula linea. No English words can picture the monstrosities which are calmly narrated in the pages of Petronius and Martial."

The conjure bag and the love powders, so dear to the African heart, are not peculiar to him.

"The use of philtres, or charms, was common in Greece. Retired courtesans often combined the manufacture of these supposed charms with the business of a midwife. They made potions which excited love, and potions which destroyed it; charms to turn love into hate, and others to convert hate into love. That the efficacy of the latter must have been a matter of pure faith need not be demonstrated, though the belief in them was general and profound. The former are well known in the Pharmacopœia, and from the accounts given of their effects there is no reason to doubt that they were successfully employed in Greece, as well by jealous husbands and suspicious fathers as by ardent lovers. A case is mentioned, by no less an authority than Aristotle, of a woman who contrived to administer an amorous potion to her lover, who died of it. The woman was tried for murder; but it being satisfactorily proved that her intention was not to cause death, but revive an extinct love, she was acquitted. Other cases are mentioned in which the philtres produced madness instead of love. Similar accidents have attended the exhibition of cantharides in modern times."

I close these descriptions with a citation from Juvenal, which for good reasons I leave in the Latin tongue:—

"Dormire virum quum senserat uxor,
Ausa Palatino tegetem præferre cubili,
Sumere nocturnas meretrix Augesta cucullos,
Linquebat comite ancilla non amplius una,
Sed *nigrum flavo crinem abscondente galero,*
Intravit calidum veteri centone lupenar,
Et cellam vacuam atque suam. Tunc nudacapillis
Constitit auratis, titulum mentita Lyciscæ,
Ostendit que tuum, generose Britannice, ventrem.
Excepit blanda intrantes, atque *aëra poposcit,*
Et resupina jacens multorum absorbuit ictus.
Mox lenone suas jam dimittente puellas,
Tristris abit, et quod potuit, tamen ultima cellam
Clausit, adhuc ardens rigidæ tentigine vulvæ,
Et lassata viris necdum satiata recessit;
Obscurrisque genis turpis fomoque lucernæ
Fœda lupanaris tulit ad pulvinar adorem."

"Babylon, Carthage, Greece, Rome, and all the older civilizations have had their periods when female virtue was a matter of laughter, when women outvied the men in their moral degradation, when evil seemed triumphant everywhere."

These extracts could be indefinitely increased by illustration of the burnings at the stake in Queen Mary's time of Catholic efforts to restrain heresy, or the disembowelings of Elizabeth's time of protestant efforts to discourage papal error, or of Catherine of Russia's vindication of her artistic temperament by human statuary; but enough has been said to show that the presence of the black man is not necessary to the cruelty, immorality, and savagery of the white man.

I have purposely drawn my illustrations from the boasted "background of European culture," but could have found plenty of material right here in the United States of America to show that the economical and moral troubles of this country are quite independent of the Negro's presence. The Anthracite Coal Miners' strike in Pennsylvania, the Miners' trouble in Colorado, and the Iron Workers' difficulties in California and Indiana are illustrations from the field of economics; and the moral atmosphere is surcharged with a "cloud of witnesses." The execution out west of a divinity student for murdering young women in a church; ditto a Baptist divine in New England for seducing and poisoning young women; ditto a Catholic priest in New York, for seeking by death, dissection, and dismemberment to hide immoralities; all are events too recent to need description. The wholesale debauchery of the electorate in an Ohio county and the bitter charges and recriminations growing out of recent Democratic primaries in the South are moral evidences of the white man's ability to sin without the black man's assistance. But, enough. The problems of sex and food are world-wide and limited to no race.

The white people of the South are as upright in their sexual and social relations as any people on earth, and the virtue of white women is safer here than in any other part of the civilized world.

"Figures show that commitments for rape are, per thousand of the population, less for colored than for white." I have seen the statement, but cannot now verify it, that "more white men in the city of Chicago are charged with rape in a year than black men in the entire South."

Sir Harry Johnston, who is so often quoted against the colored man, says on this subject: "There is, I am convinced, a deliberate tendency in the Southern States to exaggerate the desire of the Negro for a sexual union with white women, and the crimes he may commit under this impulse. A few exceptional Negroes in West and South Africa, and in America, are attracted toward a white consort, but almost invariably for honest and pure-minded reasons, because of some intellectual affinity or sympathy. The mass of the race, if left free to choose, would prefer to mate with women of its own type. When cases have occurred in the history of South Africa, Southwest, East, and Central Africa, of some great Negro uprising, and the wives and daughters of officials, missionaries and settlers have been temporarily at the mercy of a Negro army, or in the power of a Negro chief, how extremely rare are the proved cases of any sexual abuse arising from this circumstance! How infinitely rarer than the prostitution of Negro women following on some great conquest of the whites, or of their black or yellow allies! I know that the contrary has been freely alleged and falsely stated in histories of African events; but when the facts have been really investigated, it is little else than astonishing that the Negro has either had too great racial sense of decency or too little liking for the white women (I believe it to be the former rather than the latter) to outrage the unhappy white women and girls temporarily in his power. He may have dashed out the brains of the white babies against a stone, have even killed, possibly, their mothers, or taken them and the unmarried girls as hostages into the harem of a chief (where no attempt whatever has been made on their virtue), but in the history of the various Kaffir wars it is remarkable how in the majority of cases the wives and daughters of the British, the Boers, and the Germans, after the slaughter of their male relations, were sent back unharmed to white territory.

"I do not believe, as already stated, that there is any inherent tendency on the part of the Negro in America or Africa to dishonor the white woman; rather the contrary. I have already quoted the fact that *in the most densely "Black" parts of the United States white women can live alone in perfect safety.* There is not a complete absence of danger to lonely white women and girls anywhere in the United States (or in many parts of England, Germany, and France), but the danger may arise even more frequently from white tramps and social outcasts than from Negroes."

Another English observer, Mr. Archer, who is also frequently quoted against the Afro-American, says on this subject: "It is a hard thing to say, but I have little doubt it is true, that much of the injustice and cruelty to which the Negro is subjected in the South is a revenge, not so much for sexual crime on the Negro's part, as for an uneasy conscience or consciousness on the part of the whites."

Mr. E. G. Murphy, himself a cultured Southerner, a believer in race inequality, but not injustice, says ("Basis of Ascendency"): "Much of the South's talk against the Negro has therefore been the South talking to itself; it has been its rebuke, by implication, of those corrupting elements within the limits of its own life which answer to no high policy of social respect, to no fine purpose of racial conservation, but which, under the lowest impulses, would degrade the present and betray the future."

The average Southern white woman is neither afraid of a colored man nor nervous over his presence. She has only to command to be obeyed. Instinct, custom, and a sense of self-preservation make this so; to say nothing of the colored man's innate kindliness and almost frantic desire for the white man's approbation. Whatever the past history of the South or its future fate, *today,* 1915, the white inhabitants are not degenerates nor are the colored inhabitants savages.

These colored people are the grandchildren of a generation whose sufferings won the sympathy that brought freedom, whose moderation produced a tolerance that brought peace, and whose industry made a co-operation that brought wealth; a generation that was a blessing to this country and an asset to civilization. Whatever justification slavery may find in the heathenism of Africa, freedom finds its justification in the civilization of America. Whatever the social conditions of the victims of African slave-trade, the beneficiaries of Lincoln's immortal edict were *civilized Christians* whose faithfulness in slavery justified their emancipation.

History furnishes no illustration of a generation of people more entitled to be called civilized than these men and women who, in January, 1863, wept and sang,

> "Thank God Almighty,
> I'm free at last."

I call upon every Confederate soldier, living or dead, to testify as a character witness for the people of whom I speak. I call upon every mistress of a plantation from the shifting sands of the Rio Grande to the blood-stained shores of the storied Potomac, to speak for the fidelity, self-restraint, and industry of this unique generation. Well might the "black mammy" be enshrined in the affections of the Southern white people who saw "the tramping of the vintage where the grapes of wrath were stored!" These black "mammies" were the mothers of as deserving a race of men as ever endured the lash of oppression or met the shock of battle.

Grecian slaves in battle array were vanquished by their masters with whips, but the 54th Massachusetts crossed the bloody sands of Ft. Wagner, climbed the belching ramparts, endured the awful intimacy of the bayonet's charge, and felt the terrifying thrill of the cannon's death-dealing voice, retired in good order, and

"The Old Flag never touched the ground."

In the day of battle they were brave and in the night of temptation they were true. Woe worth the policy, woe worth the day that would estrange the South from the descendants of this generation! Fix the thought firmly in your minds that the *Afro-American was a civilized Christian, baptized with blood and tried with fire, when he became a citizen of the United States!*

Whatever its barbarities and tragedies, a social system that inspired such songs as "My Old Kentucky Home," "Swanee River," "Old Black Joe," and "Massa's in de Col' Col' Groun' " could exist only among civilized people. This civilization which stood four years of war with less brutality than Europe has shown in as many months, will be strong enough to eliminate criminal men, soothe nervous women, and relegate ambitious politicians whose self-seeking has complicated with passion a situation that needed only calmness of reason and the fairness of justice.

Such information as I now possess of the sciences of Anthropology, Physiology, Anatomy, Ethnology, Psychology, Medicine and Organic Evolution,[7] History, and Geography, brightened by experience, but not clouded by sympathy, leads me to believe that the Golden Age of Civilization and human achievement will find fruition in the Mississippi Valley!

---

[7] Shufeldt.

"The thing that gets fed when you are successful is your personal vanity, and the thing that gets starved when you're not successful is your self-respect. And the temptation to go wrong is always strongest when you happen to have the least to resist with."

"Liberality, courtesy, benevolence, unselfishness, under all circumstances and toward all men—these qualities are to the world what a linchpin is to a rolling chariot."—Buddha.

CHAPTER V.

DARK PAGES IN THE WHITE MAN'S CIVILIZATION.

In the preceding chapter I have shown that the physiological problems of sex and the sociological problems of slums were not created nor were they intensified by the presence of colored people. Prostitution is coeval with society. Sexual orgies have accompanied humanity wherever crowded together; in Palestine, in Egypt, in Greece, in Berlin, in London, in New York it is the same, whether the inhabitants are Caucasian or Negro. I now propose to show that the struggle for existence presents all the barbarities among Caucasian people that it does among the darker races. There are dark pages in human history, black and white. "Esquimaux and Australians, Negroes and Scotch Highlanders of former days, ancient Japanese and Hindoos, Polynesians and early Greeks,—all these appear side by side, in such comparative studies of the primitive mind of man, side by side as brothers in error and in ignorance, so soon as you proceed to study by the comparative method their early magic, their old beliefs, their early customs." (Josiah Royce, "Race Questions and Other American Problems.")

I.—Slavery.

It is often charged that the colored man is the cause as well as the victim of the white man's cruelty. It is not true. I can establish an alibi. Nature is impartial, but some fare worse than others. The spirit that established the slave-trade across the Atlantic and planted the Negro in America played no favorites, but devoured wherever lust of power and greed of pelf saw promise of gratification or gain.

"Need I be the Nemesis to remind my Christian countrymen," says a learned Scotsman, "that the sale of English men and women to the American plantation went on lucratively during the reign of the first three Georges, and that in Scotland there were slaves down till the beginning of the present century? Are the Lowland Scots of an inferior race? Are they the product of an undeveloped civilization? Are they not Christians?

"Well, not in the dim and distant ages, but in the latter end of the seventeenth century, there were hundreds of Scotsmen, mixed up with Negroes, doing the work of beasts, and reddening the lash of their drivers with the hero-blood that won Bannockburn Moor and glowed in the gules of glory on the tragic slopes of Flodden Hill. . . . You sold the Lowland Scots, whom the naked truth, apart from patriotism, compels me to claim as, take them for all in all, the finest race that exists under the circuit of the heaven. They have their faults; but a little tract that has not, and never had, two millions of population all told, and yet had produced a Wallace, a Burns, a Scott, and a Carlyle, and scores of stars which in the firmament of history can never set, is no common corner of the world, but is a land of which Man may be proud and of which God has no cause to be ashamed.

"And yet, only two hundred years ago, the Lowlands of Scotland were a hunting ground for slaves. Who hunted the slaves? Christians. Who were the slaves? Christians. In the American plantations, along with Negroes from Coromandel and Mozambique, the Scotsman of Ayrshire and Galloway toiled under the conditions of the most degraded slavery.

"At the battle of Bothwell Brig, when, for lack of gunpowder on their part, the Covenanters were compelled to allow the royal forces to cross the Clyde, there was no longer a battle; there was only a ruthless massacre. . . . Many were cut down in flight. Many were slaughtered where they stood, quoting their text or singing their psalm, determined to give their lives as an evidence that they had never retreated an inch before the Man of Sin and the hosts of Belial. But the sword grew sick of massacre, and a large number of the insurgents were made prisoners and marched off to Edinburgh, where, there being no gaol accommodation for them, they were driven into Greyfriars' Churchyard. There in the open air, exposed to semistarvation and all the inclemency of the season, they remained for well-nigh five months, the slightest attempt to escape being met by a volley of musketry.

"Demented by privation and 'religion,' some went raving mad, some tried to escape, or were supposed to have tried to escape, and were shot, and some died of wounds and disease; but, when five months had expired, there were two hundred and fifty-seven of them still alive,—the skeletons and wrecks of brave and manly men, who, whatever were their follies and errors, had the courage of their convictions, and, undrilled peasants as they were, had dared on the battlefield to try the issue against the British crown. The two hundred and fifty-seven of them who had been possessed of youth and a strength and constitution of iron were still alive. What was to be done with them? Why spend money on the wretched crusts which were flung to them daily—why waste powder in shooting them? This remnant of Bothwell Brig had a money value. These servants of God, by other servants of the same God, could be offered up on the altar of Mammon. They were bargained over to a holy man, William Paterson, a merchant of Leith. Paterson had a ship yclept the 'Crown,' and with this ship he essayed to transport his countrymen to America to be sold as slaves.

"The 'Crown' had barely accommodation for one hundred men; but into her hold were crushed the two hundred and fifty-seven who had borne arms for Christ and his covenanted Kirk. In the hold there was not room to lie down; the decencies of life were impossible; there was plenty of dirt and very little food. There was no light and no comfort; but ever and anon arose the prayers of misery and the psalms of delirium. The weather was wild, cold, stormy, and tempestuous. Day was dark and night was darker still. No sun shone through the drifting snow, no star through the dark and mist; and the wilderness of waters raged and boiled and plunged over the deck and leapt over yardarms, and the cordage was stiff with ice and grisly with snow. Wodrow has put it on record that all they had suffered since, at Bothwell Brig, the banner of Christ went down in blood was as nothing to what the devoted remnant were suffering now. So severe was the weather and so stormy was the sea that, a fortnight after leaving Leith, the 'Crown' had got no further than Orkney Isles.

"On the night of December 10, 1679, some of the inhabitants of Orkney caught, now and then, sight of a vessel through the drifting snow. The vessel was evidently in the direst distress. The sky was black, flakes of snow alternated with pelting sleet, the wind roared like an angry demon, the billows flung themselves into the mountains, and the chorus of the ocean's thunder-song shook the foundations of the world. The eye could not discern what was sea and what was land, what was mountain and what was cloud. But ever and anon, for a moment, in the comparative lull of the wind and the wave, was an interlude of human voices, pitched in the key of agony and ranging the gamut of despair. Scott of Tankerness, at the head of two or three seamen, manned a boat and led a forlorn hope into the ocean. With mighty voice Scott cried to the captain of the ship—the ship was the 'Crown'—to steer to a certain point to avoid destruction. The captain cried back, 'If the vessel cannot ride where she is, she may go to ——!' She could not ride where she was, and to —— she went. More terrible blew the wind. The anchor held fast, but the cable snapped like a thread; and, like a mad thing rushing on to perdition, the 'Crown' dashed onward, where jagged rocks stretched far out like the great saws of the god of the sea. As the 'Crown' drove before the wind to her inevitable doom, down in the darkness the Covenanters joined together and sang the hundred and thirty-seventh psalm:—

" 'By Babel's streams we sat and wept,
  While Zion we thought on;
In midst thereof we hung our harps
  The willow trees upon;
For there a song required they
  Who did us captive bring;
Our spoilers called for mirth and said,
  A song of Zion sing.
O how . . . '

"This psalm, which through years of fierce persecution had rung over the Scottish moorlands and waked the echoes of the Scottish hills, had often been interrupted before as the sentinel espied in the distance the dancing plumes and the shining blades of the men of blood; and the conventicle had, on the spur of the moment, to make up its mind whether it would fight or flee. But now the psalm was interrupted by a mightier than Claverhouse, a fiercer than Dalziel, a more merciless than Lag. The 'Crown,' drifting before the tempest, had struck, with the impact of a thunderbolt, a ledge of rock projecting into the waves. The holy and brave, the men from whose loins I am sprung, the men whose blood boils in my veins as I write, were still below in the dark, *with the hatches battened down* by the order of the captain's wife, who had had her brains dashed out by the falling rigging the moment after she gave the fiendish command.

"By now there is no deck, no hold, no mast, no hatches; that jutting rock of the Orkneys has left the 'Crown' a shattered and shapeless wreck! To the shore—to the shore! In vain. Some, by the waves, are dashed against it lifeless; some, but far fewer, are dashed against it living, and clamber up the Moul Head. But, even on the shore, the remnant who had fought under the banner of the Lord at Bothwell had not seen an end of their suffering. They were weak with hunger, faint with fatigue, their limbs stiffened under their frozen clothes, and they were blinded by the drifts of snow which were dashed in their faces by the December wind. They sank in death in the fields round Deerness; and round Scarvating, each beside his pool of frozen blood, lay more than one noble, but unknown hero of the Covenant, under the cliff from the summit of which he had fallen in the snow and darkness.

"Of the two hundred and fifty-seven more than two hundred perished on that fatal 10th of December. Their flesh never writhed under the driver's whip, they never in slavery sang the songs of Zion and Scotland. The frowning headland of the Moul is their monument, and the waves round the distant Orkneys sing their requiem forever and forever.

"And forever and forever shall the valiant and free souls of the human race execrate the accursed greed that shipped these men into slavery." (W. Stewart Ross.)

This was the spirit of the transatlantic slave-trade. That the black man was finally the victim and the white man the perpetrator was the merest incident. The white man has done nothing to the black man that the black man would not have done to the white man had the conditions been reversed. Nay, the white man has done little to the black man that the black man has not done to himself. This the white man admits, and delights to tell of the barbarities of the African slave-hunters; but he will not admit, in fact, in many cases seems not to know, what is equally true, that the white man has done nothing to the black man that he would not, under like circumstances, do to white people. In fact, there is little that is cruel and barbarous that the white man has done to the black that he has not previously done to his fellow-white.

II.—Religious Fanaticism.

Life is more psychology than physiology. This psychological portion is made up of many elements, the most important portion of which is reason; but the most important element is, unfortunately, not always the most powerful. A stoker on a great steamship may throw the captain overboard. This is exactly what may happen to the ship of our lives when language appeals solely to our "feelings;" when self-interest, greed, or passion become dominant. The emotions are to the intellect what the rabble is to a democracy; once thoroughly aroused, and everything goes down before it. This is why "blessings" frequently bring good fortune and "cursings" bad fortune. It was the misfortunes that followed the excommunicated that made Europe at one time, from the king on the throne to the beggar in the ditch, slaves of the priesthood. What man could leave a church and be fit for successful work with the following curse ringing in his ears?

"In the name of the Father, Son, and Holy Ghost, the blessed Virgin Mary, John the Baptist, Peter, Paul, and all other Saints in Heaven do we curse and cut off from our Communion him who has thus rebelled against us. May the curse strike him in the house, barn, bed, field, path, city, castle. May he be accursed in battle, accursed in praying, in speaking, in silence, in eating, in drinking, in sleeping. May he be accursed in his taste, hearing, smell, and all his senses. May the curse blast his eyes, head and body, from his crown to the soles of his feet. I conjure you, Devil, and all your imps, that you take no rest till you have brought him to eternal shame; till he is destroyed by drowning or hanging, till he is torn to pieces by wild beasts, or consumed by fire. Let his children become orphans, his wife a widow. I command you, Devil, and all your imps, that even as I now blow out these torches, you do immediately extinguish the light from his eyes. So be it—so be it. Amen. Amen." (Motley, "Dutch Republic.")

Well for mankind if religious fanaticism would only limit itself to violence of language, but alas!

The savagery of Africa! Aye! And the savagery of Europe! Even as I write this, Europe is engaged in murder upon a scale that Africa never knew. Savagery! "Oh for a lodge in some vast wilderness!" The history of the world is the martyrdom of man. In savagery man has indeed "pre-eminence above a beast," whether he is black and establishing a Ju Ju House in Gnongo (see J. Cameron Grant's "Ethiopian") or is white and is vindicating religion in Ireland. Since some are fond of quoting Grant's description of the former I will quote Macaulay's description of the latter:—

"Nor age, nor sex," writes Macaulay, "nor infancy, were spared. All conditions were involved in one general ruin. In vain did the unhappy victim appeal to the sacred ties of humanity, hospitality, family connection, and all the tender obligations of social commerce; companions, friends, relations, not only denied protection, but dealt with their own hands the fatal blow. In vain did the pious son plead for his devoted parent; himself was doomed to suffer a more premature mortality. In vain did the tender mother attempt to soften the obdurate heart of the assassin in behalf of her helpless children; she was reserved to behold them cruelly butchered, and then to undergo a like fate. The weeping wife, lamenting over the mangled carcass of her husband, experienced a death no less horrid than that which she deplored. This scene of blood received yet a deeper stain from the wanton exercise of more execrable cruelty than had ever yet occurred to the warm and fertile imagination of Eastern barbarians. Women whose feeble minds received a yet stronger impression of religious frenzy were more ferocious than men; and children, excited by the example and exhortation of their parents, stained their innocent age with the blackest deeds of human butchery.

"Some thousands of English were burnt in their houses; others were stripped naked, and, in hundreds in a drove, pricked forward with swords and pikes to river-sides, and from thence pushed headlong into the stream; some were manacled and thrown into dungeons, and there left to perish at leisure; others were mangled and left to languish in highways; some were happy enough to suffer the milder death of hanging; other more unfortunate wretches were buried alive—this was the fate of a poor little infant, who, while he was being put in the grave, cried to his dead parent,

'Mammy, mammy, save me!' Yet could not his innocent cry pierce the heart of the hardened wretch from whom he received his fate. Some were mangled and hung upon tenter-hooks; some with ropes round their necks were dragged through the woods, bogs, and ditches, till they died; some were hanged up by the arms, and then cut and slashed; some were ripped up, and their entrails left hanging about their heels. These kinds of cruelties were exercised on children of all ages, and many women with child suffered the same fate. Children were forced to carry their sick and aged parents to the place of slaughter; there were of these barbarians some so ingenious in their cruelty as to tempt their prisoners, with the hope of preserving their lives, to imbrue their hands in the blood of their relations. Children were, in this manner, impelled to be executioners of their parents, wives of their husbands, mothers of their children; and then, when they were rendered accomplices in guilt, they were deprived of that life they endeavored to purchase at so horrid a price. Children were boiled to death in cauldrons; some were flayed alive; others were stoned to death; others had their eyes plucked out, their ears, noses, and cheeks and hands cut off, and thus rendered spectacles to satiate the malice of their enemies; some were buried up to their chins, and were left to perish by degrees. Parents were roasted to death before their children, and children before their parents. When anyone on the brink of mortality desired to say a short prayer the bigoted barbarians would exult over the fearful wretch, and tell him that the agonies to be inflicted were but the beginning of infinite and eternal torments. If anyone escaped the murdering hands of these human fiends, they were hunted, baited, and worried to death by their dogs; nor could the miserable condition of these wretches' excrutiating pangs, their anguish of mind, their agony of despair, assuage the lust of cruelty, which precept, bigotry, national prejudice, and the contagion of example had kindled in the depraved nature of their brutal enemies. In the last stroke of death they expressed their malice with the following valediction, 'Thy soul to the devil!' and, at the hazard of contagion, obstinately refused burial to their mangled bodies."

I leave the reader to find out for himself wherein these civilized rites of white Christians are superior to the mad orgies of the black heathen.

And this is the civilization of which Euro-Americans boast and call Afro-Americans barbarians —whose emotional animalism, falsely named religion, will endanger the calm intellectuality of the genuine European article. Emotional fanaticism is by no means the exclusive possession of the colored man.

"The practice of public self-flagellation in church during Lent appears now to have died out entirely, but it existed in Spain and Portugal up to the early years of the nineteenth century. Descriptions of it will often be met with in old volumes of travel. Thus, I find a traveller in Spain in 1786 describing how, at Barcelona, he was present when, in Lent, at a Miserere in the Convent Church of San Felipe Neri on Friday evening, the doors were shut, the lights put out, and in perfect darkness all bared their backs and applied the discipline, singing while they scourged themselves, ever louder and harsher and with ever greater vehemence until in twenty minutes' time the whole ended in a deep groan. It is mentioned that at Malaga, after such a scene, the whole church in the morning was sprinkled with blood."[1]

If as much ingenuity had been expended in fostering art and pursuing science as has been exerted to

[1] Havelock Ellis, "Psychology of Sex."

prove the inferiority of the unfortunate victims of greed and human selfishness, we should today be living in a brighter, happier, nobler world.

Ye that think we are not progressing, take a look at the laws of a few centuries ago. Burning at the stake was common: "It was commonly regarded as an easier death than hanging, and was, therefore, inflicted on criminals of less flagitious offenses, and on women. In some instances, however, the condemned was ignited and choked simultaneously, in order to give her the advantage of both systems. Women were frequently drowned, too, especially adulteresses and witches; being generally put in a bag along with a cat or a snake, and cast into a pond. For the former, the frail delinquents whom men had seduced, smothering in mud was not infrequently prescribed. In 1599 the High Court of Edinburgh sentenced Grissel Mathon, 'to be taken to the North Loch and there drowned till she be dead.' In Bavaria, *circa* 1450, the wife of Duke Albert the Pious was, by order of her father, sacked up and dropped off the bridge; but she got free, and was about to reach the bank when the executioner thrust a long pole into her hair and held her down till life was extinct. In France, about the same period, it was legal to bury people alive, and much later a special law was passed in England conferring upon a criminal of unusual talent the distinction of being boiled in oil. Plain boiling in water was common enough; and in the executioner's expense account for the last sad rites of Friar Stone, at Canterbury, are the following items:—

Paid two men who sat at the kettle and parboiled him. . 1s. 0d.
To three men that carried the quarters to the gates
and set them up . . . . 1s. 0d.

The law under which boiling was done was repealed in the time of Edward VI, not without the gravest apprehension that the repealing act would unsettle the foundations of public security; but as late as 1786 a woman previously strangled was publicly burned opposite Newgate Prison. George III put an end to the practice in 1790. Disemboweling, which was at one time in high religious favor, has been discontinued for some centuries."[2]

Let those who claim that the Negro is contaminating the white man's Christianity read these extracts from a recent European writer: "The Romans were no religious bigots, but were well known to tolerate all speculative opinions whatever. Let us find out, then, why they made an exception in the case of the Christians. On pages 7 and 8 of 'Min. Fælix' we find the impeachment of the new sect stated thus: 'That the Christians knew one another by certain private marks and signs, and were wont to be in love with, almost before they knew, one another; that they exercised lust and filthiness under the pretence of religion, promiscuously calling themselves brothers and sisters; that, by the help of so sacred a name, their common adulteries might become incestuous; that, upon a solemn day, they meet together at a feast, with their wives, children, sisters, mothers, persons of every age and sex, where, after they have well eaten and drunken, and begun to be excited and merry, heated with excess of wine, a piece of meat is thrown to the dogs, who, being tied to the candlesticks, begin to jump and dash about till they have run away with and extinguished the lights, and then, nothing being left but darkness, the fit cover and shadow for indecency and villainy, they promiscuously run among one another into filthy and incestuous embraces; and, if they be not all alike guilty of incest, it is not the fault of

[2] Saladin, "Woman," vol. i.

their will, but the good fortune of their chance, seeing what actually happens to one is intentionally the lot of all."

"Eusebius himself bears testimony that the early Christians were, by their contemporaries, accused of feasting on the flesh of murdered infants."

"From the 'Apologies of the Fathers'[3] we learn that not only those who never had been Christians, but those who had been Christians and become apostate, asserted that at the Christian Agapæ, or love-feasts, 'a newborn infant entirely covered over with flowers was presented, like some mystic symbol of initiation, to the knife of the proselyte, who, unknowingly, inflicted many a secret and mortal wound on the innocent victim of his error; that, as soon as the cruel deed was perpetrated, the sectaries drank up the blood greedily, tore asunder the quivering members, and pledged themselves to eternal secrecy by a mutual consciousness of guilt. It was as confidently affirmed that this human sacrifice was succeeded by a suitable entertainment, in which intemperance served as a provocative to brutal lust, till, at the appointed moment, the lights were suddenly extinguished, shame was banished, nature was forgotten, and, as accident might direct, the darkness of the night was polluted by the incestuous intercourse of sisters and brothers, of sons and mothers.'

"The same protest against murder, incest, and unspeakable abomination rose not only from Rome, but from Lyons and Vienna. Eusebius,[4] quoting a letter from the Christians of Gaul, says: 'Some domestics belonging to our brethren were also seized, as the governor had publicly commanded that search

[3] See Justin Martyr, "Apolog.," i, 35; ii, 14; Athenag., in "Leg.," ch. xxvii; Tertull., in "Apolog.," chs. vii, viii, ix; "Min. Fælix," chs. ix, x, xxx, xxxi.

[4] Euseb., "Hist. Eccles.," lib. v, ch. i.

should be made for all. But these, at the instigation of Satan, for fear of the tortures which they saw the saints endure, and owing to the solicitations of the soldiers, charged us with the feasts of Thyestes and the incests of Œdipus, and such crimes are neither lawful for us to mention nor imagine.'

"Who were Thyestes and Œdipus? I shall inform the non-classical readers. . . . Thyestes violated Ærope, the wife of his brother Atreus, and fed upon the flesh of his own children, which she had borne him in adultery. He, *incognito,* ravished his daughter Pelopeia in a grove sacred to Minerva. Œdipus killed his father and committed incest with his mother."

Let those who are trying to prove that the colored man in America today is not fit for citizenship because of the savage wars waged by his ancestors in Africa read what Don Frederic did for Naarden in Europe: "Here Don Frederic established his headquarters and proceeded to invest the city. Senator Gerrit was then directed to return to Naarden and to bring out a more numerous deputation on the following morning, duly empowered to surrender the place. The envoy accordingly returned the next day, accompanied by Lambert Hortensius, rector of a Latin academy, together with four other citizens. Before this deputation had reached Bussem, they were met by Julius Romero, who informed them that he was commissioned to treat with them on the part of Don Frederic. He demanded the keys of the city, and gave the deputation a solemn pledge that the lives and property of all the inhabitants should be sacredly respected. To attest this assurance, Don Julian gave his hand three times to Lambert Hortensius. A soldier's word thus plighted, the commissioners, without exchanging any written documents, surrendered the keys and immediately afterward accompanied Romero into the city, who was soon followed by five or six hundred musketeers.

"To give these guests a hospitable reception, all the housewives of the city at once set about preparations for a sumptuous feast, to which the Spaniards did ample justice, while the colonel and his officers were entertained by Senator Gerrit at his own house. As soon as this conviviality had come to an end, Romero, accompanied by his host, walked into the square. The great bell had been meantime ringing, and the citizens had been summoned to assemble in the Gast Huis Church, then used as a townhall. In the course of a few minutes five hundred had entered the building, and stood quietly awaiting whatever measure might be offered their deliberation. Suddenly a priest, who had been pacing to and fro before the church-door, entered the building, and bade them all prepare for death; but the announcement, the preparation, and the death were simultaneous. The doors were flung open, and a band of armed Spaniards rushed across the sacred threshold. They fired a single volley upon the defenceless herd, and then sprang in upon them with sword and dagger. Men were slain, women outraged at the altars, in the streets, in their blazing homes. Hardly any man or woman survived, except by accident. A body of some hundred burghers made their escape across the snow into the open country. They were, however, overtaken, stripped stark naked, and hung upon the trees by the feet, to freeze, or to perish by a more lingering death.

"Nearly all the inhabitants of Naarden, soldiers and citizens, were thus destroyed; and now Don Frederic issued peremptory orders that no one, on pain of death, should give lodging or food to any fugitive. He likewise forbade to the dead all that could not be forbidden them—a grave, and for a long time Naarden ceased to exist."[5]

Here is fanatical literalism quenched by heartless barbarism: "On a cold winter's night (February, 1535), seven men and five women, inspired by the Holy Ghost, threw off their clothes and rushed naked and raving through the streets, shrieking 'Wo, wo, wo! the wrath of God, the wrath of God!' When arrested, they obstinately refused to put on clothing. 'We are' they observed, 'the naked truth!' In a day or two, these furious lunatics, who certainly deserved the madhouse rather than the scaffold, were all executed." (Motley.)

Woman asserted her rights in those days: "Mary of Hungary, sister of the emperor, regent of the provinces, the 'Christian Widow' admired by Erasmus, wrote to her brother that 'in her opinion all heretics, whether repentant or not, should be prosecuted with such severity as that error might be, at once, extinguished, care being only taken that the provinces were not entirely depopulated.' With this humane limitation, the 'Christian Widow' cheerfully set herself to superintend as foul and wholesale a system of murder as was ever organized. In 1535, an imperial edict was issued at Brussels, condemning all heretics to death; repentant males to be executed with the sword, repentant females to be buried alive, the obstinate of both sexes to be burned. This and similar edicts were the law of the land for twenty years, and rigidly enforced."

We close with this glance at Caucasian morals and syphilis when no Negroes were there: "At the diet of Nuremburg, . . . the honest pope declared roundly . . . 'that these disorders had sprung from the sins of priests and prelates. Even in the holy

[5] Motley, "Dutch Republic."

chair,' said he, 'many horrible crimes have been committed.' Many abuses have grown up in the ecclesiastical state. The contagious disease, spreading from the head to the members—from the pope to lesser prelates—has spread far and wide, so that scarcely anyone is to be found who does right, and who is free from infection." (Motley's "Dutch Republic.")

For some further details on this subject the reader is referred to the Bible. Read the first chapter of Paul's Letter to the Romans, beginning at the 22d verse.

III.—Modern Social Conditions.

But let us turn from ancient religion to modern society. The white man's civilization, indeed! Civilization is not a possession, but an attainment,—an attainment envisaged by many, but only reached by few. The keen-brained, clear-voiced heralds of the dawn have called in vain to the multitudes. I could set your hair on end, O reader, with horror at the bare and unvarnished recital of the refinements of cruelty invented by "man's inhumanity to man!"

Here is a side-light on Caucasian chivalry to women: "As to the prevalence of whipping in England, evidence is furnished by Andrews, in his book on ancient punishments. The public whipping of women, stripped naked and whipped till they bled, sometimes to death, was practised. Judge Jeffreys, a great conserver of good old constitutions and customs, sentencing a lady to be whipped, in his genial manner said: 'Hangman, I charge you to pay particular attention to this lady. Scourge her soundly, man; scourge her till her blood runs down! It is Christmas, a cold time for madam to strip. See that you warm her shoulders thoroughly.' "

Speaking of London, Mr. Ross[6] says: "I have

[6] W. Stewart Ross, "Woman."

more than once gone home with children I have found sleeping under dark stairways, railway arches, and under carts. 'Home' has usually been a den of drunkenness and dirt. I have never been thanked for bringing home a child from the frosty railway arch or from the frozen doorsteps. I have usually had to give the contents of my purse to prevent the child, who had not earned or stolen sufficient coppers, from getting beaten well-nigh to death; and, even after having given my last farthing, I have heard the dull and heavy blows fall upon the children I had rescued, before I had well got outside the door, and my heart had sickened under their terrible screams. I have sometimes returned to plead for mercy, and always at the risk of being done to death by villains without a gleam of human intelligence in their eye or a drop of human blood in their heart—villains that the great towns of England can furnish in hundreds of thousands, after more than eighteen centuries of the gospel of the Galilean. I should not advise Arch-deacon Farrar, or those like him, to go into such localities; but I should advise them to hold their peace about the effects of Christianity till they do. The entering of such localities is not for the halt, the maimed, the lame, or the blind. The entering such localities is not for the mere scholar and fine gentleman, with flaccid muscles and attenuated thews; but for one with, when put to it, a desperado's courage, and bones of iron and sinews of brass. I never stir out after sunset without a heavy oaken staff, the motto of which is 'Defense, not Defiance.' Not attacked, I would be the last to use it; attacked, I should be the first. Grasping it in my right hand, I have, more than once, set out on an errand of mercy, and returned with it mercilessly encrusted with blood and hair—peradventure some of the blood my own. I have had occasionally to be very cruel to be kind. With those whom society has allowed to sink lower than dogs or swine, you have to argue with a poker; you have to convince them by breaking their heads with a broken chair. You need not try to make them understand any moral canon; but, once with a broken chair and once with a poker, I succeeded in letting them know the plain, concrete fact that I objected to being murdered. Mere words, however kindly meant and spoken, are simply wasted wind. They do not want your words; they want your watch. When you appeal to their sense of right and truth you appeal to minus quantities; you may as well invoke the moral sentiment of a clam, and attempt to inflame the chivalry of an oyster. Very many of them are the result of the lecherous whim of somebody in broadcloth—a lecherous whim which fructifies into destitution and disease, degradation, deviltry and danger. The toad that spawns on the margin of the pool is more careful of its young than are the parents who spawned these creatures in the center of Debauchery's Lake of Dismal Swamp. If emmenagogues had not failed—if attempts to obtain abortion had not proved abortive, they would not have been there. They owe nothing to the fabric of society; they are not of the fabric; they are stercorous and pestilent offal that lies around its base. They owe nothing to the world, and each man or woman would set the world on fire to cook his or her own particular herring. The begetting of children, the bearing of children—all the offices of nature, all the mean gutter-crawling of 'life,' and all the groaning squalor of death, not infrequently take place in the same den, and in the sight and hearing of all. Society has dropped them through as slag and clinkers for guilt and hell, and turned her pious attention to savages in foreign lands."[7]

[7] *Ibid.*

Who with a full knowledge of such conditions, wherever man is crowded, will dare say that the slums of our Southern cities exist *because* of the Negro? The great damage done by Negro-baiting is not the propagating of false doctrine, but the creation of an atmosphere antagonistic to calm thought and free speech. It gives us an America under the tyranny of prejudice and passion instead of an America under the sovereignty of reason and conscience. The bugbear of "Social Equality" in some form or other has been used as a weapon against progress as far back as the record of man's struggle for liberty goes. Douglass used it with telling effect in his celebrated debate with Lincoln.

To those who maintain that all crimes against womanhood are committed by Negroes and would disappear with the banishment of the Negro, I commend the reading of this bit of news from Australia, where the population is entirely Caucasian: "Sentence of death has been passed upon nine young men convicted of outraging a servant-girl 16 years of age, near Moore Park, in the suburbs of Sydney. The circumstances under which the crime was committed were revolting to the last degree. A young girl of 16, of good character, was decoyed into an unfrequented suburb of Sydney, and there was violently outraged by relays of youths of 16 years old and over. As the child was alone, amid a gang of at least twelve strong young ruffians, her struggles, though violent, were unavailing. She was at first held down by her hands and feet; but after the brutality had lasted some hours she became unconscious. One man who attempted to rescue the girl was overpowered by the gang, some of whom had knives, and while he fled to inform the police another man arrived on the scene and witnessed the crime without raising an alarm. After the last of the gang left her she was found by the police sitting crying on the bank of the creek. On being removed to the police station it was found impossible to make a surgical examination. After a day in the hospital she was examined and the evidence of her injuries confirmed. It was not for sometime however, that she was able to appear in the witness-box. When she did she identified her assailants, and the result is that nine of them are sentenced to death. The law of the colony prescribes death as a penalty for this crime. The English Home Secretary has recommended that the sentences of three of the ruffians be commuted to imprisonment for life; the other six will be hanged."

This is no traveller's tale, but a plain criminal court record.

Ye who believe only Negroes are bartered, read this from a London paper: "Horrible practice was being carried on by two men in a certain house in Bethnal Green, aided by one or more agents in the neighborhood. They make a practice of decoying young girls away by means of these agents, and, in many cases, resort to the process of going about in cabs, snatching the girls, placing them inside, and carrying them off to their den. The men own a vessel which, though ostensibly an ordinary trading vessel, yet carries from London to the North of England, and in some cases to the Continent the girls thus decoyed, and hands them over to brothel-keepers for a pecuniary consideration, although more often than not they have already been outraged by the men before they are thus bartered. A large number of letters, it may be added, from heart-broken parents have found their way to the Great Assembly Hall, asking for Mr. Charrington's assistance in trying to discover the whereabouts of daughters who have been some time missing."

In another column of the same paper occurs the following: "Further and sad revelations have been made in connection with Mr. H. F. Charrington's descent on disorderly houses in the East-end.

"In a narrow turning, dignified by the title of Lady Lake's Grove, about fifty houses of ill-fame were discovered, among the unfortunate occupants of the dens being many *girls as young as 12 and 13 years of age,* who plied their wretched calling equally with their adult companions. By energetically availing himself of the powers of the law Mr. Charrington succeeded in clearing out this hot-bed of vice. Next he turned his attention to Oxford Street, another East-end purlieu. This thoroughfare, in the matter of the character of its inhabitants, is described as being even a greater disgrace to public decency than the 'Grove,' because, while the 'sisterhood' of the latter carried on their shameless trade in comparative privacy, few people passing through on account of its notorious character, Oxford Street is in the unfortunate position of being the only means of direct access to several important thoroughfares. The traffic, consequently, is considerable and continuous, and women and children have not been able to escape being witnesses of the revolting scenes arising out of the solicitation going on at every one of the houses. Two or three visits paid by Mr. Charrington for the purpose of collecting evidence, combined with the knowledge of the wholesale evictions that had been carried out in the 'Grove,' seemed to have alarmed the miserable community, who cleared out of their own accord.

"Mr. Charrington next turned his attention to Nelson Street, a turning containing some two dozen houses, the larger majority of which are, or were, dens of the worst description. Not only were the women of the very worst type of their degraded order, but they were 'protected' by ruffians of the most desperate character. Mr. Charrington's visit to the locality gave the unmitigated villains an opportunity of exercising their innate brutality. He was assaulted with decomposed fish and other filth, and was so seriously threatened that the police had to escort him away from the place. On Sunday evening Mr. Charrington intended to hold a short service in Nelson Street. The way, however, was blocked by several carts, containing men armed with sticks and stones; and, as it was obvious that a murderous attack had been arranged, Mr. Charrington prudently postponed his visit. It is current rumor that the bullies of Canal Road have threatened to drop Mr. Charrington into the water should he appear in that neighborhood, while some of the lower class of publicans, whose trade has been seriously affected by the sweeping of the Augean stables, are vowing all sorts of vengeance upon the author of their ruin. The clearances which have taken place have brought to light some revolting facts, showing the extensive character of the shocking traffic which has so long been carried on. Thus in one house were discovered no less than 45 beds, which were let from 5s. to 15s. per night. More painful than surprising were other circumstances. Here is an instance: A gentleman well known in West-end society, a year or so ago, missed his daughter. He had reason to believe that his daughter was living in a disorderly house in East-end; but the most searching inquiries were fruitless to ascertain her whereabouts. In the clearance of Nelson Street, however, a young woman answering the description of the missing daughter was discovered. The gentleman and his wife were promptly on the spot, driving in a handsomely appointed brougham, attended by coachman and footman in powdered wigs. They identified their child, who, however, was proof against all parental expostulation and entreaty. She firmly refused to leave the people with whom she had connected herself."

Let those who believe that only the lack of comeliness and virtue in colored women provoke sexual brutality in the white man read this bit of fifteen-year-old news from "Bonnie Dundee," Scotland, where possibly not one of the actors ever saw a Negro: "In the Police Court, Dundee, before Bailie White, three lads, about 15 or 16 years of age, were charged with having assaulted a young woman named Jane Sinclair, a weaver, residing in Overgate, by jostling and pushing her about, knocking her down and abusing her while in Euclid Crescent. One pleaded guilty and the other two not guilty. Jane Sinclair deposed that, between 8 and 9 o'clock on Monday night, she was set upon in Commercial Street by a gang of young lads, the accused among the number. She was knocked down and abused by the mob. Her companion, a girl named Mary Downie, made her escape, and witness took refuge behind a shooting gallery. She remained in concealment for about ten minutes, but when she came out the crowd was still waiting for her, and again she was attacked, mobbed, and abused. The mob followed her on up Commercial Street and around Albert Square. In Euclid Crescent she was knocked down and abused in an indecent manner. A man named John Gary deposed that he saw a mob of young lads, and some bearded men among them, following the girl and abusing her. There was a young man protecting her, and two policemen tried to disperse the crowd; but no heed was paid to their authority. When they got into a dark place in Euclid Crescent the mob set on the girl and knocked her down. Witness made a rush into the midst of them, and gripped one of the prisoners as he was in the act of behaving indecently. The other two were by his side and they were secured by the police. James Sword stated that he saw a mob of about 200 boys following the girl. After she came out from hiding behind the shooting gallery witness accompanied her up Commercial Street on her way to the Police Office, as the only place where she could get protection from her persecutors. He tried to keep back the mob and he was severely kicked about the legs. The mob were acting like savages. The girl was knocked down and abused in a shameful way in the midst of the crowd. In answer to the Court the witness said there was nothing peculiar in the girl's appearance. The evidence was corroborated by two police constables. In moving for sentence Mr. Dewer said he thought he was justified in asking for a sharp punishment. Attacks of this kind were far too common in Dundee. Last night, in another part of the town, another woman was attacked in a similar manner. Young women were entitled to protection, and it was monstrous to think that, between 8 and 9 o'clock in the evening, a woman should be attacked in the public street and abused in a way which could scarcely be expected from savages. The Bailie found the charge proven, and fined the accused 20s. with the option of ten days in prison, each."

In the preface of that masterly work, "The Negro in the New World," Sir Harry Johnston says: "In Chapters XIV and XV is traced the history of slavery in the United States. It was here that the battle for human freedom was fought on the grandest scale and with the most tremendous results, and consequently the history of the Negro in this part of the world is so important that it requires a more ample treatment than is necessary for similar problems in Brazil or Spanish America. I have felt it advisable, as the re-

Prominent colored Americans.

sult of reading so many books (some of them little known), to give an explicit account of the exceptional cruelties attending slavery in the United States. These cruelties, perhaps, were not greater than what went on in British Barbadoes or in the Bahama Islands, and certainly not more outrageous than the treatment of the Negroes in Dutch Guiana; but the wickedness was on a far greater scale geographically, and affected the welfare of a much larger number of human beings.

"Even this may seem a thrice-told tale and an unnecessary raking up of embers that have ceased to glow. I do not think so. I still believe that the bulk of my fellow-countrymen and the mass of my possible readers in North America have not realized (with our supersensitive, twentieth-century consciousness) how bad was the treatment of the Negro in the South-eastern States of the Union between, let us say, 1790 and 1860. This story should be rewritten ever and again 'lest we forget.' Given the same temptations and the same opportunities, there is sufficient of the devil still left in white men for the three hundred years' cruelties of Negro (or other) slavery to be repeated, if it were worth the white man's while, and public opinion could be drugged or purchased. Perhaps some day the white man's conscience may be universally educated up to the level of Christ's teachings and of the gospel according to Exeter Hall, and the subject of slavery and the slave-trade can be tacitly dropped."

This is the truth, but not the whole truth. "The devil still left in the white man" is in the black man and in the red man and in the brown man and in the yellow man. Civilization is the only thing that will eventually eradicate it. Little did Mr. Johnston think when he wrote those words that there was then reigning in Europe a sovereign who would repeat in the Netherlands, in less than a decade, the work of Don Frederic. Mr. Johnston implies that it is only against the black man that the white man shows the devil, but Sir Harry is wrong. Men do not change their dispositions with their company. Brutality is brutality and is no respecter of persons. Civilized white Belgium is oppressed just as readily as uncivilized black Congo. There is always enough devil left in a man "to do it again" if opportunity offers. It is vain to talk of *inter*national peace until we have *intra*-national justice. Until the culture of justice dominates our educational system and the spirit of fair play actuates our religion, our national welfare is in danger and the peace of the world insecure. Patterson DuBois[8] is right:—

"Justice is more than a basis of ethical training. It is essential to the full efficiency of all forms of right influences of man upon man. It underlies all true education as means and as end.

"Something that looks like social reform or moral improvement or a closer brotherhood or a truer unity or a higher freedom or a firmer peace can be accomplished through the indefinite motives that we call philanthropy and benevolence.

"But if such reform has been wrought at the expense of a true equity, it must in the end prove a delusion. Unless philanthropy has confided its cause to the exacter thought and the even, steady hand of justice, it has failed of its devine mission. Upon this distinction moral education must focus."

A sense of justice is the noblest moral sentiment in the nature of man. A willingness to put one's self in the other one's stead is the very essence of true civilization. As Emerson defines it, "Justice consists mainly in the granting to every human being due aid

[8] "The Culture of Justice."

in the development of such faculties as it possesses for action and enjoyment." Kant's great moral law is the quintessence of justice: "So act that thy deed will not contradict itself if it is made the universal act of all intelligent beings."

Segregation—"Jim Crowism"—generally, like slavery, is in direct fundamental and irreconcilable opposition to this sentiment. Like slavery, of which it is the twin-sister, it must kill or be killed by the higher civilization. They cannot survive together.

If I can get the white people to assume an attitude of justice toward my people, I shall have done them the greater service. A full sense of justice, with the will and power to bestow it, raises a man to grander heights than any other earthly possession—physical, moral, mental or spiritual. The grandeur of a nation thus endowed is beyond the power of language to portray.

The child that has been taught that injustice and impoliteness are proper when practised toward those whom he regards as inferior, will eventually regard all persons as inferior whom he can thus treat with personal advantage or safety. He is thus disqualified for a higher civilization.

"Common justice is the basis of all human relations that are right, and therefore permanent. Privilege is not the basis. Charity is not. Class interests are not. Even mercy, without justice, is not. Mercy with justice is without reproach, but mercy without justice is a knave's refuge. Party loyalty is not the basis. Neither is national allegiance. If a foundation is not to rot, it must be rock, and the bed-rock foundation of all human relations which are right and therefore permanent is common justice."[9]

Not equality, not blood, but justice is the basis of brotherhood.

---

[9] Sermon by Dr. J. I. Vance, of Nashville.

The relationship of mind to matter is just as certain as the relationship of life to matter; but the one is no better understood than the other. Life and mind alike elude the mensurations of matter. The laboratory cannot answer the whys of life nor the wherefores of mind.

"Never in the history of man has a race made such educational and material progress in forty years as the American Negro."—REV. LYMAN ABBOTT.

"I am quite resigned to our own and the Negro races occupying the South together, confident that as time passes the two will view each other with increasing regard, and more and more realize that, destined as they are to dwell together, it is advantageous for both that they live in harmony as good neighbors and labor for the best interests of their common country."—ANDREW CARNEGIE, "The Negro in America."

CHAPTER VI.

STRUGGLING TO THE LIGHT.

THE colored people of African descent, who form the so-called race problem of the United States of America, present the interesting spectacle of a cultural unity or a race variety in process of formation. *There is not yet a Negro race in America, not even in name.* Neither they themselves, nor those associated with them, have been able to agree upon a racial designation. Nomenclature is a necessity of speech and is an effort to describe, delimit, and differentiate as well as to designate.

Racial designations, like most proper names, eventually lose their original significance, and, like individual proper names, are usually derived from physical or mental traits or the dwelling-place of the designated one. Still another similarity is that races, like individuals, usually have their names thrust upon them. There seems to be no fixed rule by which racial designations obtain vogue. Why should the descendants of Abraham be called after one of his grandsons? Why was this honor conferred upon Juda in preference to Joseph or Benjamin? The Jews themselves are not fully decided between Jew and Hebrew, though outside pressure displaced Israelite for Jew.

If there is confusion in the designation of one of the very oldest human varieties, it is small wonder that the name of one of the youngest race varieties should find difficulty in settling upon a name. Colored people, Afro-Americans, and Negroes are, I think, the names from which we must finally choose.

The objections to the word Negro as a racial designation are many and serious:—

1st. *It is not true.* The prevailing color among Afro-Americans is not black, but brown.

2d. The cognate ideas associated with the word make it *per se* objectionable. It connotes the devil, was used in slavery, and is easily corrupted into "nigger," which was formerly applied indiscriminately to all people not white; and many of our best Southern people pronounce it so that the two words are scarcely distinguishable.

3d. It is not comprehensive enough to include all our racial elements. There is something grotesque as well as untrue in calling a person with white skin, blue eyes, and flaxen hair, black. (See cut.)

4th. It is an adjective that is persistently written with a small letter, showing the unsoundness of its ethnical pretensions. The word is from the Latin, Niger, meaning black, and applied to the night, sky, storm, etc. The people were called Ethiops, or Afer.

"It is often asked what races are Negro, as the meaning of the term is not well defined. . . . The word is not a national appellation, but denotes a physical type, of which the tribes of North Guinea are the representatives. When these characteristics are not all present, the race is not Negro, though black and woolly-haired." (R. N. Cust, "Mod. Langs. of Africa," p. 53).

There is, therefore, an additional sting of race prejudice in trying to fix this name upon the colored people of America. It is not used to designate a physical quality of color, but to circumscribe our ancestral home to a certain part of Africa.

The most rampant negrophobe will not write African with a small letter unless he is illiterate, yet the Century Dictionary defines Ethiop as an "African, a negro." It certainly ought to be dropped as a racial designation or spelled with a capital. Though I have used the word "Negro" in this book, I am inclined to believe the term "Colored" is more comprehensive and truer to fact, nowithstanding all the cheap wit that has been fired at it.

I.—Language.

While thought preceded and caused speech, speech reacts upon thought. Language, according to Huxley, is the most human of human attributes. In no phase of man's activities does injustice more frequently manifest itself than in language.

Here is where the newspapers become responsible for the dangers of the race problem.[1] *Any accusation of crime is made with big headlines in the newspapers.* Corrections or retractions are never thus made. The immense power of language is thus used to promote strife. Mobs originate in epithets as often as in crime. The intellectual forces of associated ideas are used to generate race antagonism. This works one of the greatest hardships the colored man has to bear, and is the most potent force for evil in the race situation.

Thought precedes action. The function creates the organ. Man has a stomach because he digests. He does not digest because he has a stomach. Organs exist because they are needed. They are not needed because they exist.

Men thought before they spoke. Thought created language. Language is the medium by which one person's thoughts may reach another; and is the most potent means by which men influence each other. It thus becomes a very forceful factor in environment, and reacts in a way to influence character. Words created by thought become the molders of thought. A man's character may be determined by his language,

[1] See Appendix E.

and is in a measure formed thereby. For instance, there is a verb in Italian which means to destroy the sight by holding a red-hot iron close to the eye. Is it not evident that cruelty was in the character of the generation that produced such a horrible verb? Is it not equally evident that the character of those learning to use that verb would be unfavorably affected by its meaning? So with the English verb "burke" which means to murder a person by suffocation for the price his body will bring at the dissecting table.

What a world of horrors lurks in the word lynch! The character of the American people has been influenced for lawlessness by the use of that word.

Can you not judge accurately the sexual morals of the Bushmen, when you find that they have but one word for "girl, maiden, wife"? Does the fruit more surely indicate the tree than conversation marks the man? Profanity is the verbal violence that is sure to injuriously affect conduct.

Slangy language begets impure morals. Each is but the disregard of the standards erected by the wisdom of the past. Rag-time was the legitimate progenitor of the tango.

Violence of language leads to violence of action. Angry men seldom fight if their tongues do not lead the fray. Mobs, as I said before, originate in epithet oftener than in crime, and the race situation is unnecessarily complicated by our language. It is right and beneficial for us to reverence the past, but it is foolish, injurious, and degrading for us to perpetuate in our conversation the epithets that an era of thraldom brought forth.

Noble language means noble thoughts and noble thoughts mean noble deeds. Impropriety of speech will eventually lead to impropriety of conduct.

The coiner of a happy phrase is a benefactor of

Successful young colored Americans.

mankind. Ben Butler's tongue was mightier than his sword when he coined the phrase "contraband of war," as the proper designation for the fugitive slaves coming into the Union lines. "Sambo's right to be kilt" from the verbal battery of some unknown Irish songster demolished the opposition to the enlistment of colored soldiers in the Union Army.

Elbert Hubbard says truly: "Emerson added to the wealth of the world when he gave us the expression, the 'law of compensation.' Herbert Spencer did the same thing when he referred to the 'law of diminishing returns.' "

Words are tools and derisive nicknames are verbal brickbats with which to demolish the respectability of those derided. A man ought not always to "holler when he is hit," but he is a fool to furnish the brickbats to his enemy. That is why the receiver of a nickname seldom enjoys it. I have heard Irishmen called "Paddies," Frenchmen called "Johnnies," Italians called "Dagoes," Jews called "Sheenies," and Negroes called "Darkies," but have never seen any of them that did not resent it. The Negro alone is blamed for so doing.

I once made an experiment to test the effect on the Caucasian of a species of linguistic harassment so constantly practised against the Negro and so bitterly resented by him. The result was illuminating.

I received a letter giving my correct address in every detail, even to my full name and title. Yet the writer added an adjective thus: Dr. Chas. Victor Roman, Colored.

That exact name and address could not be duplicated in the United States, and I owned the property indicated by the street number. Why this adjective? I was offended. Then I began to think maybe I was too sensitive and I decided to test it. I answered the letter politely and favorably and addressed it to Mr. Patrick O'Leary, Irish.

He came around to fight me. This I avoided by diplomacy.

"Oh!" said I, innocently, at the same time producing his letter to me; "I thought *you* regarded a man's race as part of his address."

He saw the point and laughed, promising never to be guilty again.

II.—A Discovery.

"The soul's strange miracle of memory
Makes me the guest of mine own past. I dream."

The textbooks and discussions of my youth are before me. There is no question as to the superiority of the white man. All other races were indifferently "niggers" and inferior. The white man then meant the European as he then was. The geographies made European and white synonymous. No nation but a white nation could stop a white nation in battle. But Prince Bonaparte went down in South Africa and Gordon met his doom in North Africa. Memories of the Sikh rebellion were revived, but the white man was eventually victorious and the proposition held good. Finally white man didn't mean "white" at all, but meant Aryan. This was a veritable find; for it made the white man the author of everything worth while in human history. Anybody that had done anything was "white" regardless of color, condition, locality, or feature.

Mr. Keane, the High Priest of racial inequality says: "The typical Gallas of Kaffa and surrounding uplands are perhaps the finest people in all Africa, tall, of shapely build, with high, broad foreheads; well-formed mouth, Roman nose, oval face, coppery or light-chocolate color, black, kinky hair, often worn in 'finger curls' or short ringlets round the head —altogether noble representatives of the Caucasic family."[2]

The logic is simple, as Butler's:—

> "Treason never succeeds. What's the reason?
> If it succeed, no one dare call it treason."

The Negro never made any history, because if anybody ever made any history he was not a Negro. Thus, by circular reasoning they make their position invincible. The ethnological status of the Japanese was subject to immediate revision after the second Port Arthur engagement; and the fate of an Italian expedition has changed the racial classification of the Abyssinians.

The advocates of white superiority are sorely put to it. Formerly, as I have just said, all people not white were indiscriminately called "niggers"; but now, not even Africans are "niggers" except they be prognathous and savage. Hence the effort is to fasten upon the American Negro this type of African ancestry. The wider significance with which the word Negro and its colloquial corruption "nigger" was formerly used is well illustrated by the language of the Confederate Constitution, which says: "The importation of *Negroes of the African race,*[3] from any foreign country other than the slave-holding States or Territories of the United States of America, is hereby forbidden; and Congress is required to pass such laws as shall effectually prevent the same."

Belief in racial superiority is a world-wide egotism. The lowest races think themselves superior. The Greenlanders think they are the only civilized

---

[2] Keane, "Ethnology," pages 387, 388.
[3] Italics mine.

people,[4] the Gallas call themselves the "Sons of the Brave,"[5] and the Hottentot Chief is as sure and proud of his superiority as a German professor or a Mississippi politician. Modern writers and German apologists are speaking with a great deal of contempt of "the inherent superficiality" of England, France, and other countries. Just now in Europe they are appealing to the Court of Mars for a decision on racial superiority.

The deepest meaning of democracy is equality of opportunity. Its greatest enemy is the spirit of the temple-worshipper that thanked God that he (the worshipper) was not like other men. The master always considers himself superior to the servant. Individual opinion easily becomes a group opinion. Caste is born of prejudice. Localities develop differences, and differences of form or differences of manner are interpreted by the average individual in terms of superiority and inferiority. Thus race prejudice is born.

Race prejudice is a superstition which only wider knowledge of mankind can cure. The individual or race takes the personal or home feature as the *norm* or standard, and condemns all deviations therefrom. The greater the difference, the more intense the prejudice. Intimate personal knowledge is the only remedy.

This I learned while a college lad. I had been taught the narrow prejudice that the Christian world then held against the Jewish race. In morals they were murderers; in business they were cheats.

It was bitterly cold (20 below) and everywhere was so icy that a lame boy could scarcely stand on his crutches. There was by the wayside a Jewish peddler occupying a small house on wheels. The front part

---

[4] Dana. [5] Keane.

was a shop, where he did soldering, umbrella and cane repairing, etc. The boy had 15 cents to get his lunch at 12 o'clock. The thought struck him to get "Isaac," as we called the long-bearded old man, to drive a nail in the bottom of each crutch, cut off the head and file the remainder to a point, thus making a brad that would prevent the crutches from slipping on the ice. Possibly he would not charge more than ten cents. This would leave five cents for the lunch.

When approached, the old man said our ideas were all right and it would work fine, but would not look well nor last long. He, however, would fix it all right. When we saw him reach up and get two brass collars, we anxiously asked would he not do what we requested, for we had but ten cents to spare. He laughed at us and proceeded over our protest to do a job worth seventy-five cents or a dollar while we saw visions of "a pound of flesh" exacted with no Portia to plead our cause. Finally the job was done to the satisfaction of the mechanic and the lad was bidden to test it. This he could hardly do for dread of the bill.

"How much?" he tremblingly asked, amid the breathless silence of his companions.

"How much?" kindly repeated the old man. "Nothing," said he, gently but firmly, adding: "Only this, always be kind to people in trouble." We departed in silence, gratitude, and wonderment, thinking not of Shylock, but of the Good Samaritan.

Thus was sown the seed that liberalized my mind and made me one of those

> "Who dream the dream of true democracy,
> Of happy workers in a happy state,"

and who look forward to the day when

> "Knowledge hand-in-hand with truth
> Shall walk the earth abroad."

With races as with individuals, happiness is best conserved by a knowledge of each other's virtues. Science knows no innately superior race, nor any hopelessly inferior one, and the world has not yet seen a thoroughly civilized one. Basicly, men are much alike. Accomplishment is oftener the result of environment and superior opportunity than of superior capacity or innate effectiveness.

III.—The Indian.

The Negro's docility is often used as an argument against him, and he is disadvantageously compared with the American Indian. Courage is conditional and valor is circumstantial. The spirit of the bravest man may be broken by oppression. Hear what Professor Ross says of the South American Indian:—

"There could be no more eloquent testimony to the barbarities of Pizarro and his ruffians than the timid, propitiatory attitude of the Indians toward all white men. Every man, woman, and child we met on the road doffed the hat as we passed, and respectfully wished us 'Buenos dias' or 'Buenos tardes.' In the remoter districts an Indian who sees a white man coming toward him along the trail will make a long and toilsome detour to avoid meeting him. If you approach an Indian abruptly to ask him a question, he will fall on his knees, put up an arm to shield his face, and cry, 'Don't hurt me, master!' The Indian never thinks of chaffering over the price of his services. The patron pays a porter what he chooses; and if the Indian murmurs, a harsh 'Begone,' causes him to shrink away." (Edward A. Ross.)

The editor of the *New Republic* (Nov. 28, 1914) quotes a sentence about racial traits from E. A. Ross, and comments pungently thereon:—

"PRIDE OF RACE.—There were so many sugar-loaf heads, moon-faces, slit mouths, lantern-jaws, and goosebill noses (among the gatherings of the foreign-born) that one might imagine a malicious jinni had amused himself by casting human beings in a set of skew molds." (Professor Edward A. Ross, in "The Old World in the New.")

Professor Ross has come from the Middle West, looked upon man made in the image of God, and proclaimed that except as produced in America he does not justify the Divine craftsmanship. He has watched the poor immigrants struggling up the gang-plank, has seen them herded in the roped enclosures of Ellis Island, has studied them as they issued, workworn, from factory gates and sweat-shops, and has from some gallery or other looked down upon them, as brushed and combed and clothed in their best, they gathered to celebrate weddings and christenings and funerals, occasions when common people are wont to laugh or cry. And as he looked down upon these men and women, Professor Ross, who is of a race of which he is justly proud, studied their faces, their hands, and their manners, and noted that these were "sub-common" people, "hirsute, low-browed, big-faced, of obviously low mentality,—in short, of the Caliban type." Foreigners, he observes, at least those foreigners who come as immigrants to America, are in the main unbeautiful. There is a certain "fleeting, ephemeral bloom of girlhood," but otherwise among the women "beauty is quite lacking." He fears that American good looks will disappear as all this European ugliness works to the surface. "It is unthinkable," writes Professor Ross, "that so many persons with crooked faces, coarse mouths, bad noses, heavy jaws, and low foreheads can mingle their heredity with ours without making personal beauty yet more rare among us than it actually is."

Nor is it in good looks alone that the immigrant is deficient. These foreigners, as Professor Ross observes, are undersized, especially the Italians, who are dwarfish, and the Jews, who are very poor in physique. The Slavs, he admits, have vitality, are "immune to certain kinds of dirt" and "can stand what would kill a white man"; but even this vitality disappears in a generation or two of American life. As for honesty, fair play, decency, and morality, Professor Ross is certain that the new immigrants are below the earlier types. The Syrian is a liar and a cheat, the South Italian is a liar and a cheat, the Greek and the Jews are liars and cheats, and these are the races which are to people America, and bear the children that Americans, dismayed by this immigration, refuse to bear. America is itself to blame. "A people that has no more respect for its ancestors and no more pride of race than this, deserves the extinction that surely awaits it."

After reading Professor Ross, we wonder whether pride of race, however justifiable, is in itself a sufficient equipment for passing judgment upon a problem as intricate as that of immigration. We do not wish to prejudice the question, for Professor Ross's inadequate defense still leaves that policy defensible. But Professor Ross, entering the arena armed with racial snobbishness, should know that it is exactly such facile generalizations as he has made which becloud knowledge, and evoke equally offensive and absurd assumptions from the other side. From an ignorant disputant nothing better might be expected, but Professor Ross is an erudite and brilliant man, with access to the learning of the world. A scholar so equipped has no more excuse for meeting difficult anthropological problems with the superficial observations of a cub reporter than a wealthy man has excuse for turning counterfeiter.

Cettiwayo, Zulu chieftain who annihilated British regiment.

When we seriously seek to unravel the infinitely complex problem of the effect of racial intermixture upon national character, many perplexing questions present themselves. What, for example, is the effect of good food upon good looks? What is the influence of the better economic conditions of America upon cleanliness, courage, truthfulness, and physical vitality? To what extent has our declining birth rate really been the result of immigration, and to what extent has it been due to other economic and social causes equally operative elsewhere? What are the interactions between social environment and heredity, and what are the economic and historical roots of that very race-snobbishness which takes the form in each nation of assumed racial superiority and a contemptuous attitude toward lesser breeds?

IV.—Reaping Where Others Sow.

I lay no claim to originality. The fields of erudition that have sustained my intellect and refreshed my spirits were ready for harvesting when I was born. The cities of my residence I did not build and the vineyards of my comforts I did not plant. I have never built a railroad nor launched a steamship, and while I have enjoyed them both, I have never wrecked the one nor scuttled the other.

"Sometimes when we look back over the gulf of the centuries, . . . a feeling of hopelessness and despondency is apt to dampen the ardor of the boldest and most sanguine among us. It would seem sometimes that our work is that of Sisyphus, destined forever to roll the heavy stone up the steep, which always, when we have, by intense toil, raised it to a certain height, rolls down again and crushes us. But be of good cheer, fellow-soldiers in the vanguard of Liberty, fellow-workers in the field of Humanity. True, much is to be overcome; but already much has been won. . . . .

"The day is dawning, though the clouds obscure it. . . . . The fires of martyrdom are quenched, the light of day has flashed through the roof of the dungeon, the gibbet is overthrown, and the torture engine is broken."[6]

There is an heroic race of men who are doers of the world, the flower of their kind. They stood in the Pass of Thermopylæ and made a hundred spears deadlier than a million. They held the Alpine highways against the covetous Austrian hordes. They forgot arithmetic at Balaklava and transmuted four hundred Sheffield sabers into magic falchions. They lighted the torch of learning while the battle for freedom was raging and opened the Halls of Knowledge to manumitted slaves. They sped the triremes at Salamis and redeemed a race at Ft. Wagner. They lashed the sails of Drake and manned the cannon of Perry. They crawled across the Arctic ice. They cut their way through the tangles of mid-Africa. Few of their names are known and few of their graves are marked, but the glory of their courage is imperishable—a heritage for all tomorrows—a spark to heat the blood and to fire the future generations with inspiration.

They are of no particular sect, nor caste, nor race. They are born alike from the loins of peasant and of peer. Their fraternity is not of breed, nor brain, nor brawn, but of truth. Duty is their mission and its fulfillment their ultimate hope.

"They wage for the ages and not for the wages."

Like the number that John saw, they have come up through great tribulations, from every kindred and tongue and people.

---

[6] Saladin, "God and His Book."

"Fellow-soldiers in Liberty's Army, shoulder to shoulder, let us march on, undaunted, unsubdued! Our dower is the splendid heroism of our fathers. . . . Let us hand it down to our children with its glory undimmed, so that a not remote future may shout for joy that the long war is over, that the victory is won, that the world is free!"[7]

The great forces of heredity and evolution are still at work. As Pennsylvania outlived her black laws, so will Louisiana. Mississippi will as certainly quit Negro-baiting as Massachusetts quit burning witches. Negro social equality with the white man is no more real and menacing than witchcraft, and will finally take its place in the limbo of forgotten superstitions that have marred the happiness and retarded the progress of mankind. Civilization will yet come into its own.

"America has still a long vista of years stretching before her in which she will enjoy conditions far more auspicious than any European country can count on. And that America marks the highest level, not only of material well-being, but of intelligence and happiness, which the race has yet attained, will be the judgment of those who look not at the favored few for whose benefit the world seems hitherto to have framed its institutions, but on the whole body of the people."[8]

---

[7] *Ibid.*

[8] James Bryce, "Social Institutions of the United States."

"Woe unto the world because of offences, for it must needs be that offences come, but woe to that man by whom the offence cometh. If we shall suppose that American slavery is one of those offences which, in the providence of God, must needs come, but which, having continued through His appointed time, He now wills to remove, and that He gives to both North and South this terrible war as the woe due to those by whom the offence came, shall we discern there any departure from those Divine attributes which the believers in a living God always ascribe to Him? Fondly do we hope, fervently do we pray, that this mighty scourge of war may speedily pass away. Yet if God wills that it continue until all the wealth piled by the bondsman's two hundred years of unrequited toil shall be sunk, and until every drop of blood drawn by the lash shall be paid by another drawn by the sword, as was said three thousand years ago, so still must be said, that the judgments of God are true and righteous altogether."—LINCOLN's 2d Inaugural Address.

"Law is not law if it violates the principles of eternal justice."—LYDIA MARIA CHILD.

CHAPTER VII.

AFRICAN SLAVERY IN AMERICA

I.

"No plague that ever tainted the globe, nor war that ever devastated our planet, has, to the extent that slavery has done, left its blight and curse upon the race of man. . . . Christian slavery is the Golgotha of History." The very name, Christian slavery, is a tragedy. Nor has the white man been the only offender, nor has the black man been the only victim.

John Wesley very vividly and truly described slavery as "the sum of human villainies." It is certainly the climax of injustice. There is one absolutely unanswerable argument against slavery. It is unfair. The ethics of Moses made slavery possible; the ethics of Paul made slavery endurable; the ethics of Jesus made slavery impossible.

In his second inaugural address Abraham Lincoln stated fully this phase of the case: "It may seem strange that any men should dare to ask a just God's assistance in wringing their bread from the sweat of other men's faces; but let us judge not, that we be not judged. . . . The Almighty has His own purposes."

Wm. Henry Seward said: "One of the chief elements of the value of human life is freedom in the pursuit of happiness. The slave system is not only intolerable, unjust, and inhuman toward the laborer, whom, only because he is a laborer, it loads down with chains and converts into merchandise, but is scarcely less severe upon the freeman, to whom, only because he is a laborer from necessity, it denies facilities for employment, and whom it expells from the community because it cannot enslave and convert into merchandise also. It is necessarily improvident and ruinous, because, as a general truth, communities prosper and flourish or droop and decline, in just the degree that they practise or neglect to practise the primary duties of justice and humanity."

To show the picture is not overdrawn, I will introduce three items from the other side:—

1. Robert Toombs, in a speech to the United States Senate on January 7, 1861, made five stipulations or demands, as follows: (1) That the Southern people be allowed to emigrate and settle in any part of the United States with any property they possess (including slaves) and be protected by the United States government. (2) That property in slaves receive the same treatment from the United States government as any other property. (3) That persons who commit crimes against the slave property in one State and flee to another State shall be delivered to and tried by the State wherein the crime was committed. (4) That fugitive slaves be returned to their masters without the right of habeas corpus proceedings or trial by jury or "other similar obstruction to legislation." (5) That laws be passed to punish any persons in any State who aid or abet invasion or insurrection in any other State.

2. The Supreme Court of North Carolina in 1829 laid it down that "The end of slavery is the profit of the master, his security, and the public safety. *The subject is one doomed in his own person, and his posterity to live without knowledge and without the capacity to make anything his own, and to toil that another may reap the fruits.* The power of the master must be absolute to render the submission of the slave perfect."

3. Even as late as 1856 the Constitution of Maryland enacted that a Negro convicted of murder should have the right hand cut off, should be hanged in the usual manner, the head severed from the body, the body divided into four quarters, and the head and quarters set up in the most public places of the county where such act was committed.

The descent of the white man upon the west coast of Africa and the east coast of America was a sad day for humanity; for it ushered in "the bloodiest chapter in the book of time." The native American was ruthlessly murdered and robbed of his patrimony, and the African was thought to have no rights that a white man should respect. How the African survived this ordeal is one of the mysteries of that mysterious land. To get an idea of what the African really endured in America, let us see how the natives were treated by the European invaders. I quote from a Catholic Bishop:—

"The West Indies swarmed with a multitude of people as an emmet-hill swarms with emmets. But they were murdered, and most cruelly made way with by the Spaniards and the priests, though they never committed any offense that deserved punishment by man. When the country was discovered these murderers entered like wolves and tigers long famished, and did nothing but tear them in pieces and torment them by cruelties never read nor heard of before. . . . The miserable people died on the road when carrying burdens for their oppressors. If, through faintness, they sank down, they had their teeth broken by the pommels of the Spanish sword to make them rise and go. These tormentors spared neither children nor old persons, nor even women with child, nor such as lay in child-bed; but would rip them up and chop them in pieces as if they had been butchering lambs. They would lay wagers who would most readily and nimbly despatch them. They kept dogs for hunting down the Indians, and fed them on the bodies they caught; keeping great numbers in chains, whom they murdered like swine when their dogs were hungry. One man wanting meat for his dogs, took a child from its mother, and, chopping it in pieces, flung it down for their eating. A woman who was sick and dreaded the dogs hung herself, having tied her child to her feet. An especially gratifying deed was to set up thirteen low gibbets *in honor of Christ and His twelve apostles,* and to hang and burn thirteen persons on each. They threw down from a high cliff seven hundred men together, who fell like a cloud to the ground and were battered to pieces. *In three months they famished seven thousand infants.* On one day they massacred two thousand sons of the chief natives, and dishonored and slaughtered thousands of females in a manner that cannot be mentioned. In the island of Cuba a prince, having called his people together, showed them a cask full of gold and jewels, and told them it was the Spanish God. After they had danced around it he threw it into the river, because, said he, if the Spaniards know we have it, they will kill us to get it. This prince was afterward taken by them and burned. At the stake a friar told him about Christ and the matters of our faith, which, if he would believe, he might go to heaven; if not, he must needs go to hell. The prince, after a pause, asked the friar if the Spaniards went to heaven. The friar said they did. The prince then, without any pause, replied that he would not go to heaven, but to hell, that he might be free from such a cruel people.

. . . "Thus more than ten realms greater than Spain are turned into a wilderness. *Twenty-seven millions* of souls perished within the space of forty years. In Hispaniola, also three millions. In five small islands near it half a million. In another district, fully five millions. In Peru, above four millions."

Macaulay says: "In Britain the conquered race became as barbarous as the conquerors." It was even so in America. During the height of the African slave-trade across the Atlantic, the lights of *morality burned low and the fires were quenched upon the altars of justice.* Savage and heathen red men, savage and heathen black men, savage and Christian white men united in a carnival of injustice and barbarities without a parallel in history. If the heathen were desperately resisting, the Christians were unrelentingly cruel. If the heathen savages were cunning, the Christian savages were powerful. The result was what might have been expected—the invading savages from Europe and Africa triumphed and the native heathen were vanquished. No wonder that the first European nation (French) to raise its voice against the African slave-trade spoke against the Christian religion also.

So closely were the Church and slavery united that opposition to slavery and *free-thought* became synonymous. The rising tide of freedom and democracy flowed *away* from the Church. The Declaration of Independence was the work of Thomas Paine, Benjamin Franklin, and Thomas Jefferson, all of whom were profoundly religious but as anti-church as they were anti-slavery. Washington signed a treaty with the Barbary States stipulating that the United States of America was not a Christian nation, and Abraham Lincoln's name is not on the roll of any church. The advance guard of modern thought, both within and without the Church, is still very indifferently orthodox.

This does not mean the death of faith, but that

faith in *man* is as important as faith in God. In fact, faith in God unaccompanied by faith in *man* is an injury, not a benefit, to human society.

II.—The White Man Degraded Africa and the African.

"Commodore Owen, who was employed in the survey of the eastern coast of Africa in the years 1823 and 1824, gives an insight into how the peaceful industries were fostered and encouraged. 'The riches of the Zulimaine,' he writes, 'consisted in a trifling degree of gold and silver, but principally in grain, which was produced in such quantities as to supply Mozambique. But the introduction of the slave-trade stopped the pursuits of industry, and changed these places where peace and agriculture had formerly reigned into the seat of war and bloodshed. Contending tribes[1] are now constantly striving to obtain by mutual conflict, prisoners as slaves for sale to the Portuguese, who excite these wars and fatten on the blood and wretchedness they produce." . . .

Slavery has "produced the most baneful effects, causing anarchy, injustice, and oppression to reign in Africa, and exciting nations to rise up against nations, and man against man; it has covered the face of the country with desolation. All these evils, and many others, has slavery accomplished; in return for which the Europeans, for whose benefit and by whose connivance and encouragement it has flourished so extensively, have given to the artless natives ardent spirits, tawdry silk dresses, and paltry necklaces of beads."

[1] This implies what all investigators know, that the slaves brought to this country were of different tribes and nations of Africa; and not all of one tribe, as is so frequently asserted by anti-Negro writers.

Against the charge of innate debasement of the African character I quote one of the brainiest and most learned men of the nineteenth century, William Stewart Ross, of London, than whom no more ardent devotee of the truth ever lived:—

"I have contended that the fire of the domestic and social affections is more intense in savage and untutored than in civilized and educated man. The attachment of the Negroes to their homes and families was proverbial. In defence of their hearths and their dear ones they fought with the most desperate of courage. The turtledove of the idyl pines away and dies when her mate is no more; but the Negro woman of authenticated fact cared nothing as to what became of herself when her husband was slain. The family instinct was intense and the very children felt that all that was worth living for was gone when their father's blood was poured out under the steel or the bullet purchased by Christian gold. When attacked they were no cravens. A year of slavery would degrade a demigod, and the enslaved Negro, under the lash and the gospel, was as spiritless and disgusting a specimen of humanity as the most morbid imagination could picture; but the Negro, unenslaved and unchristianized, was simple, artless, manly and brave, and attached to his straw hut and his children and their dusky mother with a heroic passion to which the phlegmatic blood of civilization is a stranger. Against their enemies 'they throw,' writes T. Fowell Buxton, 'their long, poisoned javelins, covering themselves with their shields; while their wives and children stand by them and encourage them with their voices. But, when the head of the family is killed, they surrender without a murmur.' . . . 'When the Negroes are taken their strong attachment to their families and lands is apparent. They refuse to stir, some clinging to the trees with all their strength; while others embrace their wives and children so closely that it is necessary to separate them with the sword; or they are bound to a horse, and are dragged over brambles and rocks until they reach the foot of the mountain, bruised, bloody, and disfigured. If they still continue obstinate (not to leave their homes) they are put to death.'[2] It was notorious that, even after they had been put aboard ship, many of the exiles died of nostalgia, or home-sickness,—a malady which has hardly ever been known to carry off a civilized man or woman with his or her wider, consequently less intensified, loves and sympathies. It is further notorious that, when the slaves, during their voyage across the Atlantic, were allowed to go upon deck, high and strong nets were placed along the bulwarks to prevent their leaping overboard, and that these nets, supplemented by loaded muskets and drawn swords, were not sufficient to prevent great numbers from finding death by leaping into the roaring ocean rather than meet the endurance of life, torn away from their native land and those who were the objects of their simple and vehement love."

Pride of race and love of native land are not confined to "civilization's" simpering products in silk hats, kid gloves, and patent-leather boots.

"We can sympathize with our own Caractacus, torn away from his home in Britain to grace a Roman triumph, for he was one of our own kith and kin, and those who vanquished and exiled him were not Christians, and the event reaches way back into ancient history. But we have no sympathy with many a nameless brave as patriotic as Caractacus, who was vanquished and exiled by Christians, and that not in the far-off epochs of the ancient world. Abyssinia had

[2] "The Slave Trade."

her warriors, Soudan had her heroes, no whit less noble, no whit more savage, than Caractacus. It ill-becomes a Christian poet to sing of their misfortunes and their valor; only one poet, as far as I am aware, has ventured so to sing. When a boy I was wont to recite the following lines by William Cullen Bryant, which I now inscribe from memory":—

"Chained in the market-place he stood,
  A man of giant frame,
Amid the gathering multitude
  That shrunk to hear his name—
All stern of look and strong of limb,
  His dark eye on the ground;
And silently they gazed on him,
  As on a lion bound.

"Vainly but well that chief had fought—
  He was a captive now;
Yet pride, that fortune humbles not,
  Was written on his brow.
The scars his dark-brown bosom wore
  Showed warrior true and brave;
A prince among his tribe before,
  He could not be a slave.

"Then to the conqueror he spake,
  'My brother is a king;
Undo this necklace from my neck,
  And take this bracelet ring,
And send me where my brother reigns,
  And I will fill thy hands
With store of ivory from the plains
  And gold-dust from the sands.'

"'Not for thy ivory nor thy gold
Will I unbind thy chain;
That bloody hand shall never hold
The battle spear again.
A price thy nation never gave
Shall yet be paid for thee;
For thou shalt be the Christian's slave,
In lands beyond the sea.'

"Then wept the warrior chief, and bade
To shred his locks away;
And, one by one, each heavy braid
Before the victor lay.
Thick were the platted locks and long,
And closely hidden there
Shone many a wedge of gold among
The dark and crisped hair.

"'Look, feast thy greedy eye with gold
Long kept for sorest need;
Take it, thou askest sums untold,
And say that I am freed.
Take it—my wife, the long, long day,
Weeps by the cocoa-tree,
And my young children leave their play
And ask in vain for me.'

"'I take thy gold; but I have made
Thy fetters fast and strong,
And ween that by the cocoa-shade
Thy wife will wait thee long.'
Strong was the agony that shook
The captive's frame to hear,
And the proud meaning of his look
Was changed to mortal fear.

"His heart was broken—crazed his brain;
At once his eye grew wild;
He struggled fiercely with his chain,
Whispered and wept and smiled;
Yet wore not long those fatal bands,
And once, at close of day,
They drew him forth upon the sands,
The foul hyena's prey."

So much for the typical Caractacus of the Negro race.

"A survey of African tribes exhibits to our view cultural achievements of no mean order. To those unfamiliar with the products of Native African art and industry, a walk through one of the large museums of Europe would be a revelation. None of our American museums has made collections that exhibit this subject in anyway worthily. The blacksmith, the woodcarver, the weaver, the potter,—these all produce ware original in form, executed with great care, and exhibiting that love of labor, and interest in the results of work, which are apparently so often lacking among the Negroes in our American surroundings. No less instructive are the records of travellers, reporting the thrift of the native villages, of the extended trade of the country, and of its markets. The power of organization as illustrated in the governments of native states is of no mean order, and when wielded by men of great personality has led to the foundation of extended empires. All the different kinds of activities that we consider valuable in the citizens of our country may be found in aboriginal Africa. Neither is the wisdom of the philosopher absent. A perusal of any of the collections of African proverbs that have been published will demonstrate the homely, practical philosophy of the Negro, which is often proof of sound feeling and judgment." (Boas.)

III.—The Slave Trade.

In spite of the buccaneering spirit of iconoclasm and expansion that characterized the Middle Ages, slavery in the United States began as a patriarchal serfdom including all the races, Negroes, Indians, and Caucasians. It became an industrial system for monetary and not for ethical nor ethnical reasons.

"Here it was that the fatal mistake of compromising with slavery in the beginning, and of the policy of *laissez faire* pursued thereafter, became painfully manifest; for, instead of a healthy, normal, economic development along proper lines, we have the abnormal and fatal rise of slave-labor large-farming system, which, before it was realized, had so intertwined itself with and braced itself upon the economic forces of an industrial age, that a vast and terrible civil war[3] was necessary to displace it. The tendencies to a patriarchal serfdom, recognizable in the age of Washington and Jefferson, began slowly but surely to disappear; and in the second quarter of the century Southern slavery was irresistibly changing from a family institution to an industrial system.

"The development of Southern slavery has therefore been viewed so exclusively from the ethical and social standpoint that we are apt to forget its close and indissoluble connection with the world's cotton market. Beginning with 1820, a little after the close of the Napoleonic wars, when the industry of the cotton manufacture had begun its modern development and

---

[3] It is often asserted that the war was not caused by slavery; yet if any man that ever lived in this country ought to know the cause of the war, that man was Abraham Lincoln. (See quotation at front of this chapter.)

Arts and crafts among the Kaffirs. (Deniker.)

the South had definitely assumed her position as chief producer of raw cotton, we find the average price of cotton per pound, 8½d.

"From this time to 1845 the price steadily fell, until in the latter year it reached 4d; the only exception to this fall was in the years 1832-1839, when, among other things, a strong increase in the English demand, together with an attempt of the young slave power to 'corner' the market, sent the price as high as 11d. The demand for cotton goods soon outran a crop which McCollough had pronounced 'prodigious,' and after 1845 the price started on a steady rise, which, for the checks suffered during the continental revolutions and the Crimean War, continued until 1869. The steady increase in the production of cotton explains the fall in price down to 1845. In 1822 the crop was a half-million bales; in 1831, a million; in 1838, a million and a half; in 1840-1843, two million. By this time the world consumption of cotton goods began to increase so rapidly that, in spite of the increase in Southern crops, the price kept rising. Three million bales were gathered in 1852, three and a half million in 1856, and the remarkable crop of five million bales in 1860.

"Here we have data to explain largely the economic development of the South. By 1822 the large-plantation slave system had gained footing; in 1838-1839 it was able to show its power in the cotton 'corner'; by the end of the next decade it had not only gained a solid economic foundation, but it had built a closed oligarchy with political policy. The changes in price during the next few years drove out of competition many survivors of the small-farming free-labor system, and put the slave *régime* in position to dictate the policy of the nation. The zenith of the system and the first inevitable signs of decay came in the years

1859-1860, when the rising price of cotton threw the whole economic energy of the South into its cultivation, leading to a terrible consumption of soil and slaves, to a great increase in the size of plantations, and to increasing power and effrontery on the part of the slave barons. Finally, when a rising moral crusade conjoined with threatened economic disaster, the oligarchy, encouraged by the state of the cotton market, risked all on a political *coup d'état,* which failed in the war of 1861-1865.

"The attitude of the South toward the slave-trade changed with this development of the cotton trade. From 1808 to 1820 the South half wished to get rid of a troublesome and abnormal institution, and yet saw no way to do so. The fear of insurrection[4] and the further spread of the disagreeable system led her to consent to the partial prohibition of the trade by severe national enactments. Nevertheless, she had in the matter no settled policy; she refused to support vigorously the execution of the laws she had helped to make, and at the same time she acknowledged the theoretical necessity of these laws. After 1820, however, there came a gradual change. The South found herself supplied with a body of slave laborers whose

---

[4] Nat Turner's rebellion in Virginia and the efforts of the slaves for freedom in South Carolina show the growing restlessness of the slaves and the increasing barbarity of the masters that characterized this period.

"The loss of South Carolina was occasioned by a terrible civil excitement in 1822, which was produced by the discovery of a contemplated insurrection on the part of certain slaves for the overthrow of slavery in that State. The ringleaders, six in number, were arrested, tried and convicted, and hung on a single gallows at a single blow. Chief of these were Denmark Vesey and Gullak Jack. Subsequently twenty-two of the conspirators were convicted of the same offense, to-wit: a combination to overthrow the most villainous system of oppression beneath the sun. They, too, were hung on the same gallows, and at the same moment. They had not shed a drop of their so-called masters' blood, nor had they taken up arms or committed one act of violence; but they had conspired against the infernal system, and that was a crime in itself sufficiently heinous to be punished with death."—Payne, "History of the A. M. E. Church," page 45.

number had been augmented by large illicit importations, with an abundance of rich land, and with all other natural facilities for raising a crop which was in large demand and peculiarly adapted to slave labor. The increasing crop caused a new demand for slaves, and an interstate slave-traffic arose between the Border and Gulf States, which turned the former into slave-breeding districts,[5] and bound them to the slave States by ties of strong economic interest.

"As the cotton crop continued to increase, this source of supply became inadequate, especially as the theory of land and slave consumption broke down former ethical and prudential bonds. It was, for example, found cheaper to work a slave to death in a few years, and buy a new one, than to care for him in sickness and old age; so, too, it was easier to despoil

---

[5] In 1843 the famous Irish advocate and emancipator, Daniel O'Connell, nearing the limit of his long and useful life, made an appeal to his countrymen in America, from which I extract the following eloquent words: "You say the Negroes are naturally an inferior race. That is a totally gratuitous assertion on your part. In America you can have no opportunity of seeing the Negro educated. On the contrary, in most of your States it is a crime—sacred Heaven!—a crime to educate even a free Negro! How, then, can you judge of the Negro race, when you see them despised and condemned by educated classes—reviled and looked down upon as inferior? The Negro race has naturally some of the finest qualities. They are naturally gentle, generous, humane, and very grateful for kindness. They are brave and as fearless as any other of the race of human beings. . . . .

"We ask you to exert yourselves in every possible way to put an end to the internal slave trade of the States. *The breeding of slaves for sale is probably the most immoral and debasing practice ever known in the world.* It is a crime of the most heinous kind, and if there were no other crime committed by the Americans, this alone would place the advocates, supporters, and practisers of American slavery in the lowest grade of criminals. . . . .

"Irishmen! sons of Irishmen! descendants of the kind of heart and affectionate disposition, think, oh! think only with pity and compassion on your colored fellow-creatures in America. Offer them the hand of kindly help. Soothe their sorrows. Scathe their oppressors. Join with your countrymen at home in one cry of horror against the oppressor; in one cry of sympathy with the enslaved and oppressed,

> ''Till prone in the dust slavery shall be hurl'd,
> Its name and nature blotted from the world.'

"Irishmen, I call upon you to join in crushing slavery, and in giving liberty to every man and every caste, creed, or color."

rich, new land in a few years of intensive culture, and move on to the Southwest, than to fertilize and conserve the soil. Consequently, there early came a demand for slaves and land greater than the country could supply. The demand for land showed itself in the annexation of Texas, the conquest of Mexico, and the movement toward the acquisition of Cuba. The demand for slaves was shown in the illicit traffic that noticeably increased about 1835, and reached large proportions by 1860. It was also seen in a disposition to attack the government for stigmatizing the trade as criminal, then in a disinclination to take any measures which would render our repressive laws effective; and finally in such articulate declarations by prominent men as this: 'Experience having settled the point, that this *trade cannot be abolished by the use of force,* and that blockading squadrons serve only to make it more profitable, and more cruel, I am surprised that the attempt is persisted in, unless it serves as a cloak to some other purposes. It would be far better than it now is, for the African, if the trade were free from all restrictions, and left to the mitigation and decay which time and competition would surely bring about.' "[6]

The efforts today to evade and repeal the Thirteenth, Fourteenth, and Fifteenth Amendments to the Federal Constitution are similar in method and spirit to the efforts to revive or re-establish slave-trade; as the pro-slavery cruelty of 1835 which made it a crime for a colored man to educate his own children finds its rebirth in the segregation laws which forbid white people to teach colored people.[7]

---

[6] DuBois, "Suppression of Slavery."

[7] In the beginning the Negro slaves were taught to read and write as freely as they were taught Christianity. That epoch continued until about 1835, and it produced some brainy persons of color, such as Phyllis Wheatley, the poet, and Benjamin Banneker, who, in 1770, made the first clock manufactured in the United States. Another instance

"No man who is correctly informed as to the past will be disposed to take a morose or desponding view of the present."[8]

IV.—The Movement Against the Slave-trade Laws.

It was not altogether a mistaken judgment that led the constitutional fathers to consider the slave-trade as the backbone of slavery. An economic system based on slave labor will find, sooner or later, that the demand for the cheapest slave labor cannot long be withstood. Once degrade the laborer so that he cannot assert his own rights, and there is but one limit below which his price cannot be reduced. That limit is not his personal well-being, for it may be, and in the Gulf States it was, cheaper to work him rapidly to death.[9] The limit is simply the cost of producing him and keeping him alive a profitable length of time. Only the moral sense of a community can keep helpless labor from sinking to this level; and when a community has been debauched by slavery, its moral sense offers little resistance to economic demand. This was the case in the West Indies and Brazil; and although better moral stamina held the crisis back longer in the United States, yet even here the ethical standard of the South was not able to maintain itself against the

---

is that of James Durham, who spoke French and Spanish fluently, as well as English, and was a distinguished physician of New Orleans. The noted Dr. Benjamin Rush, of Philadelphia, once deigned to converse with him professionally and afterward confessed: "I learned more from him than he could expect from me." About 1835, however, the dark age set in, when it became a crime even for a Negro to teach his own children to read and write.—*The New York Times,* July 18, 1915.

[8] Macaulay's History of England.

[9] Sir Harry Johnston says the slaves were not only poorly fed and driven under the lash to the limit, but on the plantations, and even by public roads, men, women, and children were worked absolutely naked.

demands of the cotton industry. When, after 1850, the price of slaves had risen to monopoly heights, the leaders of the plantation system, brought to the edge of bankruptcy by the crude and reckless farming necessary under a slave *régime,* and baffled, at least temporarily, in their quest of new land to exploit, began instinctively to feel that the only salvation of American slavery lay in the reopening of the African slave-trade.

"It took but a spark to put this instinctive feeling into words, and words led to deeds. The movement first took form in the ever-radical State of South Carolina. In 1854 a grand jury in the Williamsburg district declared, 'as our unanimous opinion, that the Federal law abolishing the African slave-trade is a public grievance. We hold it has been and would be, if re-established, a blessing to the American people, and a benefit to the African himself.' This attracted only local attention; but when in 1856 the governor of the State, in his annual message, calmly argued at length for a reopening of the trade, and boldly declared that 'if we cannot supply the demand for slave labor, then we must expect to be supplied with a species of labor that we do not want,' such words struck even Southern ears like 'a thunder-clap on a calm day.' And yet it needed but a few years to show that South Carolina had merely been the first to put into words the inarticulate thought of a large minority, if not a majority, of the inhabitants of the Gulf States."

"The first piece of regular business that came before the Commercial Convention at Knoxville, Tennessee, August 10, 1857, was a proposal to recommend the abrogation of the eighth article of the Treaty of Washington, on the slave-trade. An amendment offered by Sneed, of Tennessee, declaring it inexpedient and against settled policy to reopen the trade, was voted down, Alabama, Arkansas, Florida, Louisana, Mississippi, South Carolina, and Virginia refusing to agree to it. The original motion then passed; and the radicals, satisfied with their success in the first skirmish, again secured the appointment of a committee to report at the next meeting on the subject of reopening the slave-trade. This next meeting assembled May 10, 1858, in a Gulf State, Alabama, in the city of Montgomery. Spratt, of South Carolina, the slave champion, presented an elaborate majority report from the committee and recommended the following resolutions:—

"1. *Resolved,* That slavery is right, and that, being right, there can be no wrong in the natural means of its formation.[10]

"2. *Resolved,* That it is expedient and proper that the foreign slave-trade should be reopened, and that this Convention will lend its influence to any legitimate measure to that end.

"3. *Resolved,* That a committee consisting of one from each slave State, be appointed to consider the means, consistent with the duty and obligations of these States, for reopening the foreign slave-trade,

---

[10] There was no hesitancy in arguing both the necessity and justice of slavery. James Henry Hammond, of South Carolina, said in the United States Senate, March, 1858: "In all social systems there must be a class to do the mean duties, to perform the drudgery of life; that is, a class requiring but a low order of intellect and but little skill. Its requisites are vigor, docility, fidelity. Such a class you must have or you would not have that other class which leads progress, refinement, and civilization. It constitutes the very mudsills of society and of political government; and you might as well attempt to build a house in the air as to build either the one or the other except on the mudsills. Fortunately for the South, she found a race adapted to that purpose to her hand—a race inferior to herself, but eminently qualified in temper, in docility, in vigor, in capacity to stand the climate, to answer all her purposes. We use them for the purpose and call them slaves. We are old-fashioned at the South yet; it is a word discarded now by polite ears; but I will not characterize that class at the North with that term; but you have it; it is there; it is everywhere; it is eternal."

and that they report their plan to the meeting of this Convention.

"Yancey, from the same committee, presented a minority report, which, though it demanded the repeal of the national prohibitory laws, did not advocate the reopening of the trade by the States.

"Much debate ensued. Pryor, of Virginia, declared the majority report 'a proposition to dissolve the Union.' Yancey declared that he was 'for disunion now.' (Applause.) He defended the principle of the slave-trade, and said: 'If it is right to buy slaves in Virginia and carry them to New Orleans, why is it not right to buy them in Cuba, Brazil, or Africa, and carry them there?' The opposing speeches made little attempt to meet this uncomfortable logic; but, nevertheless, opposition enough was developed to lay the report on the table until the next convention, with orders that it be printed, in the meantime, as a radical campaign document. Finally the convention passed a resolution:—

" 'That it is inexpedient for any State, or its citizens, to attempt to reopen the African slave-trade while that State is one of the United States of America.' "

"The Convention of 1859 met at Vicksburg, Mississippi, May 9-19, and the slave-trade party came ready for the fray. On the second day Spratt called up his resolutions, and the next day the Committee on Resolutions recommended that, 'in the opinion of this Convention, all laws, Federal or State, prohibiting the African slave-trade, ought to be repealed.' "

V.—Public Opinion in the South.

"This record of the Commercial Conventions probably gives a true reflection of the development of extreme opinion on the question of reopening the slave-trade. First, it is noticeable that on this point there was a distinct divergence of opinion and interest between the Gulf and Border States, and it was this more than any moral repugnance that checked the radicals. The whole movement represented the economic revolt of the slave-consuming cotton belt against their base of labor supply. This revolt was only prevented from gaining its ultimate end by the fact that the Gulf States could not get on without the active political co-operation of the Border States.

"Congressmen and other prominent men hastened with the rising tide. Dowdell, of Alabama, declared the repressive act 'highly offensive'; J. B. Clay, of Kentucky, was 'opposed to all these laws'; Seward, of Georgia, declared them 'wrong, and a violation of the Constitution'; Barksdale, of Mississippi, agreed with this sentiment; Crawford, of Georgia, threatened a reopening of the trade; Miles, of South Carolina, was for 'sweeping away' all restrictions; Keitt, of South Carolina, wished to withdraw the African squadron, and to cease to brand slave-trading as piracy; Brown, of Mississippi, 'would repeal the law instantly'; Alexander Stevens, in his farewell address to his constituents, said: 'Slave States cannot be made without Africans. . . . My object is to bring clearly to your mind the great truth that without an increase of African slaves from abroad, you may not expect or look for many more slave States.' Jefferson Davis strongly denied 'any coincidence of opinion with those who prate of the inhumanity and sinfulness of the trade. *The interest of Mississippi,' said he, 'not of the African, dictates my conclusion.'* He opposed the immediate reopening of the trade in Mississippi for fear of a paralyzing influx of Negroes, but carefully added: 'This conclusion in relation to Mississippi is based upon my view of her *present* condition, *not* upon any *general* theory. It is not supposed to be applicable to Texas, to New Mexico, or to any *future acquisitions* to be made south of the Rio Grande; John Forsyth, who for seven years conducted the slave-trade diplomacy for the nation, declared, about 1860: 'But one stronghold of its (*i.e.*, slavery's) enemies remained to be carried, to complete its triumph and assure its welfare,—that is, the existing prohibition of the African slave-trade.' Pollard, in his 'Black Diamonds,' urged the importation of Africans as 'laborers.' 'This I grant you,' he said, 'would be practically the reopening of the African slave-trade; but . . . you will find that it very often becomes necessary to evade the letter of the law, in some of the greatest measures of social happiness and patriotism.' "

In 1857 the committee of the South Carolina Legislature to whom the governor's slave-trade message was referred made an elaborate report, which declared in italics: *"The South at large does need a reopening of the slave-trade."*

"We have followed a chapter of history which is of peculiar interest to the sociologist. Here was a rich, new land, the wealth of which was to be had in return for ordinary manual labor. Had the country been conceived of as existing primarily for the benefit of its actual inhabitants, it might have waited for natural increase or immigration to supply the needed hands; but both Europe and the earlier colonists themselves regarded this land as existing chiefly for the benefit of Europe, and as designed to be exploited, as rapidly and as ruthlessly as possible, of the boundless wealth of its resources. This was the primary excuse for the rise of the African slave-trade to America.

"The colonists averred with perfect truth that they did not commence this fatal traffic, but that it was imposed upon them from without. Nevertheless, all too soon did they lay aside scruples against it and hasten to share its material benefits. Even those who braved the rough Atlantic for the highest moral motives fell early victims to the allurements of this system.

"For the solution of this problem there were, roughly speaking, three classes of efforts made during this time,—moral, political, and economic; that is to say, efforts which sought directly to raise the moral standard of the nation; efforts which sought to stop the trade by legal enactment; efforts which sought to neutralize the economic advantages of the slave-trade. . . .

"An appeal to moral rectitude was unheard in Carolina when rice had become a great crop, and in Massachusetts when the rum-slave-traffic was paying a profit of 100 per cent.

"In 1774 and 1804, the material advantages of the slave-trade and the institution of slavery was least. . . . A fatal spirit of temporizing, however, seized the nation at these points. . . . It was only a peculiar and fortuitous commingling of moral, political, and economic motives that eventually crushed African slavery and its handmaid, the slave-trade in America. . . .

"The political efforts to limit the slave-trade were the outcome partly of moral reprobation of the trade, partly of motives of expediency. . . . On the whole, these acts were poorly conceived, loosely drawn, and wretchedly enforced. . . .

"Economic measures against the trade were those which from the beginning had the best chance of success, but which were least tried. They included tariff measures; efforts to encourage the immigration of free laborers and the emigration of the slaves; measures for changing the character of Southern industry; and, finally, plans to restore the economic balance which slavery destroyed, by raising the condition of the slave to that of complete freedom and responsibility. . . .

"The one great measure which stopped the slave-trade forever was, naturally, the abolition of slavery, *i.e.,* the giving to the Negro the right to sell his labor at a price consistent with his own welfare. The abolition of slavery itself, while due in part to direct moral appeal and political sagacity, was largely the result of the economic collapse of the large-farming slave system."[11]

African slavery in the United States of America was born of cupidity and died of self-inflicted economic strangulation. With it justice and morals had little to do; and ethnic considerations were the merest incidents.

This does not mean a disparagement of the abolitionists nor of those noble-hearted conservatives who wished in their hearts that all men might be free, but the fact remains that the Proclamation was a "war measure called forth by military necessity in the time of actual armed rebellion against the United States." It is a question if the President's action issuing the Proclamation met the approval of a bare majority of those who favored the Federal Cause at that date. Certainly there was bitter opposition at the North as well as the most intense anger and consternation in the South.

Harrisburg Union said: "The proclamation of the President is an outrage upon the humanity and good sense of the country."

The Richmond Inquirer said: "Murder is a term of honor compared to Lincoln's crime."

[11] DuBois, "Suppression of Slave-trade."

A resolution was introduced in the Confederate Senate declaring it "a gross violation of the usages of civilized warfare and declaring it ought to be held up to the execration of mankind."[12]

"Neither party expected for the War the magnitude or the duration which it attained. Neither anticipated that the cause of the conflict might cease when, or even before, the conflict itself should cease. Each looked for an easier triumph and a result less fundamental and astounding."

---

[12] Wilbur, "President Lincoln's Attitude Toward Emancipation and Slavery."

"Lo, now thine enemy
Hath surely found the place that weakest is
In those strong walls that rampart 'round thy life;
Thou ow'st him much, see thou repair the breach."

*　　*　　*　　*　　*　　*

"Have we not done the right
By feeling no resentment in this case?"

A. D. WATSON, "Love and the Universe."

"The position of women in Central Africa is quite enviable compared with the lives of drudgery from morning till night of hundreds of thousands in Europe and America. They labor in the field as a rule from choice, not compulsion. Their influence in the home over their children, and often over their husbands also, is very great. It is not uncommon to find women chiefs of tribes and villages, and the succession always runs through the sister to the king's nephew rather than to his son. Children are members of their mother's family, and when old enough to shift for themselves are handed over to their maternal relations."—DOUGLASS M. THORNTON, "Africa Waiting."

CHAPTER VIII.

THE PRESENCE OF THE NEGRO AND PROGRESS IN THE SOUTH.

I.

THERE is a collective or tribal mind as truly as there is an individual or personal mind. This tribal or racial mind is just as dominantly determinative of the group career as the individual mind is of the personal career. The same laws govern both. We can study one from the other.

Man's sole right to pre-eminence over his animal kinsmen is his intellectuality. The mind makes the man. "As a man thinketh in his heart, so is he." Not his looks, nor his stature, but his thoughts make the man. It is not the shape of his head, whether it be dolichocephalic[1] or brachycephalic; it is not the texture of his hair, whether it be ulotrichous or leiotrichous;[2] it is not the facial contour, whether it be angular and sharp and European or broad and flat and African; it is not the color of the skin, whether it have the achromatic pallor of the Norwegian or the midnight hue of the sun-kissed Senegambian; no, neither facial angles, nor brain-weight, nor set of teeth, nor length of arm, nor arch of foot,[3] nor any other outward physical characteristic is the determining factor in life's complicated equation. As a man

---

[1] Long-headed. "This word is applied in ethnology to the persons or races having skulls the diameter of which from side to side, or the transverse diameter, is small in comparison with the longitudinal diameter, or that from the front to the back. . . . Broca applies the term dolichocephalic to skulls having a cephalic index of 75 and under, and this limit is generally adopted."—Cent. Dist., vol. i. The opposite is brachycephalic, short-headed.

[2] Huxley's divisions of mankind.

[3] All of these have been used to differentiate races.

thinks, not as a man *looks,* finally fixes his status. Thoughts and not bites win the battles of life. This is as true racially as individually. Racial distinctions are psychical rather than physical. Slav, Saxon, and Latin are far more dissimilar in mental habit than in physical contour. Mental habit rather than physical form differentiated Greece and Rome. Many attempts have been made to classify mankind, but the intellectual division into sensorimotor[4] and ideomotor[5] is the most far-reaching. Just as the ideomotor mind is the winning one in the individual, so it is in the race. *Reason* should dominate *sensation* and *will* guide *emotion* if the individual or race is to keep the orbit of success. Such a mind never loses its sense of proportion nor thinks the troubles incident to human existence its peculiar besetments.

When a person gives himself over to prolonged and exclusive emphasis upon one or two ideas, he eventually ceases to have ideas. This is as true of a community or race as of an individual, and is the only real danger with which the race question threatens the South; that is, this section may become monomaniac (crazy) on the Negro.[5a] The greatest problem the

---

[4] Moved by feelings or sensations.

[5] Moved by thoughts or ideas.

[5a] No other explanation can be given of the power in the South of what the learned contributing editor of the *New York Age* calls "Bogeyman" politics and economics. Here are three recent examples from widely distributed Southern points:—

(*a*) A group of colored citizens, taxpayers, called a meeting to discuss some city-welfare problems and invited the mayor to address them. He did so. The next day his political opponents set forth a full-page argument in the local press showing he should be defeated "because he addressed niggers as 'ladies and gentlemen.'"

(*b*) A conservative and prosperous daily in a Southern city with a large colored population added a page of news about respectable colored people, and though this page appeared only in the papers distributed to colored patrons a campaign was inaugurated to put this paper out of business.

(*c*) A laundry found colored washerwomen serious competitors. To overcome this, little printed slips were put in packages from the laundry systematically slandering the colored women, even going so far as to charge one with using a baby's dress for a shroud for her own

Full-blood types: a brilliant high-school teacher and a winner of intellectual prizes.

South has had to face was the fateful transition from an oligarchy to a democracy. The governmental *principle* of *slavery* and not the ethnological classification of the slave was, and is, the vexing question.

The serfs in Russia were manumitted two years before Lincoln's famous edict. Neither the color question nor the passions of war complicated the situation there, and yet the Russian serfs have not made nearly so much progress toward democracy as the American Negroes.

Before the war the South was an aristocracy or oligarchy. The slaveholders formed an upper or ruling class. There were two subject classes: the non-slaveholding whites and the enslaved blacks. The poor whites were nominally free; but, beyond the control of their own bodies, they had few more privileges than the slaves. It was the irony of fate that these subject classes should assist in their own degradation by mutual enmity. It was easy for the ruling class to use one of the subject classes to oppress the other. A common degradation and a common ignorance intensified ethnic differences. Each was ever ready to curtail the other's happiness. The slaves rejoiced in the poverty and squalor of the "po white trash," and the poor whites delighted in the sufferings of the "niggahs." It was the overseer and the "patroller" rather than the masters that put the terror in "those agonizing cruel slavery days."

There were many and happy exceptions, but this condition was the rule.

The war freed the slaves and broke the power of

---

dead child and then returning it after the funeral to her patron without washing it again. This villainous rascality was exposed by an accident. One of the slips was placed in the package of a colored patron. Yes! This laundry did work for colored people.

Only an abnormal popular sensitiveness could make such transparent trickery profitable.

the masters, but left the poor whites and old-time enmities untouched. "The Reconstruction was a bridge of wood over a river of fire." Slavery was tyranny with order. Emancipation was freedom without order. The carpet-bagger sought to restore order and establish government by using the freedman. The natural result followed. The former aristocracy united with the poor whites on racial grounds.

The uncultured and irresponsible part of this latter combination being the most numerous, eventually came into control. Shrewd leaders found them as susceptible to a *class* appeal against the former leaders as the former leaders had found them susceptible to a *race* appeal against the Negroes;[6] and the cultured aristocracy ceased to dominate the "white primary." Things went from bad to worse. Plebeian leaders of brains and character, but without breadth or culture, who had succeeded men with all four qualifications, were now themselves displaced by men with neither qualification. By the cry of "nigger domination" all opposition was silenced and the demagogue was in clover. The nightmare of new constitutions and Jim Crowism followed.

"Dark indeed must be the fate of any land if compelled to approach the solution of any significant problem of its life with its lips sealed and its reason bound." It was just under these conditions that the South attempted to establish democratic government. "The

---

[6] Class distinction, and not racial purity, is the actuating motive in most of the Jim Crow laws. Take the Texas definition of a separate car as defined in the act of 1890: "Each compartment of a coach divided by a good and substantial wooden partition, with a door therein, shall be considered a separate coach within the meaning of this act."

The drawing-room of a sleeping-car fulfills these conditions better than any of the Jim Crow cars in use. Yet in this State the use of the drawing-room is usually denied colored passengers. The writer was denied the use of an unoccupied drawing-room even at the request of a Southern white passenger who had polled the car and assured the conductor that there was no one who objected to his occupying it.

ignorant were assertive and the educated were silent." Small wonder that she grew hysterical and "saw red," and confused every manner of social and economic question with the Negro problem. Woman suffrage, child labor, prohibition, party government, illiteracy, the drug habit, prison reform, minimum wage, poverty, crime, prostitution, any of these subjects provoked but discussion of the Negro problem. In a large measure this is the condition now, though there are signs of improvement.

This condition was intensified by two phases of outside interference:—

1. Those inexperienced but good-natured "wiseacres," who proposed to solve at once the ethnical riddle for the South, "judging where they did not know and advising where they had not suffered." Though no two of them could agree, each thought the South ought to accept his remedy.

2. Those Job's comforters that kept telling the South how bad off she was, and pitying her awful condition, encouraging the hysteria without offering a remedy.

Past history and current events were alike ignored. The judgment was starved and the imagination stimulated. The South failed to recognize that the difficulties with which it was dealing were, in a large measure, common to every civilization. It was simply struggling "with the age-long divisive fate of racial cleavage," that by no means included all its social, economic, and political problems.

But notwithstanding all this, there are few spots on earth today where the people are happier and better off than here in the South. *There is no land of more promise.*

II.

It was inevitable that the Negro should be left out in the South's first strivings after democracy. It is just as inevitable that he must be taken in ere she attain that desirable goal. Under what conditions is this possible, if possible at all? Is there anything in the *blood* or *beliefs* of the Afro-American incompatible with the progress of the South? It is purely a matter of *blood* and *belief;* for *color* and *feature* have long been eliminated from the race question in the South. Black is white and white is black. Black people (Aryans) in North Africa are white, and white people (Octoroons, etc.) in the South are black. (See illustration, page 125.)

Nobody with any pretensions to intelligence will claim that the average Afro-American is ulotrichous (woolly haired) and characterized by "a dark-brown to black color, an abnormal length of arm, projection of the jaws, a short flat nose, thick and everted lips, a full black eye, a thick skull, small cranial capacity, and early closure of the cranial sutures." (Standard Dictionary.) (See Chapter XIV.)

The brain-weight argument has died of inanition. That size of brain does not necessarily indicate brain-capacity the following statement from Dr. Bean will show:—

"So then the brain weights do not necessarily represent the exact racial differences between the Negro and Caucasian, but do perhaps show that the low-class Caucasian has a larger brain than the better class Negro." (R. B. Bean, "Racial Peculiarities of the Negro Brain.")

This construction is inevitable unless we credit Dr. Bean with the monstrous contention that low-class Caucasians are intellectually superior to the better class Negroes, or the equally untenable proposition that Negro men have more sense than white women; for "the average brain weight is greater in the Caucasian male, least in the Negro female, and intermediate in the Negro male and Caucasian female." (Bean.)

Prof. Boas has truly said: "If we were to assume a direct relation between size of brain and ability,—which, as we have seen before, is not admissible,—we might, at most, anticipate a lack of men of high genius, but should not expect any great lack of faculty among the great mass of Negroes living among the whites, and enjoying the advantages of the leadership of the best men of that race."[7]

Mr. Josiah Royce ("Race Questions and Other American Problems") says: "For after all it is a man's mind" rather than his skull, or his hair, or his skin, that we most need to estimate. And if hereupon we ask ourselves just how these physical varieties of human stock, just how these shades of color, these types of hair, these forms of skull, or these contours of body, are related to the mental powers and to the moral characteristics of the men in question, then, if only we set prejudice wholly aside, and appeal to science to help us, we find ourselves in the present state of knowledge almost hopelessly at sea. We know too little as yet about the natural history of the human mind, our psychology is far too infantile a science, to give us any precise information as to the way in which the inherited, the native, the constitutional aspects of the minds of men really vary with their complexions or with their hair."

Only those intimately associated with the Negro know of those latent capacities by which he so often

---

[7] Franz Boas, "Mind of Primitive Man."

transcends the limitations of his heritage and makes the prophets lie.

But what is democracy, and who is entitled to its privileges? A democracy is a government of the people, by the people, for the people; and every man is entitled to participate in the exact proportion to the manhood his character will show under the test of civic duty. His value as a citizen depends upon his value as a man.

"Democracy in its essence has arrived when the rich man and the poor man, the man of the professions and the man of trade, the privileged and the unprivileged, unite to build the common school for the children of the State."

Democracy's peril is injustice, not color. The South is not yet by any means fully committed to the doctrine of popular education. The acuteness of the race problem is greatest where popular education has the least hold on the ruling classes. The spirit that refuses public-school accommodation to the colored children of Atlanta is the spirit that made the Atlanta mob. Injustice feeds on itself. Unfairness has ever sought to justify itself by cruelty. Neither color nor race has anything to do with it.[8] The poor whites were as illiterate as the colored people under the slave oligarchy.

"Democracy does not mean the erasure of individuality in the man, the family, or the race. Its unity is truer and richer because not run in one color or expressed in monotony of form. Like all vital unities, it is composite. *It is consistent with the individuality of the man; it is consistent with the full individuality and the separate integrity of the races.* No one has ever asserted that the racial individuality

---

[8] In his "Two Years Before the Mast," Dana describes "a flogging at sea" that shows this point very clearly.

of the Jew, preserved for sixty centuries and through more than sixty civilizations, by convictions from within and by pressure from without, was a contradiction of democratic life. Democracy does not involve the fusion of the races any more than it involves the fusion of the creeds or the fusion of the arts. It does not imply that the finality of civilization of man is in the man who is white or in the man who is black, but in the man, white or black, who is a man. Manhood, in democracy, is the essential basis of participation." (Murphy.)

Democracy means co-operation, individual integrity, *peace*. Fitness, not race, is the test. Opportunity, not fusion, is the aim. "Intelligence is the only safe foundation upon which free institutions can rest," said Jefferson.

This nation was "conceived in liberty and dedicated to the proposition that all men are created equal." We are now "testing whether any nation so conceived and so dedicated can long endure." Let us work and pray "that this nation, under God, shall have a new birth of freedom and that government of the people, by the people, for the people, shall not perish from the earth." The acid test of American civilization is the Negro question in the South.

III.

The charge that the presence of the Negro detracts from civilization is not well founded. *The colored man is just as anxious as the white man to preserve American civilization. The Negro knows that his own safety depends upon Caucasian civilization.*

What has morality to do with the texture of the hair? Suppose the Negro's hair is woolly. A sheep is as moral as a goat and less odorous. Some dogs are woolly and some have straight hair, but they are all dogs.

Why must the Negro be like the white man? What has facial angle to do with brain-capacity? Is prognathism any more prevalent among the Afro-Americans than among the people of Southeast Europe?

As for this country being better off without the Negro; so the Germans think of the English, and *vice versâ.*

There is no need of any new principles in the Negro's case. The general program for the good of mankind and of the nation without any modification reaches the colored man's needs.

There are two sides to every shield. The Negro's presence in this country has advantaged the white man, and the white man's opposition has inured to the progress of the Negro.

IV.

In man's fight with nature, environment is his greatest aid or greatest hindrance. The world is divided into six continents: three northern,—Asia, Europe, and North America; three southern,—Australia, Africa, and South America. A generation ago the great geographer, Guyot, said:—

"Asia, Europe, and North America are the three grand stages of humanity in its march through the ages. Asia is the cradle where man passed his infancy, under the authority of the law, and where he learned his dependence upon a sovereign master. Europe is the school where his youth was trained, where he waxed in strength and knowledge, grew to manhood, and learned at once his liberty and his moral responsibility. America is the theater of his activity

Editorial staff of the Journal of National Medical Association.

during the period of his manhood; the land where he applies and practises all he has learned, brings into action all the forces he has acquired, and where he is still to learn that the entire development of his being and his own happiness are possible only by willing obedience to the laws of his Maker. . . .

"The geographical march of history must have convinced us:—

"1. That the three continents of the North are organized for the development of man, and that we may rightly name them pre-eminently the historical continents.

"2. That each of these three continents, by virtue of its very structure, and of its physical qualities, has a special function in the education of mankind, and corresponds to one of the periods of his development.

"3. That in proportion as this development advances, and civilization is perfected, and gains in intensity, the physical domain it occupies gains in extent and the number of cultivated nations increases.

"4. That the entire physical creation corresponds to the moral creation, and is only explained by it.

"The three continents of the South, outcasts in appearance,—can they have been destined to an eternal isolation, doomed never to participate in that higher life of humanity, the sketch of which we have traced? And shall those gifts nature bestows on them with lavish hand remain unused? No; such a doom cannot be in the plans of God. But the races inhabiting them *are captives in the bonds of all-powerful nature;*[9] they will never break down the fences that sunder them from us. It is for us, the favored races, to go to them. Tropical nature cannot be conquered and subdued, save by civilized men, armed with all the

[9] Italics by the author.

might of discipline, intelligence, and of skillful industry. It is, then, from the northern continents that those from the South await their deliverance; it is by the help of civilized men of the temperate continents that it shall be vouchsafed to the men of the tropical lands to enter into the movement of universal progress and improvement, wherein mankind should share.

"The three northern continents, however, seem made to be the leaders; the three southern, the aids. The people of the temperate continents will always be the men of intelligence, of activity, the brain of humanity, if I may venture to say so; the people of the tropical continents will always be the hands, the workmen, the toil." . . .

Assuming the biological unity of man, environment becomes the deciding factor in human hegemony (leadership). The rise of Japan and the awakening of China seem to indicate the intention and ability of Asia to maintain her historic primacy over her southern counterpart, notwithstanding the world-conquering white man has supplanted the black man there. White encroachments upon Africa, whether north, south, east, or west, give no indication of the probability of that continent endangering the relative historic importance of Europe in the annals of the human race. The geographical march of civilization will not be changed by the distribution of races, and North America will become the scene of man's third and greatest efforts to

> "Build his life with love and gladness
> Into the structure of the universe."

"Thus we may, perhaps, foresee that the American Union, already the most numerous association of men that has ever existed voluntarily united under the same law, will hereafter become, even within the limits of its present confines, a true social world, transcending in grandeur and unity the most impressive spectacles of human greatness the history of the past ages holds up to our view." (Guyot.)

This glorious destiny will be the triumph of humanity. All nations and kindreds and tongues will be contributing factors. The African will be no exception. In this glorious destiny of her exiled sons and daughters will be fulfilled the prophesy that "Ethiopia shall stretch forth her hands unto God." The historic meaning of the slave-trade is that the African shall be a participant in the triumphs of civilization in North America. And neither heights nor depths, nor principalities nor powers, nor things past nor things to come shall separate him from this glorious privilege. A privilege he has won by faithful service and shall enjoy as a distinctive ethnical entity—not as the mongrel spawn of a despised miscegenation. So the Negro believes.

The Negro at his best neither hates nor fears the white man at his best; but, *mirabile dictu, they love and trust each other.*[10]

V.

The doctrine of heredity as taught by some phases of modern science seems destined to teach in terms of biology the faith-killing doctrine of predestination that was once fastened upon mankind in the name of religion.

In sociology and statescraft it is even worse. There is not an argument made by a politician today that was not old in the Golden Age of Greece, and trite when Cæsar paused upon the banks of the Rubicon. Just the other day the Governor of South Carolina was setting forth what "God Almighty intended" with as

[10] See "Address before Am. Economic Assoc.," Dec. 29, 1903, by Edwin A. Alderman, LL.D., Pres. Tulane Univ., New Orleans, La.

much assurance as Bishop Usher fixed the date of creation.

Our enemies are persistent in their reference to our savage ancestry. Science believes in the *rise* of man rather than in the *fall* of man. The Golden Age lies before us and not behind us. How long does it take for a man to become civilized? It depends upon the opportunities and the method. A thousand generations of Europeans lived and died having never reached America, and *vice versâ;* but now it is a matter of a few days. The Negroes of the United States of America are a civilized people regardless of ancestry.

But is there anything in the blood of the Afro-American to disqualify him for the duties and restraints of civilization? Let us take a look at the native African.

First, there are many "races, tribes, and peoples" in Africa. The Afro-American ancestry is drawn from all of these sources. It is historic ignorance, if not malicious mendacity, to claim the lowest types of "Guinea Nigger" as the sole ancestor of the American Negro.[11]

"Africa is the one continent whose population is composed almost entirely of dark people. For, although Africa is his home, the black man, the pure Negro, has not been left to live there alone during the centuries. The result is that through the mingling of Negro blood with that of lighter races the population of Africa is more brown than black."[12]

"In any description of the African himself it must be remembered that there is a difference between the primitive native of the interior, away from outside influences, and the native who, through long contact

---

[11] See Chapter XIV.
[12] "Daybreak in the Dark Continent."

with Christian or Mohammedan civilization, has in a greater or less degree altered his primitive mode of life. . . . Changes in dress, in customs which endanger human life, and in industries are the most apparent."

Bishop Taylor closes the first chapter of his "Flaming Torch in Darkest Africa" with these words: "Yet amid all the shadows which we have faintly portrayed there are many beautiful bright lights, shining all the brighter from the somber hue of the background. Even amid the moral darkness there shine forth virtues which would do honor to society in its most refined and exalted state. Domestic affection generally pervades African society, and generous hospitality is often shown to travellers. The varieties of nature and character, the alternations of nature's wildness and beauty, of lawless violence and the most generous kindness, render travelling in this continent more interesting than in any other quarter of the globe."

"Their (the Kaffirs) features were almost European," says Barrow, "and their dark, sparkling eyes bespoke vivacity and intelligence. The men were the finest figures that the travellers had ever seen, considerably above the middle size, robust, and muscular, yet marked with elegant symmetry. Their deportment was easy, and their expression frank, generous, and fearless." (See also Chapter XIV.)

I was a young man when an entire British regiment was annihilated in a war with these people. I remember distinctly an oft-quoted sentence credited to a British officer: "The Zulus are the finest race of savages the world has ever seen."

Mr. J. W. Work, professor of history in Fisk University, who is a great singer and has met many people, told me of the following experience: "An English lady whose husband was an officer in the

English Army during the South African War, told me this story:—

" 'My husband lost his life early in the war and I served as nurse. I had to trek many, many miles, and often I was miles and miles from any white people, with no protection other than black Zulus. Many a night I have passed in the black forest with them, and not once was there any suspicion of harm to me. They were always careful, particular, and brave, and I came to the conclusion that I, under the protection of the Zulus, was in the safest place in South Africa.

" 'They have a tremendous standard of morality. The white men in South Africa care for no other bond or pledge than the *word* of the Zulu. I have seen them ply the Zulu with "Give me your word; give me your word." When this is given, it is enough. The Zulu keeps his word and has nothing to do with any man who breaks his word.' "

There is in the native African blood no menace to female chastity.[13] Crime is sociological and not ethnological. The remedy is even-handed, inflexible justice; swift, deliberate, and sure, but under the established forms of civilization. If any scoundrel rocks the boat of social security, let us not upset the boat to drown him, but *deliberately throw him overboard.*

Of the Hottentots, Sanger says: "Intelligent and well-conducted women have attracted the notice of travellers." The same author says: "It is important to mention that where these people have embraced Christianity, their manners have totally changed; polygamy has been renounced, and they manifest an inclination to conform to the morals taught them."

Dorothy Amaury Talbot, a white woman, writing

[13] See also what Sir Harry Johnston says on this subject in Chapter IV.

from personal knowledge of the Ibibios of Southern Nigeria, says: "This strange race, comprising some three-quarters of a million souls, inhabits the south-eastern part of Southern Nigeria. Before our arrival at the Eket district, which forms the southernmost stretch of Ibibio Country, we had been informed that the natives of these regions were of the lowest possible type, entirely without ethnological interest, and indeed little better than 'mud-fish.' Saving the more civilized Efiks, it is indisputable that Ibibios occupy a low rung on the ladder of culture, and are as brutal and blood-thirsty as any people throughout the Dark Continent. Yet, to our minds at least, it would appear that their present condition is due to gradual descent from a very different state of things. Fragments of legend and half-forgotten ritual still survive to tell of times, shrouded in the midst of antiquity, when the despised Ibibio of today was a different being, dwelling not amid the fog and swamp of fetishism, but upon the sunlit heights of a religious culture perhaps hardly less highly evolved than that of ancient Egypt.[14]

"The child cult is by no means so much in evidence among the Ibibios as among the gentler-natured semi-Bantu Ekoi, where unkindness to little ones was practically unknown, and parents vied with each other in tender care of their children. Yet even here, in spite of the almost ceaseless drudgery of their lives, the women lavish care on their little brown piccans, and no case of a neglectful mother has come to our notice.

"Ibibio babies are nearly always well nourished, and roll and creep contentedly in the warm sand. They take considerable part in the lives of their elders, proudly riding to market astride the hip of a busy mother, safe girdled in the curve of her arm." (*Harper,* March, 1915.)

[14] Sir Harry Johnston expresses the same idea.

"The native African is a good smith and potter when occasion requires. Modern investigation points to the African as the first smelter of iron. The primitive African in grazing sections cares for small herds, that he himself may occasionally fare sumptuously, or may set a feast for an honored guest.

"Domestic slavery, degrading to morals, unfair to the rights of man, and cruel as it often is in its practice, cannot be said, taken all in all, to be the unmitigated curse to the continent that foreign slavery has been.

"Perhaps the family relations are closer than the observer deems them to be. With all its looseness of connection, the family has cohesive features. The African's sense of honor is displayed. Crafty to a foe, he is exceedingly loyal to a friend."

Bishop Hartzell says: "The most interesting thing in Africa is the native himself; the more I see him and study him, the more I respect him. If I had a thousand tongues and each of them were inspired by the gifts of the prophets of old, all should be dedicated to pleading for this people."

The facts of history clearly prove that there is nothing bad in the white man's makeup which has come to the surface in his association with the African but what he has manifested in the absence of the African;[15] nor is there anything good in the character of the African coming to the surface in touch with the white man that the African has not manifested without the touch of the white man.[16] There is nothing in the history of either Europe or Africa to justify the claim that civilization is the product of the one and beyond the attainment of the other.

There is nothing in the blood or beliefs, ancestry or

[15] See Chapter V.
[16] See Chapter VII.

A group of university men.

heredity, of the Afro-American incompatible with the highest civilization.[17] "So far as the original endowment of the Negro is concerned, I would conclude that there is nothing in kind to differentiate him particularly as a different psychic being from the Caucasian."[18]

From savagery to civilization is a long way. The time required depends upon the method of travel. The dugout and ox-cart are no match for the steamboat and the motor-car. The question then is, not where did he start from, nor how long has he been on the road, but *has he arrived?* (See illustration, "university men.")

VI.

My mother taught me faith in God; but experience taught me faith in man. I am not old; yet my memory of men and events covers the realization of many things deemed impossible. I have talked with men who saw the first steamboat, and who heard the speeches against granting the first railroad the right to run at the "dangerous speed of twelve miles an hour." My father told me about the first matches, and my mother told me of the first sewing-machines. My uncle was arrested as a "dangerous incendiary," because he prophesied that the slaves in the South would be free. I had a teacher who saw the first iron boat

---

[17] Perhaps the climax of heartlessness was found in the white masters selling their own children by slave women; but that this was not peculiar to his association with the African the following will show: "At the time of the Norman conquest, such was their degradation and such the irreverence with which the half-converted barbarians conformed to the religious usages of the age, that the nobles, instead of attending at church would have matins and mass performed in the chambers where they were in bed with their wives and concubines. . . . . It was common for these petty tyrants to sell their female vassals for prostitution at home, or to foreign traders, even though they were pregnant by themselves." Southey, "Book of the Church." (See also Chapter V.)

[18] Dr. Herbert Miller, "Bibliotheca Sacra," April, 1906.

and who talked with men that saw the first telegraph. I knew a travelling man who was chased out of a town because he insisted that he had seen ice made in hot weather. Lamp-chimneys and coal-oil were marvels of my boyhood days. The bicycle, the automobile, the telephone, the electric light, the gas stove and the electric car are well within my personal recollection. I have talked with physicians that knew the discoverers of ether and chloroform, while Lister and Pasteur are only recently dead. I have seen the impossibility of flying demonstrated "ultimately and fundamentally." Talking-machines and moving pictures were considered impossible by a generation that is still young. The demonstrated efficiency of submarine ships and large-caliber guns is alike beyond the tales of Munchausen and the dreams of Jules Verne.

This physical development is but a reflex of mental and moral development. *A creed that will control conduct and a government that will do justice are among the probable attainments of mankind.*

The psalm-singing, witch-burning, rum-selling, man-stealing slave-trader no more envisaged the ethical ideals of today than did the victims of his rapacity and rum. The white master and the black slave were both changed by their experiences.

There is in the nation today a new white man as much as there is a new Negro. They present a new phase of an old subject, that must be met by a new application of old principles. The newness of the men and the newness of the problems are matters of attitude and relationship, and not of intrinsic values. "Am I my brother's keeper?" is not a new question, nor is murder a new crime. Justice is as old as crime. Both are coeval with the history of society.

How to secure the triumph of justice and the elimination of crime is the Gordian knot of human relationship,—the puzzle of the ages. Man is slowly learning that justice must exist for all or exist for none—and crime against the humblest individual is against society itself; that the only just government is by the consent of the governed, and this can be secured only by equality of opportunity. This new child of man's wisdom, *fairplay,* is now face to face with the older child of his folly, *privilege.* Their conflicting claims constitute the apparently irreducible factors in human relationship. The fate of civilization depends upon the adjudication of their respective claims. The race question is but a factor of this larger problem. In Belgium, in Ireland, in the Balkans, and in Russia conditions are incomparably more acute than in the South.

In some ways, however, the American situation is without precedent or parallel. Slavery is common enough in human history and even among animals.[19] But the slave has either been subdued and oppressed in his native habitat or been carried to the master's native habitat. *Never have both master and slave been permanently expatriated as in America.* That they gradually became acclimated together accounts for *the strange miracle of friendship between master and slave.* Common dangers and hardships overcame mutual antagonisms and mistrusts. Common experiences bind men more closely than blood.[19a] Not only

[19] Darwin, "Origin of Species," ch. viii, "Slave-making Instinct."

[19a] Some years ago when the actual participants in the great Civil War were numerous and active in public affairs, a forlorn and battered specimen of the *genus homo sapiens Africanus* was haled into a Texas court charged with hog-stealing. The prisoner's wrinkled face and withered limbs showed plainly the many hardships he had passed, while his tattered raiment told the tale of his poverty.

The prisoner was arraigned without any evidence of emotion or sympathy on the part of the court officials or spectators, except the passing comment at the prisoner's apparent indifference to the proceedings. The prosecution stated its case. A perfunctory defense, in which the prisoner took neither part nor interest, was conducted by a court-appointed lawyer. The judge delivered his charge and the jury retired. The

did the white man and the black man unite to fight the Indian, but also to fight the European. The first victim of the Revolutionary War was Crispus Attucks, a Negro. With Perry on Lake Erie and Jackson at New Orleans, the white men and the black men fought, side by side, an European government. At

---

prisoner, dazed and listless, awaited the fate that, except for an emphatic "Not guilty," he had done nothing to avert. His revery was broken by the verdict of the jury: "We find the defendant guilty and assess his punishment at two years in the penitentiary." The old man's eyes dilated in astonishment.

"Prisoner at the bar, stand up," formally commanded the judge. The old man shuffled to his feet. Was it a court formality or a touch of sympathy, that led the judge to ask the delapidated and now thoroughly alarmed prisoner:—

"Prisoner at the bar, have you anything to say?"

The silence following the judge's question was immediately broken by an earnest "Yes sah!" from the prisoner, who then began a speech that at once gripped court and audience. On and on he went, the courtroom filled amid profound silence except for the broken voice of the prisoner. He was telling the story of his life. In graphic and picturesque language he described the childhood gambols of "young Marse Bill," how he had attended him through his schoolboy days to young manhood, how he had gone with him as a body servant into the war, how he had travelled on foot two hundred miles to tell "ole Miss" that "Marse Bill" was not dead as reported, but the yankees had him. How when "Marse Bill" was sick and wounded he had carried him to a place of safety and "foraged" a pig for his nourishment. After the war he had lost track of his "white folks," but on coming into court had recognized the judge as "Marse Bill": had thought surely "Marse Bill" remembered "Joe" and would see that he got "justice." If it was right to "take" a pig to keep "young Marse" from starving, how was it wrong to take one to keep his wife and children from starving?" The last words of the speaker, an appealing question to the judge, rang through the silent courtroom as the old man dropped exhausted into his seat:—

"If it was *foraging* then, how come it *stealing* now?"

No oration pronounced in the English language ever went straighter to the heart of an audience than the simple tale of this unfortunate prisoner. He had struck a responsive chord in every heart. Tears glistened in the eyes of more than one grizzled old warrior of the "Lost Cause." Amid the profound silence that followed the old man's speech, which no one had thought of interrupting, the judge said to the clerk, "The prisoner's motion for a new trial has been granted and he is discharged on his own recognizance." Then addressing the prosecutor, "Colonel," he said, "you'll have to get you another pig."

"He can have the rest of the litter," said the colonel, as much moved as the judge.

The spell was broken. With enthusiastic approval of everybody, the judge bade the prisoner "come home (the judge's house) and get food and clothes."

Joe's remaining days were spent in peace and comfort. His soldierly conduct in war had made the survivors, regardless of race, his friends.

El Caney and San Juan the same thing happened—and should a foreign foe invade our soil tomorrow, history would repeat itself.

Mr. Isaac Fisher, a full-blooded Afro-American says: "Looking backward—away back to the spot on Boston Commons, where a Negro—Crispus Attucks—was the earliest to shed his blood for American liberty, I get a point from which to count the black patriots slain. I see 5000 Negroes 'dead on the field of honor' in the Revolutionary War; I hear General Jackson say to the black boys in blue in 1812, 'I expected much from you. . . . But you have surpassed all my hopes.' I see a list of sable heroes marching against Mexico; and later, when, amid the shot and shell and carnage and ruin and misery of the terrible Civil War, God purged the nation of slavery, I see them still—black men, with hearts that did not quail, striving to defend this Union which had given them, in fullest measure, nothing but the gall and wormwood of physical chains. And then, later still, in Cuba, at Santiago, and charging up the heights of San Juan Hill, I see them marching, marching, marching, while the band played, 'There'll be a Hot Time in the Old Town Tonight,' and the world applauded their valor.

"And when I turn to history and ask if the black boys—yes, if my race—have ever sulked in their tents when the country called them, and there is but one answer: 'They have ever been ready to die in defense of the Stars and Stripes.'

"So far, the Negro's record as a patriot, as one who will lay down his life for this country, is *clean!*

"The Negro . . . has been charged with many crimes. . . . But, blessed be our Father, the Negro has not yet been called a man afraid and unwilling to die for his country. . . .

"I am opposed to wars and bloodshed. I hope that

the American sword has been drawn for the last time; but if this is not to be, I want my race to have part in any struggles which are for the national good. . . .

"America is the land of our birth—she must have our loyalty. . . . We defend her flag, not for the crimes against us which it shelters and protects, but for the best in our government of which it is a sign."

All other colored peoples in all other countries have, as a class, hated and fought and died in the presence of the white man. But the Afro-American has actually fallen in love with the white man and has waxed and grown fat and increased and multiplied in his presence. Stranger still! The white man, the *real Southern white man,* fell in love with the Negro—the real manhood in ebony—not the mulatto, nor any kind of "oon" but black.

In the year of grace 1915 I saw the Legislature[20] of a Southern State accept the hospitality of a Negro school. I saw them make a minute and critical examination of the grounds, buildings, students, and teachers. I saw them file into the dining-room and enjoy a dinner cooked and served by teachers and students to the inimitable harmony of Negro music. I saw them enter the chapel, more than a quorum of both houses, and listen to a brief program of music and recitation by the school, after which the principal turned things over to the visitors. I heard their speeches; sometimes witty, sometimes wise, and sometimes hortatory, sometimes pathetic, but always sincere; and at times tenderly compassionate and reverential as the memory of "Aunt Susan," "Aunt Rachel," or "Aunt Liza" welled into consciousness. Pledges of sympathy and support were given, amid praises for duty well done to faculty and students.

[20] See cut of Legislature.

This splendid program of reminiscence, sympathy, and helpfulness formally closed with a speech of rare eloquence and beauty, but full of sound and much appreciated advice to the colored people. The final words of the speaker fell like a benediction upon the grateful teachers and students, many of whom were personally known to individual legislators. The speaker was a Georgian and quoted Henry W. Grady: "If I forget these people, may an infinite God forget me."

I said, "This is neither ethnology, anthropology, nor evolution, but *humanity.*" Herein hath man "preeminence above a beast."

Strange miracle of the centuries, the love that grew up in America between the exiled children of Europe and Africa—a love without a parallel in the annals of the world—a love that constrained rugged old Senator Tilman to say he would give his life in defense of *some* negroes he knew—a love that moved the Confederate soldiers to propose a monument to *Negro* fidelity in the "days that tried men's souls,"—a love that will yet find a way for these people to live in helpful, hopeful peace, though ethnically separate, yet geographically one—"races to whom coexistence seems imperative, but between whom coalescence would be intolerable."

"Culture is everybody's creed and democracy is everybody's chance to put the creed to work." Religion is the melting-pot of passions—the only alembic that can transmute the antagonisms of the races into co-operation, while preserving their integrity and self-respect. In this country Euro-Americans and Afro-Americans have a common language, a common religion, a common country, and a *common destiny.*

"The formative assumptions, the ultimate dogmas of a civilization are to be determined, however, not from the failures of the few, but from the conceptions, the laws, the habits of the many."[21]

The vast majority in both races in the South are deeply religious. "Where difficulties are so great, none but the great and elemental human forces will prevail. It is, therefore, of deep and hopeful significance that the power and influence of religious institutions are so general. As these come to deal more definitely and explicitly with the phases of social need, there will enter into social enthusiasms a high and serious confidence, a touch of authority, and yet a touch of tenderness which will draw the world to the Church while it draws the Church to the quickening and freeing of the world."[22]

Herein is our assurance of peace and co-operation. It is so significant that "where we find the Negro in relation to the trained and educated representatives of the stronger race, we find few of the evidences of racial friction."

A sound heart and a clear head mean the same thing to races as to individuals,—peace with yourself, peace with your neighbor, and prosperity for both.

The following incident shows the unifying power of religious sentiment over the warring elements of races speaking a common tongue:—

"The Holy City."

"Thirty men, red-eyed and disheveled, lined up before a judge of a San Francisco police court. It was the regular morning company of 'drunks and disorderlies.' Some were old and hardened, others hung their heads in shame. Just as the momentary disorder attending the bringing in of the prisoners quieted

[21] Murphy, "The Present South," page 272.
[22] *Ibid.*

A summer school for colored teachers. Nearly 1000 in attendance (1915). (See page 194.)

Visit of the Legislature to the State Normal School (colored).

down, a strange thing happened. A strong, clear voice from below began singing:—

'Last night I lay a-sleeping,
There came a dream so fair.'

"Last night! It had been for them all a nightmare or a drunken stupor. The song was such a contrast to the horrible fact that no one could fail of a sudden shock at the thought the song suggested.

'I stood in old Jerusalem,
Beside the temple there,'

the song went on. The judge had paused. He made a quiet inquiry. A former member of a famous opera company, known all over the country, was awaiting trial for forgery. It was he who was singing in his cell.

"Meantime the song went on and every man in the line showed emotion. One or two dropped on their knees; one boy at the end of the line, after a desperate effort at self-control, leaned against the wall, buried his face against his folded arms, and sobbed, 'O mother, mother!'

"The sobs cutting to the very heart of the men who heard, and the song, still welling its way through the courtroom, blended in the hush. At length one man protested:—

" 'Judge,' said he, 'have we got to submit to this? We're here to take our punishment, but this—' He, too, began to sob.

"It was impossible to proceed with the business of the court, yet the judge gave no order to stop the song. The police-sergeant, after a surprised effort to keep the men in line, stepped back and waited with the rest. The song moved on to its climax:—

> 'Jerusalem! Jerusalem! Sing, for the night is o'er!
> Hosanna in the highest! Hosanna forevermore!'

"In an ecstasy of melody the last words rang out, and then there was silence.

"The judge looked into the faces of the men before him. There was not one who was not touched by the song; not one in whom some better impulse was not stirred. He did not call the cases singly—a kind word of advice, and he dismissed them all. No man was fined or sentenced to the workhouse that morning. The song had done more good than punishment could have accomplished."

Civilization is the altruistic fruition of the ages and rests upon man's unselfish service to man. Everyone who does a kind deed is a contributor, from the humble slave that did his duty in the dim and distant past to the brilliant inventor of today; and while it is the patrimony of mankind, the white man is the present administrator. He must, however, deal fairly with all the heirs or vacate his office; for *civilization is the product of no particular breed of men* and is therefore the heritage of all. Universality will mean perpetuation. World-wide peace can only come with world-wide democracy.

There is no middle ground for the Negro. He must go up to a citizen or down to a serf. He is not going to die out. The Negro preacher and the Negro teacher stand at the moral gate to keep the race back from fatal corruption; the Negro doctor is keeping the pass against disease, and the hosts of civilization are camped round and about.

The Negro is not going to leave here for two

reasons: In the first place *this is his home,* and in the second place *there is nowhere to go.* He is not going back to Africa any more than the white man is going back to Europe or the Jew is going back to Palestine. Palestine may be rehabilitated and Europe be Americanized, but the Jew will not lose his world-wide citizenship, nor America fail of her geographical destination as the garden-spot of the world. The Negro will do his part to carry the light of civilization to the dark corners of the world—especially to Africa; dark, mysterious, inscrutable Africa; the puzzle of the past and the riddle of the future; the imperturbable mother of civilizations and peoples.

The slave-trade was the diaspora of the African, and the children of this alienation have become a permanent part of the citizenry of the American republic. Fate holds the welfare of America as hostage to insure final justice and fair play to all citizens, regardless of color, creed, or sex.

"A culture that long ignores its own context will not be taken seriously even by itself."[23]

The spirit that enables the white man to modestly write himself down as belonging to "the most potent race the world has known,"[24] finds no difficulty in accepting as a fundamental principle of race adjustment "the absolute and unchangeable superiority of the white race."

Fundamentally erroneous and mischievous as I believe this assumption to be, I am not disposed to quarrel over it with such men as Messrs. Page and Murphy. We believe in the same thing for different reasons and can easily act in harmony.

Mr. Page says: "The Negroes will always have

---

[23] Murphy, "The Present South."

[24] Thos. N. Page, "The Negro," page 204.

their leaders, and it is better to have enlightened leaders than ignorant. . . .

"The alleged danger of the educated Negro becoming a greater menace to the white than the uneducated is a bugaboo which will not stand the test of light."

And again: "In the first place, it seems to me that our plain duty is to do the best we can to act with justice and a broad charity and leave the consequences to God."

My experience is exactly like Mr. Page's: "When the writer first began to study the conditions of the race problem they appeared to be most disheartening. As, however, he surveyed the entire field, he has become more hopeful, and certainly more firm in his convictions as to a few principles."

My guiding principles on this question are six:—

1. Mankind is one in blood and capable alike of the same vices and the same virtues. It is a matter of topography and temperature.

2. Races, like individuals, are prone to prate of their own virtues and enlarge upon their neighbors' vices.

3. The reverse process would eliminate most of their marginal troubles; namely, study to correct their own vices and to find out the others' virtues.

4. Misunderstanding, rather than meanness, makes them unjust to each other.

5. There is but one proposition in human reason that is settled "ultimately and fundamentally," namely, *man has never yet settled anything that way.* It is not wise to try to look too far ahead. The cryptograms of the book of destiny have not yet been opened to man's inspection. Ultimate problems are as inscrutable today as of old.

Successful men in various lines of endeavor.

6. I have accepted as sound the conclusions of the Greeks: "These things are not of today nor yesterday, but evermore, and no man knoweth whence they came.

"The ways of His thoughts are as paths in a wood thick with leaves, and one seeth through them but a little way."

Knowledge is harmonious and truth is a unity. Any subject pursued far enough and understood well enough will liberalize the mind and humble the spirit, making us charitable and patient. From different starting points Mr. Page and I reach the same conclusion. "Our plain duty is to do the best we can to act with justice and a broad charity and leave the consequences to God."

The presence of the Negro is not a menace to the prosperity of the South.

"The absolute supremacy of intelligence and property, secured through a suffrage test that shall be evenly and equally applicable in theory and in fact to white and black—this will be the ultimate solution of the South for the whole vexed question of political privilege."—MURPHY.

"The cultured class of white society in the South, as a rule, comes in contact only with the hewers of wood and drawers of water of the Negro race, and are prone to judge the rest by what it sees. A great mistake. There is a large and growing cultured class of Negroes in the South, which can mingle only with itself. When the strength of these cultured classes—living in the same section, but separate and distinct, and ignorant of each other—become more equal, as it surely will in the future under the present specially fine educational advantages now being engaged by the Negro, what is going to be the effect? I believe that, in time, we will have in the South two almost universally cultured races. That is the trend."—SMITH CLAYTON, Atlanta, Ga.

CHAPTER IX.

WHAT THE NEGRO MAY REASONABLY EXPECT OF THE WHITE MAN.[1]

LIBERTY has ever been the dream of man—the theme of philosophy, the ideal of poetry, the goal of statesmanship. It has enhanced the dreams of the great and powerful as well as the poor and oppressed.

Slaves in their chains have cried for it,
Kings on their thrones have sighed for it,
And soldiers on gory fields have died for it;
  Yet the world knows it not.

"Liberté, egalité, fraternité" (liberty, equality, fraternity), is written in the blood of Frenchmen, and yet France is not free. "Fiat justitia ruat cœlum" was a motto of ancient Rome, but justice came not; neither did the heavens fall, but Rome did.

"In the beauty of the lilies,
  Christ was born across the sea,
With a glory in his bosom
  That transfigures you and me.
As he died to make men holy,
  Let us die to make men free."

So sang the Union soldiers in the bloody days of the sixties. But, alas! where is the freedom for which they died?

The glory that was Greece, and the grandeur that

---

[1] The substance of this chapter formed an address at the Semi-centennial Emancipation Celebration, at Philadelphia, Pa., Sept. 17, 1913.

was Rome, alike passed away in a maddening wail for liberty. Rivers of blood have not been sufficient to bear Irish citizenship to that desired goal. Labor leaders seeking it travel like one lost in a wilderness—moving in a circle and coming ever to the same point.

Why has man's quest for liberty ever been a fool's errand? Is human liberty like the bag of gold at the end of the rainbow? A barren and unattainable ideality to lure the foolish and amuse the wise?

On the contrary, liberty is within easy reach of mankind, but the conditions upon which she will abide with an individual or nation are fixed and unalterable. She cannot be induced to tarry unless these conditions are met.

Man's unwillingness to *be* just is the explanation of his failure to *obtain* justice. Liberty is a sun that shines for all or shines for none. The white people in the United States of America will never enjoy liberty and justice until they are willing to concede liberty and justice to all.

In the face of this eternal truth, written with blood in the annals of time, why do men seek justice by indirection, and liberty by oppression? What men *expect* of each other is at the bottom of the tragedy.

I.

The Negro expects the white man to make good as a civilized man—to materialize into tangible objectivity the ideals of human brotherhood. The white man has not done this, though he has made some progress in the past fifty years.

In July, 1863, the *Boston Courier* said: "As no white man ought to consent to be a slave, so, in our opinion, no Negro ought to desire to be a free man in

Twentieth-century civilization. ("Causes and Cures of Crime," Mosby.)

the United States. Freedom to them can have no other meaning than misery, degradation, and final extermination." (See *Independent,* July 24, 1913, p. 225.)

In July, 1913, Dr. Elliott said: "We may reasonably hope, therefore, that the moral atmosphere in which the political and industrial struggle of the colored race is to be conducted during the next fifty years will be more favorable than it has been during the past fifty. The policies which the race should follow, and all its leaders should incessantly urge, are the acquisition of private property by the individual; the accumulation of capital in the hands of the race as a result of industry and frugality; the education of all its children far beyond the narrow limitations imposed by present State legislation; the preparation of colored men for all the learned and scientific professions in order that the race may be independent as regards the possessions of all safeguards of society against physical and moral evils, and of all the means of intellectual and moral progress. . . . If in another fifty years these liberties shall have been won, the Americans of African descent will have passed from slavery to freedom more quickly than any white race has ever done, and with much less suffering by the way." (Chas. W. Elliott, Pres. Em. Harvard Univ.; see *A. M. E. Review,* July, 1913.)

But all white men have not made the advance here indicated. Witness this extract from a governor's message in 1913: "I warn you today, passing as I am rapidly from State politics, that if I go higher it will be to a broader and national field, where I will fight the education of the Negro. God Almighty never intended that he should be educated, and the man who attempts to do what God Almighty never intended will be a failure. God made that man to be your servant.

The Negro was meant to be a hewer of wood and a drawer of water. If God had intended him to be your equal, he would have made him white and put a bone in his nose."[2]

Over against this ignorant and brazen attempt to read the Book of Fate and interpret the ways of the Almighty, I set the words of the pious revelator, St. John, the *Divine:* "And I saw a strong angel proclaiming with a loud voice, Who is worthy to open the book, and to loose the seals thereof?

"And no man in heaven, nor in earth, neither under the earth, was able to open the book, neither to look therein." (Rev. 5: 2, 3.)

Who can penetrate the Arcana of God and read the cryptograms of the Book of Destiny? God is His own interpreter. Not even the angels of glory are considered worthy to open the Book of Fate; but there *is* a class of men who "rush in where angels fear to tread." The Negro expects the white man to reach a stage of civilization when that type of men will not be leaders.

"The God who knows our wrongs seems—and but seems—to have abandoned us."

But the white man hopes to make still more progress.

Rev. Henry Stiles Bradley expects flying machines to establish peace; humanitarianism to make human brotherhood a living actuality, and eugenics to bring universal health.[3]

Truly a great vision! Somewhat in advance of repealing the Fifteenth Amendment! The two things are incompatible.

---

[2] Subsequent events proved this gentleman as short on prophecy as he was on human anatomy. He "passed from State politics," but not to "the broader national field."

[3] At Southern Sociological Congress, Atlanta, Ga., Apr., 1913.

He also places mastering your neighbor in the first or lowest stage of civilization.

The Negro is willing to rest his case in the *court of civilization,* and expects the white man to be influenced by the ideals of civilization's choicest spirits, such as Dr. Elliott and Dr. Bradley.

II.

The Negro expects the white man to preserve the chivalry of the strong.

In the fifth canto of the "Lady of the Lake," Scott describes a scene between Roderick Dhu, an outlawed highland chieftain, and Fitz James, the King of Scotland, incognito, where each refused to take advantage of the other. After calling up his army to suddenly confront the boasting Fitz James, the chief dismissed them and said:—

"Fear naught—nay, that I need not say—
But—doubt not aught from mine array.
Thou art my guest;—I pledged my word
As far as Coilantogle Ford!

"Nor would I call a clansman's brand
For aid against one valiant hand,
Though on our strife lay every vale
Rent by the Saxon from the Gael."

When they reached Coilantogle Ford, "Far past Clan Alpine's outmost guard," the irate chieftain proposed a duel, throwing down his shield because Fitz James had none. Fitz James was now within calling of his retinue, but refused to wind his horn, and, single-handed, closed in mortal combat with this chivalrous but vengeful and powerful chief. Thus—

"Shine Martial faith and Courtesy's bright star, . . .
Through all the wreckful storms that cloud the brow of war."

The strong man demands only a square deal and willingly concedes to others the same thing. On this principle, the *Negro expects of the white man a man's chance to be a man.*

"Ill fares the land, to hastening ills a prey,
Where wealth accumulates and men decay."

Is the United States a decadent nation? Has gangrene set up in the body politic?

The keynote to an ideal man's character is courage. Neither virtue nor wisdom is of much avail without this fundamental quality. Wealth, position, power, and opportunity are all naught unless courage is present. Cowardice is the most fatal defect of human character and is a presage of disaster. Success, whether individual, communal, or national, cannot live in the absence of courage. So true is this that, in our language, courage and manhood are synonymous.

"Peace hath higher tests of manhood,
Than battles ever knew,"

sings the Poet, Whittier. Habits may change the qualities of character, and nations may lose the characteristics that made them great. Sin is a reproach to a people and vice may ruin a state.

One of the chief characteristics of true bravery is a love of fair play. When courage hesitates to give opponents a fair chance, deterioration has set in. Cruelty and oppression as national traits are sure precursors of national decay.

The latest phases of the lynching evil in the United States seriously raise the question of manhood deterioration in this country. It is the note of decadence in the oratorio of American progress. Patients are dragged from hospitals and tortured to death as a Sunday evening's amusement. Innocent women and even little children are murdered in noon daytime. Manacled prisoners are assaulted and murdered in the temples of justice. Has the white man reached his zenith and retrogression set in? Has the gift of wealth destroyed alike his heart and his brain? Has the battle for justice and freedom been lost in the Western World?

The Memphis *Commercial Appeal* said recently: "When the Negro enters into the contest with the white man he is already at a disadvantage, and therefore the truly brave white man never seeks a quarrel with Negroes. He knows that the Negro is at a disadvantage and he does not want to take advantage of him.

"Furthermore, the white man of courage can almost always control the Negro without being compelled to resort to violence."[4]

III.

The Negro expects the white man's sympathy rather than his pity.

Every man has a right to be graded according to the amount of manhood his character may show when assayed by the standards of civilization; or, as Mazzini put it, "The standard of civilization is the value of man as man." The Negro expects the dominating spirit of this nation to be democratic in this sense. (See "Who is a Democrat?" by Dr. Dillard, in *Southwestern Christian Advocate,* July 17, 1913.)

[4] Quoted in *New York Age*, Aug. 5, 1913.

IV.

The Negro expects of the white man a reasonable measure of consistency.

Currency reform and manhood degradation form an incongruous program of "progressiveness."

Paleontology has established the fact that the primitive man showed far more skill in depicting animals than in drawing human beings. In fact, "Amid the quaternary works of art, compared with animal figures, human figures are extremely rare. Primitive artists evidently had no skill in this direction." This seems to be a phase of a still more general and puzzling fact; civilized man often shows more interest in and sympathy with the brute creation than with humanity. The suffering of frogs in a physiological laboratory excites more interest than the agony of working girls in a sweat-shop. The imagined torturing of dogs in laboratories arouses more humane activity than the actual torturing of men in prisons.

A striking illustration of this phase of human nature came under my observation recently in a Southern city, famed for culture and refinement. A colored man was driving a mule. The latter did not do to suit the former, whereupon the man began to beat the mule. This attracted the attention of a member of the Humane Society, who at once protested, and called a policeman. The muledriver was arrested and ordered to proceed immediately to the police-station. The colored man did not move fast enough for the policeman, who at once began to club his prisoner far more severely and with much less excuse than the mule was clubbed. Humane Society interested itself to protect the mule, but not the man. The driver was fined, but the policeman was not even prosecuted. *The*

Negro expects the white man to give him as much consideration as he does a mule.

This inconsistency sometimes takes the form of dishonesty and cruelty. Take the question of separate accommodations for the races. The laws declare or presume *equal* accommodations, and all the arguments in favor of these laws assume such a condition as a fact, whereas the opposite is true. With few exceptions, *separate accommodations mean inferior accommodations.* The most diabolical example of this is an illustration of national greed rather than local prejudice; for the ownership of the guilty railroads is by no means limited to the South. In fact, the Southern-owned railroads are usually the least culpable. Few civilized men could be found to maintain that a Negro should receive only 10 ounces of sugar for a pound, while everybody else received 16 ounces for the same price. Yet this is what the railroads do for the colored people every day in the year. The Negro expects, and has a right to expect, the white man to make a change in this condition.

V.

The Negro expects the white man to concede him the right to stay on the earth. The Negro has earned this right by long residence.

The origin of the Negro is as mystical as Sappho's leap from the Leucadian Rock, and the beginning of his troubles as undiscoverable as the name of the valiant antedeluvian who first tasted an oyster. Before Hercules set up his pillars with his *ne plus ultra;* before Rameses conceived the pyramids of Egypt or the Collossus of Rhodes fell; before Homer sang or Moses received the Ten Commandments; before Joseph's flight into Egypt or Herod's slaughter of the innocents; before Leonidas stood at the Pass of Thermopylæ or Xenophen led the Retreat of the Ten Thousand; before Confucius taught or Buddha lived; before the wise men journeyed from the east, or the Roman discovered Britain; before Job had his troubles or Jeremiah his lamentations; before the Red Sea parted or the walls of Jericho fell; before the Sermon on the Mount or the Cross on Calvary—in fact, before history began, *the Negro race was.* And when Macaulay's South Sea Islander sits on the broken arch of London Bridge to sketch the ruins of St. Paul, the Negro will be there, as he was with Columbus, Balboa, and Perry. Who knows but that last man so graphically described by the poet will be a Negro?

Virtues do not change, but the conditions of their exercise do. Hence, each generation needs its own ethical interpreters of conduct. I am an American and speak and write as an American to Americans. I shall, however, attempt to promulgate no new doctrines nor establish any novel ethical standards. On the contrary, I shall attempt the strictest adherence to the universal tenets of modern civilization and the ethos of the American people. But the *ethos* of a people is not stationary,—knighting Hawkins for establishing the transatlantic slave-trade and immortalizing Lincoln for the Emancipation Proclamation could hardly spring from the same ethical standards.

"The ethos of a people constitutes the universe of their moral activities. The man who conforms to the morality of that world is a good man." In that sense I hope to be good and strive to be patriotic. I seek not revolution, but evolution. *I ask not the white man to change his ideals, but to live up to them.*

I believe the American people want positive and absolute advancement, not negative and relative advancement by holding somebody else back.

Prominent colored Americans.

The highest individual conduct is manifested when reason controls personal action, and the greatest general good comes to a people when the brainiest and best men control the state. May God pity this country if certain ignorant and erratic demagogues, United States Senators, or would-be senators, shall ever become truly representative of the majority sentiment of the American people!

VI.

The Negro expects the white man to cease parading universal human frailties as peculiar Negro vices.

This is a national failing that is used sometimes unconsciously to increase race prejudice. Suggestion has a powerful influence on belief and conduct.[5]

"If the many-footed worm which rolls up into a ball when you touch it is pricked with a needle, and the aching tooth is touched with the needle, the pain will be eased."

Was this remedy for toothache proposed by an African voodoo? No, indeed! It is from the "Rose Anglica," a book by "John of Gaddesden (1280-1361), member of Merton College, Master of Arts, Bachelor of Theology, and Doctor of Medicine, Court Physician to the King of England."

The author modestly says of this book: "As the rose overtops all flowers, so this book overtops all treatises on the practice of medicine, and it is written for both poor and rich, surgeons and physicians, so that there shall be no need for them to be always run-

[5] An auto accident was caused by a boy running in front of the machine. The published account emphasized the fact that it was a Negro boy. The Hot Springs fire started in a small dwelling. The published account emphasized the unimportant detail that it was a Negro dwelling. Mrs. O'Leary's race has never been emphasized in connection with the Chicago fire.

ning to consult other books, for here they find all about curable disease, both from the special and the general point of view."

The Negro is often accused of ignorance and egotism. There are others.

A strange fact of physiological interest is that memory sometimes becomes subservient to the imagination, the wish becomes father to the thought, and a man believes his own lies, whether he is an angekok (sorcerer) in Greenland or a demagogue in Mississippi; a voodoo in Nigeria or an office-seeker in South Carolina, especially if the doctrine bring power and pelf, is utility preferable to truth.

Somebody has defined heaven as a point of vantage from which some folks may enjoy watching the misery of others. This is a witty fling at a very widespread human perversity, a perversity that receives the hell-fire doctrine with complacency among Christians, and sustains the torture feast among savages; that made the down-trodden white man and the down-trodden black man hate each other in ante-bellum days; that leads the poor white man in the South today to reward with official prominence the politician who promises the most harm to the colored people; that leads Northern and Western Chautauquas to pay Southern platform agitators to abuse the Negro.

VII.

The Negro expects of the white man a reasonable interpretation of the Declaration of Independence.

Governments derive their *just* power from the *consent* of the governed.

Equality of men in reference to *life, liberty,* and the *pursuit of happiness,*—the right to *live, labor,* and *laugh* is the heritage of all men.

Mankind is ever given to extremes in humanitarianism, as in everything else. It is either the frothy sentimentality that is afraid to draw its breath, lest it give pain to the ephemera of the air, or the hard-hearted cruelty that justifies the strong in despoiling the weak. The square deal seems yet to be a barren ideality or a convenient party slogan. Public good is inextricably mixed with private whims. My inalienable right to bread is continually confused with the social privilege of my neighbor's table. The first is the heritage of every human; the second is the dowry of the chosen. To deny the former to anyone is an injury to all; the latter may follow the taste of an individual or the custom of the locality without serious disturbance to the general welfare.[6]

The War Amendments to the Constitution and the Civil Rights Bill marked the culmination of the American wave of the world-wide humanitarianism that characterized the first two-thirds of the nineteenth century; a movement that had for its object the brotherhood of man—or, as the French put it, "Liberty, Equality, Fraternity." Reaction set in in 1876, and the friends of liberty have yielded in the forum what they had won in the field. The slaveholder did not call the roll of his slaves at the foot of Bunker Hill, but the lynchers did do their fiendish work within the sound of Liberty Bell.

VIII.

The Negro expects the white man to get over his obsession that Negro progress is inimical to American civilization.

---

[6] See *Independent,* July 24, 1913, page 225.

A well-nigh universal human stupidity is the belief that our neighbor's success is the cause of our failure. This is the tap-root of envy, and can be made to flourish incredibly when properly stimulated. Thus poor white folks situated in communities by themselves are led to believe that the prosperity of colored people in other parts of the State is a menace to them. They eagerly vote into State and national prominence the cunning and conscienceless, though poorly educated, politicians who promise to head off the colored man's prosperity.

The supreme test of civilization is the attitude of the strong toward the weak.

The self-sufficiency of the Negro is the only sane and equitable solution of the race problem in this country. The white man himself is responsible for the ethnological bugaboo of social equality. His effort to keep all colored people to a dead level, and that level below the aspirations and capacities of modern civilization, brings the inevitable reaction of effort to escape; whereas, if the Negro were let alone he would be content to be a man and flock with his kind.

Politics, ethnography, and religion seem a trinity of discord in human history. Races and individuals are frequently sane on one of them, but rarely on all three.

The South still wants to treat the Negro as a slave; the North wants to treat him as a *freed* man; neither wants to recognize him for what he is striving to be, namely, *a free man.*

IX.

The Negro expects the white man to make the average salary of the Negro school-teacher at least what the contract price for a convict is.

The United States government refused to pay the first Negro soldiers employed (54th Mass.) the same wages that white volunteers were receiving. This unexplained discrimination of the secretary of war is well-nigh universally imitated by those who employ Negro brawn and brain. 'Tis a national vice that the Negro expects the white man to remedy.

"While much has been done for us along the lines of education, yet our chance for an education is sad. The average salary of colored teachers in the public schools in the South is just about $25.00 per month, while a Negro convict is rented out for $46.00 per month."[7]

We have no playgrounds for our children:—

"Plenty of room for dives and dens,
Glitter and glare and sin;
Plenty of room for prison pens,
Gather the criminals in;

"Plenty of room for jails and courts—
Willing enough to pay;
But never a place for the lads to race,
No never a place to play.

"Plenty of room for shops and stores,
Mammon must have the best;
Plenty of room for the running sores
That rot in the city's breast;

"Plenty of room for the lures that lead
The hearts of our youth astray;
But never a cent on a playground spent,
Nor never a place to play."[8]

---

[7] R. S. Lovinggood, *Southwestern Christian Advocate,* Jan. 16, 1913.
[8] Mr. S. Waters McGill, Nashville, Tenn., Gen. Sec. Y. M. C. A.

The Negro expects the white man to help remedy this condition.

X.

The Negro expects the white man to remember the facts of history. The Negro has played many a noble rôle in the drama of human history. A general knowledge of this fact would tend to lessen prejudice.

As the Negro troops broke Hood's center and made Union victory possible at the battle of Nashville, so the Negro's brawn broke the wilderness of this continent and made possible the splendid civilization of our subtropical region.

"Gen. Jas. B. Steadman, of the Union army, commanded the colored troops at the battle of Nashville. . . . Gen. Thomas was viewing from Ft. Negley the strategic maneuvers of Gen. Wood just before the engagement. He called his staff and asked if some general would volunteer to take his brigade and break Hood's left center, stating that the loss of men would be so great that he would rather not order troops in, but have them volunteer. While the generals were considering it he turned to Gen. Steadman and asked him what the colored brigade would say. 'I'll ask them,' said Steadman. 'When can you be back?' 'In twenty minutes, sir,' said Steadman. Gen. Steadman rode away to his men, explained the extreme danger of such a charge, and asked them whether they would be willing to make it. They accepted the offer with prolonged and tremendous cheering. When Gen. Steadman had conveyed the message, Gen. Thomas said: 'And will you lead them?' 'Certainly, I will, sir.' 'Then make the charge tomorrow morning.'

"The colored troops charged the Confederate batteries. It was a desperate hand-to-hand fight. Some of the batteries were captured. Then a fierce bayonet charge followed upon the Confederate trenches behind the batteries. It was one of the most daring feats of the great war. The Confederate lines finally retreated. *Steadman's colored brigade had turned Hood's left wing and made it possible for Thomas to win the battle of Nashville."*[9]

The Negro has played his part as a soldier. We have Kipling's word for it that "He's a first-rate fighting man."

The 54th Massachusetts at Ft. Wagner and Steadman's colored brigade at Nashville are as glorious in the annals of war as the charge of the Six Hundred, or the stand at Thermopylæ.

XI.

The Negro expects the white man to help him pass the zone of incapacity.

There comes a period in the history of organizations and races when conflicting interests make united action for the general good difficult, if not impossible. 'Twas such a period that destroyed the solidarity of Greece, broke up the Saxon heptarchy, rendering the Norman conquest possible, defeated Protestantism in the Romance countries, overthrew the Netherlands, disintegrated the Spanish empire, brought on the American Civil War, delays home rule in Ireland today, and renders impotent the anti-Tammany forces of New York City. Such a period is at present upon the Negro. The Negro justly expects the white man to help him pass this zone of incapacity.

To separate the sheep from the goats we need and

---

[9] C. H. Bennett, Ph.D.

expect the white man's help. Slavery tended to level the race. We must get trusted and capable leaders to succeed in freedom. We expect the white man's help to make them.

The American Negro needs sane, conservative, unselfish, patient, Negro leadership. The greatest help that can be given the race is to assist in the development of these leaders. Wholesome Negro ideals must be created by men of Negro blood. These ideals may be assisted from without, but cannot be superimposed. Masters may be aliens, but *leaders* must be patriots. Leaders must know the people they lead. A race without leaders of its own blood is lost. No masterpiece was ever written in any language but the mother-tongue of the writer; and great leaders are always kindred of the led. Moses was a Jew, Cromwell was an Englishman, Lincoln was an American, and Toussaint L'Overture was a Negro.

It has been said in a good many ways and with a good many different kinds of emphasis how grateful the Negro ought to be for being transformed from an African savage to an American citizen, notwithstanding the limitations with which prejudice has hedged that citizenship. Much has been written on the benefits the Negro derived from slavery, and how grateful the race ought to be therefor. As for the benefits, I am like the Irish sergeant, willing to let it go at that; but as to our gratitude, I feel like the archer in the chronicles of Monstrele.

An archer was condemned to death for poaching, but before execution it was discovered that he suffered from stone in the bladder, a disease which afflicted many prominent personages of that time. A surgeon suggested the advantage that might accrue from examining the condition in a living man. Consequently, the condemned prisoner was given over to a real vivisection, carried on by the surgeon in the presence of the distinguished persons suffering from the disease. The victim was simply held and cut open until the stone was found and removed. The parts were examined to the satisfaction of those present and then sewed back together. As strange as it may appear, the prisoner recovered, after which the king graciously pardoned him. He was not only a free man, but a well man. But how much gratitude he owed to those who cured him is a question in casuistry too complicated for me. *This is the Negro's position in reference to his freedom.*

The cold facts of North American slavery will chill the heart of the historian of the future; and the somber hierarchs of misology who sought to harmonize the highest humanitarianism with chattel slavery, and to justify the selling of men by the tenets of philosophy and religion, will be cited in the archives of the future as queer examples of the intellectual aberration and moral obliquity of mankind.

XII.

The Negro expects the white man to help him train the rising generation to conserve the virtues of their ancestry and transmit them with increased number and added luster to posterity.

The colored people are headed away from slavery. The clash often comes with white people who are headed toward slavery. The bitterest opposition to Negro education comes from uneducated or poorly educated Caucasians.

Men rise to fame by getting in the right place as well as by energy, ability, and endurance. Hans Wagner, the great baseball player, was a failure as a pitcher, but a world-beater as a batter and short-stop. So with the races. *We have earned an honorable place in American civilization, and we expect the white man to help us maintain it.*

Will not some of our wealthy millionaires establish some *foundations* with this end in view? Why not endow a medical research laboratory in connection with the Douglass or Mercy Hospital of Philadelphia, or George W. Hubbard Hospital of Nashville, or Andrew Memorial Hospital of Tuskegee Institute? Is it too much to expect the white man in his magnificence of wealth and culture to establish some "foundations" for development of Negro brains and morals?

A nation's strength is in men—a leisure class is necessary for the improvement of the race. I mean men who are not vexed by the questions: "What shall we eat? What shall we drink? And wherewithal shall we be clothed?"

We need the highest development of professional men. For highest usefulness, men need to be de-developed indigenously. Education in our great Northern schools among white people seems, temporarily at least, to unfit some of our men for the exigencies of life among their own people in the South. There are men of our race who could do the race and country inestimable good could they devote their time to the work of race improvement, unvexed by the insistent question of making a living.

The Jewish Agricultural and Industrial Aid Society, supported by the Baron Hirsch Fund, finds employment, aids Jews in purchasing homes, loans money, etc. Such an effort would be of inestimable benefit to the Negro, relieving the congestion of the

South and obviating the loss of vitality of industrious Negroes in the slums of Northern cities.[10]

The Negro expects the white man to learn and act upon the ineluctable truth that no man nor race can permanently obtain justice that will not give justice. People are more active as enemies than as friends. Let the friends of humanity wake up. The reactionaries are active.

The Negro expects of the white man the *liberality of success.* Why should not some wealthy philanthropist place within the reach of the Negro the blessings of the Knapp School of Country Life?[11]

Finally, *the American white man is a distinctive ethnic entity. The American Negro is sui generis. Their relationship is unparalleled and has furnished two unique incidents in human history that are a credit to humanity and deserve a memorial slab in the corridors of time. Each race contributed one.*

The annals of the human race contain no more glorious chapters than those recording:—

(*a*) The disinterested zeal and self-sacrificing enthusiasm of the early abolitionists and the educational missionaries to the manumitted slaves. These heroes were by no means all Northern, as is generally believed.

(*b*) The conduct of the slaves during the Civil War and immediately thereafter. Loyalty to home, self-restraint, protection of women and children, characterized the "black daddies" as well as the "black mammies."

Can't we get together and furnish a third unique event in human history, viz., justice, fraternity, equality, with racial integrity?

---

[10] See *Independent,* Aug. 14, 1913, page 402.
[11] See Editorial in *Southern Workman,* July, 1913.

In this country we believe in short cuts to any desired goal. We believe law is omnipotent, hence the incessant agitation for new laws. An insistent and noisy minority may easily put almost any law on the statute book. Their effectiveness, however, depends upon another force, more powerful but less pliable. It is what we vaguely call public opinion, but which is more accurately expressed by the German Sittlichkeit and the Greek ethos.

While "the totality of existence is in perpetual flux," there is a reasonable degree of permanency in the physical world. This results from the gradual operation of physical laws. A gallon of water suddenly exposed to a freezing temperature turns to ice gradually. Ice subjected to high temperature will return to water before becoming steam.

In like manner is a reasonable degree of social permanency preserved. Lasting changes in public opinion cannot be made suddenly; the Sittlichkeit of a people changes slowly. The fiery eloquence of Toombs could not avert the doom of slavery nor the erudite ardor of Sumner bring civil rights to the freed men. Neither will ignorant and malicious diatribes of ambitious politicians stay the rising tides of justice and righteousness in this glorious Southland of ours.

Racial co-operation is not incompatible with racial purity. Make the Negro self-sufficient and the thing is done. Give him a man's chance and he will do a man's work.

We boast a reunited country. The peace of Appomattox in 1865 was the unconditional surrender of the South to the power of the North. The peace of Gettysburg in 1913 was the unconditional surrender of the North to the propaganda of the South.

May we not hope there is to come a real peace without subterfuge or reaction, when righteousness will so fill men's hearts that the Northern ideal of freedom and equality will join hands with the Southern ideal of racial integrity and power, and together march in perfect harmony to a glorious national destiny, that shall embrace all true citizens, without regard to *race, color, sex,* or *previous condition of servitude?*

"Friendship does not grow where former differences are thrust into sight. There are wounds of the mind as of the body; these, too, must be healed. Instead of irritation and pressure, let there be gentleness and generosity. Men in this world get only what they give,—prejudice for prejudice, animosity for animosity, hate for hate. Likewise confidence is returned for confidence, good-will for good-will, friendship for friendship. On this rule, which is the same for the nation as for the individual, I would now act."—CHARLES SUMNER.

"Spiritual kinship transcends all other relations among men."—KELLY MILLER.

"Every step in the history of political liberty is a sally of the human mind into the untried future."—EMERSON.

CHAPTER X.

THE SOLUTION.

I.

THE indispensable factor in unity of action is unity of purpose, not unity of blood. A unity of brains brings that intelligent difference which makes peace possible and co-operation imperative. The Euro-American and the Afro-American of this country are closer together in ideals and aspirations than any two separate peoples on earth. They speak the same language, are attached to the same country, adapted to the same climate and like each other.[1]

In popular governments, ambitious men in all ages have played upon the prejudices of the populace for power and place. Post-bellum reaction and reconstruction in the South created a favorable atmosphere for the demagogue to exploit race prejudice for personal gain. Nothing is easier than to make a man feel that he is mistreated. The poor white man was made to believe that the degradation of the Negro meant elevation of the white man; and the nation reversed itself on the fundamental question of human justice. So fifty years after a successful war of emancipation, the Negro finds the path to civil liberty barred by discriminating legislation and himself a despised suppliant at the closed gate of justice. The United States Supreme Court, by technical ingenuity, is picking its way through the War Amendments back to the

[1] "There is a certain amount of race hatred, of course, and there are reasons for this, but the best Southern people not only do not hate the Negro, but come nearer to having affection for him than any other people." (Edwin A. Alderman, LL.D., President of Tulane University, New Orleans, La., before the American Economic Association, Dec. 29, 1903. Quoted by Mr. Murphy, in "The Present South.")

Dred Scott Decision, which furnished the popular slogan of ante-bellum days. *"The Negro has no rights the white man is bound to respect."*[2] Spain lost her world-wide political dominion by religious fanaticism, the jewel of religious freedom sought by the Pilgrim Fathers was lost in the smoke of the burning witches, and America is endangering democracy by an unreasoning reaction against the progress of the colored people.

Archimedes thought he could move the earth if he could get a fixed point from which to operate. So Descartes thought he could solve the fundamental problems of human life if he could get a fixed point from which to start; that is, an indisputable, elemental proposition as a premise;—something that everybody would accept as true. This he thought he had in *"cogito, ergo, sum"* (I think, therefore I am). But he was wrong, and so is that school of political philosophy that assumes the degradation of the Negro as an essential condition of American progress. The spirit that insists on segregation of colored govern-

[2] Since the above was written the Supreme Court has given a decision favorable to the rights of the colored people.

"At last the Supreme Court of the United States, forced to squarely face the issue involved in the 'grandfather' clause of Oklahoma's election law, has rendered a definite decision. It decided in the only way it could without revoking the Fifteenth Amendment. The 'grandfather' clause had no other object than to disfranchise Negro voters for the sole reason that they happen to be Negroes."—*The Public,* July 2, 1915.

The *New York World* (June 22, 1915), speaking editorially of this decision, said among other things: "The Republic is to be congratulated upon having at last a Constitution that is alive in all its parts. For forty-five years, first by violence and then by legislation, we have endured the reproach that one article of the fundamental law was blank paper wherever it pleased a local sovereignty to ignore it. Today, by the unanimous decree of a court presided over by a great Chief Justice who was once a Confederate soldier, we have a Constitution that for the first time since the Civil War guarantees equal rights to all, irrespective of race or color. Thousands of white men have as much reason to applaud this judgment as any Negro. Every outcast in a Republic, for color or religion or race alone, gives oligarchy, bigotry, and aristocracy an excuse for banishing others on any ground that prejudice may name."

Individual types.

ment employés is the same spirit that in bygone ages had attendants carry scented sponges on poles in front of dignitaries when they went about, "lest the smell of common people rise up and offend them."

II.

At the siege of Quebec, when a messenger told the French commander that the English were coming up from the rear, he said it was impossible, for nobody could get up there. But another messenger said the English were at that moment in possession of the Plains of Abraham, and the boom of guns soon confirmed the story. Quebec fell because the keepers underestimated the possibility of courageous effort and determined purpose. So the enemies of democracy, the hierarchs of heredity, mistaking the favors of fortune for the merits of blood, have undervalued the power of culture and the force of environment. But the Fort of Prejudice will fall.

In the year of grace 1904, one Mr. William Benjamin Smith, of Tulane University of New Orleans, La., U. S. A., asks the question, "Is the Negro inferior?" and with perfervid rhetoric, albeit logical limping and historical strabismus, maintains the affirmative, claiming as follows:—

"*At present there rolls between the historical development of the black and the white species an impassable river of ten thousand years.* Possibly the former might catch up in the course of the ages, if only the latter stood still. But will they stand still? Can they afford to wait? Is there not every reason to hope that they will forge steadily ahead and widen still more and more the interval between? Is not such the obvious teaching of history? Does not the tree of life bud and bloom and put forth new boughs at the top? For our part, we believe in the Overman, Him who is to come—not, however, from the lower, but from the higher humanity. Such, at least, seems of necessity our working hypothesis." (Smith, "*The Color Line.*")

Men seek to answer their own prayers and to make their own prophecies come true. Herein is the bane of false doctrine and the reason that believing a lie leads to damnation. (See II Thess. 2:11, 12.) The man who believes his neighbor is foreordained for hell is prone to raise hell for him. So the man who believes himself, or race, superior gives this doctrine material objectivity by blocking the other fellow's path and stealing his patrimony. Strong delusions have fallen upon nations, and they have been damned for not believing the truth. As I have just said, Spain lost her world-wide dominion from the "strong delusion" wherewith the Inquisition destroyed her brightest minds. America may follow suit unless she regain her sanity on the race question. The inferiority doctrine is the child of tyranny.

Self-interest has a power of metamorphosis. What a man at first advocates from policy he may later defend from principle. The punishment of every liar is that he eventually believes his own lies; and selfishness finally construes its own aims to be for the general good.

Mr. Smith's rhetoric has submerged his logic. His sentiment of racial snobbishness has destroyed his sense of human justice. Investigating the past and reconnoitering the future, he has overlooked the present. The river of years between the historical development of the Euro-American and the Afro-American has been bridged by the altruism of modern civilization and the progressive march of the races, moving on parallel lines, has overlapped. The white race is still in the lead, but the vanguard of the blacks is farther ahead of the rear of the white procession than it is behind the white lead; and all fair-minded, intelligent people want an unobstructed race. Why should the white man stop? Why should the black man stop? Why should either try to stop the other? If the Caucasian *evolved* his civilization the Negro *absorbed* his; as did the German from the Greeks, and the Britons from the Romans. One possession is as secure as the other. There are two ways to arrive—two qualities that win success. The faith to follow is as sure a passport to success as the brains to lead. The Negro and Esquimaux reached the North Pole as surely as did the Caucasian.

Sir Sidney Oliver, in "White Capital and Colored Labor," says (after talking with Americans visiting Jamaica and himself visiting the Southern United States): "I found myself, as a British West Indian, unable to account for an attitude of mind which impressed me as superstitious, if not hysterical, and as indicating misapprehensions of premises very ominous for the United States of the future." He proceeds: "The theory held in the Southern States of America, and in some of the British Colonies, comes, in substance, to this—that the negro is an inferior order in nature to the white man, in the same sense that the ape may be said to be so. *It is really upon this theory that American negrophobia rests, and not only upon the viciousness and criminality of the Negro. This viciousness and criminality are, in fact, largely invented, imputed, and exaggerated, in order to support and justify the propaganda of the race exclusiveness.*"

And again, in another part of his book: "My argument has been that race prejudice is the fetish of the man of short views; and that it is a short-sighted and suicidal creed, with no healthy future for the community that entertains it."

The hexiology[3] of the Negro is distinctive. He has an adaptability to circumstances unsurpassed by the children of men. It is admitted by all, even his enemies, that the Negro was faithful as a slave—a beau-ideal of a servant—the best the world has ever seen. He has received the most magnificent reward that ever fell to the lot of an oppressed people—the friendship of the world's best spirits. The freedom of the Negro was bought at a higher price, in white men's blood and treasure, than any people ever paid, of their own blood and treasure, for their own liberty.[4] The emancipation of the Negro marked the crest of the highest wave of altruism that the ocean of human effort ever knew.

The Negro has been blessed with the brains and heart of the white race. Washington was his Commander-in-Chief in the Revolutionary War, Perry led him on Lake Erie, and Jackson praised him at New Orleans. Jefferson said that the edict of his freedom was written in the Book of Fate, and Lincoln died believing the emancipation "an act of justice too long delayed." Since men stood in battle array and knew the marshalling of armies, no regiment of men was ever more gloriously officered than the *Fifty-fourth Massachusetts* at Ft. Wagner.

"The Negro has been given a chance, never before given to any destitute race in all history, and *he has*

---

[3] "Every living creature has relation with other living creatures, which may tend to aid it, or indirectly to destroy it, and the various physical forces and conditions exercise their several influences upon it. The study of all these complex relations to time, space, physical forces, other organisms, and to surrounding conditions generally, constitutes the science of hexiology." Hexiology is, therefore, "the behavior of living creatures in the presence of their environments."

[4] George W. Cable, "The Negro Question," page 69.

shown his native worth by taking that chance. Schools have been opened and he has been to school. Twenty thousand are today in the higher schools and colleges established by Northern benevolence.[5] Several noble institutions have been opened by denominations of colored people. And we must gratefully recognize the fact that the Southern people are gradually taking hold, also. At Paine and Lane Institutes and Tuscaloosa Seminary the noblest talent of the Church is giving itself with devotion to this work."[6]

III.

The real problems of the South today are economical, political, and educational, and not ethnological. It is a poor workman that quarrels with his tools and a poor statesman that abuses his constituents.

In the transition from a slave-holding oligarchy to an equal-suffrage democracy, things got mixed up and the South became "wool-gathered," confusing absence of constructive statesmanship with the presence of the Negro. It is the *spirit of slavery* and the *spirit of freedom,* and not the races, that are struggling in the South. The rogue with stolen property in his possession often joins in the pursuit of an innocent party crying loudly "Stop thief"! Thus, he makes good his escape. So in politics it is common for ambitious men to cover their unfitness by raising a false issue and gain power by fooling the people. Mr. DuBois, in his "Quest of the Silver Fleece," shows how the cotton-

---

[5] "As nearly as we can calculate from imperfect records there were 281 colored men and women who received the Bachelor's degree in arts and science this spring as compared with 250 reported at this time last year." (*The Crisis,* July, 1915.)

[6] Rt. Rev. Wilbur P. Thirkield, D.D., New Orleans, La., on the subject, "Present Weaknesses of Negro Ministry Squarely Faced."

mill owners kept wages down by threatening the white help with Negro competition. *In our refusal to be just, we lose our opportunity to obtain justice.* The spirit of democracy is to grade each individual according to the amount of manhood his character will show. But your *negrophobe* says, "*No!* Manhood is not the test."

Mr. William Benjamin Smith, in his book "The Color Line," defies the spirit of modern civilization, wounds the soul of democracy, and repudiates the principles for which Messiah died, when he prophesies the destruction of the nation "if the individual standard of personal excellence be established." Thus would race prejudice abrogate the decrees of fate, and deny even the hope of light to those "that sit in darkness." This is religious foreordination reincarnated in a political body.

Mr. Smith gets so excited that he overlooks what he is seeking. In quoting Mr. Bryce to prove the inferiority doctrine, he overlooks the settled "*conclusion,*" "That races of marked physical dissimilarity do not tend to intermarry," and throws all his emphasis on "*if we were to suppose,* etc."[7]

No one conversant with racial conditions in the South can fail to be impressed with the soundness of Mr. Bryce's *conclusion,* and the improbability of his "if we were to suppose." The spirit of ethnic solidarity is growing by leaps and bounds in the colored people of the South. The tendency to miscegenation is dying out. There is a marked decrease in the concubinage of colored women by white men.

Slavery was the arch-mixer of the races. The intimate relationship between sexual lust and cruelty is well known to modern medicine. The helplessness

---

[7] "The Color Line," page 63.

of the slave was a temptation to the master, but the habit of stripping grown women and adolescent girls stark naked for flagellation at the whim of mistress, master, or overseer[8] was a tax upon the sexual restraint of the whites that weighed heavily upon the integrity of the races. This was not all: the system of Negro slavery in the South tempted lust with lucre. White men begetting children by slave women not only escaped the responsibility of paternity, but received the reward of cupidity. The child followed the condition of the mother, and the bastardized offspring frequently went into the pocket of the lecherous father.

The condition of slavery, and not the morals of the slave, promoted the hybridization of the race. Freedom changed this; but the spirit of slavery still lingers. Only the initiated know how difficult and dangerous it is in certain sections for respectable colored men to protect their women.[9]

"And yet," says Mr. Murphy, "the Negro home exists. Those who would observe broadly and closely will find a persistently increasing number of true families and real homes, a number far in excess of the popular estimate, homes in which with intelligence, probity, industry, and an admirable simplicity, the man and the woman are creating our fundamental institution. Scores of such homes, in some cases hundreds, exist in numbers of our American communities—exist for those who will try to find them and will try, sympathetically, to know them. But one of the tragic elements of our situation lies in the fact that of this most honorable and most hopeful aspect of

---

[8] See "Negro in the New World," Sir. H. H. Johnston, ch. xiv and xv.

[9] Not long ago, according to press dispatches, a Negro woman, (under 20) shot a white man in her room, where he had broken into while she was undressing. She was arrested, taken to jail, and *lynched,* and her brothers had to flee for their lives.

Negro life, the white community, North or South, knows practically nothing."[10]

Thus has the Negro met squarely the severest test of Western civilization, for, as Mr. Murphy says in the same connection: "All promise and all attainment are worth while, but the only adequate measure of social efficiency and the only ultimate test of essential racial progress lie in the capacity to create the home; and it is in the successful achievement of the idea and the institution of the family, of the family as accepted and honored under the conditions of Western civilization, that we are to seek the real criterion of Negro progress."

I am not a miscegenationist; neither as it applies to America nor in the world-wide sense of a "pan-mixture." I believe in the comity of races, rather than the obliteration of races, as the basis of universal brotherhood.

IV.

Racial comity is the solution of the race question in the South.

I believe in the comity of cultural units as a basis for national co-operation in this country. No precedent, you say? Can't we set one? Any precedent for the discovery of America or the foundation of this *union?* for the Civil War or Emancipation? The vanguard of civilization must move without precedent.

Few conclusions of ethnology are apodictic. The efforts to place the findings of inferiority doctrinaires in this high class have failed utterly—whether considered historically, ethnically, morphologically, or functionally, the argument has invariably broken

[10] Murphy, "The Present South."

down. Neither brain-cells nor surface gyri, nor sulci have any distinctive racial traits.

Notwithstanding the numerous attempts that have been made to find structural differences between the brains of different races of man that could be directly interpreted in psychological terms, no conclusive results of any kind have been attained. The status of our present knowledge has been well summed up by Franklin P. Mall. He holds that on account of the great variability of the individuals constituting each race, racial differences are exceedingly difficult to discover, and that up to the present time none have been found that will endure serious criticism. (Boas.) (See Chapter XIII.)

"A culture, a civilization, to be helpful and healthful, must proceed from within and not from without. It must be an internal evolution, not an external imposition. The impulse may, indeed, be given by contact; it may proceed from another; but it must strike upon a nature prepared, responsive, and kindred. It must release energies and potencies already present and in high tension,—it cannot create them; it may be an occasion, it cannot be a cause. You may ignite a match by friction, but not a piece of chalk."[11]

This is exactly what happened to the Negro. In the fiery furnace of slavery the savage was destroyed. The Negro emerged with the pure gold of civilization burned into his nature. The beneficiaries of Lincoln's proclamation were a civilized people.

In a notable address delivered May 10, 1900, at the First Annual Conference held at Montgomery, Ala., under the auspices of the Southern Society for the Promotion of the Study of Race Conditions and Problems in the South, Professor W. F. Wilcox, of Cor-

---

[11] Smith, "The Color Line."

nell University, Chief Statistician of the United States Census Office at Washington,[12] truly said: "Divers races of men may be roughly graded according to their value to humanity and their ability to improve."

I am perfectly willing to rest the case of my people on this principle. *The Negro is just as indispensable to the South as the white man, and is just as willing and just as able to improve.* The concession of this fact by the white man is the first step in permanent racial comity. It means racial integrity, co-operation, and peace.

The words of a distinguished Southern Baptist minister are pertinent here: "We are the Negro's debtor for services rendered; we have been, and are and shall continue to be, the beneficiaries of his toil. For generations the Negro was our slave. He felled our forests, tilled our soil, gathered our harvests, tended our homes. It is largely through his sweat and toil that our country, North and South, has become what it is. The planter of the South received the product of his labor in the abundant yield of the cotton fields. The manufacturer of the North received that same product, put it through his looms, and sent it back to the South, levying large profits, both upon the Negro and upon his master. Neither North nor South is justified in making wry faces at the other, about this matter. Every section of the republic profited equally from the Negro's slavery. No thoughtful American can ignore the debt and the obligation that we owe the race, unless he has a heart of stone. . . . . Our millions have come to us largely through the Negro's toil. Our civilization is largely his achievement, view it as you will. As he has been and is the producer of our civilization, he of right

[12] *Ibid.*, page 180.

ought to receive, and we both of privilege and of debt ought to bestow, a full measure upon him, until he shall realize the highest and best things possible to him as our brother."[13]

"The South is a solid South in more than a political sense. We are a solid South in a social sense. I mean whatever affects the social welfare of one man affects the social welfare of every other man in the section. We are bound together by the facts of proximity; we are bound together by economic relations; we are bound together by the traditions of the past; we are bound together by all the forces of present life which demand the guarding of our health, our ideals, and our civilization. We are not eight million negroes and twenty-one million whites; we are twenty-nine million human beings, and whatever affects one of our company must of necessity affect all the other 28,999,999." [14]

"As all races have contributed in the past to cultural progress in one way or another, so they will be capable of advancing the interest of mankind, if we are only willing to give them a fair opportunity."[15]

A bi-racial democracy is not only possible, but practicable and desirable. It is the sane and equitable solution of the ethnic puzzle of the South—the one thing necessary to complete the establishment of democratic government in this section.

Nothing in history shows the white too good for such a government; nothing shows the black man too bad. How can it be? What can we do to bring it about? The question naturally resolves itself into several elements:—

---

[13] Rev. A. J. Barton, D.D., "The White Man's Task in Uplift of the Negro."

[14] W. D. Weatherford, Ph.D., "How to Enlist South's Welfare Agencies."

[15] Boas, "Mind of Primitive Man."

1. What can the *Negro do?*
2. What can the *Caucasian do?*
3. What can they do *together?*

Each of these questions may be still further divided into two questions, as follows:—

1.

(*a*) What can the Negroes do for themselves?
(*b*) What can they do for the Caucasians?

2.

(*a*) What can the Caucasians do for themselves?
(*b*) What can they do for the Negroes?

3.

(*a*) What can the Negroes and the Caucasians co-operating do for the Negroes?
(*b*) What can they do for the Caucasians?

To answer these questions in detail would greatly simplify matters. Space will permit only generalizations here.

Beginning with the third question—What can the races do together?

The first thing is to resolve to be fair and just to each other, to rededicate themselves to the ideals of democracy and the welfare of their common country. Human rights and racial privileges must be sharply differentiated. Neither our geographic unity nor our ethnic separateness should ever be lost sight of. Helpful co-operation should characterize the one and mutual respect and courtesy promote the other. *Let us encourage interracial co-operation on matters appertaining to the common good.* May not the intelligent and conservative members of both races form a kind of clearing-house for the debits and credits of racial contact? A knowledge of a friend's virtues may give us patience with his vices. Mutual respect is a prerequisite to mutual fair play. The problem can be solved better in detail.

Let us find the facts. This is no easy task. The races know so much about each other that *is not so.* The average individual "reasons but to err." Bacon described four kinds of errors or false notions that seduce men's minds from the truth. Race adjustment in the South is hindered by all four forms; but what he calls idols of the market-place and idols of the theater are the most troublesome. The first are the loose inaccuracies of ordinary gossip—erroneous opinions that men communicate to each other in social and business intercourse. The second are the systematically taught tenets of false philosophies and unsound political creeds.

The effectiveness of opposition to one's progress is in inverse ratio to one's speed. A stone thrown at less than a mile a minute shatters a window-pane against which it strikes; a pistol-bullet at 40 or 50 miles a minute goes through with little disturbance, while light at a rate of twelve million miles a minute passes through with no perceptible disturbance whatever. A candle hurled with sufficient speed will pass uninjured through an oak plank.

Apparently insurmountable opposition often indicates that we have too little momentum—are, in fact, moving too slowly. That is what is the matter with the country today. It has slackened its pace toward that ideal government which "derives its just powers from the consent of the governed"; "a government of the people, by the people, and for the people," under which any individual, whatsoever, may have "life, liberty, and the pursuit of happiness" unhindered and unhindering.

"The lust of other things entering in has choked the word." "For the love of money, we have denied the faith and pierced ourselves through with many sorrows," and

> "Man's inhumanity to man,"

has again postponed the day

> "When truth and worth o'er a' the earth
> Shall bear the gree and a' that."

"The real solution of the trust question, the race question, and all the great problems of our government today is a rededication of the thought of the country to the ideals of *justice* and *fair play.*"

If we set our eyes on *justice for all men,* the momentum of righteousness will overcome all obstacles, even the *race question.*

V.

All things being equal, a white man is more apt to believe a white man than he is a black man, and *vice versâ.* Herein lies the great good of interracial missionaries and biracial conferences. Such men as Mr. W. D. Weatherford and Prof. A. M. Trawick, of Nashville, Tennessee, are real heralds of a glorious dawn. They study the colored people and then tell their own people the truth about them.

The Southern Sociological Congress is a positive asset to modern civilization and the progress of democracy. Its founders and promoters are benefactors of mankind. That magnificent woman, Mrs. Anna Russell Cole, whose wealth and wisdom made it possible; the energetic and gifted secretary, Rev. Jas. E. McCulloch, and the matchless chairman of the Race Problem Section, Dr. J. H. Dillard, deserve a niche in the Valhalla of their country's glory.

"Battling for Social Betterment," "The Human Way," and "A New Voice in Race Adjustment" are the books on the race question which the nation should read and which patriotic editors, especially Southern editors, should try to popularize.

Mutual respect, mutual understanding, and mutual confidence are necessary to effective co-operation. People who destroy these qualities either by ignorance, ambition, greed, or malice are enemies of their kind and country. The general welfare demands their suppression. Dixon and Johnson have been drawbacks to their race and country. It was an unfortunate thing for the country that popular notice was given to the Leopard Spots or the Reno Battle. If neither had been noticed, the subsequent "bad eminence" of the chief actors would not have marred the country's history.

VI.

Each race should reject instantly and utterly any leadership that abuses or proposes injury to the other race.

"The culture of the South will find the occasions of its supreme and immediate interest, not in the issues presented by the Negro, but in the problems presented by the undeveloped forces of the white race." (Murphy.)

The acuteness of the race question has been greatly accentuated and exaggerated in the South by the white people elected to office, men whose only qualification is their ability to abuse the Negro. I have in mind two notable illustrations. Their governmental and senatorial campaigns were both won by abusing the Negro, though they were appealing to democratic primaries where Negroes could not vote.

Senator —— went so far in one of his speeches, for home consumption only (I have it from an ear and eye witness), as to say that the Negro has no more right to coffined sepulture or funereal ceremonies than a dog or a horse. I reproduce only his ideas, not his words. Our vocabularies are different.

VII.

Each race should discourage and discountenance the traitors of the other. White people who go among Negroes to abuse white people, and Negroes who go among white people to abuse Negroes, are undesirable citizens and enemies to the general welfare. The races are equally guilty. Black perfidy has fed white prejudice. It is no more creditable to the white people to quote and believe an immoral and discredited Negro preacher than it is to the colored people to have produced him. Each race can serve itself and serve the other race by scanning cautiously the motives and morals of interracial messengers.

> "Alas! that Scottish maid should ever sing
> Of combat where her lover fell,
> That Scottish bard should wake the string
> The triumphs of our foes to tell,"

was a just comment upon Scott's "Marmion," because the author, a Scot, had celebrated an English victory over Scotland.

Interracial messengers should talk and exemplify the virtues of the race they represent. Negroes need to learn more about the virtues of the white people, and the white race need to learn more about the virtues of the Negroes. Each knows enough of the other's vices. They are already, indeed, deep forces of racial suspicion.

The chief glory of the educational missionaries the white people have sent among the colored people is that they have been messengers of peace. I forgive their egotism when I contemplate their enthusiasm. They sang the glories of the white man until the Negro became so enraptured that he confounded *race* with *attainment,* and thought it necessary to be white to be a man. A mad desire seized him to be white. The skin-bleacher and hair-straightener were in glory. The white man got scared and thought the whole world was after "his squaw."

The intraracial agitators and the interracial liars got in their work. Ignorance and malicious "recriminative entanglement" of unrelated subjects put new danger into an old situation. White men forgot that the Negro had never shown any intention or desire to break over the racial barriers even when he was most ignorant and most powerful. This attitude of the white man, coupled with the desire of the Negro for freedom and security in that freedom, "threw him, intoxicated with more importance and power than either friend or foe intended him to have, into the arms of political hypocrites and thieves.

"It is this attitude that has demonstrated with ghastly clearness the truth, counted suicidal to confess, that even the present ruling class is not strong enough or pure enough to establish and to maintain pure government without the aid and consent of the governed. I admit that the Negro problem is not always and only political. No problem can be. It is not in the nature of politics for any question to be only political. The Negro question is fundamentally a question of civil rights, including political rights as the fortress of all others. It is not always a peculiarly African proneness to anarchy; nor is it always race instinct; it is often only traditional pride of a master-class, that remands the Negro to separate and individual tenure of his civil rights; but it is to perpetuate this alienism that he is excluded from political copartnership; and it is the struggle to maintain this exclusion that keeps the colored vote solid, prevents its white antagonists from dividing where they differ as to measures, and holds them under a fatal one-party idea that rules them with a rod of iron." [16]

We need a new Peter the Hermit to preach a new crusade, not to rescue an empty tomb from infidels, but to rescue the jewel of democracy from the demon of prejudice. It is the slavery thought, and not the slave race, that is hindering democracy. To remove the unnecessary discrimination against the Negro will loose the white man in the race of life and not endanger racial integrity.

In October, 1851, speaking of woman suffrage, Wendell Phillips said: "Every step of progress the world has made has been from scaffold to scaffold, and from stake to stake. It would hardly be exaggeration to say that all the great truths relating to society and government have been first heard in the solemn protests of martyred patriotism or the loud cries of crushed and starving labor. The law has been always wrong. Government began in tyranny and force, began in the feudalism of the soldier and the bigotry of the priest; and the ideas of justice and humanity have been fighting their way, like a thunderstorm, against organized selfishness of human nature. And this is the last great protest against the wrong of ages. It is no argument to my mind, therefore, that the old social fabric of the past is against us." [17]

---

[16] Cable, "The Negro Question."
[17] Wendell Phillips, "Woman's Rights."

VIII.

Democracy means equality or disaster. Equality in what? Americans lack discrimination in what the French call *nuance.* A French actress won great applause by appearing perfectly nude *in the play,* but was hissed when she responded to a curtain call in the same attire. The first was art; the second vulgarity. But we cannot distinguish between an intelligent interest in the personal welfare of our neighbors and having them as social guests. *We confuse the right of life with the privilege of place.*

Public utilities are "incriminatingly entangled" with private privileges. A seat at the family fireside or a meal at the family board involves, or may involve, everything; but a seat in a theater or a railroad coach, or a meal at a hotel, or a public banquet involves nothing, or should involve nothing, beyond the occasion itself. An Englishman will ride all day with you in a compartment of a railway carriage, eat with you at the hotel, and not know you the next day. There is a difference between public civility and private sociability. It is moral petulancy to expect the denial of public rights to conserve private virtues.

"A little discrimination, a little poise, a little of that equable capacity which can note the distinction between incidents great and small, *a little clear-headed appreciation of perspective events*, a due sense of proportion, will aid—as nothing else can aid—in the secure establishment of the doctrine of race individuality and integrity. No doctrine or dogma can be so injuriously compromised as by its wanton and unintelligent exaggerations. *A doctrine is always held most strongly when it is held most sanely.*"[18]

---

[18] Murphy, "The Present South."

The bulwark of racial integrity in the South is equal opportunity and a square deal in all matters of human rights and public welfare.

Civilization connotes fair play, equality of opportunity. Unfair distribution of benefits is the canker that has destroyed the civilizations of the past. Unwillingness to let the other fellow have a show, injustice, immorality, and "man's inhumanity to man" are but different names for the hydra-headed monster that has ever stood in the pathway of human progress and is now seeking to bar out our glorious Southland from the most splendid career in the history of nations.

IX.

The white man has been brutalized by power and misled by egotism. It is an injury to civilization to make an ignorant, immoral, shiftless man believe that because of his color he is superior to an intelligent, upright, thrifty man. It is a serious atavism of morals as well as of manners to teach white children that it is belittling to be polite.[19] It is only the atavistic, uncultured, or downright ignorant who refuse to use Mr., Mrs., and other polite verbal coin of social or business exchange when thrown into contact with respectable people of whatever color, social condition, or nationality. This is the beggar-on-horseback, nouveau-riche form of culture that bases its claim to good breeding upon pretension and not upon possession. The real culture of the South seldom offends here; and when it does, it is usually through some degenerate scion that seeks to uphold racial and family dignity by passing *assumption* for *worth.*

---

19 See footnote, page 367.

Business intercourse is hampered and friction needlessly engendered by this racial Chauvinism *that leads many white people to disregard the ordinary amenities of civilization in their dealings with Negroes.*

This is not in accordance with the ideals of ethics, nor the traditions and conduct of the great men of the South. The sun is not injured by shining upon the lowly; neither is politeness degraded when extended to the humble. The supercilious airs of pompous but petty satraps "puffed up with a little brief authority," such as ticket agents, clerks, street-car conductors, etc., make life at times unnecessarily burdensome to colored people. Were it not for the exceptions, life would be unendurable. It is a strange superiority of blood that rests upon such inferiority of manners.

The imagination of Dante seconded by the pencil of Doré draws an awful picture of the tortures inflicted upon the souls of women who in life tortured and corrupted other women. The human intellect is overawed in an effort to portray the final doom of those who willfully block the avenues of culture and mar the happiness of human beings merely to gratify some whim of assumed superiority of blood.

X.

More than twenty years ago George W. Cable[20] said: "Can the Southern question be solved? There are men in the North and South who say No, and, without being at all able to tell what they mean by the phrase, think it must be 'left to solve itself.' But careful thinkers on either side of the question never so reply. Their admission, whether tacit or expressed, is

[20] Cable, "The Negro Question."

that 'can be' is out of the debate; it *must* be solved. It is a running, not a healing sore; one of those great problems 'whose solution strains the bonds of society and taxes the wisest statesmanship'; that kind of problem with which every nation must deal. *We* must solve it.

"*The Negro question is three-quarters of a century old.* Within that period a vast majority of the nation have totally changed their convictions as to what are the Negro's public rights. Within that period the sentiment of every community and the laws of every State in the Union, as well as the Federal Government, have been radically altered concerning him. In their dimensions, in their scope, in their character, the problem's original relations have passed through a great and often radical change. So far from the problem still existing in its original relations, only two or three of those original relations any longer exist.

"The problem is being solved; slowly, through the years, it is true; in pain, in sweat, in blood, with many a mistake, many a discouragement, many an enemy, and, saddest of all, many a neutral friend in North and South. Yet *it is being solved.*"

To hasten this solution, the *Negro stands ready, anxious, and able to contribute his part; and in the interest of harmony is willing to concede everything except his self-respect as a man and his rights as a human being.*

XI.—Mulattoes.

The blanco-negro composite[21] seems to be the bugbear of the ethnologist and the nightmare of anthropology. The exigencies of tyranny have evolved some

[21] This word is coined in the interest of scientific accuracy, and may be used to designate a mixture of Caucasian and Negro blood in any proportion.

strange logic and exemplified some queer morals. But the rarest specimen of intellectual light seeking to adjust the straight ways of reason to the circuitous paths of moral obliquity is found in the ante-bellum discussion of the servile status of the Afro-American mixed blood.

It was in the early fifties of the last century, Dr. Channing, an anti-slavery advocate wrote: "But the worst is not told. As a consequence of criminal connections, many a master has children born into slavery. Of these, most, I presume, receive protection, perhaps indulgence, during the life of the fathers; but at their death, not a few are left to the chances of a cruel bondage. These cases must have increased, since the difficulties of emancipation have been multiplied. Still more, it is to be feared that there are cases in which the master puts his own children under the whip of the overseer, or sells them to undergo the miseries of a bondage among strangers.

"I should rejoice to learn that my impressions on this point are false. If they be true, then our own country, calling itself enlightened and Christian, is defiled with one of the greatest enormities on earth. We send missionaries to heathen lands. Among the pollutions of heathenism, I know nothing worse than this. The heathen who feasts on his country's foe may hold up his head by the side of the Christian who sells his child for gain, sells him to be a slave. God forbid that I should charge this crime to a people! But, however rarely it may occur, it is a fruit of slavery, an exercise of power belonging to slavery, and no laws restrain or punish it. Such are the evils which spring naturally from the licentiousness generated by slavery."

Mr. Fletcher, an eloquent and learned pro-slavery writer, quotes the words of Mr. Channing and comments as follows: "The owner of slaves who acts in conformity to the foregoing picture, to our minds, displays proofs of very great debasement, and his offspring, stained with the blood of Ham, we should deem most likely to be quite fit subjects of slavery; we cannot regret that the laws do not punish nor restrain him from selling them as slaves; we should rather regret that the laws did not compel him to go with them.

"That there are instances in the slave States where the owner of female slaves cohabits with them, and has offspring by them, is true. There may be instances where such parent has sold them into slavery,—they in law, being his slaves; yet, we aver that we have never known an instance in which it has been done. That such offspring have been sold as slaves, by the operation of the law, must certainly be acknowledged; and that such instances have been more frequent since the action of the abolitionists has aroused the slave States to a sense of their danger, and thereby caused the laws to be more stringent on the subject of emancipation, is also true. And are you, ye agitators of the slave question, willing to acknowledge this fact? And that your conduct—even you yourselves—are even now the cause, under God, of the present condition of slavery, which many such persons now endure? Is not he who places the obstruction on the highway, whereby the traveller is plunged in death, the guilty one? In what light, think ye, must this class of slaves view you and your conduct? But we wish not to upbraid you. If you are ignorant, words are useless. If you are honest men and know the truth, we prefer to leave you in the hands of God and your own conscience.

"We hold that cohabitation with the blacks, on the part of the whites, is a great sin, and is proof of a great moral debasement; nor will we say but that *the conservative influences of God's providence may have moved the abolitionists to the action of forever placing a bar to the emancipation of this class of slaves, such colored offspring, in order that the enormity of the sin of such cohabitation may be brought home, in a more lively sense, to the minds of their debased parents."*[22]

This is vicarious atonement with a vengeance.

Lincoln's proclamation freed the slaves from domination by their masters, but left the mixed blood in the toils of bad logic and pseudo-science. There continually creep into the current discussion of the race problem two mutually contradictory and equally unwarranted assumptions concerning him.

The first is that the evident primacy of the mixed bloods in Afro-American progress indicates the inferiority of the full blood. The other assumption is that the mixed blood is inferior to both parent stocks. There mutual contradiction has no effect upon their use by the same author.[23]

The conditions these assumptions attempt to explain are easily explainable upon simpler and more rational grounds. The principle of *selection* and *survival of the fittest* explains the first condition, and *heredity* explains the second.

It is not only reasonable but highly probable that the slave woman selected by the master or overseer would be above the average in form, feature, or endowment. *Consciousness* of kind would tend to soften the rigors of serfdom imposed upon the offspring and open to them avenues of improvement denied their fellow-servants. Many of these people are the descendants of common-law marriages or morganatic unions, and have had lavished upon them all the love

---

[22] Fletcher, "Studies on Slavery."
[23] Archer, "Through Afro-America."

and care of parenthood. Some of the best blood of both races got together at times in these unions. Out of this condition grew the necessity in certain localities of defining the word Negro.[24]

No assumption of inferiority is necessary to explain the frequent leadership of this class. In fact, it is no mean argument for the very opposite contention when we recollect the frequency with which these children were dependent upon the mother for moral, spiritual, and intellectual guidance. It is a well-known principle of heredity that good children often have bad fathers, but seldom, indeed, bad mothers.[25] Add to this the equally well-known fact that mixed bloods are usually though not invariably[26] classed as Negroes, with all the handicaps and restrictions this implies, and you are forced to the conclusion that in all fairness the colored people should be credited with the major part of the virtues and debited with the minor part of the vices of this class. That the opposite rule obtains is but another item in the long chapter of unfair discriminations which handicap the Afro-American in the race of life.

Another fact in this connection worth noting, is that many mixed bloods of this type have figured in

---

24 See Appendix A.

25 "What we owe to the great men of the world, we owe primarily to their mothers. The history of the human race is twined like a garland around the hearthstones of humanity. A man may pride himself upon a son whose good traits bespeak a great and good career; but it is now a fairly accepted law of heredity, established by the researches of modern science, that in most cases of normal heredity, the male offspring borrows its traits from the female parent and not from the father. Unfortunately, we know too little of the great mothers of the world. Like the violet, they blossom in secret places; and, as the whereabouts of the shrinking flower is often disclosed only by the fragrance it exhales upon the passing breeze, so do we often discover these modest women only by the perfume of those good works which have gone forth from a secluded home, to scatter sweetness and light along the ways of life and breathe a benediction to the world. One such there was in Nazareth."—Mosby in "Causes and Cures of Crime."

26 See "The Facts of Reconstruction," by Major Jno. R. Lynch, ch. xxiv.

history. The intellectual hierarchy of the ages contains more than a "dash" of Negro blood.[27] One of the most virile and able men of that remarkable group who founded this government was a West Indian hybrid. There seems to be indisputable documentary evidence that Alexander Hamilton was an octoroon. There was a Russian writer of international fame who belonged to this class,—Alexander Sergelevitch Pushkin (1799-1837), a Russian Count, poet, dramatist. The celebration of his one hundredth anniversary was made a national event. The educated world knows of Dumas. The first martyr for American liberty was Crispus Attucks,[28] a mixed blood. W. E. B. DuBois and Booker T. Washington are both men of more than national fame. Coleridge Taylor in Music and Henry O. Tanner in Painting are both contributors to the artistic world; while Dr. Daniel H. Williams, of Chicago, undoubtedly advanced the frontiers of surgery[29] and Dr. S. C. Fuller, of Massachusetts, has widened the horizon of pathology.

Now, as to the inferiority assumption, heredity is the simple and full explanation of its undoubted occurrence every now and then. No fanciful theories of racial deterioration by mongrelism are necessary to explain the inferiority of the bastard spawn of Legree and Topsy. When each of the parents is below the average in his or her race, it is human experience to expect offspring inferior to either race. This is but an illustration of the well-known principle that like produces like. So we come back to the established principles of ethnology,—variations within the race. Mixed bloods are good, bad, and indifferent, just as other people, black or white.

---

[27] See Appendix, "Color Problem in United States."
[28] See page 296.
[29] "International Textbook of Surgery," vol. i, page 895.

There is an historical aspect of their existence, however, whose importance seems not sufficiently noted.

> "God moves in a mysterious way
> His wonders to perform."

The mere existence of the blanco-negro composite destroyed the chief arguments in favor of African slavery in America. It was then claimed that the *color* and *features* of the Negro permanently fixed his servile status. About 1840 De Tocqueville wrote: "The abstract and transient fact of slavery is fatally united to the physical and permanent fact of color. The tradition of slavery dishonors the race, and the peculiarity of the race perpetuates the tradition of slavery.

"That the Negro transmits the eternal mark of his ignominy to all his descendants; and although the law may abolish slavery, God alone can obliterate the traces of its existence.

"The modern slave differs from his master, not only in condition, but in his origin. Nor is this all; we scarcely acknowledge the common features of mankind in this child of debasement whom slavery has brought among us. His physiognomy is to our eyes hideous. I despair of seeing an aristocracy disappear which is founded upon visible and indelible signs."

He was quoted approvingly by pro-slavery writers as late as 1860.[30] Justification for different political status was found in different ethnic appearance. Black and white were interpreted in terms of inferiority and superiority.

The presence of the mixed blood destroyed this argument.[31] Uncle Tom's character alone pleaded

---

30 Williams, "Letters on Slavery," page 26.

31 "I preached recently to a large congregation of slaves, the third of whom were as white as myself. Some of them had red hair and blue eyes." (Rev. John H. Aughey, in a letter from Mississippi dated Dec. 25, 1861.)

A typical family group.

for him and his fellows. Not only did Frederick Douglass make an equally strong appeal with character, but his personality made an appeal of blood. Henry Ward Beecher's spectacular illustrations of the methods of the slave auctioneer would not have thrilled his audience to popular frenzy had the victim been black. The light face as well as the suffering of Elizabeth Blakely, the run-away mulatto girl, fired the eloquence of Wendel Phillips and moved the heart of Frederika Bremer. The mistreatment of a mulatto slave-girl kindled in Abraham Lincoln's bosom the fire of an unquenchable resentment against slavery. The sufferings of "Eliza" "put a million tongues in the wounds" of "Uncle Tom." The octoroon on the auction block gave a dynamic verity to the appeals of golden-charactered pure bloods like Sojourner Truth and Harriet Tubman.

The prostitute has been termed the vestal virgin of civilization. Her sufferings quenched fires that would otherwise have destroyed the foundations of society. So the mixed blood, bearing the double burden of oppression and betrayal, by his suffering fanned the smoldering and almost extinct embers of justice into a torch of liberty that enlightened the world. The friends of humanity everywhere, North, East, South, and West, saw that the *race* of the slave was no justification of the *principle* of slavery. The American and French Revolutions irrevocably condemned the principle of slavery as an economic system; and the blanco-negro hybrid condemned it as a political necessity of ethnic adjudication. The slaves in America were no longer *black*. They were of all colors, from coal black to blonde white, and from blonde white to coal black again. Thoughtful people then perceived that slavery was based on *caste,* and not on *color* or *race*. Then a great fear arose that solidified and aroused the divided and indifferent North. The poor-white blood of the South gave it voice. Abraham Lincoln's great speech about a house divided against itself sealed the doom of slavery. The fear that the laboring white man would become a serf, and not love for the Negro or the American Union, manned the armies of the North. *To save the white man's freedom, the nation destroyed the black man's slavery.*

Who could have foreseen that the raping of slave-women would have ripened the fruit of freedom and renewed the altars of civilization? But the work is not done.

"A little leaven leaveneth the whole lump." The sluggish tropical blood has been sufficiently energized for adaptability to the more arduous existence in a temperate climate. All indications point to a wider diffusion of the white blood already incorporated in the Negro race, but *no fresh inoculation.* In other words, the Afro-American is tending to racial homogeneity and racial exclusiveness. Growing race pride is surely killing miscegenation. The numerical excess of light-colored females and their tendency to marry the darker males is evident to the most superficial observer.[32] Race instinct and moral soundness have given this class the good sense to prefer a black husband to a white paramour. Thus the colored American is growing more distinctive and at the same time more self-sufficient socially. This means increasing ethnic cleavage, and consequently increasing racial contentment.

"In general, whatever tends toward the sharp demarcation of the two races, toward the accurate delimitation of their spheres of activity and influence, will unquestionably make for peace, for prosperity, for

---

32 See typical family group.

mutual understanding, and for general contentment. On the other hand, every attempt to blur these boundaries, to wipe out natural distinctions, to mix immiscibles, must always issue in confusion, discord, failure, reciprocal injury, and final ruin."[33]

The presence of the mixed blood in the slave-pen wrought the destruction of that vile monument to man's "inhumanity to man." His presence in the racial ghetto may have the same effect. History often repeats itself, and the world grows freer as it grows wiser. Freedom and intelligence are the bulwarks of racial integrity and peace.

The stone which the builders rejected became the head of the corner; and the despised hybrid may become the means by which this Southland will travel safely the long and dangerous road from oligarchy to democracy.

---

[33] Smith, "The Color Line." page 108.

"What I want to impress you with is, the great weight that is attached to the opinion of everything that can call itself a man. Give me anything that walks erect, and can read, and he shall count one in the millions of the Lord's sacramental host, which is yet to come up and trample all oppression in the dust. . . .

"They tell us that this heart of mine, which beats so unintermittently in the bosom, if its force could be directed against a granite pillar, would wear it to dust in the course of a man's life. The Capitol of Injustice is marble, but the pulse of every humane man is beating against it. God will give us time, and the pulses of men shall beat it down. Take the mines, take the fishing-skiffs, take the mills, take all the coin and the cotton, still the day must be ours, thank God, for the hearts—the hearts are on our side!"—WENDELL PHILLIPS.

Members of Faculty of Meharry Medical, Dental and Pharmaceutical College, Walden University (1915).

CHAPTER XI.

PERSONALITY AND CRITICISM—"A CLOUD OF WITNESSES."

In a previous chapter we discussed some methods and analyzed some testimony. We will now pay some attention to critics and criticism. The value of a man's testimony is to be determined not only by his *desire* but by his *ability* to tell the truth; by what he *knows* as well as by what he *says*. Ignorance is often assertive and malevolence is active, while knowledge is silent and benevolence immobile.

Last night (March 26, 1915) I sat on the platform in the auditorium of Meharry Medical College and listened to the following program:—

INVOCATION .... S. M. Pitt
Medical Department.

REMARKS—Master of Ceremonies .... J. H. Griffin
President of Medical Class.

"LOVE'S WILFULNESS" .... R. Barthelemy
Meharry Orchestra.

ADDRESS—The Ideal Nurse .... Miss E. A. Barnett
Nurse Training Department.

GLEE CLUB ....
Dental Department.

CORNET SOLO—Holy City .... T. Monte Rivera
Medical Department.

ADDRESS—Effectiveness of Dental Pursuits ..... Henry Bullock
Dental Department.

LUCIA DI LAMMERMOOR .... G. Donizetti
Meharry Orchestra.

ADDRESS—The Modern Trend of Medicine ..... Walter L. Brown
Medical Department.

GLEE CLUB ....
Dental Department.

HISTORIAN .... A. E. Thompson
Medical Department.

MOSZKOWSKIANA—M. Moszkowski ....
Meharry Orchestra.

No Repetition of Numbers.

It was the Class Night Exercises of 1915. The audience of more than eight hundred people taxed the capacity of the building. The students and their friends were there.

Modestly but conventionally arrayed, the speakers and performers took their various parts. There was no noise, no announcements. From the first word of the prayer to the last full-toned diapason of the orchestra there was not a hitch. Wit was there and eloquence and epigram and pathos. Melody and harmony were there. When the clear and high-pitched but mellow tones of the cornet solo flooded the house with music, the audience felt a perceptible thrill.

"My higher self, emergent,
Rose to new life ineffable.
Beyond all signs, beyond descriptions,
Soul dimness and depression changed
To ecstasy of flight and soaring exaltation.
I felt the impact of strong-surging truth
Upon the gates of my poor utterance."

My soul went out to each participant and I said by thought-telepathy:—

"Why should you snub opportunity
Or fear to be interested in yourself?
Let not the bane
Of fear lay waste your heart and desolate
Your soul."

These young people of my race, speakers and audience, were running with skill and patience the race set before them; but where was "the great cloud of witnesses" St. Paul describes as compassing about those who run the race of life?

With tireless eyes I searched the audience. There were but three white people present,—the venerable Dean of Meharry with his noble consort and the duteous daughter of the founder of the school, Miss Mamie Braden.

The past rose before me and

> "Fond memory brought the light
> Of other days around me."

I saw forms and heard voices of blessed memory. (I speak only that which I know and testify only to what I have seen.)

No better or truer or braver men and women have ever been born than those who manned the watch-towers of learning erected for the manumitted slaves of this Southland. They were the ripest fruit of altruism, the very flower of civilization. But they are gone!

> "How are they blotted from the things that be!
> How few, all weak and withered of their force,
> Wait on the verge of dark eternity,
> Like stranded wrecks, the tide returning hoarse,
> To sweep them from our sight!
> Time rolls his ceaseless course."

Phillips, of Roger Williams; Cravath, Morgan, and Spence, of Fisk; Braden and Patterson, of Old Central Tennessee College; Father Robinson, who taught in Edgefield; Miss Kate Lyon and the Southern white physicians, Tucker, Sneed, Stevens, and Baskette,—all of Meharry; where are they? They have received "the last cold kiss that awaits us all" and entered into that rest which remains for the people of God.

President Cravath and Prof. Patterson sleep with the soldiers of the Union in the National Cemetery. Dr. Braden and Miss Lyon await the trump with the grateful beneficiaries of their service, in beautiful Greenwood.

Father Robinson lies in an unknown and unmarked grave in the old City Cemetery. Most of the others rest in Mt. Olivet. They are, however, together in the spirit-world; and all died believing they had served a deserving people. But—

"Still there are some few remaining."

Prof. Tefft and Miss Dyer, Prof. Wright and Miss Wells, and dear old Sister Joanna P. Moore are still with us, but "out of harness."

Dean Hubbard and the two ladies mentioned are not only with us, but are still on the watch-towers and still believe in my people.

II.

The conclusions of ethnology and sociology are largely assertory judgments.[1] The character and experience of the witnesses become of first importance in weighing their testimony. The testimony for and against the Negro must therefore be judged largely by the personality of the witnesses giving it.

The scene that I have attempted to describe was typical and familiar to the class of people I have just enumerated and might be duplicated in any city where schools for the freedmen exist. There are, however, other scenes and other sides to Negro character. There is the thoughtless, happy, honest, hard-working, good-natured, mellow-voiced, music-loving, easily-imposed-upon, trusting, emotional child of nature; faithful unto death in personal attachment, uninterested and unknowing in matters of deep thought or abstract duty; while at times neglectful of minor details, he is thoroughly reliable in large ones, and grows into

[1] See Introduction.

the heart of his employer until a rugged old sinner like Senator Tillman softens his diatribes against the race by declaring that he and the Negro foreman on his farm would, if necessary, die for each other.

It is the white people who know this type of Negro, who make it hard for emigrant agents and labor agitators that try to induce the Negro to leave the South.

But there is a darker picture. I have described the top and middle strata of Negro society. Let us go down to the bottom where scenes of the Berlin[2] dance-house are duplicated. The Negro can duplicate the white man's vices as well as his virtues. There is the Negro brothel, the gambling hell, the dens of vice, thievery, and drink, where human frailty is coined into gold,—dives of infamy, usually owned by white men and frequently conducted by them in person, and always a source of revenue to some white man.

Here is the heart of the Negro problem. From these places are graduated alike the Negro criminal and the negrophobe. It is rather significant that the anti-Negro writer always knows of the dens, but not of the colleges. Even many fair-minded people think the slum problem is all there is to the Negro problem, and believe the Negro to be all there is to the slum problem. Our efforts and arguments must be directed to the rational, though at times uninformed and thoughtless, people who can and will see the matter in its true light if it is properly presented.

There should be just sufficient publicity on this subject to keep the thinking man in possession of the true facts. If this is done we can have nothing to fear. "A good cause can sustain itself upon a temperate dispute." The agitator dearly loves controversy and attention. Without these he dies of inani-

---

[2] See Chapter V.

tion. In the name of justice and the general welfare, I ask the patriotic, fair-minded, intelligent, American people to let him die. *Let the public carefully scan the moral character and cautiously weigh the intellectual accomplishments of those who attack the Negro.*[3] It is an unfortunate thing that the voice of the anti-Negro agitator, though in a minority, is the only voice on the race question heard in some parts of the South. Free speech is only an ideal. People who are willing to speak *only* the truth must therefore, on some subjects, preserve a discreet silence.

In examining the personal side of this racial controversy I shall discuss the *character and credibility of the Negro's friends only.* "By their fruits ye shall know them." The devotees of a doctrine may furnish a key to its acceptability. The Negro has reason to be proud of his champions. "Let others sing the arms of Cæsar, I will sing the altars of Cæsar and those days which he has added to the calendar!" My heart goes out in gratitude to the good white people who have been and are still our friends, rather than in

---

[3] How many anti-Negro writers ever attended a concert by the Mozart Society of Fisk University at Nashville, Tenn., or any like function?

The following is from the Nashville, *Tenessean and American,* the leading morning paper of Middle Tennessee, May 1, 1915:—

"FISK CONCERT IS MUSICAL TREAT.

'ELIJAH' RENDERED IN BEAUTIFUL MANNER

BY

MOZART SOCIETY BEFORE LARGE AUDIENCE.

"The Mozart Society rendered its seventy-third concert in Fisk Memorial Chapel, Friday night, the building being well filled with a representative Nashville audience of music lovers, that were thoroughly pleased with the entertainment. Several hundred white people, mostly from the various local educational institutions, were present.

"Mendelssohn's oratorio of 'Elijah' was rendered by the society, and the music department scored one of its greatest musical triumphs in the successful rendition of the composition. . . .

"Although the program lasted nearly three hours, the audience seemed not to tire in the least, every listener being so thoroughly pleased with the excellence of the singing."

revenge to those who for various reasons are our enemies.

Mr. Murphy is right: "The consciousness of grievances is not an inspiring social asset for a class or for a race."

"My marvelling childhood's legend store" was indeed of "strange ventures hapt by land and sea." But no "Jack the Giant Killer's" thrilling feats, nor wandering Gulliver's exciting bewilderments, carried my "budding, golden hours on fairies' frolic wings." No King Arthur and the Knights of the Round Table, nor Robinson Crusoe and his man Friday; but Negro men and Negro women, wounded and bleeding, pleading at the *closed gate* of *justice*.

My maternal grandfather anticipated the Proclamation by more than thirty years. My father, also, prayed "heel-prayer" successfully before Lincoln was known to fame or the forces of freedom had converged toward the immediate and unconditional liberty for the Southern slaves. The disquietudes of my childhood were often soothed by crooning lullabies, breathing gratitude to God for Lincoln and 1863. My ears often tingled at the thrilling narrative of some quandam fugitive slave. I had not reached my teens when I wondered

"Why was man given the power to make his brother mourn?"

My mind was saturated with the tales of tyranny and scenes of blood. My grandfather, though cheated and robbed and betrayed, escaped actual physical violence. My father was not so fortunate. Out of this medley of sorrows there arise two clear notes that dominate my repertoire of slavery-day tales. The fidelity, courage, and self-sacrifice of the poor white man that went from Canada to Virginia for my grandmother, and brought her safe to her husband, is one; and the second is like unto it, only more so. My father's life was a deeper tragedy and brought out higher virtues. Shifting fortunes changed the ownership of my father from the Sinclair class of master to one of the Legree type. This new master planned to give him an exemplary scourging and then sell him to the traders for the far South.

Some *finesse* was necessary to avoid resistance on the part of the slave—a resistance that might not only involve monetary loss through damage to the slave, but physical suffering through damage to the master. There was mutual dislike and determination—and suspicion. Each had accurately gauged the other; for the slave was planning to run away—and, while punctiliously obedient, his manner was not satisfactory. He did not sing. He used his words with too much care. He was too observant. In short, he knew too much.

Perhaps an earlier incident will prove illuminating here. When he was a mere child ("a shirt-tail chap," according to the local vernacular) there was a runaway. For the evident purpose of intimidation, the punishment to be inflicted upon the fugitive when captured was freely discussed in the hearing of the slaves. The child's unexpected comment after hearing a conversation of this kind chilled his mother's heart (I got the story from her): "Mammy, I'm going to run away when I get big." The desire grew with the years; but good treatment, lack of opportunity, and maternal attachment prevented an overt attempt at realization.

The new master's ways crystallized the desire into purpose. Each was on the alert—but, "on the oppressor's side there was power." It was a game of wits, but the master loaded the dice. He took advantage of the slave's obedience to practise treachery. The slave was ordered to take a load of whisky from

Noted musicians.

the distillery on the farm to the warehouse in town. Men were secretly hired to rush upon him from their hiding places in the warehouse and tie him. He could then be tortured into submission and humiliation without being damaged for the market.

The acquiescence of the poor-white men thus employed was a foregone conclusion and no questions were asked. One of them did not, however, agree to this program and, at the risk of life, notified the slave.

This poor-white man and his wife—living from hand to mouth, scorning the thousand-dollar reward, hiding and feeding this hunted slave until the chase subsided—make the most vivid and lasting picture of the slavery days' experience of my forbears. It is the star of hope in the night of oppression. Civilization rests upon the spirit of these people—the Golden Rule incarnate—the word made flesh.

That my father's life won such a friendship is more to me than the gnashing teeth of a defeated and cruel master. So I feel that my race should be encouraged by its friends rather than discouraged by its enemies.

The fate of the American Negro will be decided largely by people who do not and can not personally know the facts, but are dependent upon the testimony of others. Is it too much to ask that the character, the capability, and motives of the witnesses be carefully scrutinized? Is it unreasonable to ask fair-minded people, who want to know the truth, to scrutinize carefully both the sincerity and the sanity of a man who denounces such men as DuBois and Washington as traitors to their race, and quotes approvingly a discredited Negro preacher who "for a handful of silver" betrayed his race?

The American public is bound by personal interest and the welfare of civilization to find out the truth about the Negro.

I introduce first Mr. Wm. Benjamin Smith, the ablest of the anti-Negro blancoids,[4] who admits that "three-fourths of the virtue, culture, and intelligence of the United States" is against him, and that "England has no word of sympathy," "Europe looks on with amused perplexity," and, "worst of all, the South herself appears to have no far-reaching voice," on his side. He also reluctantly admits that Mr. Franz Boas is not only our friend, but "speaks from the pinnacle of Science." In the face of these handicaps, he seeks by "counter-plea" of racial inferiority to demolish the Negro's claim for a man's chance to fill a man's place.

I leave the witness without comment except to say, that he professes to be a democrat and to believe in the rule of the majority.

I call next the noted scientist, Prof. Boas, just mentioned. He thus deposes: "There is, however, no evidence whatever that would stigmatize the Negro as of weaker build, or as subject to inclinations and powers that are opposed to our social organization. An unbiased estimate of the anthropological evidence so far brought forward does not permit us to countenance the belief in a racial inferiority which would unfit an individual of the Negro race to take his part in modern civilization. We do not know of any demand on the human body or mind in modern life that anatomical or ethnological evidence would prove to be beyond the powers of the Negro."[5]

I will next introduce Mr. Arthur J. Barton, Corresponding Secretary of the Education Board of the Baptist General Convention of Texas. Because of his

---

[4] The antonym of the etymological monstrosity negroid. He is of course as far from actual white as Mr. DuBois is from actual black. Few normal human beings are either.

[5] Franz Boas, "Mind of Primitive Man."

extraordinary qualifications we will allow the witness full latitude:—

"Personal words are not quite in place on such occasions as this. But, owing to the nature of my subject, dealing as it does with the relation of the races, you will cheerfully indulge me, I think, in a word or two of a personal nature. I speak as a Southern man to Southern men. I was born and reared in the South; my father belonged to a South Carolina slave-holding family. While I, myself, was born and reared in Arkansas and was not in constant association with the Negroes during my childhood, I have nevertheless been constantly thrown with the race for nearly thirty years. In addition, I have inherited that genuine love for the Negro that was cherished in the bosom of the better class of the white people of the South in the olden days. I speak, therefore, in full sympathy and genuine affection for the Negroes. I have visited their religious associations and conventions in almost every State in the South. I have never missed an opportunity, in season and out of season, to speak a word of hope and cheer to the race or in behalf of the race. From my point of view, therefore, I feel quite untrammeled in speaking of the white man's task in the uplift of the race. I feel equally free as far as your attitude is concerned, for you come as the representatives of the best element of the white people of the South. Before the War there were three classes of people in the South: the first-class white folks (most of whom owned slaves), the negroes, and the 'po' white trash' (as the Negroes were accustomed to call the less frugal element among the whites). *Whenever you hear any white man of Southern ancestry abusing the Negro, you may know that he comes from the latter element.*[6] All the first-class white people

[6] Italics mine.

have a genuine love for the Negro. Recognizing you as belonging to this class, and knowing your sentiment, I feel that I may speak with the greatest freedom.

"As expressing my own feeling, I give this incident: About the same time my father moved from South Carolina to Arkansas, which was just before the War, a great-uncle of mine, Col. Wilson Barton, together with the other members of the family, moved from South Carolina to Williamson County, Texas. They carried with them some of the old family servants.

"A few years ago I was holding evangelistic meetings at Liberty Hill, Williamson County, Tex., and those colored friends were much interested in my visit, coming from far and near to talk with me. As you know, even to this good day, the crown prince of a Negro's heart is his 'young master' who is a preacher. One day I was taking dinner with a cousin in the country. One of these descendants, a good-natured woman of ample proportions, was assisting my cousin about the kitchen and dining-room. After dinner she asked me to take a seat on the porch near the kitchen-door, so that as she passed in and out doing her work she could talk to me. Some of the children of the family observed the situation and twitted me sharply about my sitting out there talking to the cook. The good-natured black woman shook her ample sides with laughter and said: 'Lor, yes, honey, cose he is. Don't you know us Bartons is all kinfolks anyhow?' That expressed her feeling and expresses mine. I have a feeling of kinship for the Negro that is nigh to the ties of blood. As far back as I can remember, my child heart glowed with enthusiasm and joy as I heard my father tell of Jerry and York, of how many chestnut rails they could cut and split in a day, and of what mighty tasks they could do. They were his heroes; they are mine. I love their names, their memories. So I come today to speak to you, feeling that we, the first-class white folks of the South, and our Negro neighbors and friends, descendants for the most part of our old family servants, are bound together not only by the indissoluble, industrial, commercial, and civic bonds of the present day, but by many of the tenderest and sweetest memories of the past. We may, therefore, deal in the utmost frankness with every phase of the relation of the races."[7]

Accepting Mr. Barton's testimony as an introduction to the *purposes* and *personnel* of this session of the Southern Sociological Congress, I introduce without further comment the following witnesses:—

Prof. C. H. Brough[8]: "I believe that by the recognition of the fact that in the Negro are to be found the essential elements of human nature, capable of conscious evolution through education and economic and religious betterment, we will be led at last to a conception of a world unity, whose Author and Finisher is God."

Dr. W. D. Weatherford[9]: "I wish to make clear in the very beginning that the same type of agency which can improve the conditions for the white people can also improve the conditions of life for the Negro. Humanity is humanity, whether the color be white or black, and I know no fiat of God that makes white any more valuable as a color or any easier to deal with than black. Every social agency which is working for the uplift of the white race should also be working for

---

[7] Rev. Arthur J. Barton, "The White Man's Task in the Uplift of the Negro."

[8] Prof. C. H. Brough, Ph.D., University of Arkansas, "Work of Com. of Universities."

[9] W. D. Weatherford, Ph.D., Nashville, Tenn., "How to Enlist Southern Welfare Agencies."

the uplift of the colored race, unless there is a special branch of that organization working for the Negroes."

Prof. Wm. M. Hunley[10]: "The present economic status of the Negro shows marvelous advancement and holds great promise."

Prof. J. H. DeLoach, Ph.D.[11]: "As a general thing Negroes are easily taught and can be led to adopt any kind of information in their practices if the teacher is in sympathy with them and understands them."

Prof. E. C. Branson[12]: "The Negro has suffered from the zeal of retained attorneys for preconceived opinions; almost as much from indiscreet friends as from hostile critics. The skies ought to be cleared by impersonal, impartial acquaintance with the facts, whatever they are, concerning the Negro problems and progress. Many good people in the South stand hesitatingly aloof because they are insufficiently informed and honestly in doubt about what is really best for the Negro and the community in which he lives."

Prof. Josiah Morse[13]: "The Negro is a human being, and modern anthropology has shown that the differences among human beings—anatomical, physiological, and mental—are insignificant as compared with their fundamental resemblances and identities. We shall certainly not need a Negro science of medicine. The things that breed disease among the whites —poverty, ignorance, overcrowding, immorality, alcoholism, insanitary premises, neglect, and malnutrition of children, etc.—will breed disease with equal facility

---

[10] Prof. Wm. M. Hunley, Ph.D., University of Virginia, "Economic Status of Negro."

[11] Prof. DeLoach, Ph.D., University of Georgia, "Negro as Farmer."

[12] Prof. E. C. Branson, A.M., Pres. State Normal School, Athens, Ga., "Negro Working out his Own Salvation."

[13] Prof. Josiah Morse, Ph.D., University of South Carolina, "Social and Hygienic Condition of the Negro."

among the Negroes. And we may rest assured that the measures and remedies that prevent and cure diseases among the whites will do the same for the blacks."

Prof. W. O. Scroggs[14]: "Our hope lies in further education for white and black, in co-operation between the best elements of both races, in the greater publicity for those whose views are rational, and last, but not least, in the development of an infinite amount of patience. Civic progress for the Negro is to be secured by educational and economic improvement rather than by political methods. His condition as a citizen will improve with his economic progress; his economic progress is dependent upon an increase of his wants, and an increase of his wants will come with better education. Where the white man is guilty of injustice no merely external reforms will suffice. Such injustice is an outward sign of a lack of internal grace. There must be a reform of men's souls. Better education, higher moral ideals, a general awakening of mind and spirit, the substitution of reason for prejudice and tradition, the socialization of religion,—these are the fundamental needs of the hour. Above all, we must realize that as a race we cannot live wholly unto ourselves; that if the black man is sinking we are not rising; that if he is going backward we are not going forward; and finally, that no social *régime* can long endure that is not founded on justice."

Rev. John Little[15]: "The most remarkable thing in connection with the whole work is the fact that the white people of this community have volunteered as teachers. One by one, men and women from Presby-

---

[14] Prof. W. O. Scroggs, PhD., University of Louisiana, "Desirable Civic Reforms in Treatment of the Negro."

[15] Rev. John Little, Louisville, Ky., "Our Church Work for the Negro."

terian and other evangelical churches in the city have volunteered their services. Our sewing classes and cooking classes are taught by white women who have volunteered to give one afternoon each week. Other men and women volunteered as instructors on Sunday afternoon in the Sunday school. Many of these people rarely see each other because they come on different days, but their hearts and services are united in their ministry to the needy people. A nobler group than the seventy consecrated men and women who are cheerfully donating their services to this work could not be found in the whole land."

Mrs. J. D. Hammond[16]: "Long ago an old English bishop said of the children in London's slums that they were not born into the world, but damned into it. It is an old trick of the privileged class—this allowing children to be damned into the world. Damnation is not particular about the color line; it is as swift for black as for white.

"Our duty to the Negro is as clear as day. It is the duty of strength to weakness, the world around; of knowledge to ignorance; of the privileged to those shut out; plain, simple, human duty that cuts through prejudice and sophistry as a sword cuts threads. We must give him justice and opportunity; and we have not given them yet."

I will next call attention to a group of witnesses. To save time I will not have them testify individually, but invite the closest scrutiny of their *character, conduct,* and *capabilities.* I refer to the Northern and Southern white people, men and women, doing educational and religious work among the colored people.

These people are not only sound in morals and upright in conduct, but clear in brains and capable of

---

16 Mrs. J. D. Hammond, Augusta, Ga., "The Test of Civilization."

Harriet Tubman tablet.

the highest efficiency in other callings. Such men as John Braden, of Central Tennessee College; Erasmus M. Cravath, of Fisk University; Samuel Chapman Armstrong, of Hampton Institute; Edmund Asa Ware, of Atlantic University; Daniel W. Phillips, of Roger Williams, and G. W. Hubbard, of Meharry Medical College, were born leaders and would have attracted attention in any field of endeavor. *That men of such ability should not only become converted to a cause, but earnestly espouse it and give their lives for it without reward, and in the face of ostracism and contumely, ought certainly to commend that cause to the respect of their countrymen, and to the considerate judgment of mankind.* Not only did the Negro win the love and respect of this noble band, but their children after them.[17] The son of Fisk's first president, though a successful lawyer in a metropolitan city, is not too busy to serve on the trustee board of the school his father built. The president of Atlanta University is the son of its founder.

That the Negroes were susceptible to culture and amenable to kindness is shown by their devotion to the persons and doctrines of these teachers. Rarely was one disobeyed and never was one dishonored. That miscegenation grew not in this atmosphere of kindness and culture shows the security of racial integrity in an atmosphere of racial self-respect.

Let us call Bishop Haygood, whose testimony may explain this fact[18]: "I have seen the Negroes in all their religious moods, in their most death-like trances, and in their wildest outbursts of excitement. I have preached to them in town and city, and on the plantations. I have been their pastor, baptized their chil-

---

[17] Read inscription on Tubman tablet.

[18] Bishop Atticus G. Haygood, Atlanta, Ga., quoted by Bishop Thirkield.

dren, and buried their dead. In the reality of religion among them I have the most entire confidence, nor can I ever doubt it while religion is a reality to me."

III.

There is no alternative between the growth of what Mr. Albert Pike,[19] of Alexandria, Va., in 1875 called "Negrophily" and the failure of civilization. There is no brotherhood of man with the black man excluded. Justice only to white men means, in the last analysis, justice to nobody. There is no middle ground. Justice and fraternity are for all or for none. Civilization must become world-wide or perish. The doctrine that led Germany to rape Belgium will justify the undoing of Germany by some greater power. By this greed strife is continuous and inevitable; sometimes kinetic, sometimes latent, but always potential and immanent. Ossa is piled on Pelion and Pelion is piled on Ossa till all tumble into inextricable ruin. Peace can only reign where justice is secure, and justice is only secure when available to all. Fate has given man the alternative of living or dying with his brother. She has permitted him to take his choice, but has steadfastly refused to permit separation. By pestilence, by famine, by war, by the rise and fall of nations, by every movement of matter or mind, from the simplest monad to "the stars in their courses"; by revelation, by history, by great men, by great women, by great events, *nature* has everywhere, at all times and under all circumstances, steadfastly refused to alter this decision.

All reason and all human experience unite in the

[19] Letter of Gen. Albert Pike, Sovereign Grand Master A. & A. Rite on Negro Masonry.

judgment that *the American white man and the American black man may live together or may die together; but they will do neither separately.* If the Negro dies, the white man will perish with him; if the white man lives, the Negro will survive with him. To deny this is to deny all history and all experience; to ignore it is to make a futile attempt to repeal a natural law.

The world is undergoing a change on the color question.[20] The great European War may evolve a complete metamorphosis on this subject.

I now call Mr. Saint Nihal Singh[21]: "As the reports of the terrible carnage that is taking place on the continent of Europe reach me, day by day, I sit and ponder whether the human blood that is being so wantonly shed is going to wash away some of the prejudices that divide men of different colors.

"The mere employment of black and brown troops on European soil implies a revolution in the attitude of the white man toward the colored races. Nothing shows this transformation so significantly as the inner history of the Boer War, sedulously kept from the knowledge of most people. It was proposed then to convoy troops from India to fight in South Africa; but the idea had to be abandoned, because Hindoostan's swarthy sons were considered not good enough to fight white men.

"It happened in this way: Lord Curzon, at that time the Viceroy and Governor-general of India, knew that the South African veldt was much like the plains of the Indian Peninsula, and he considered that the Indian cavalrymen would be able to distinguish themselves fighting on South African soil. He therefore proposed to the Prime Minister of England, at that

---

[20] See note at end of chapter.

[21] See *Southern Workman,* April, 1915.

time Mr. Balfour, that Indian troops should be taken to the field of battle to assist the British in putting down the obstreperous Boers. The authorities in England, however, would not listen to such a proposition. I am informed by an officer whose authority is above question that this attitude was largely dictated by Emperor William of Germany, who was scandalized at the idea of putting colored men against whites, and threatened to go to the aid of the Boers if the British adopted such a course of action. Be this as it may, the whole plan fell through, and the best that could be done under the circumstances was to transport the British garrison from India to South Africa, trusting to the loyalty of the Indians during the absence of the troops not to make any trouble.

"And now, less than fifteen years later, over two hundred thousand Indian soldiers are fighting in Europe, Asia, and Africa; side by side with British, French, and Belgian troops, against the Germans! Besides these Asiatic soldiers there are also African troops, or Senegalese, as they are called, who have been brought over by the French from their possessions in Africa to help them fight the Germans." . . .

Many instances show that "the attitude which the French, British, Belgian, and Russian peoples are assuming toward the dark-skinned men who are helping them is that of a comrade for a comrade. It is not that of a superior for an inferior race. The life and death struggle in which Europeans are at present engaged has obliterated, not only for the time, but let us hope, forever, the old feeling of superiority and inferiority. The white and colored men have been thrown into each other's arms. Fighting shoulder to shoulder they are realizing that they have a community of interest which they have never comprehended before."

IV.

I will conclude this chapter by introducing some testimony to show the similarity of the present discussion of the Negro's citizenship to the discussion of his emancipation that preceded the War. Let us have first the psychology of the situation:—

Rev. Wm. A. Smith[22]: "A false principle may be honestly believed by minds which, at the same time, adopt antagonistic principles that are essential truths; but owing to various causes calculated to confuse the ideas, the inconsistency is not perceived. Now, in such a case as this, the principle of essential truth is really brought into practical antagonism with essential error, and that in the same minds and upon the same subject. And as truth is more powerful than error in the minds of all honest people, the truth holds its way in practical results, in defiance of false principle, which is relatively powerless in the presence of truth. The antagonism between the false principle and the practical results of things may be perceived and acknowledged; whilst the antagonism of the false principle with the true principle, which underlies and produces these practical results by a law of its own operation, is not only not perceived, but actually denied to exist. Now, so long as this false principle is honestly believed to be true, and clearly perceived to be in conflict with the *practice,* but not perceived to be in conflict with other and more latent principles, which are in themselves *truths,* and admitted to be *truths,* and which produce this *practice,* just so long will this false principle wage war, by the simple law of belief, against this *practice.* But as this war is not suffi-

[22] "Philosophy and Practice of Slavery, as Exhibited in the Institution of Domestic Slavery in the United States, with the Duties of Masters to Slaves," by William A. Smith, D.D., Pres. Randolph-Macon College and Professor of Moral and Intellectual Philosophy.

ciently potent to overturn this practice, because it is founded on the belief of principles *true* in themselves, the practice will remain; and so long as this false belief remains, the strife with the practice must remain. Hence, if this be the state of the public mind in this country on the subject of African slavery, and it finds no efficient remedy, we can see nothing awaiting us but interminable strife—men against themselves—the country against the country! We forbear to sketch the future."

Substitute "Afro-American citizenship" for "African slavery," and you have an exact statement of the case today. Excuse this interruption.

Proceed Mr. Smith: "In maintaining the institution of domestic slavery, we are either right or wrong, in a moral point of view. We ask no mere apology on the score of necessity, and we can certainly claim none on the ground of ignorance. . . .

"We are told that all men believe slavery to be wrong in principle; that is, wrong in itself! and that all men feel that it is wrong! And certain it is, there is more truth than fiction in all this! It is strictly true, as to the citizens of the so-called free States. The same doctrine is not without advocates at the South; whilst many more, as we have before stated, who may not be said to believe it, are nevertheless often subjects of painful misgivings. They *fear* it may be true. . . . The men of whom I speak, both North and South, are candid, honest men."

Yet this gentleman believed that Thos. Jefferson and the "candid men, North and South," were all wrong. He proves to his own satisfaction the correctness of the *principles of slavery*.

Mr. James Williams[23]: "Let not the honest and

[23] "Letters on Slavery from the Old World," etc., by James Williams, Late United States Minister to Turkey. (1861.)

well-meaning opponents of slavery delude themselves or others into the belief that there can be any essential modification of the existing relations between the whites and the blacks, while they inhabit a common territory. . . .

"When Great Britain introduced Africans into her American Colonies, she designed that their enslavement should be perpetual. . . .

"Any change in the relative condition of the European and African races in America would be fatal to both."

One more question, Mr. Williams. How long have the colored people been in this country?

"Upon the establishment of the independence of the United States, about one-fifth of the population, in round numbers, were slaves. . . . These Africans were totally unfit, by nature, habit, and education, to enter upon the discharge of the responsible duties of free citizens. . . .

"Soon after the establishment of the new government, the Congress enacted a law fixing upon a period, not remote, after which no slaves should be introduced from abroad into any State or Territory of the Republic. Of the nearly four millions of slaves now held as such in the United States, not five hundred have been introduced in contravention to that enactment."

Mr. John Fletcher[24]: "Philosophy knows no obligation that binds one man to another without an equivalent. If one man could be subjected to another who is not bound to render anything in return, it would be subversive to good morals and political justice. Such a relation cannot exist, only so far as to reach the immediate death of the subjected. But it has been

[24] "Studies on Slavery, in Easy Lessons," etc., by John Fletcher, Louisiana. (1852.)

the error of some good men to suppose that slavery presented such a case. It has been their misfortune also to receive the following succedaneums as axioms in search for truth:—

" 'All men are born equal.'

" 'The rights of men are inalienable.'

" 'No man has power to alienate a natural right.'

" 'No man can become property.'

" 'No man can own property in another.'

" 'The conscience is a distinct mental faculty.'

" 'The conscience infallibly distinguishes between right and wrong.'

" 'No man is under obligation to obey any law when his conscience dictates it to be wrong.'

" 'The conscience empowers any man to nullify any law; because the conscience is a part and parcel of the Divine mind.'

" 'Slavery is wholly founded on force.'

" 'Slavery originates in the power of the strong over the weak.'

" 'Slavery disqualifies a man to fulfill the great object of his being.'

" 'The doctrines of the Bible forbid slavery.'

" 'There is no word, either in the Old or New Testament, which expresses the idea of slave or slavery.'

" 'Slavery places its subjects beyond moral and legal obligation; therefore, it can never be a legal or moral relation.'

" 'Slavery is inconsistent with the moral nature of man.'

" 'To hold in slavery is inconsistent with the present state of morals and religion.'

" 'Slavery is contrary to the will of God.'

" 'No man can hold a slave, and be a Christian.'

"Averments of this order are quite numerous.

Fanatics receive them; and some others do not distinguish them from truths."

The intelligent sentiment of Western civilization is today overwhelmingly for genuine democracy, as it was in 1850 in favor of emancipation. *Every man should be dealt with according to his character and not according to his color.* Are we going to repeat the blunders of those days?

In 1851 the publishers of Mr. Fletcher's masterful "Studies on Slavery" lamented "that a general league against the institution of African slavery has been entered into and consummated between most of the civilized nations of the earth, and public opinion in many of the sister States of our own National Union has taken the same direction."

How like the words of Mr. William Benjamin Smith in 1905![25] Then the opponents of emancipation were entrenched in power as the opponents of civil rights are now. The moral forces of the nation were then in a political minority as now. *But slavery fell!*

From the misty mountain-top of antiquity the horrid form of tyranny leers adown the valley of the ages, but his expectations have ever vanished like bubbles blown from soap; for mankind finally hears the testimony for justice and liberty, which throughout the ages has been borne by "a great cloud of witnesses."

A fond devotion to the mistaken customs of the past is all that prevents the South from taking the lead in the advancement of this nation.

Since so much disturbance was created by a Negro holding the World's heavyweight championship, it will not be out of place to introduce as a witness the "white hope" who recently restored the belt to the white race. I quote from a recent article in a New

---

[25] See page 266.

York daily, entitled, "Willard Tells Why He Will Not Fight Another Negro."

After declaring all the heavyweights not to be in his class, he says: "But this is my real reason—a championship fight between a black man and a white man makes bad blood between the races. . . .

"I am not saying this in a mean way. I am not excusing white men for feeling that way. I think it shows ignorance. But lots of white men did feel that way. Who doesn't remember all that sickening 'white hope' business?

"That's why I am going to draw the color line. I say this because I don't want anybody to think that I'm doing it from any mean, dirty little prejudice.

"It isn't race or color that counts. It's brains. A sober, decent Chinaman looks better to me than a drunken bum of an American. A Negro who uses his intelligence is a finer man than a white man who soaks his mind in a whisky glass.

"Some of the greatest fighters in the history of the ring have been black men. And I want to say that they have always showed up as game and as square as white fighters. A hundred years ago the Jack Johnson of the ring was a big black named Molineaux. And the sole thing that kept him from being champion was a dishonest trick played by white men.

"We've also had some mighty great Negro fighters in our own day. They didn't make them better than Peter Jackson in his prime, and Joe Wolcott was certainly some terror.

"And when you are talking of champions, what about George Dixon? I don't suppose any more intelligent boy ever drew on a glove. The same goes for Joe Gans. Both of them, they tell me, were quiet-mannered, well-behaved lads, and far more of a credit to the ring than many of the white fighters they met."

After giving many reminiscences of the ring, illustrating the fact that fighting ability is not dependent upon race, he summed up his opinions about race prejudice in the following words:—

"I just mention these things to show how foolish we all are when it comes to thinking that one race is better than another. Or that it proves anything when a man of one race whips a man of another race. Everything depends on the man. And what the man amounts to depends on his brains."[26]

---

[26] I fully agree with the following comment of James W. Johnson, contributing editor of the *New York Age:* "Those are words you would not expect from a prize fighter; and it is exactly for that reason that we reproduce them here. If they had been said by a college president they would not be nearly so important. For, in the first place, everybody expects a real college president to talk like that; and, in the second place, what real college presidents say reaches comparatively few people; and they would be the kind of people who, if they had strong racial prejudices, would be rather ashamed to assert them, at least forcibly. But what the champion prize fighter of the world says in a widely circulated newspaper reaches a great mass of people who not only have racial prejudices, but boast of the fact. And what he says will carry more weight with them than the words of all the college presidents in the country."

"Gentlemen, when you trust fully in the democratic principle that every man is entitled to one vote, and when no man fears to have that vote counted, there will be less danger of the continued control of ignorance over intelligence than there is when resort is had to any other method; and only when such is the rule will free institutions be fully established. . . .

"Liberty and justice shall surely govern this fair land. . . .

"I had read the Scriptures where it is written that men should convert their swords into ploughshares and their spears into pruning-hooks; but in your neighboring city of Chattanooga I also saw the battery that had belched forth fire and death converted into a fountain of living water to nourish the new industry of the New South.

"As you convert the darkness of oppression and slavery to liberty and justice, so shall you be judged by men and by Him who created all the nations of the earth."—HOWARD ATKINSON, "The Basis for Prosperity for the New South," in the Senate Chamber, Atlanta, Ga., 1880.

CHAPTER XII.

WHAT HAS THE AMERICAN NEGRO DONE? WHAT OUGHT HE TO DO? WHAT WILL HE DO?

THE Negro's civil and political rights and his racial relation to the public weal are the pressing and perplexing phases of the Negro problem. Therefore in answering these questions I will limit myself to those phases of racial conduct that reflect racial tendencies or touch the general welfare.

A.

The Negro has met the fundamental prerequisite of a successful career. *He has stayed on the earth.* Whether in slavery or in freedom, he has increased and multiplied. While his relative number has diminished, his absolute number has increased. At the close of the Revolutionary War he was one-fifth of the total population; he is now less than one-tenth; yet the four millions in 1860 are now ten millions. The peculiar hexiology[1] of the Negro has enabled him to thrive in all climates and live among all peoples.

> Born on the earliest dawn of time,
> He will be till time is o'er;
> He has sung his songs in every clime
> And dwelt on every shore.

If the Negro has made little history directly, he has made a good deal indirectly; failing to write himself, he has made the other fellow write. The annals

[1] See definition of this word, Chapter X, page 228.

of the human race contain no parallel to the great Civil War fought in this country about the Negro's condition.

The Negro has been grateful to his friends, forgiving to his enemies, and has frequently disappointed the prophets.

B.

A great deal has been said about Reconstruction and the Negro in politics; yet the following historical facts stand out to the Negro's credit:—

"He has accepted his freedom[2] in the spirit of those who bestowed it; that is, limited by, and only by, the civil and political rights and duties of American citizenship equally devoid of special privileges and special restrictions."

"The freedman never by legislation removed the penalties from anything that the world at large calls a crime, and here it may be added that he never put upon the statute book a law hostile to the universal enjoyment of American liberty. *In the darkest day of his power he established the public-school system.*"

"The Negroes never did and do not now draw a strict color line in politics. Even in reconstruction days, when everything favored Negro supremacy, the colored man generally entrusted the public offices of county and State to the white man."

"If the Negroes are too ignorant to fill the offices themselves, surely no better testimony than this to their wisdom and public spirit could be asked for."

Let us face the facts. Such phrases as "Negro domination," "The political supremacy of the Negro," "A black oligarchy at the South," "To Africanize the States of the South," etc., all belong to the hysterics of

[2] See page 26.

the subject, and can be at once dismissed by reasonable investigators today.

"Whatever may be said of Sumner, Stevens, and the men who gathered around them, they were not a herd of perfect fools with a total lack of foresight."

Their object was: "*To put race rule of all sorts under foot,* and to set up the common rule of all,"—or rather, "the consent of all to the rule of a minority the choice of the majority, frequently appealed to without respect of persons."

In other words, they sought to establish a free democracy. They were right in purpose, whatever their errors in method.

In all candor, "this scheme was never allowed a fair trial in any of the once-seceding States."

There are "impersonal public rights which belong to every man because he is a man, and with which race and its real or imagined antagonisms have nothing to do. . . . There is a Negro question which belongs to private society and morals and to the individual conscience; the question what to do to and with the Negro within that realm of our own private choice where public law does not and dare not come. But *the Negro puestion which appeals to the nation, to the laws, and to legislation, is only, and is bound to be only, the question of public, civil, and political rights.*"

The acceptance of this truth is the *soul of democracy* and its denial is the *spirit of slavery.*

The difficulties of the problem are persistently and immeasurably increased by "a recriminative entanglement of these two matters, one entirely within, and the other entirely beyond, the province of legislation."

Governor Colquit, of Georgia, struck the nail squarely on the head more than twenty years ago when he said, "Friendly relations habitually exist between our white and black citizens, and are never disturbed except on those occasions when the exigencies of party politics call for an agitation of race prejudices.

"The question of the Negro's entrance into private white society, we again protest, is entirely outside the the circle of his civil rights."

I know my people, their hopes, their fears, their aspirations, and their desires; and from my youth up I have preferred a discreet silence to false or dishonorable speech. With all candor and earnestness I say to the American public: *the Negro has no desire to break over social barriers. In this regard he is, if possible, more strongly prepossessed in favor of his own than the white man.* In these matters the Negro is not only pleased but happy to work out *his own equivalent rights.* But in civil, political, and economical matters the Negro insists, and for the good of the country ought to insist, upon *equal,* not *equivalent,* rights.

"Equal civil rights inhere in the individual and by virtue of individual conditions and conduct. Equivalent civil rights are fictitiously vested in *classes* and without regard to individual conditions and conduct.

"Politics is what we do or propose to do in and for the various relations of public society. What do the American white people want? Must the average mental and moral caliber of the whole Negro race in America equal that of the white race before *any* Negro is entitled to the civil and political standing decreed to all citizens of the United States except the criminal and insane? Shall the Negro, through the domain of civil rights, enjoy impersonal and individual consideration, or be subjected to merely a class treatment?

"The popular assumption that a certain antagonism between the white and black races is natural, inborn, ineradicable, has never been scientifically proven. Even if it were, that would not necessarily fix a complete and sufficient rule of conduct. *To be governed merely by instincts is pure savagery.* . . .

"Why then, in strictly public relations, should not this expensive color-line be removed and the Negro given treatment based on individual merit?"

C.

Civilization means justice and fair play to all, even the most humble. True democracy estimates a man's value as a man.

The Negro is not an alien in this country. He began his residence here concurrently with the white man. The Dutch slaver landed at Jamestown the same year the English adventurer landed at Plymouth —1620. There has been practically no reinforcement from Africa for more than a hundred years.

"Soon after the establishment of the new government, the Congress enacted a law fixing upon a period, not remote, after which no slaves should be introduced from abroad into any State or Territory of the Republic. Of the nearly four million slaves now [1860] held as such in the United States, not five hundred have been introduced in contravention of that enactment."[3]

Negroes were with the early voyagers and discoverers of America. Crispus Attucks, a Negro, fell in the front of the first battle for American Independence. Benjamin Banneker, a Negro, assisted in fixing the boundaries of the District of Columbia, selecting the site of the Capitol and in locating the Executive Mansion. A Negro sentinel guards the tomb of

[3] Williams, "Letters on Slavery," pages 19 and 20.

Washington and Negro soldiers defend the Philippines. There is not a break in our residence nor a flaw in our patriotism.

It is the *spirit* of *slavery* and not the *race* of the slave that makes difficult the attainment of democracy. Slavery itself, not the slave; the principle, and not the man, is the evil. The fathers all knew this and expected gradual, peaceful emancipation. Washington, Jefferson, Madison, all so held and so believed. *Greed and circumstances, and not race or section, finally riveted the chains of slavery on the Afro-American.* The process was not only similar but practically identical with the evolution of the sweat-shop and factory victims.

Mr. Archer, of England, after a hurried trip "through Afro-America," talks oracularly of the injustice and ill prospects of the South, and boasts of the superiority of civilization in England because it is "monochrome." He seems to forget that notwithstanding the "polychrome condition of the South," it is more prosperous than England and just as peaceful. While some of our laws are bad and some of our practices worse, monochrome England has surpassed us in both. Why, it was not long ago that "Beggars who were vagabonds were whipped, burnt through the gristle of the right ear with a hot iron, and virtually made slaves of by being apportioned to some employer to work without wages for a year, to be imprisoned if they ran away once, treated as felons for the second offence of the kind, and very summarily hanged if they ran away the third time."

And these barbarities were honestly thought necessary to make men work and to preserve the integrity of society. The abolition of these cruelties increased both the comfort and security of society. So it was with chattel slavery in this country, and so it will be with the civic and political discrimination against the Negro.

Emancipation was not a failure, *because it was accepted in good faith by the slaveholders.* Enfranchisement and reconstruction met the opposite fate for the opposite reason. *They were not accepted in good faith and were never fairly tried.*

"One of the most conclusive proofs that the changes that have been made in the Negro's status have been generally in the direction of true progress, is that wherever and whenever these changes have been complete and operative, opposition to them has disappeared and they have dropped out of the main problem, leaving it by so much the lighter and simpler. The most notable instance, of course, is the abolition of slavery; but there are many lesser examples in the history of both Northern and Southern States,—the teaching of Negroes in private schools; their admission into public schools; their sitting on juries; their acceptance as court witnesses; their riding on streetcars; their enlistment in the militia; their appointment on the police force, etc. It is a fact worthy of more consideration than it gets from debaters on either side of the Negro question, that such changes as these, which nobody finds any reason for undoing in any place where they have been fully established, were, until they were made, as fiercely opposed and esteemed as dishonorable, humiliating, unjust, and unsafe to white men and women, as those changes which, in many regions of our country, not all of them Southern, still remain to be made before the Negro question will let itself be dismissed. This fact no one will dispute. Yet thousands shut their eyes and ears, or let others shut them, to the equal, though not as salient, truth of this fact's corollary, to wit: that every step toward perfecting of one common public liberty for all

American citizens is opposed and postponed only where it has never been fairly tried. Even the various public liberties intended to be secured to all men alike by the Civil Rights Bill have rarely, if ever, in any place been actually secured and made operative and afterward withdrawn and lost. Only where they have been merely legalized and not practically established, but bitterly fought and nullified throughout reconstruction days, have they since been unlegalized, condemned, and falsely proclaimed to have been fairly tried and found wanting.

D.

"To describe without rising to the causes, or descending to the consequences, is no more science than merely and simply to relate a fact of which one has been a witness."[4]

Heredity and *evolution* are antagonistic but complementary forces.[5] *Conservatism* and *progress* are their legitimate representatives. They are mutually corrective though mutually depreciative of each other's virtues. To the ultra-conservative, the ultra-progressive are recklessly iconoclastic. On the other hand, the progressives think the conservatives ignorantly opposed to all advancement.

Among intelligent and sincere people of different temperaments and experiences these things may *honestly* be. Now, mix with these qualities, *ignorance, obstinacy, selfishness, fear, ambition,* and all the thousand and one moods and tenses that swell the diapason of human passion, and we see why civilization ebbs and flows; and why the history of human progress is a martyrology of earth's choicest men.

---

[4] Arnold Guyot, "Earth and Man."
[5] See Chapter II.

Conservatism or cowardice always predicts disaster at every attempt to advance the frontiers of knowledge or move the landmarks of limitation. It has been gravely argued that relieving the pains of childbirth would destroy female chastity, and crossing the equator would turn men black. "And if no kindly cloud will parasol me, my very cellular membrane will be changed; I shall be negrofied."

Ancient Mythology wrote *ne plus ultra* (nothing more beyond) upon the Pillars of Hercules, and modern Science has removed it to the outer rim of the Milky Way; but there has been a throb of pain for every inch of that awe-inspiring distance. Every advance toward liberty and freedom has aroused fear and provoked opposition.

Nowadays, a workingman may live in splendors Cæsar never knew, and conquer worlds of privilege beyond the dreams of Alexander; but mankind is not yet free, and the croaker is still busy. Man has not yet learned the truth that will make him free nor felt that universal throb of sympathy that will make him everywhere and at all times his brother's keeper. Hungry children still tug at the lean breasts of starving mothers; and State governments still coin the quivering flesh of convicts into gold.

Bacon said of the ancient philosophies, that they "ended in nothing but disputation; that it was neither a vineyard nor an olive ground, but an intricate wood of briars and thistles, from which those who lost themselves in it brought back many scratches and no food." This seems particularly true of political philosophy. There seems to be some essential thing left out of man's makeup, or something wrong put into it, that prevents him from having faith in himself and being just to his brother. "All is life for him who is alive; all is death for him who is dead. All is spirit for him who is spirit; all is matter for him who is nothing but matter. It is with the whole life and the whole intellect that we should study the work of *Him* who is life and intellect itself." Man must concede humanity to man to win that concession for himself.

E.

Religion is a determining factor in political destiny. Religion is the surest basis for morality, and without morality civilization is impossible. Religion softened the lot of the slave. Religion brought emancipation. Religion built our schools and colleges. And, if we ever reach the goal of real citizenship. it will come through religion.

Right thinking is the chief factor in the advancement of a race or nation. Not only is the Negro religious, but he is thoughtful. He has not only contributed to the physical wealth of this country by his muscle, but he has contributed to its moral wealth by his character, and to its intellectual wealth by his brains. Character is not only a personal asset, but a national asset. The conduct of the Negro race during the Civil War was a contribution to the moral wealth of the world. A nation with all its citizens of high moral character would be

"As rich in having such a jewel as twenty seas,
If all their sands were pearl,
The water nectar, and the rocks pure gold."

The courage of Crispus Attucks, the knowledge of Benjamin Banneker, the eloquence of Frederick Douglass, the genius of Booker T. Washington, the learning of Burkhardt DuBois, the art of Henry O. Tanner, the music of Coleridge Taylor, and the poetry of Paul Laurence Dunbar are national contributions to the elemental forces of civilization.[6] The Jubilee Music is a contribution to the joy of the world. The folk-songs of the Afro-American find a responsive chord in every human breast.

A sympathetic and painstaking study of American history[7] will show the Negro has produced the exceptional individual with a frequency that is little suspected even by his friends. The story of Abram Grant from the ox-cart (where he was born) and the slave-pen to the bishopric is of as great educative value as the story of James A. Garfield from the tow-path to the presidency. The principles of true government are nowhere in literature more plainly and forcibly expressed than in the words of Martin R. Delaney, a black man.[8] The American boy should know all. From every walk of life they come. Why, here on the banks of the Cumberland River, at Nashville, Tenn., dwelt for many years an humble fireman who risked his life a score of times for others, and rescued a dozen people from the clammy clutch of engulfiing waters. The local papers made special note of his death.

It is a long way from a log cabin in Kentucky to the presidency of these United States, but from the slave-pens of Maryland to the marshalship of the District of Columbia is farther. While we justly honor Lincoln for the first, we should remember Douglass, "the noblest slave God ever set free," made the second.

> "'Make way for liberty,' he cried;
> Made way for liberty and died,"

---

[6] See also page 251.
[7] See page 47.
[8] See "Life and Public Service of Martin R. Delaney," by Frank A. Rollin, page 329.

is as true of Crispus Attucks' rush upon the British bayonets at Boston as of Arnold von Winkelried's plunge upon the Austrian pikes at Sempach. Toussaint L'Overture is as worthy a place in the history of war as Napoleon Bonaparte. Of those turbulent and erratic souls that sacrifice themselves for the righting of others' wrongs, Nat Turner is as worthy of remembrance as John Brown. When the roll is called of great and good women whose spiritualized lives have blessed their generation, Sojourner Truth is as worthy a place as Frances E. Willard; and for pure heroism and self-sacrifice to save others, Harriet Tubman is as worthy a place in the Sacred Fanes as Grace Darling, Florence Nightingale, or Joan of Arc.

F.

The Negro has learned that racial self-sufficiency is the road to racial peace and prosperity. Especially is this true socially. Mr. Murphy has sententiously formulated a doctrine that intelligent Negroes generally understand and preach to the masses.

"As the race comes to have within itself, within its own social resources, a world that is worth living for, it will gain that individual foothold among the families of men which will check the despairing passion of its self-obliteration; and instead of the temptation to abandon its place among the races of the world it will begin to claim its own name and its own life. That is the only real, the only permanent security of race integrity for the Negro. Its assumption is not degradation, but opportunity."

'Tis a long way from slavery to freedom. Sometimes the freedman is absolutely incapable of becoming a freeman.

Hon. Fred Douglass.

"Chains do not a prison make,
Nor iron bars a cage."

Manacles and shackles cannot by their presence alone make a slave, nor by their absence alone make a free man. The caged canary sings, but the caged sparrow dies. Why? Out of his cage the canary makes a meal for the first hungry cat that passes his way. Cats, dogs, boys with toy guns, are not sufficient to diminish the number of sparrows. Why? Adaptability to environment is the explanation.

Fifty years of freedom have not entirely abolished the virtues of slavery nor established those of freedom. These qualities are antagonistic and do not yield readily one to the other. While the virtues are struggling for the mastery, the vices of both estates have united upon the most intimate terms, and are producing a numerous progeny of illegitimate troubles just as the respectable white people and respectable Negroes are afraid to co-operate for the public good, but the ignorant and vicious of both races do not hesitate to commingle to the detriment of all.

Slavery taught the Negro to accept without question the white man's opinion on every subject. This he too often does yet, to the injury of both races. When a white man believes the white people are the best looking people on earth, he is wise and in harmony with nature; but when a black man believes it he is a fool and out of harmony with nature. Because that belief will make the white man proud of himself and his race, while that same belief will make of the black man a creature that neither God nor man has yet found any use for, namely, a man ashamed of his race.[9] This by-product of the slave system has confused ethnic values and hindered social progress. It is an

---

[9] See page 60, "Undesirable Variations."

insidious poison that has perverted the reason of many men, so that they have not only forgotten justice, but are blind to their own interests. The white man is right when he insists that a black man cannot be a white man, but wrong when he insists that *all men are white.* The Negro who does not accept the first proposition is a fool; but the Negro who accepts the second is both a fool and a menace.

Socially the Negro has loosened the sealed fountains of knowledge and is earnestly striving to

> "Drink deep, until the habits of the slave,
> The sins of emptiness, gossip, and spite,
> And slander die."

"Even under the artificial and undiscriminating pressure of public caste he is developing social ranks with wide moral and intellectual differences, from the stupid, idle, criminal, and painfully numerous minority at the bottom, to a wealth-holding, educated minority at the top; each emerging or half-emerging from a huge middle majority of peace-keeping, but uneducated and unskilled farmers, mechanics, and laborers, yet a majority unestranged from the more cultured and prosperous minority of their own race by any difference of religion, conflict of traditions, or rivalry of capital and labor, and harkening to their counsels more tractably than the mass listens to a few among any other people on the continent."

G

The Negro has been very unfortunate in the administration of justice. Little is done to lessen crime. The lack of simple justice is appalling.

"There are State prisons in which you may find the

colored convicts serving sentences whose average is nearly twice that of the white convicts in the same place for the same crimes."

The pendulum swings from indifferent laxity to vengeful severity, seldom indeed resting at the perpendicular of even-handed justice. All the weaknesses of popular government are reinforced by class prejudice and racial antagonism. There are several distinctive phases of criminal administration:—

1. Crimes by whites against whites.
2. Crimes by blacks against blacks.
3. Crimes by whites against blacks.
4. Crimes by blacks against whites.
5. Crimes committed by whites and blacks together: (*a*) against whites, (*b*) against blacks.

In the first place, purse, position, and interest being equal, justice, though somewhat belated, is apt to arrive. In the second case indifference is apt to clog the wheels of justice, though partiality does not often mar the findings. Under the third head prosecution is rare and conviction difficult. Under the fourth heading prosecution is vigorous (unless the offense is trivial or personal friendship intervenes), conviction easy, and escape practically impossible.

5 (*a*) usually represents headings 1, 2, and 3 combined, while 5 (*b*) is usually a duplicate of conditions under 3.

A belief that the Negro is unable to defend himself often makes white people tyrannical. A belief that the courts are unfair often makes the Negro desperate. By magnifying petty offenses, petty criminals are often made grave and incorrigible offenders. Thus the seed of race antagonism and anarchy are sown. The records of the inferior courts of our country will prove painful reading to those who love justice and fair play. Fred Douglass said that as a boy he discovered that the slaves oftenest whipped were not the ones most deserving punishment, but those most easily whipped. This is largely true of our administration of justice. This fact, rather than race prejudice or Negro criminality, explains the frequency with which Negro crap games are raided and Negro vagrants incarcerated.

The administration of justice is one of the weakest and darkest spots in our national life. In the Poet Dante's day there was current a superstition that if a murderer were to eat on the grave of his victim a sop of bread and wine within nine days from the murder he would thus escape the penalty of his crime. Similarly in our day there is an effort to escape the consequences of injustice to the present generation of colored people in freedom by a sop of praise to the character of their grandparents in slavery. But the warning of Dante holds good today: "Hope not to scare God's vengeance with a sop." In the face of it all, the Negro has never turned back on the thorny road from *freed*man to *free*man. With increasing literacy and decreasing death rate, he has kept his face to the morning.

H

About twenty-five years ago Mr. Geo. W. Cable, a learned and patriotic Southern gentleman, discussed the Negro problem in a series of magazine papers. I have drawn freely upon this material in the first part of the present chapter, and now enumerate largely from the same source the following imperative obligations of the Negro:—

1. To reach full citizenship he must make most of the liberties he has.

Sojourner Truth. (Courtesy of "The Crisis.")

"The intelligent Negro may well ask of our public opinion a larger measure of discrimination; and yet he may well lay the greater stress upon his gains rather than upon his losses. Certainly his gains will be of small avail if the contemplation of his wrongs shall supersede in his life the positive acceptance and the definite using of his rights."[10]

2. Be patient and work persistently and intelligently for his manhood rights.

"In the politics of a great nation even the greatest questions must take their turns, according as now one and now another gains the lead in the public attention, and the more sagaciously and diligently any worthy question is pressed to the front by the forces that dictate to the daily press, the stump, and the national and State legislatures, the sooner and oftener will its turn come round to lay uppermost hold upon the national conscience and policy. There always was good reason, but now there is the greatest need, that you give and get this kind of backing for the question of your civil and political rights. We say give and get, because every endeavor should be used to secure by personal solicitation not the condescension—there has been enough of that—but the friendly countenance and active co-operation of white men well known in their communities for intelligence and integrity."

3. So frame his propaganda as to include his racial welfare program *within* a program for the general welfare.

"Nothing else can so hasten the acquisition of all your rights as for you to make it plain that your own rights and welfare are not all you are striving for, but that you are at least, equally with the white man, the student of your individual duty toward every public question in the light of the general good."

[10] Murphy, "The Present South."

4. Make his intentions clear.

"There are tens of thousands of intelligent people who today unwittingly exaggerate the demands made by and in behalf of the Negro into a vast and shapeless terror. Neither he, nor his advocates, nor his opponents have generally realized how widely his claims have been, and, sometimes by and sometimes without intention, misconstrued. He needs still to make innumerable reiterations of the facts that seem to him too plain for repetition; as, for example, that he does not want 'Negro supremacy,' or any supremacy save that of an intelligent and upright minority, be it white, black, or both, ruling, out of office, by the sagacity of their counsels and their loyalty to the common good, and, in office, by the choice of majority of the whole people; that, *as to private society, he does not want any man's company who does not want his;* or that, as to suffrage, he does not want to vote solidly unless he must in order to maintain precious rights and duties denied to, and only to, him and all his."

5. The Negro ought to show political sense.

"This means several things. It means, that, without venality or servility, he must hold his vote up for honorable competitive bid of political parties. *A vote which one party can count on as a matter of course, and the opposite party cannot hope to win at any price, need expect nothing from either.* In no campaign ought the Negro know *certainly* how he will vote before he has seen both platforms and weighed the chances of their words being made good. He will never get his rights until the white man does not know how he is going to vote. *He must let him see that the Negro vote can divide* whenever it may, and *come together again solidly whenever it must.*

"Keeping his vote alive means, also, that while to be grateful is right and to be ungrateful is base, he must nevertheless stop voting for gratitude. The debts of gratitude are sacred, but no unwise vote can lighten them. A vote is not a free-will offering to the past; it is a debt to the present."

Again, the Negro must make himself a part of his country.[11]

"What makes great parties if it be not the combination of various political interests consenting to concern themselves in one another's aims and claims for the better promotion of those designs in the order of their urgency and practicability? Now, here is the colored man charged, at least, with rarely—almost never—making himself seen or heard in any widespread interest except his own. Small wonder if other men do not more hotly insist upon his vote being cast and counted. The Negro may be not the first or the principal one to blame in this matter, but he is largely the largest loser."

Once more this means that whenever practicable or possible he should vote, pay poll-tax, register, etc.

"He must practically recognize two facts, which if the white man had not recognized in his case long ago he would be in slavery today; that there is an enormous value in having votes cast: first, even though they cannot win; and, secondly, even though they are not going to be counted. A good cause and a stubborn fight are a combination almost as good as victory itself; better than victory without them; the seed of certain victory at last. Even if he has to cope with fraud, make it play its infamous part so boldly and so fast that it shall work its own disgrace and destruction, as many a time it has done before the colored man ever voted. *Vote!* Cast your vote, though taxed for it. Cast your vote, though defrauded of it, as many a white man is today."

---

[11] See page 34, especially footnote.

"In most of the Southern States the colored vote has been diminishing steadily for years, to the profound satisfaction of those white men whose suicidal policy is to keep you in alienism. In the name of the dead, black and white, of the living, and of your children yet unborn, not as one party or another, but as American freemen, *vote!* for in this free land the people who do not vote do not get and do not deserve their rights!"

The ballot-box should become a holy shrine to the Afro-American. "Three hundred thousand white men died that you might not touch it; other three hundred thousand died that you might approach it." *As no other people since time began was ever the beneficiaries of so much blood not their own, so we should stand for purity and patriotism as no people has ever stood. The Negro should cherish the ballot as he does his own life.*

6. He must spend his money willingly and wisely to advance his own citizenship.

"No full use of the liberties you now have can be made without co-operation, however loose that co-operation may have to be; and no co-operation can be very wide, active, or effective, without the use of money. This tax cannot be laid anywhere upon a few purses. Falling upon many it will rest too lightly to be counted a burden. White men may and should help to bear it: but if so, then all the more the Negro must spend his own money. Half the amount now idled away on comparatively useless societies and secret orders will work wonders."

Money is essential especially for two matters: First, for the stimulation, publication, and wide distribution of a literature of the facts, equities, and exigencies of the Negro question in all its practical phases. This would naturally include a constant and diligent keeping of the whole question pruned clear of its dead matter. From nothing else has the question suffered so much, at the hands both of friends and of foes, as from lack of this kind of attention. And, secondly, money is essential for the unofficial, unpartisan, prompt, and thorough investigation and exposure of crimes against civil and political rights.

7. He must intelligently and patiently, but eternally and watchfully, press the contest for equal rights and duties in his home State.

"The claim need by no means be abated that the national government has rights and duties in the matter that have yet been fully established; but, for all that, he can urge the question's recognition in State political platforms, and, having made his vote truly and honorably valuable to all parties, can bestow it where there is largest prospect of such recognition being carried into legislation and such legislation being carried into effect."

8. The Negro ought to learn that *self-interest (mutual benefits) is the only sane basis from which to predicate successful co-operation.*

No man is ever going to think more of you than he does of himself. The highest ethical ideal ever lived or preached enjoined that you love your neighbor as yourself. Sane *altruism* is the highest and truest *egoism.*

"There is a strong line of cleavage already running through the white part of the population in every Southern State. On one side of this line the trend of conviction toward the establishment of the common happiness and security through the uplifting of the whole people by the widest possible distribution of moral effects and wealth-producing powers. It favors, for example, the expansion of the public-school system, and is strongest among men of professional callings and within sweep of the influences of colleges and universities. It antagonizes such peculiar institutions as the convict-lease system,[12] with that system's enormous political powers. It condemns corrupt elections at home and abroad. It revolts against absolutism of political parties. In a word, it stands distinctly for *the new South, of American ideas,* including the idea of material development, as against a new South with no ideas except that of material development for the aggrandizement of the few and the holding of the whole Negro race in the South to a servile public status, cost what it may to justice, wealth, or morals. Let the Negro in every State and local issue strive with a dauntless perseverance intelligently, justly, and honorably to make his vote at once too cheap and too valuable for the friends of justice and a common freedom to despise it or allow their enemies to suppress it. He should remember that his power in the nation at large must always be measured entirely by his power in his own State."

---

[12] Few people outside of those intimately connected with it have any conception of what this system is. The following editorial from *The New Republic* (Oct. 16, 1915) gives only a faint inkling:—

"The convict-lease system has survived many exposures, but the arraignment of the treatment of State prisoners just made by the Alabama Legislative Investigating Committee is not likely to make the practice more popular. The committee members were sickened by the stupid brutality and greed which they discovered. They found farmers' sons, young mountaineers, accustomed to living in the sunshine, condemned to work underground in the coal mines, beginning before sunrise and laboring until long after sunset, with insufficient and ill-prepared food, and treated so brutally that "the skin was literally beaten from the backs." In the turpentine camps conditions were even worse. The convicts "were made frequently to rise at four in the morning, day in and day out, walk five or six miles to work, toil all day long with insufficient water and food, in the heat of the sun, until darkness comes, and then forced to walk into camp for their supper." Inexperienced and untrained short-term convicts were put at extra-hazardous work, and a case was cited in which two boys arrested for stealing a ride on the train were blown up on their second day of work in a mine explosion. The Alabama Committee, who were not philanthropists but rather conservative, hard-headed men, declared the convict system to be "a relic of barbarism, a species of human slavery, a crime against civilization."

Finally, the Negro ought to exalt individual excellence.

"It is perfectly natural that the Negro, his history being what it is, should magnify the necessity of co-operation in multitudinous numbers to effect any public result. He has not only been treated, but has treated himself too much, as a mere mass. While he has too often lacked in his organized efforts that disinterested zeal, or even that semblance of it, which far-sighted shrewdness puts on, to insure wide and harmonious co-operation, he has, on the other hand, overlooked the power of the individual and the necessity of individual power to give power to numbers."

Individual excellence has ever been the hope of progress and the dread of tyranny. The bulwark of the slave system was its ability to destroy individual initiative and keep the slaves *en masse*. We are now prone to hope too much from mass movement. We must learn the value of individual excellence and effort.

"Do not wait for the mass to move. The mass waits for the movement of that individual who can not and will not wait for the mass. You may believe your powers to be, or they may actually be, humble; but even so, there are all degrees of leadership and need of all degrees. There is work to be done which is not in the nature of violence or votes or any mere mass power, organized or unorganized, you can accomplish."

Isaiah was right: "And a man shall be as an hiding-place from the wind and covert from the tempest; as rivers of water in a dry place, as the shadow of a great rock in a weary land." (Is. 32: 2.) The efforts of an individual thinker may be more victory-compelling than "an army with banners." The biological researches of Prof. Ernest Everett Just, of Washington, D. C., give promise that such men are coming.

The Negro ought not to talk too much, especially about prosperity. We are still poor. A man without a home or any other earthly possessions may feel very rich over his first ten-dollar bill. Whatever his feelings, he is still a poor man. This was our condition as a race. Turned loose with nothing after working without wages, we were so proud of our first earnings that we failed to see the gulf between our actual possessions and our urgent needs. In an effort to prove our industry we overstated our possessions.

Overemphasis sometimes defeats its own ends. Some years ago a lurid temperance orator illustrated the dangers of drinking alcoholic liquors by the vivid portrayal of a terrible accident. A man had drunk so long and much that the tissues of his body were saturated with alcohol to such an extent that his breath was laden with its fumes. One night in a drunken stupor he attempted to blow out a candle, when his breath took fire and he met a most agonizing death. At the conclusion of the address an old toper in the rear tottered to the platform and said to the lecturer: "Pardon, but is that candle story straight?" Being assured that it was, he cordially thanked the lecturer and congratulated himself for coming. As he reeled from the platform he solemnly declared, amid breathless silence: "As long as I live, I'll never, *never, never blow out another candle!*"

Like the lecturer, we have talked too much or talked the wrong way. Our boast of industry brought discrimination against us in getting work. Our call for sanitation brought segregation of our habitations and persons. *Let us be cautious of how we emphasize unduly either our needs or our deeds.*

Wearing diamonds may not only excite envy, but invite robbers; and exposing sores may not only offend taste, but drive away friends. Too much attention prevents progress. *The Negro should not seek admiration by boasting nor sympathy by whining.*

Finally, the Negro ought to cultivate unceasingly a racial sense of spiritual values. "Thrice is he armed who has his quarrel just." To deserve success is eventually to get it. We must be careful not to exalt material prosperity or possessions unduly. The most durable stone will not make a substantial wall unless good mortar be used. *Moral rectitude and spiritual insight are the mortar that make material wealth a wall of protection.*

The curse of this age is the apotheosis of the dollar.

The fight against alcohol is not so much a fight against appetite as against dollars. Venality, not Venus, is the bulwark of prostitution. The red-light district is a monument to the triumph of money over morals. Money produces the turmoil in the race question. It *pays.* It is a source of revenue. *Prejudice produces profit.*

When all things are for barter, destruction is imminent. To arrest ruin, a change must come. The Negro should make every effort to enhance and strengthen the moral forces of the nation. What we lack in silver and gold we should try to make up in the fruits of the spirit.

Babylon fell because the souls of men could be bought in her market-place.

> "In Babylon, mad Babylon,
> What get you for your pence?
> A moiety of cinnamon,
> Of flour and frankincense.
> But let the shekels in your keep
> Be multiplied by ten,
> And you shall purchase slaves, and sheep,
> Yea, and *the souls of men.*"

There are some things that must not be bartered if civilization is to endure. The price is immaterial. It matters not whether a man gets a mess of pottage or a kingdom for his honor; the condemnation holds. Men shirk responsibility by doing collectively what they would hesitate to do individually. Yet the units make the mass, and division of guilt is not destruction of guilt. The number of defendants does not change the character of a crime, and racial misdeeds are as sure of a Nemesis as individual misconduct.

While the great white race cannot escape the penalty if it barter its honor for the privilege of exploiting, suppressing, or even destroying the Negro, neither can the Negro escape if he contribute to this end by moral turpitude or spiritual blindness.

I

The historian can say what a man has done, the philosopher can say what he ought to do, but only God can say what he will do. And yet prosperity depends in a measure upon foresight, and peace is helped or hindered by prophecy. What then will the Negro do? What is the racial program of the present-day leaders of the Afro-American?

Assertory judgments[12] are the reflexes of our moral and intellectual experiences. Our opinions of what the other fellow will do may be but the overtones of our own desires. That is, we credit the other man with *intending* to do what *we think he ought or ought not to do.* A man's own character is often strikingly portrayed by his description of other men's motives and intentions. In spite of all this, however, associations beget similarity and like experiences produce like desires. One touch of nature makes all the world

[12] See Introduction, page 5.

akin. An individual may speak for a group, and one man may voice the sentiment of a nation. This psychological truth is one of the basic facts of representative government.

Without egotism and vainglory, and with a full knowledge of the limitation of my representative capacity, I essay to answer the third question at the head of this chapter.

The Afro-American will continue his struggle for a man's place in the sun.

"God has implanted in man an infinite progression in the career of improvement. A soul capacitated for improvement ought not to be bounded by a tyrant's landmarks."

> We are resolved to be ourselves,
> Knowing well that he
> Who knows himself loses his misery.

The Romans distinguished the *cives ingenui,* or unrestricted citizen, from the *jus quiritium,* the wailing or supplicating citizens; those who were "continually mourning, complaining, or crying for aid or succor."

The Negro has no intention of abandoning the thorny road to full citizenship in this his native land. He will struggle the more and more earnestly and more and more intelligently to deserve the considerate judgment of mankind. He is going to lose the embarrassment of self-consciousness and cease to be a "wailing citizen."

> Unaffrighted by the forces around us
> And undisturbed by the sights we see,
> Self-poised we'll live;
> Bounded by ourselves, and unregardful
> In what state God's other works may be;
> In our own tasks all our powers pouring,
> And thus attain our citizenship to be.

The Negro is going to live.

Notwithstanding the prophets, the American Negro is not going to die out.

Mr. P. A. Bruce, in his "Rise of the New South" (Philadelphia, 1905), says: "The vaster the growth of the Southern States in wealth and white population, the sharper and more urgent will be the struggle of the black man for existence. In order to hold even his present position as a common laborer he will have to exert himself to the utmost, and in doing so he will have to submit to a manner of life that will be even more unwholesome and squalid than the one he now follows, and sure to lead to a great increase in the already very high rate of mortality for his race. The day will come in the South, just as it came long ago in the North, when for lack of skill, lack of sobriety, and lack of persistency, the Negro will find it more difficult to stand up against the white workingman. Already it is the ultimate fate of the Negro that is in the balance, not the ultimate fate of the Southern States in consequence of the presence of the Negro. The darkest day for the Southern whites has passed. The darkest day for the Southern blacks has only just begun." (Archer.)

As civilization advances laboring men, white and black, will stand less and less *against* each other and more and more *with* each other. The laboring white man is gathering the apples of Sodom for the golden fruit of Hesperides, if he expects to secure his rights by destroying the black laboring man's rights. *The wail of the hungry is dangerous music* for a banquet. The Negro intends to strive *with* and not *against* the white man for the advancement of this country.

Destruction is not nature's final decree in equity for the black man. Race prejudice hopes that the warp of ignorance and the woof of disease will be so placed

The Public-school Principals of a Southern city. (1915.)

in the loom of civic oppression that time may weave the winding sheet of the Negro race. The people who so think are like a German friend of mine once said about his prayers. He had talked the value of prayer to me until under stress of other duties my patience gave way and I petulantly asked, "Do you ever get any answer to your prayers?" His face lighted with an innocent eagerness that at once soothed my irritation as he said, "Yes, yes! I answer him myself."

It is a painful fact that those who declare the Negro cannot utilize the agencies of modern civilization are ever ready to block his upward path; and while prophesying his engulfment in the cesspool of vice, corruption, and death, they never reach an arm to save.

But we shall not die. The Negro doctor is rallying a successful army to attack the strongholds of physical disease, the schoolteachers and preachers are keeping the passes against moral degeneracy, and our lawyers and civicists, albeit somewhat belated and ill-equipped, are protecting us from political suicide. We shall not die! The spirit of the race was breathed in the good old revival song of our fathers:—

> "I will go and I shall go,
> To see what the end will be."

Sojourner Truth, "the most singular and impressive figure of pure African blood that has appeared in modern times," said: "People ask me how I live so long and keep my mind; and I tell them it is because I think of the great things of God; not the little things."

She spoke for her race.

It is not without significance that the largest work of man's hand in the world and the only remaining one of the seven wonders of the ancient world is the work of Africans.[13]

A knowledge of history should have a restraining effect upon prophetic enthusiasm. History is hard on the prophets of tyranny. Cotton was king and the slave power apparently invincible when Mr. Toombs, of Georgia, prophesied that he would call the roll of his slaves at the foot of Bunker Hill. In 1855 Mississippi was dictating the nation's policy on the race question as it is in 1915. The right of petition was denied in the House when Giddings was censured, and free speech was challenged in the Senate when Sumner was assaulted. The execution of John Brown wrecked the Underground Railroad, and the Dred Scott Decision struck the note of doom for the abolitionists. The sentiment of this famous decision, denying to the slave and his descendants forever even the right of litigants, was so sweeping and revolutionary that it was popularly interpreted to mean that "the Negro had no rights that a white man was bound to respect." Yet Lincoln was elected, and the slaves were emancipated; Judge Taney slept with his fathers, and his successor in office, with the acquiesence of his associates, admitted a Negro lawyer to the bar of that august body. All of this happened in less than eight years after Dred Scott was remanded to involuntary servitude.

What is coming, who can say? I only know the American Negro has no intention of dying out; nor of moving out. I am speaking of present intentions, not future contingencies.

The Negro intends to stay in the United States.

"In August, 1778, Adjutant-general Scammel's roster showed seven hundred fifty-five free Negroes in

---

[13] Pyramid of Ghizeh, 481 feet high and nearly 756 feet square.

Washington's main army fighting in the line of white companies." Pennsylvania, New York, New Hampshire, and even Maryland, all following the lead of little Rhode Island, had Negro regiments in the Revolutionary War. In 1814 Louisiana furnished General Jackson, at his own request, a levy of free colored troops. Negro soldiers shared the death and disease of more than two hundred battles in our Civil War. The blood of these men was not shed in vain.

The Negro is not going to abandon the land which his own blood has hallowed.

The Negro is going to stick to his religion. He is not going to abandon his belief in the human brotherhood.

The General Conference of the African Methodist Episcopal Church convened in Baltimore, April, 1826. Among its deliberations was the trial of an elder for calling in a white preacher to administer the sacrament. He was acquitted. Thus early did the Negro commit himself to racial comity.

The Negro will continue to grow in ethnic consciousness and teach race pride until he produces a racial scholarship that will bring him that positive assurance of a respectable seat in the hierarchy of civilization as a distinct racial entity, and not as the tolerated contamination of some nobler race. *Racial solidarity, and not amalgamation, is the desired and desirable goal of the American Negro.* Phyletic triumph through racial solidarity, rather than phyletic oblivion in the Lethean waters of miscegenation, will be the teaching of that scholarship.

The Negro will continue his struggle for racial self-sufficiency.

Let us look to nature for analogy and instruction and hope.

Down in the sunless retreats of the ocean—way

down, down, where the sunlight never penetrates and eternal night holds sway—in this cheerless region may we find a useful and inspiring lesson. The multitudinous inhabitants of this inhospitable place may be divided into two general classes, sedentary and migratory; the former have no eyes—beautiful adaptation of organism to environment—nature's economy. What use are eyes in a region of perpetual darkness? The migratory ones, however, not only have eyes, but have the power of making a light. They thus supply by their own phosphorescent energy that luminosity denied them by the sun, because of the intervening waters. It is my hope that Negro scholarship will become self-luminous with a brilliancy that will give our race correct historical perspective, and lead us to that ethnological respectability and racial solidarity which the floods of prejudice have so persistently washed beyond our grasp. In that hope I believe the Negro will labor earnestly, and patiently await the triumph of justice.

Finally, the Afro-American is going to complete his evolution from *freed* man to *free* man. He is now passing through a period of adjustment—racial moving, as it were—from bondage to freedom. The freedman is becoming a freeman. Losses always attend moving. As we get settled in the house of freedom we will surround ourselves with more of the virtues and fewer of the vices of that condition. There are distinctive slave virtues that are not virtues in freedom. All observers see that the Negro is throwing off the former; only those associated with the best of the Negro race know that he is putting on a glorious substitute, the virtues of a freeman.

Forced to come against his will, compelled to stay when he wanted to go, the Negro has decided on America for his home. From the politician he hears:

"This is a white man's country and the white man is going to rule it." From the preacher he learns that the devil "is the prince of the power of the air." (Ephesians II, 2.)

With the white man ruling the ground and the devil ruling the air, the Negro has decided to stand still and see the salvation of God.

Suppose we have no historical antecedents, what then? Does this give certitude to Huxley's "assuredly" uttered in 1856? Conceding relationship, but not fraternity, he says of the American freedman: "The highest place in the hierarchy of civilization will assuredly not be within reach of our dusky cousins, though it is by no means necessary that they should be restricted to the lowest."

Let us see. If the Negro has never made any history he has certainly been in the white man's history from the beginning of that history. He has won the right to the earth by long residence if by no other right. He has been here so long that, in the words of Uncle Remus, "Twill time has quit runnin agin him." This is sufficient answer to Ingalls' lugubrious prophecy: "Destruction is nature's final decree in equity for the black man."

As black contains by absorption all the colors of the rainbow, though it does not reflect them; so the Negro has in him all the elements of civilization and may yet reflect them as brilliantly as any of the sons of men. It is a beautiful metaphor that likens civilization to light. "The light of civilization" is a phrase as suggestive as beautiful. The similitude is apt. So let us study the action of light closely. If all the light falling upon an object pass through it, the object is transparent and invisible. Imperfect transparency indicates the reflection or absorption of some of the incident rays. Color arises the same way. If all the rays are reflected the object is opaque and white; if all the rays are absorbed the object is opaque and black. So really the white man has no more light than the black man, though he is more luminous. He knows no more of his origin and nature's ultimatum for him than does the black man.

Light needs to strike against something to become manifest. Take a cylinder six inches long, and painted black within. Have a hole in the side equidistant from each end. Darken the room until only a single beam of light is permitted to enter. Now place the cylinder in the path of this beam of light in such a way that the beam of light will traverse the cavity of the cylinder. Look through the hole in the side, and notwithstanding the evident fact that the light is passing through this cavity it is completely dark. No trace of the light is visible. Now introduce a pencil so as to obstruct the pathway of the beam and a ball of light will at once appear. Obstruction has made the light manifest.

The American white man may be the necessary obstruction to make the Negro reflect the light of civilization.

The first number of the *Christian Recorder,* the official organ of the African Methodist Episcopal Church, issued in July 1, 1852, contained an article by a New School Presbyterian minister, one Dr. J. W. C. Pennington, entitled "The Destiny of the Colored Race in the United States." It opens as follows:—

"It was remarked by a distinguished statesman that the future destiny of the colored race will be identified with the interests of the Anglo-Saxon race in America. That sentiment will be verified. The colored race will never be entirely separated or removed from this country as a race, and located somewhere else. History forbids the indulgence of the supposition. Nowhere in the history of nations, where slavery has existed, have the enslaved been entirely separated or removed from the land of their oppression, except in the solitary instance of the Hebrews from Egypt."[14]

After showing that this was true of the Greeks and Romans, etc., and admitting that some colored people would leave during the impending struggle between truth and error, he closes as follows:—

"But the millions will remain in this country, and be identified with the history of the white race, be that history what it may."

This is as true today as when written. *The Negro intends to stay in the United States of America.*

---

[14] See Appendix B.

"Humanity appears to move in a confused medley of the most diverse and composite forms, without any one of them being able to persist."—DENIKER, "The Races of Man," p. 120.

"Oh, my friend, why will men not see that there can be no true civilization while any men in the world are left out of it, and that no race or no nation can go far forward while other races and nations lag behind?"—RAY STANNARD BAKER.

CHAPTER XIII.

RACIAL DIFFERENCES.

In the beginning of this work we established three fundamental propositions in relation to man generally:—

I. In his bodily makeup man is an animal. His anatomy and physiology are practically identical with that of the higher animals.

II. There is an immense and unbridged gulf between the lowest man and the highest animal. No "missing link" has ever been discovered between living and non-living matter, nor between man and beast.

III. There are distinctively human traits and faculties which no animal possesses and which no type of man, however low, is without. This fact substantiates the second proposition and establishes a third, namely, *there is but one species of man.*

These propositions are so firmly established that no one with any just pretense to a scientific education would attempt to dispute them. Moreover, these propositions would seem to furnish an impregnable foundation to the advanced political tenet that "all men are created equal" in three respects. "Life, liberty, and the pursuit of happiness" are common inheritances.

Upon this impregnable scientific foundation rests the political wisdom and moral soundness that demand full citizenship rights for the colored man in America.

But the cohorts of oppression lack neither ingenuity nor industry. They *now* admit all three of the above-mentioned propositions, claiming, however, that while there is but one human family, nature has favorite children, and that she has written the decree of favoritism in the tissues of their bodies. In other words, they concede the Negro's theoretical rights as a man, but deny his capabilities as a citizen. They claim that the artifice of man is built upon the necessity of nature.

A careful scrutiny of the data of anthropology, however, will show that nature has not separated her human children by impenetrable walls. Racial differences are not innate and permanent; but are superficial, environmental, and transitory. *Race discrimination rests on no firmer foundation than caste distinction.*

Humanity passes with facility from one *variety* to another, as it does from one class to another. From whatever angle we approach, scientific investigation forces us to the conclusion that *the only just way to measure men, either physically, mentally or morally, is to measure them individually.* Society is measured by the individual; the development of the individual man is the model of social progress.

The advocates of race prejudice have sought assiduously for scientific justification of the tenets of racial inequality. Violent controversialists are seldom accurate thinkers. Whatever of truth they start with is apt to be lost in the heat of battle. Where little is known much is asserted. The history of thought shows a strange relationship between vehement controversy and accurate knowledge. They are mutually exclusive. They never do and never can flourish bountifully in the same field.

The average theorist is like the little girl that cried so hard she forgot what she was crying about, which was then new cause for weeping.

We have reached a stage of scientific knowledge when evolution is accepted as "an elementary truth at the foundation of a rational conception of the universe." Yet wild theories of emotional ethnology still persist among us. In the absence of accepted first principles we give loose reins to the imagination and replace sober reasoning by extravagant speculation. "The power of error under the mask of truth is often decidedly greater than that of truth itself."

I.—There Are No Pure Races.

"We are loath to accept the facts as they are. Racial purity as a practical entity is a myth. Mankind has been so long on the earth, and has been subject to such endless migrations, displacements, and interminglings of all sorts, that in the opinion of many sound ethnologists few if any pure races now survive." (Keane.)

Take the United States as an instance. The mixing of the whites and blacks is an accomplished fact. It is estimated that the white blood infused into the Negroes of this country is equivalent to the blood of half a million white people; and that there is in the white race, through mixed bloods passing as white, the equivalent of fifty thousand full-blooded black people. According to Finot, "If the word halfbreed was strictly applied to the progeny which has really issued from a mixture of varieties, it would be necessary to include under this denomination all human beings, with rare exceptions."

Blumenbach, true founder of scientific anthropology, has summed up the whole question from the physical standpoint in words that have lost nothing of their force since they were penned a hundred years ago. He asks whether everywhere in time or place mankind has constituted one and the same, or clearly distinct species; and he concludes: "Although between distant people the difference may seem so great that one may easily take the inhabitants of the Cape of Good Hope, the Greenlanders, and Circassians for peoples of so many different distinct species, nevertheless we shall find, on due reflection, that all, as it were, so merge one into the other, the human varieties passing gradually from one to another, that we shall scarcely if at all be able to determine any limits between them."

There is black blood in the whites as assuredly as there is white blood in the blacks.

Dr. Frederick Ratzel in his "Anthropogeographie" (human geography), speaking of the contact of higher and lower culture, says: "The evil of culture lies in halfness. . . . . In all mission fields the observation has been made that those who accept the European customs entirely, as well as those who live in original, unbounded savagery, suffer less than those straying here and there and vacillating between the settlements of the whites and their own hunting grounds."

So with our mixed bloods, those who become unreservedly either white or black prosper best. The least happy and the least successful are those who play back and forth across the racial lines.

How to distinguish one race from another is an important question in America today. Mankind has been studied from every angle to discover distinctive racial features.[1]

Waitz says that "for the classification of mankind philological research has given much more certain and harmonious results than the physical study of man."

Schwiker concludes that "speech remains the most conspicuous distinctive indication of European affinities."

[1] The evidence on this subject is necessarily technical. The reader may follow the thought by noting the headings and reading the conclusions. After completing the work he may return and examine the evidence at leisure.

Sayce also observes that "the physiological races of the modern world are far more mixed than the languages they speak; the physiologist has much more difficulty in distinguishing his races than has the glottologist [2] in distinguishing his families of speech."

But in the United States practically all speak one language; in fact, there are fewer people in the United States who can't speak English than there are people in Germany who can't speak German.

Keane wisely cautions that "too blind trust in philology may lead to as erroneous results as too blind a trust in craniology or in other physical characters."

Racial distinctions have been sought in *form, function,* and *thought.* The sciences of anatomy, physiology, and psychology have been examined by various observers with a view of finding ineradicable racial differences. Thus an effort is made to establish upon a permanent scientific basis a doctrine of human inequality. Do the obvious inequalities of individuals extend to classes and races? In other words, *Are there any permanently inferior or superior races?*

Keane says: "The size as distinct from the shape of the skull gives its volume or 'capacity,' which, although to be carefully distinguished from mental capacity, stands, nevertheless, in close association with mental characters. . . . And if gradation can here be shown between the different races, we shall be able to speak on solid grounds of high and low varieties of the Hominidæ.[3] The limitations of each will also be more closely seen, and the *inherent inequality of the various members of the human family* made evident against the preconceived theories of sentimentalists."

He thus places himself squarely on the affirmative

[2] One learned in the Science of Languages.
[3] Mankind.

side of the question and, while admitting the inadequacy of the anatomical findings to substantiate his erroneous contentions, appeals confidently to psychology as follows: "A better index of difference between the mental capacity of the various human groups is afforded by the reasoning faculty, of which articulate speech is at once the measure and the outward expression. . . . Linguistic anthropology is the 'only science of man.'"

To test the validity of this doctrine of inequality, we must examine the evidence offered by anatomy, physiology, and psychology.

The word *race* as we now use it is a modern word. It was the writings of Buffon, Camper, Blumenbach, and their contemporaries and successors which gave it vogue.

The beginning of the nineteenth century was the epoch of great travels and fruitful explorations. It was likewise the epoch of the blossoming of the natural sciences. The struggle revolving round the unity and the plurality of the human species set going several generations of savants. Does humanity descend from a single primitive type (monogenesis), or has it several distinct ancestors (polygenesis)? Here is a quarrel which has brought us a most imposing literature.

All the vicissitudes of this desperate struggle reacted on the sciences of races.

If the multiplicity of human origins had triumphed, what arguments there would have been in favor of the superiority of certain human stocks! There was even a time when slave-merchants and the barbarous governments which protected their commerce used polygenesis to justify the traffic in Negroes, who were regarded as having originated outside white humanity.

But the theory of monogenesis was established

with the most convincing arguments by Prichard, in his classical "Researches into the Physical History of Man" (1837. 5 vols.), and in the luminous studies of Quatrefages, "l'Espéce humaine." These two authors completely exhausted the subject.

The word race is really inappropriate as a designation of *human varieties. The permanent characteristics of mankind are common to all the varieties; and the differences that characterize the varieties are transitory. A man always remains a man, but a few generations may change his variety.* Five generations of continued cross-breeding will make a black person white, and four generations of reverse crossing will make him black again. "Intelligence cements the unity of the human species. Its influence even fashions their morphology."

II.—Racial Classification.

At the present time it is a vain task to seek distinctive characteristics among certain products of Negroes crossed with whites. Their resemblance to the whites in the United States baffles every artifice resorted to in order to recognize them. Dr. Pearce Kintzing proved by over five hundred experiments the falsity of being able to detect Negro blood by the color of the nails. A rather wide personal experience of the author in genito-urinary medical practice convinces him of the equal falsity of the claim of a persistent distinctive coloration of the genitals.

Blumenbach divided mankind into five races: the Caucasian, Mongolian, Malay, American, and African, or "Ethiopian." Cuvier, while retaining Blumenbach's word "Caucasian," admits only three instead of five: Caucasian, Mongolian, and Negro. Bory de Saint-

Vincent, starting from the position that Adam was only the father of the Jews, divided humanity into fifteen species, and these in their turn into a number of races and sub-races.

Subsequently the classification in being, multiplied and ramified to suit the convenience of savants and of their more or less exact notions of human conformation and qualities, varied from the three races of Cuvier, the four of Leibnitz and Kant, and the nine centers of Agassiz, and at length reached a hundred. Even a hundred and twenty have been proclaimed in certain anthropological congresses.

Isadore Goeffroy Saint-Hilaire divided human beings into *Orthognathic*[4] (oval face with vertical jaws), *Eurygnathic* (high cheek-bones, Mongolian type), *Prognathic* (projecting jaws, Ethiopian type), *Eurygnathic* and *Prognathic* (cheek-bones far apart, projecting jaws, Hottentot type). All of these types are readily seen among Afro-Americans.

Gratiolet distinguished *Frontal, Parietal,* and *Occipital* races, characterized by the prominence of the front, middle, and back parts of the skull and brain.

According to Huxley, men are divided into two capital sections: the *Ulotrichi,*[5] with woolly hair, and the *Leiotrichi,*[6] with smooth hair.

As the science of man develops, the desire to classify and simplify the collected facts encourages more and more numerous demarcations of men.

As morphology is no longer sufficient for this task,

---

[4] "The profile of the face of the Calmuck is almost vertical, the facial bones being thrown downward and under the fore part of the skull. The profile of the Negro, on the other hand, is singularly inclined, the front part of the jaw projecting far forward beyond the level of the fore part of the skull. In the former case the skull is said to be orthognathous, or straight-jawed; in the latter it is called prognathous, a term that has been rendered with more force than elegance by the Saxon equivalent—snouty." (Huxley, "Man's Place in Nature.")

[5] From two Greek words meaning woolly and hair.

[6] From two Greek words meaning smooth and hair.

Prominent colored men, full-blood and mixed-blood. Which is which?

they have recourse to the psychological and mental life in order to find in them new standpoints. Thus it is that the ideal tendencies and aspirations of human beings are taken into account, and so contribute to render more difficult the pass in which the classifiers find themselves. Among the anthropo-psychologists the number of divisions becomes incalculable; for fancy and caprice replace in a decided manner the measurements of the savants. We remember in this connection the attempts of M. Fétis to divide humanity according to the musical systems of its representatives, and that of César Daly advocating, with the same object in view, the differences according to *Architectonic*[7] works.

The systematic study of the salient parts of our organism allows us to grasp vividly the difficulties which the science of races has to combat.

III.—The Skull.

The war of anatomical classification has naturally enough raged about the skull; craniometry (measuring the bare skull), with its fellow cephalometry (measuring the whole head of living beings or corpses), has assumed the dominating place in anthropology. This literature overflows with errors and dogmatisms. It would require a large volume even to summarize it. Finot accurately and fairly sums up the matter and expresses my views: "What conclusions can be drawn from this except that all these craniological measurements teach us almost nothing concerning the mental capacity and the moral value of peoples? . . . Immediately," says he, in another place, "we admit the possibility of the evolution

[7] Pertaining to architecture; hence, pertaining to construction or design of any kind.

of the brain under the influence of occupation, craniological differentiation loses its force. *The truth is that the skull and the brain furnish no arguments in favor of organic inequality.*"

IV.—The Face.

Nor does examination of the face give any better results. With the exception of those organically diseased, normal humanity is with difficulty divided into clearly marked categories. *Prognathism* ought, in the eyes of its authors, to correspond with a nobleness or baseness of origin, with a superior intellectuality, or one which is limited forevermore. For prognathism is an hereditary stain and serves as a distinction between the privileged races and pariahs.

Prognathism, as we know, is the protuberance of the face in front of the brain, in the horizontal position of the skull. This slight inclination of the facial profile can only be measured at first with much difficulty. On the other hand, it has scarcely any relation with the development of the brain. Prognathism presents a whole series of variations, beginning with that which is limited to the nasal region, such as is met with so often in Jews, and to the modifications which include the super- and sub- nasal regions. Therefore, those who consider prognathism as signifying lack of intelligence, or simply inferiority of mind, allow too much to the Jews, who are prognathic.

Moreover, all the classical types which are placed before us as models of plastic beauty and moral character are abundantly endowed with it. We elsewhere meet with the so much dreaded prognathism among royal families, like the Bourbons, who ought exactly to combine nobility of birth and superiority of origin.

The wider observation of prognathism discovers

it under all latitudes and among all peoples.[8] Certain of its most accentuated forms are merely to be found in immediate correspondence with stature. After careful observation and study I am convinced that not more than 10 per cent. of American Negroes are pronouncedly prognathic.

Deductions from the form of the face and the theory of angles give no better results. Of these the facial angle of Pierre Camper[9] is the best known. According to this the whites have a facial angle of 85 degrees, the yellow 80 degrees, and the blacks 75 degrees. He would thus make a difference of 5 degrees define a race: yet Jacquart demonstrated a difference of 10 degrees among the white inhabitants of Paris.

In addition to the facial angle, anthropometry offers us a quantity of others due to the ingenuity of savants of all lands.

Let us note some of them as they come to our mind: the sphenoidal angle of Welcker, the craniofacial angle of Huxley and of Ecker, the parietal angle of Quatrefages, the angle of Barclay, the metafacial angle of Serres, the angle of the condyles, the nasobasal angle of Virchow and Welcker, etc. However curious the results obtained by this numerous series of measurements may be, they all resemble one another from that special point of view which for our

[8] Shortly after writing the above I had occasion to notice a gang of men doing public work, twenty colored men and four white ones. The colored men varied in complexion from quite black to nearly white. A study of their features was intensely interesting. I was so situated that I got a good profile view several times of each individual. The *most nearly orthognathous individual in the group was nearly black* and, beyond all cavil or doubt, the most prognathous person was one of the white foremen.

[9] "The angle of Camper is formed by two lines, one horizontal from the auditive canal to the root of the nose; the other tangent, called facial, from the forehead to the nasal bone. In other words, one of the lines is from the auditive aperture to the lower edge of the nostrils, and the other is to the most salient points of the face, the top of the forehead, and the anterior face of the two lower incisors."

present purpose is foremost. They do not allow us "to seriate" humanity into superior and inferior races. And if they fail to establish irreducible differences between races, they only end in securing the triumph of the theory of individual differences which divide human beings, and which nobody disputes.

"Space will not even permit a definition of these angles, much less a technical discussion of the attempts to determine the length, breadth, and thickness of the face. Suffice it to say that the orbital index, popularized by Broca,[10] enjoyed and still continues to enjoy a certain success. It is concerned with the measure which is obtained in the following manner: After having measured the vertical diameter of the orbit, the result obtained is multiplied by 100 and is afterward divided by the horizontal diameter. From this standpoint Broca divided humanity into three races according to the size of the index thus obtained, viz., the Megasemes,[11] whose average index is 89 and over; the Mesosemes, 83 to 89, and the Microsemes, below 83. But when we pass from these classes to their concrete application, we perceive here also, as elsewhere, that nature has not willed to establish privileged human races. The figures of the orbital index are displaced in a capricious way, and bring together peoples and races separated in our eyes by great gulfs. . . . The Parisians, tread arm-in-arm with Negroes and Hottentots," etc. (Finot.)

V.—The Nose.

The Nose has also been examined with a view to establishing racial distinction.

10 "Sur l'Indice orbitaire," Rev. d'Anthrop., 1879.

11 These words are from the Greek. The last part of each means sign and the first part "great," "medium," and "small," respectively.

Broca, starting from the relation of the maximum width of the nose to its total height, has gone so far as to attempt to divide humanity into three different sections: men with long and narrow nose, the leptorrhinians (thin-nosed), corresponding to the white race; the platyrrhinians (broad-nosed), with wide and low nose, a characteristic peculiar to the black races; and, lastly, the mesorrhinians (middle-nosed), comprising the yellow races.

He develops a nasal index, with the white man as the norm or measure.

After having multiplied by 100 the width of the nose taken at the opening of the nasal chambers, he compared it with the length between the spine and the nasofrontal articulation. The result is what he calls the nasal index. The mean of the nasal index is 50, but it varies according to races from 42.33 to 58.38.

While the nose is an important and prominent organ and is, in a certain measure, an index to individual character, it furnishes nothing of any value as an aid to racial division.

VI.—The Ears.

Ears, like noses, vary to infinitude in individuals, but not in races; and *all attempts to deduce racial characteristics from the formation of the ear have proved unavailing.*

A conclusion forces itself on us when we compare the results obtained by the measurements of all parts of the head. It is that the skull, which is subject to variations, leaves an impression during its evolution on the face which is only its complement. Consequently, inasmuch as we no longer see about us any races which are clearly defined from a craniological point of view, it is impossible that there can be any such races from the point of view of the other measurements taken from the component parts of the head. *The differences among individuals belonging to the same human variety are thus always greater than those perceived among races regarded as distinct units in themselves.*

VII.—The Body.

The study of *bodily characteristics* for distinctively racial features has been equally fruitless. The height of the body, the weight of the body, the length of the limbs, the structure of the feet, the color of the skin, the color and texture of the hair; the development of the muscular system, the deposits of fat; the size, shape, and consistency of the breasts; the color and shape, position and size of the genitalia; the composition of the blood, and the histological structure of the skin have all been scanned in vain for some definitely racial organ or quality. *Anatomy discloses no distinctively human structure that is not common to the species wherever found, neither does it discover a single structural characteristic peculiar to any one human variety.*

VIII.—Function.

Physiology is equally against the advocates of inherent inequality.

"*The physiology of man is the same in the case of all his representatives;* he who would speak of a special physiology of yellow men, or black men, would run the risk of making himself ridiculous. Far from seeking distinctions of all sorts under this heading, we find completest harmony of all physiological functions among all the representatives of humanity, whatever their race or color. Their functions of breathing and digesting, the period of gestation and of growth through successive phases of age, in one word, the evolution of their physiological life between the two most solemn moments of their terrestrial existence, birth and death, undergo the same laws." (Finot.)

The functions of nutrition and assimilation, the temperature of the body, the capacity of the lungs and the respiratory function, the circulation of the blood, muscular force, gestures serving to express emotions, the attitude of the body, the acuteness of the special senses, the functions of reproduction, the climacteric or change of life, and the fertility of women have been examined for distinctively racial characteristics, but to no purpose.

All attempts at dividing humanity according to faculty of speech, singing, good sight, good hearing or good smelling have completely failed. All kinds of varieties are found in all races.

All men are equal physiologically at their birth, and never cease to be so till they die. Death appears everywhere under the same conditions. The mean duration of human life varies, particularly owing to climate, comfort and hygiene, and not because of racial differences. It is our way of living, not our way of being born, which lengthens or shortens life. Longevity is sometimes hereditary, but the same phenomenon is found both among civilized and uncivilized. Health stored up by the parents often profits the children, but it is a capital which is not very secure, and one which a second generation may tamper with and squander.

There is *no such thing as racial immunity or susceptibility to disease. Immunity and susceptibility are both products of environment that affect humanity individually and not racially.* Health and disease, like birth and death, are endured individually.

IX.—Art.

Art, as well as science and religion, has its apostles of inequality.

The measurements of artists have preceded those of anthropologists by many centuries. Under their influence came the conception of artistic beauty, which has not failed to leave its traces on anthropological canons.

"The study of man as well as the comparisons of human beings having been established and directed by white men, it follows that all the traits observed in and among Whites are thereby idealized and regarded as essentially superior. *The idea of beauty being essentially subjective, there is nothing astonishing in the fact that everywhere and always, whenever Whites have been engaged in its definition, they have borrowed its essentials from their immediate surroundings. Starting from this basis, they have declared all human types beautiful or ugly which approximate or diverge from formulas established by white artists and authors, from white exemplars."* (Finot.)

We are born with certain sentiments of plastic beauty, engendered by tradition and the opinions of those who surround us. The sheepish nature of man rarely revolts against admitted ideas which often equal in force innate ideas. We find beautiful everything which those who are before us find beautiful. This applies to women, pictures, and masterpieces of sculpture. Which of us has not admired the plastic beauty of Laocoon?[12] Yet his right leg is much shorter than the left, whereas, obviously to keep him company, one of his children has, on the contrary, a "more pronounced" right leg.

---

[12] A famous Greek statue in the Vatican, Rome, showing the priest of Apollo and his two sons.

G. Audran[13] makes this curious remark, that in the most beautiful figures of antiquity details are found which would be readily regarded as faults if found in the work of a modern. Apollo, for example, has the left leg too long by about nine lines: the Venus of Medici has the "curved leg longer by about three lines than that on which she stands," etc.

It would be intensely interesting to study the various canons of beauty of different ages, races[14] and individuals. For Ch. Blanc the length of the body equals 30 noses or 7½ heads. For Gerdy, 32 noses and 8 heads. Here is Blanc's canon:—

Height			100.0
Head	The crown to the hair's limit, ¼ head	3.3	13.2
	Hair to root of nose	3.3	
	Root of nose to its base	3.3	
	Base of nose to below chin	3.3	
Neck		6.6	
Trunk		30.0	
Lower limbs		50.0	
		——	99.8

But nature, which takes no account of our canons of beauty, nearly always diverges from them. Not willing to regard as false our particular conceptions as to the proportions of the different parts of the body, we declare those which diverge from them to be ugly or inferior.

The Negroes, whom it is desired to place at the bottom of the human scale, are in many respects much more removed from monkeys than the purest whites.

It is enough to confront human beings in their many aspects to perceive that nature does not recog-

[13] "Les Proportions du Corps humain," Paris, 1693.

[14] One of the interesting phases of race evolution in America is the developing by the colored people of independent canons of beauty. The cover pictures of *The Crisis* magazine and the beauty contests of the *New York Age* are illustrations.

nize superior and inferior races. *This gradation, which means nothing physiologically, is equally inadmissible esthetically.*

The fable which is current on the subject of the tail attributed to savage or primitive peoples can be turned against the whites themselves. This anomaly, due to troubles in embryonic evolution, is, according to Bartels' studies, especially frequent among the whites; not that these are themselves "inferior," but simply because of the special care given to the deformed, who among primitive peoples perish so easily, left as they are to their own resources.

Negroes who from all time have enjoyed the sorry privilege of passing as the race nearest the monkeys have had the advantage, among other things, of a defect with which certain anthropologists lightly reproach them. For, as Burmeister and so many others tell us, not only have they very long arms, but these even exceed the length of their lower limbs.[15] It will be understood that under these conditions they would only have to use their hands to walk like monkeys. Place their front limbs at right angles on the ground

---

[15] The official measurements of Jack Johnson (black) and of Jess Willard (white) heavy-weight pugilists, as published in Associated Press dispatches, are instructive.

"Physicians tonight took the measurements of the pugilists; this is how they stand:—

JOHNSON.		WILLARD.
6 feet ½ inch	Height	6 feet 6 inches.
225 pounds	Weight	243 pounds.
73½ inches	Reach	83¼ inches.
40 inches	Chest normal	39 inches.
43½ inches	Chest expanded	44½ inches.
38 inches	Waist	37 inches.
15 inches	Biceps normal	14 inches.
17⅜ inches	Biceps flexed	15½ inches.
17 inches	Neck	17¼ inches.
6⅞ inches	Wrist	8¼ inches.
25 inches	Thigh	25½ inches.
15½ inches	Calf	17½ inches.
9 inches	Ankle	9½ inches.
No. 11	Size shoe	No. 10.
38	Age	28."

with fingers stretched out, and behold, animals with four feet! But this mirage of Negro-monkeys has vanished since impartial comparisons have been started. Let us remember, first of all, that *the length of the arms surpassing that of the legs among Negroes is a pure myth,* and, what is more important, that the differences between the races measured in this respect never exceed 8.9 per cent., whereas they attain 13.8 among representatives of different professions in the same country. And if one persists absolutely in making this trait a mark of monkey ugliness, we must acknowledge, what Ranke confirms, namely, that the French and Germans are in this matter nearer the monkeys than the Negroes, Australians, or Bushmen. The English and French are on the same level as Negroes, whereas much below Negroes and other primitive peoples must be counted the Chinese.

In general, as we study human beings in the matter of regularity and harmony of features, we perceive the great influence exercised by their daily occupations. Gould, in comparing bodily proportions among divers representatives of the American people, states that *there are greater differences between sailors, agriculturists, and men of culture than between Negroes, Redskins, and Whites.*

Among civilized peoples the intellectual classes, quite apart from the color of skin, are distinguished by a relatively longer trunk, shorter extremities, and more voluminous head.

According to our ideas of beauty, what contributed to enhance our esthetic value is the difference of the diameters of chest, hips, and waist. Now, in this respect numerous Negro tribes surpass the English themselves.

Racial inequality reaches the climax of absurdity in the mutual recriminations about personal odor, each race declaring the other smells bad; the Japanese find the whites as offensive as the whites find the blacks. Finot shrewdly observes: "Americans no longer complain of odor among certain Negroes, not because they have lost the capacity of smelling it, but merely because the Negroes who surround them have entirely lost it. They no doubt exhale another odor like that of their neighbors, for which reason these last are no longer affected by it."

Diet, cleanliness, and environment control the personal odor of individuals in all races.

X.—Color and Environment.

Man is a creature of environment, or, as the French call it, *milieu.* All of the features which we call the physical criteria of a race are the result of this force.

According to Virchow, the *milieu* wherein a person lives makes him brown or fair. Prüner[16] has shown that Europeans dwelling in Egypt become darker at the end of a certain time; in Abyssinia they develop a bronze tint; in the highlands of Syria a reddish tint, etc. As a boy I noticed the dark complexion of British soldiers after long service in India. According to Sir Harry Johnston, the American Negro is developing a lighter color. ("Negro in New World," p. 462.)

Waitz[17] claims the color of the skin is especially due to heat, nourishment, atmospheric humidity, the abundance or scarcity of forests, and also geographical latitude. The Negroes of Bongo have skins nearly red from the color of the soil of their country, which is

[16] *Die Krankheiten des Orients.*
[17] *Anthropologie der Naturvölker.*

impregnated with iron ore. And Livingstone says the humid heat deepens the coloration of the Negro populations of Africa, and Simpson[18] affirms the same as to the Jews, whose complexions vary from the white of Caucasians to the black of Negroes.

We are developing two distinct race types in America. There is a white type[19] tinctured with black blood and a black type inoculated with white blood; though the direct mixing is now practically at an end.

The American white man today is not a European and the American black man is not an African. New conditions have made a new race. *The mixing has been done.*

Todd[20] tells us that the true Yankee is to be distinguished from the Englishman by the pointed and angular cut of his face. He approaches the aborigines of America, and is also marked by this characteristic trait that the lower part of his face is almost square, as opposed to the oval form of the Englishman. Knox has noticed among the Yankees the diminution of the adipose tissue and the glandular apparatus, while Desor mentions a lengthening of the neck.

Prüner-Bey states that the Anglo-American shows from the second generation characteristics of the Indian type, which bring him nearer to the Lenni-Lenapes, Iroquois, and Cherokees. Later on the glandular system is reduced to the minimum of its normal development. The skin becomes dry like leather, losing its glow of complexion and redness of cheek, which are replaced by a muddy tint and among women by an insipid pallor. The head becomes smaller or rounded and pointed, being covered with hair,

---

[18] "Narrative of a Journey Around the World."
[19] A. Murray, "The Geographical Distribution of Mammals."
[20] "Cycl. of Anat. and Physiol.," iv.

smooth and dark in color. The neck lengthens. There is observed a large development of the zygomatic bones. The eyes sink deeply into the sockets and are somewhat close to each other. The iris is dark. The bones become particularly elongated at their upper extremity, so much so that France and England manufacture a peculiar kind of glove for North America, the fingers of which are exceptionally long.

The pelvis of the woman becomes like that of the man.[21] And while Jarrold recognizes this influence of *milieu* even in their unmelodious voices,[22] Kriegk[23] dwells on their thinness and pallor and also on their precocious development physically and intellectually.

This is the result of what may be called natural environment, but man in a measure creates his own environment. This in turn reacts upon those subject to it.

The moral causes, such as liberty which people enjoy, the consideration of which they are assured, and the wholesome sentiment of equality before the law and the respect of human dignity, the instruction which is given them, the national system of taxation which contributes to their comfort, the facility of internal and external communications, the way in which the State exercises its privileges and monopolies, jus-

---

[21] It is interesting to note that according to the disciples of racial inferiority this is one of the anatomical peculiarities of a low race. Here is a list of anatomical traits "more or less Simioid" as indefinite as false:—

"1. Cranial sutures simple and uniting early.
2. Nasal aperture wide, with nasal bones ankylosed.
3. Jaws unduly projecting and chin receding.
4. Wisdom teeth well developed, appearing early and permanent.
5. Humerus unduly long and perforated.
6. Calcaneum (heel-bone) elongated.
7. Tibia flattened.
8. Pelvis narrow." (Shute, D. K., "Racial Anatomical Peculiarities," American Anthro., vol. ix.) (1896.)

[22] "Anthropology, or On the Form and Colour of Man."

[23] Lüddes, *Zeit. für Erdkunde,* i, 484.

tice which respects all the legitimate aspirations of citizens, and as many other conditions of a healthy development of a country, have all likewise their counter-effect on the physiological formation of human beings.

Here are certain striking examples:—

Norton[24] assures us that in the country studied by him the Negro children born in liberty have more beautiful eyes, a more elegant appearance, and an easier bearing like that of Europeans, than in the countries where they are ill-treated. The same remark has been made by Lewis and d'Orbigny. Day[25] improves on this fact, and states that Negroes who hold higher situations are distinguished by their features,[26] which resemble those of the Caucasian races, and are not unlike those of very dark Jews.

Lyell, in his account of his second voyage to the United States, tells us that Negroes who have had continual relations for a long time with Europeans become like these physically, and he insists on the fact that even their encephalon (brain) undergoes similar changes.

This same idea is advanced from another angle by Prof. J. H. DeLoach, of the University of Georgia. He says: "It is interesting to learn that in the counties generally, though not always, where the majority of landowners are Negroes the farm crop yields per acre are greater than in the counties where the majority of landowners are white. Where the Negroes are mostly tenants, the crop yields are not so high as where they own their own land."

Stanhope Smith[27] maintains that Negro slave-

---

24 "A Residence at Sierra Leone."

25 "On the Causes of the Variety of Complexion and Figure."

26 A group of the post-bellum United States Senators and Congressmen illustrate strikingly the truth of this assertion.

27 "Five Years' Residence in the West Indies."

merchants are distinguishable from the other Negroes in a striking way. Whereas those sold continue to keep all their characteristic traits, the vendors lose, after the second and third generations, their woolly kind of hair, and the characteristic Negro smell. "With the change in their material and moral situation, Negroes have altered considerably during the last two centuries" (Stephen Ward).[28] There is no doubt in my mind but that the color and features of the unmixed Afro-American are changing.

Dr. Warren[29] states the fact that the skulls of Negroes of past times found in New York have a cerebral capacity much less than those of modern Negroes.

XI.—Effects of Crossing.

A favorite proposition of the advocates of inequality is that the crossing of races produces degeneration. *They ignore the fact that all races are now crossed.*

Many years ago Quatrefages[30] said: "Well, we estimate that already one-seventieth of the total population of the globe are mixtures, resulting from the cross of the whites with indigenous peoples."

"Who will ever estimate the quantity of blood of all origins which flows in the veins of a white, yellow, or black man." (Finot.) An inconsistent negrophobe recently said: "Of the ten millions of Negroes in the United States more than half are hybrids."[31]

The Ethiopians, who have so largely influenced the

---

28 "The Natural History of Mankind."
29 *Quarterly Review,* June, 1851.
30 Quatrefages died in 1892.
31 "America's Greatest Problem: The Negro," page 64.

Childhood in colored America. (Courtesy of "The Crisis.")

formation of Negro races, are merely half-breeds of Negroes and Hamites. Their reaction on the ethnical composition of the whites is indisputable, which fact opens out new horizons for savants who will one day wish to explore the many links of relationship uniting the Negroes with European peoples, and, through these white intermediaries, with all humanity.

In the present state of science the place of honor assigned to pure races could only be claimed by certain savage or primitive peoples whose history is buried in oblivion.

Fertility is held a test of species.

"Fecundation is *abortive* when the fetus is born before its time; *agenesic*[32] when fecundation is relative in the sense that the progeny remain sterile among themselves or with individuals of one or the other of the parent races; *dysgenesic* when the hybrids, although mutually sterile, are fecund when crossed with an individual of one or the other of the parent races; *paragenesic* when the results are fecund among themselves, but only for two or three generations; and *eugenesic* when the progeny are normally fertile." (Finot.)

So far as human knowledge and experience go, all human varieties are perfectly fertile in crossing with each other,—eugenesic. The renewing of blood nearly always gives good results. "Wherever crossing is done under normal conditions, inferior types become better without causing any degeneration." (Waitz, Havelock Ellis, Doubleday, Benoiton de Chateauneuf.) This accounts for the present superiority of Americans —black and white—compared with those of the same blood in other countries.

---

[32] The last part of these words comes from a Greek word meaning origin, source, beginning, nativity, generation, production, creation; also the act of begetting, originating, or creating; generation, procreation, production, formation, creation. The prefixes mean, respectively: a, without; para, besides; dys, hard, difficult, bad, ill; eu, well, easily.

The more we study the transformation of man down the ages, the more we perceive that the *milieu* has changed the surface of his biological organization without ever succeeding in changing its essential character. Man always remains man. His thoughts, habits, and features vary, but only within certain limits.

Man evolved like all organized beings, but his evolution takes an ideal and mental form rather than a concrete and physiological one. If he varies, these modifications bear in particular on his intellectual faculties, and on the vast domain of their conquests, that is to say, his social, moral, and intellectual life. The gulf which separates human beings is particularly deep on the intellectual and moral side. The general laws of anatomy, physiology, and environment are as applicable to man as to all other living beings on earth; yet the intellectual, moral, and spiritual powers of man give him a latitude of action entirely beyond the animal world. *The laws of mind are superior to the laws of matter, and man's psychic life is superior to his physical life.* In considering human welfare these higher laws must be reckoned with. Psychology is more important to man than physiology, yet physiology is as indispensable as psychology. No one would maintain that a man's legs were as important as his brain. The legs are, however, just as indispensable to a man as the brain if he is going to walk. Man is both psychical and physical. Any philosophy of life ignoring either element will of necessity fail.

"The evolution of man has never resulted in irremediable or insuperable deviations in the matter of brain. *In reviewing all the craniological scales and in studying all the foundations whereon is based the division of humanity, nowhere have we met with an organic condemnation of any race whatever on the ground of its intellectual faculties.* Man, however backward he may be found in the matter of his intellectual development, never loses the right of aspiring to elevate himself above his surroundings. *Twenty years of intellectual work has often proved sufficient for a representative of the Maori, Zulu, Redskin, or Negro races to win back in his individual self the centuries of mental arrest or mental sleep experienced by his congeners. This property common to all human beings provides them at once with a trait of ineffaceable equality.* One might speak of these faculties as the common foundations whereon the circumstances of physiological and psychical life construct all kinds of buildings." (Finot.)

These higher spiritual and moral interests of both races condemn political and economic discrimination against the Negro in the United States.

All the condemnations of peoples and races in virtue of an innate superiority or inferiority have in reality failed. Life has taught us to be more careful and circumspect in our judgments. A savant who presumes to pronounce a verdict of eternal barbarism against any people deserves to be laughed at. *The Afro-American is just as capable of playing an honorable part in the future development of this country as the Euro-American.*

Civilization, indeed, has had some singular experiences during a century. Let us remember, for example, that in the time of the encyclopedists, savants like d'Alembert and even Diderot refused to concede to the Russians the possibility of becoming civilized after the European manner.

The American Negro, against whom has been directed all the forces of racial inequality, has "stolen the keys of destiny and made the prophets lie." John C. Calhoun predicted that "if the slaves were set free they would become a race of beggars unable to provide themselves with food, clothes, or shelter." These slaves have, nevertheless, not only mastered American civilization, but become a part of it. Though coming late into the vineyard of civilization, the extra vigor of his services has earned for the American black man a full day's pay. From the time of Julius Cæsar and Tacitus until Charlemagne—that is, eight centuries—Germany realized less progress than the American Negroes have done since 1860. This only shows the basic unity and innate equality of capability of mankind. The difference in pace was the result of difference of opportunity and environment.

The history of civilization is only a continual come and go of peoples and races! All, without distinction of their biological characteristics, are summoned to this great struggle for life, wherein we fight for human progress and happiness. All the ethnical elements can take part in it; all can contend for places of honor in it. Such is the general import of our biological and psychological equality, which remains intact underneath all our superficial divisions.

"*In the present state of science it has become impossible for us to distinguish the ethnical origins of peoples.* The constituent elements are so much intermingled that the most ardent partisans of inequality must admit the relationship of all the races. The 'purity of blood' which we create at will, and which we find in the animal world, becomes impossible in the human *milieu. The Negroes are related to the whites, who are linked to the yellows, as these last have common links both with Negroes and whites. On the road which separates them we only meet with links which unite them.*" (Finot.)

XII.—Race Psychology.

The last stand of the prophets of inequality has been in race psychology, which has proved a sandy foundation; for, here as everywhere else, *the variations within the different races are greater than any variations among the separate races.*

In every walk of life some Negro has made good. The unmarked credits of the American Negro would fill a large volume. The ignorance of prejudice is as astonishing as its meanness is persistent.[33] The very ones that deny Negro capability seek to bar Negro progress. I must withhold the names of many Negroes who hold positions of honor and trust to protect them from the persecutions of the people who declare the Negroes incapable of such attainment. The ignorance that says "the Negro can't" is backed by the meanness that determines he sha'n't. The amount of evidence in support of this proposition is simply astounding, but to submit it would defeat the ends for which this book was written—the promotion of justice.

The true scientific position in reference to the permanent inequality of races is correctly stated by Finot. After a searching and impartial analysis of the evidence, he thus concludes: "Some time will no doubt elapse before science, emancipated from the prejudices which have prevailed and multiplied for centuries, will succeed in making the truth triumph. All these measurements, with their imposing numbers, as also the theoretic observations and deductions, resolve themselves into a nebulous doctrine which affirms many things and explains nothing.

"The exact instruments which anthropologists and

---

[33] See Appendix F.

especially craniometrists use offer us fantastical data. The results of their operations are deposited in thousands of volumes; and yet what is their real bearing? In examining them closely one can hardly attribute to them even a descriptive value, so much do they contradict and destroy each other.

"We have seen, for example, how precarious are the affirmations of craniometry, which constitutes, however, the most developed section of anthropometry. Although the instruments which it places at the disposal of savants are very numerous, yet the ways of using them are still more varied. The lack of unity in the observations and the contradictory ends which those who use them seem to pursue, cause numerous misunderstandings, which end in chaotic affirmations. In bringing forward the most indisputable data and in proceeding to a kind of cross-examination, we arrive at a conclusion quite different from that which the adherents of the dogmas of races are anxious to impose upon us, and which so many learned demographs, politicians, novelists, and statesmen blindly accept.

"*When we go through the list of external differences which appear to divide man, we find literally nothing which can authorize their division into superior and inferior beings, into masters and pariahs.* If this division exists in our thought, it only came there as the result of inexact observations and false opinions drawn from them.

"*The science of inequality is emphatically a science of white people.* It is they who have invented it and set it agoing, who have maintained, cherished, and propagated it, thanks to *their* observations and *their* deductions. Deeming themselves greater than men of other colors, they have elevated into superior qualities all the traits which are peculiar to themselves, commencing with the whiteness of the skin and the pliancy of the hair. But nothing proves that these vaunted traits are traits of real superiority."

Quatrefages expresses a similar opinion: "If the Chinese and the Egyptians had judged our ancestors as we too often judge foreign races, they would have found in them many traits of inferiority such as this white skin in which we take so much pride, and which they would have regarded as showing an irremediable etiolation."[34]

Science builds no impassible walls between men with wide and narrow skulls, yellows and whites, tall and short men, those with thick and thin joints, those with small and large nostrils, those with straight and curved foreheads. But life passes above all these artificial partitions, and marches on their ruins toward unity.

"In Nature's infinite book of secrecy
A little I can read" . . .
"The waters pass—
Currents will have their way;
Nature is nobody's ally; 'tis well."

NOTE.—To those who may wish further evidence on this interesting subject I commend "Race Prejudice," by Jean Finot, whose elegant language and accurate data I have so frequently quoted.

---

[34] An unhealthy whitening of the skin.

"From a general survey of the various schemes, it appears that special, if not paramount, importance is given by these systematists to the three elements of complexion, character of the hair, and shape of the skull. And, in general, physical features are relied on, not merely in preference to, but to the total exclusion of, mental qualities. Yet in determining the relative position of ethnic groups these cannot be overlooked."—KEANE, 171.

"Negro blood, instead of standing at the bottom of the list, is entitled, if judged either by its great men or its masses, either by its courage, its purpose, or its endurance, to a place as near ours as any other blood known in history."—PHILLIPS.

A social club of self-supporting young women (teachers, stenographers, bookkeepers) who have made good. This picture is eight years old. One of the group is dead, eleven are married and four are successful "bachelor maids." While the club is still intact, the original membership here presented is scattered from New England to Panama and from Georgia to Colorado.

CHAPTER XIV.

THE AMERICAN ENVIRONMENT.

"The European and Negro races have the aptitude of acclimatization in all countries." (Deniker.)

The scientific data submitted in the preceding chapter and other parts of this work establish by incontrovertible evidence the Negro's innate capability to meet the conditions of a favorable environment. America is such an environment. It is proper, then, to submit some further evidence that the Negro is manifesting his capabilities by responding to this environment.

I.—Personal Appearance.

From nothing has the American Negro suffered more than from misrepresentation;[1] and no phase of misrepresentation has been more persistently malicious and willfully erroneous than that of the Negro's looks. The exceptional, the abnormal, the ugly, are continually exploited; while the average, the normal, and the beautiful are as continually suppressed or distorted.

The superficial or untrained mind dwells on resemblances rather than differences. After a certain distorted caricature of the accepted European standard of human features has been impressed upon the public

---

[1] "There are tens of thousands of intelligent people who today unwittingly exaggerate the demands made by and in behalf of the Negro into a vast and shapeless terror. Neither he, his advocates, nor his opponents have generally realized how widely his claims have been, sometimes by and sometimes without intention, misconstrued. He needs still to make innumerable reiterations of facts that seem to him too plain for repetition." (G. W. Cable, "The Negro Question," page 78.) The importance of these words of Mr. Cable justifies their repetition here. (See page 302.)

23

mind as the "typical Negro," it is easy to identify with such caricature every person called Negro.

How the public mind may be wrongly impressed by this misrepresentation is well illustrated by an incident in a Western State. A religious convention was to be held. After all preparation had been made for accommodating the visitors, it developed that one of the delegations contained a Negro. Consternation pervaded the ranks of the committee on homes. There was much discussion until the tension was relieved by a liberal-minded citizen accepting the responsibility of housing the brother in black.

Assuming so grave a duty was, of course, a matter for local distinction. For days talk about the coming event occupied the attention of the household. In fact, the event set the town agog. When the day came 5-year-old Willie objected very seriously to going to bed before the early evening train arrived with the guest. Being assured, however, that he could see the stranger in the morning he finally retired. Arising early the next morning, Willie, unbeknown to the other members of the household, approached the guest-chamber. Stealthily opening the door, he cautiously peeped in, when to his utter astonishment a cheery "Good morning" came from the guest, who was already up and dressed. Thus reassured, the child boldly opened the door and, after a careful survey of the visitor, precipitately retreated. Reaching his mother's room, he said, disappointedly, "Why mamma, *that* is a *man* in the guest-chamber!" That child announced a truth that the American people as a whole have yet to learn. *The Negro is a man;* no more, no less.

To the child's mind there was no more trouble in the situation after that discovery. If he was a man like the rest, why not treat him the same way? This logic is unanswerable.

Does the American Negro look like a man according to the accepted standards? What does the American Negro look like? Let us waive all questions of ancestry, heredity, and previous condition, and answer this question from present data. What does the American Negro look like?

Three conditions or phases of the race question make this point important:—

1. The determining influence in the nation's final decision on the race question must come from people not in position to obtain the facts directly.

2. Anti-Negro agitators are noisy and persistent. The avatars of hate are more active than the apostles of love. Self-interest is more industrious than altruism, and a lie is swifter of movement than the truth.

3. The first colored people to get into purely white sections are apt to be unfavorable representatives of the race: contract-laborers (strike-breakers), domestic servants, fugitives from justice (or oftener from injustice), or wanderers, vagabonds, or tramps. These may be "typical," but they are not characteristic, and it is unfortunate for the race if an intelligent neutral mind receives its first impression of colored Americans from these classes.

Flower and Lydekker ("Mammals Living and Extinct," p. 744) wisely observe: "A large proportion of mankind is made up, not of extreme or typical, but more or less of generalized or intermediate forms." Keane ("Ethnology," p. 12) quotes this approvingly and admits "there is no perfect embodiment of the Caucasic or of the Mongolic type." Implying, of course, that there is such a "perfect embodiment" of the Negro type.

Hasty generalization is the fruitful source of prejudice and injustice. *The average colored Ameri-*

can does not look like the textbook pictures of the "typical Negro."

Well do I remember my first geography with its vivid pictures of the "Five Races of Mankind." Caucasian (white), Mongolian (yellow), American (red), Malay (brown), Ethiopian (black). Europe was the home of the white race; Asia was the home of the yellow race; Africa was the home of the black race; America was the home of the red race; while the brown race inhabited the extreme southern part of Asia and the main islands of the Pacific Ocean.

There was a definiteness about this knowledge that left no doubts in our young minds. The pictures did not, however, exactly harmonize with our personal experience. The Caucasian was illustrated by a very good picture of a conventional family group (father, mother, and child) of white people dressed in the prevailing style. Such a sight could be duplicated at any time and was perfectly familiar to us. The Mongolian was a conventional Chinaman that looked like the laundryman "dressed in his best Sunday clothes." This gave no trouble. The American was drawn as we had seen the Indians many times,—buckskin tights and moccasins, face paint, head feathers, bow and arrows, etc. The Malayan (brown), though somewhat scanty of clothing, duplicated with more or less faithfulness "a wild man from Borneo" seen at a circus. But the Ethiopian (black), "also called Negro," was a poser. None of us had ever seen anybody like him. Entirely nude except for a loin-girdle of grasses, his gaunt figure supported by calfless legs, presented a weird appearance. Heels projecting backward and toes spread out, his feet seemed disproportionately large. His lengthy but slender arms terminated in claw-like fingers, the right group of which clutched a long spear, while the left one held a shield. His ample flat nose had a large ring through its exposed septum and his large and rolling lips showed plainly their mucous lining.

As the members of this class with few exceptions had never seen a Negro, this picture was accepted as true. Two questions we could not solve; and, after several days' discussion on playground, at home, and by the wayside, the teacher was appealed to.

First, Did not the yellow man and the brown man and the black man have a wife and baby like the white man (we knew about Indians)? When the teacher answered yes, we wanted to know why they did not put them all in the picture? She answered frankly that she did not know.

We hesitated about the second question and would have retired without asking it had not the good-natured teacher tactfully removed our embarrassment, an act she would not have performed had she had any idea of the question. A bright little Irish boy was spokesman, "What is Charley Roman?" "Charley is a mixed blood," said the teacher, with some embarrassment. "What is a mixed blood?" countered Joe. "That is a question for you to answer when you are grown up men," said the teacher, as she cautiously dismissed us to the playground.

We retired more puzzled than we entered. Why didn't they put all the mammas and babies in the picture? What is a mixed blood?

Though these questions antedate by several years the "*why*" puzzle described in the opening chapter of this book, I confess that I have not yet found a satisfactory answer to them. For many years I have understood man's domination of the animal world; but his persistent misrepresentation and persecution of his brother man is still a puzzle to me.

I have never seen any of those boys since the close

of that school year. Doubtless many of them still reside in that quiet and beautiful, but sequestered district, and still retain that geographical picture as the typical Negro.

What does the American Negro look like?

Keane truly says: "Type stands apart from all other terms in ethnological nomenclature. It is not a race, a tribe, or a family, or any concrete division whatsoever; but is rather in the nature of an abstraction, a model or pattern to which all possible divisions are referable. Originally meaning a mould or matrix, or rather a casting from a mould, it is taken as a summary of all the characters assumed to be proper to a given class or group. Thus type becomes the standard by which we measure the relative position of individuals in a group."

One of the meanest phases of the race question in this country is the urgent effort to make the colored American fit this caricature of a "typical Negro." Even Mr. Keane, high priest of racial inequality though he be, when discussing a general proposition where the Negro is not specifically involved admits:—

"In practice no individual exists, or ever did exist, who is entirely conformable to any given standard. *Hence type necessarily resolves itself into a question of averages; individuals possessing most of the characters peculiar to a group are said to be typical members of that group, and even this only in a relative sense.* They approximate nearer than other members to the ideal, but none absolutely reach it."

Thus while there are orthognathic individuals, there are no orthognathic races. It is the purest egotism to claim the *average* Caucasian in this country is orthognathic; and while there are extremely prognathic Negroes, it is mere prejudice to claim that the *average* colored American is extremely prognathic.

A recent anti-Negro writer, speaking of the colored man, says, boastingly: "The jaws exhibit decided prognathism or projecting forward, the facial angle being seventy degrees against the eighty-two of the average white man."[2]

When we remember that ninety degrees is the standard of orthognathism we can see how fatuous is this boast; eight degrees behind his own standard and bragging about being twelve degrees ahead of the black man! Even this is not true; for as Deniker says[3] prognathism "presents too many individual varieties to be taken as a distinctive character of race."

Many full-blood Negroes are orthognathic.

The widespread belief that colored Americans are black and (as some people reason, *therefore*) ugly, arises from the wellnigh universal tendency to dislike, disparage, or repudiate that which is strange or different; and the other almost equally universal tendency to accept without question or investigation the judgments and opinions, assertions, and prejudices of others. This charge of ugliness contains two fundamental errors, viz., that colored Americans are black and that black is necessarily ugly. *The average colored American is not black* and *black does not necessarily imply ugliness.* The prettiest dog I ever saw was black and the most beautiful horse I ever owned was coal black; and, finally, the most accurately proportioned human form I ever examined was a 17-year-old black girl. The symmetry of her body was perfect. She met every item of the Caucasian canon of beauty except color and hair. Both of these were very beautiful, but not according to European canons.

The truth of the whole matter is this: humanity conceded, *personal appearance depends upon physical*

---

[2] Shufeldt, "America's Greatest Problem: The Negro," page 28.

[3] Deniker, "Races of Man," page 65.

environment, intellectual habit, moral customs, and such other human associations as are involved in politics, economics, etc. When these conditions are similar or identical, and so continue, human beings, however diverse their antecedents and heredity, will grow to look alike in personal appearance. *The colored man is reacting to the American environment and in personal appearance is becoming a normal dweller in a temperate climate.*

Of the mixed bloods, Finot says: "Their resemblance to the whites in the United States baffles every artifice resorted to in order to recognize them."

Of the full-bloods Sir Harry Johnston[4] says: "The best types of Negro in bodily structure are almost as beautiful as the best types of European with (at present) the striking exception of the face. Morally, the Negro is nearly on an equality with the white race, and perhaps slightly superior to the yellow." (See also Chapter VIII.)

This brings us to the first clear truth in opposition to assertion and prejudice, that greets the honest investigator in this field. *The colored people in America do not all look alike.* Individual variation is great[5]—greater than in white people. This is true as to both facial form and bodily stature; and as to color, the words of the witty minstrel are strikingly descriptive: "We runs from ebo to city cream."

Dr. Robt. Bennett Bean, a devoted worshipper at the shrine of racial inequality, admits "the American Negro may be divided into two groups, each with subdivisions."[6]

"The first group includes the Guinea Coast Negro

---

[4] Sir Harry Johnston, "Negro in the New World."

[5] See Chapter III.

[6] "Racial Peculiarities of Negro Brain," *American Jour. Anat.*, vol. iv, No. 4.

"Friends"—Meharry Medical College (1915).

and maybe the few Hottentots in America, and is divided into three classes. First the Hottentot, or Bosjesman, having gray or old yellow skin resembling dirty varnished oak; low, dwarfed stature, either weak or squat and muscular; long, woolly hair, in small obliquely inserted tufts; very dark eyes, wide apart; extraordinarily broad, flat nose; large mouth, with thick, projecting, turned-out lips; enormous prognathism; heads extremely *dolichocephalic;* the smallest brains (weighing 900-1000 grams) of any human beings probably; and lastly, having the distinctive *steatopyga* and the *tablier* which are not always present. Secondly, the low-class Guinea Coast Negro, most ancient and most classical Negro type, having a cool, velvety skin, glassy, and varying from reddish, yellowish, or bluish black to jet black; low stature, well knit and muscular; black hair and eyes; platyrrhine nose; thick lips; prognathous face; beautifully white, sound teeth; small, square ears (Hrdlicka); long upper and short lower extremities; flat feet; heads dolichocephalic, or even approaching sub-brachycephaly; and brains weighing from 1000 to 1200 grams, possibly more. Thirdly, the high-class Guinea Negro, similar to the low class, but developed along broader lines, and instead of being ugly, diminutive, with large or squat limbs, and a round or short face, they are comparatively handsome, taller, with well-proportioned limbs and a long face.

"*The second group* is made up of Kaffirs and other Mulattoes, and Mulattoids, or Mulatto-like individuals. The Kaffirs are represented by the Zulus in Virginia and North Carolina, being particularly noted for their height and intelligence. They have various shades of dark-brown skin; very high stature, slim and well made; thick, woolly hair, and dark-brown eyes; broad, flat nose, sometimes highly arched, Romanesque, or

Arablike; thick lips; long, oval face; slight prognathism and platyrrhiny; long, high heads, with narrow foreheads, and median frontal protuberances; and large brains, weighing from 1300 to 1500 grams.

"The mulattoes are such a heterogeneous conglomeration as to beggar description.

"There are all sorts of mixtures of all the classes mentioned above, forming a not inconsiderable part of the Negro population. There may be a few other types of Negroes here and there, such as the Ethiopians, Papuans, Nigritos, and perhaps Australians, and occasionally one sees a red Negro, probably a Foulah from the heart of Africa in the region of the Soudan, or a Dahomian from near there, but these are so rare as to be inconsiderable. A few mixed bloods with Indian characteristics are occasionally observed."

Truly a variagated multitude. I have quoted at length Dr. Bean's unfair description for the sake of emphasizing the extent of individual variation in American Negroes. With this amount of variation *every dictate of justice and common sense demands individual treatment.*

"Outside the question of what the pure Negro type is, the Negro American represents a very wide and thorough blending of nearly all African people from north to south; and more than that, it is, to a far larger extent than many realize, a blending of European and African blood." This is a perfectly natural condition when we remember that "The slaves thus procured came from all parts of Africa—the Soudan, Central and South Africa. Distinct traces of Arab and even Malay blood could be seen side-by-side with the tall Bantu, the yellow Hottentot, and the African dwarfs."

The scholarly Burkhardt DuBois has differentiated the following American Negro types:—

A. *Negro types.*
B. *Mulatto types.*
C. *Quadroon types.*
D. *White types with Negro blood.*

He has subdivided these types as follows:—

A. 1. Full-blooded Negroes.
2. Brown Negroes, full-blooded or with less than one-fourth of white blood.

B. 1. Blended types.
2. Negro-colored.
3. Negro-haired.
4. Negro-featured.

C. 1. The chromatic series.
2. Blended types.

D. Latin.
Celtic.
English.
German, etc.

These types are described in detail and illustrated by photographs.[7]

Of type A, *Negro types,* he says: "These present perhaps sixty-six and two-thirds per cent. of the colored people of this country. A really adequate study would lead to an investigation of all the African types, most of which are represented in America, and subsequently changed by intermingling, and possibly by climate and surroundings. We can still catch glimpses of the original African—the straight-nosed, dark Nubian; the tall, massive Bantu; the small, sturdy West Coast Negro, and others. All these types agree in dark color and crisp hair. The color we usually

[7] Atlanta University Reports.

denominate black, although it is in reality a series of browns, varying between black and yellow as limits."

Of type B, *Mulatto types,* he says: "The mulatto types of American Negroes have from three-fourths to one-half Negro blood and form in this country, to hazard a guess, about twenty-seven and seven-ninths per cent. of the colored population. In some, white and Negro blood is evenly distributed in color, hair, and features, making light-brown or yellow persons, with hair in small but minute curls or waves, features rounded or half European. In others the Negro blood has asserted itself in one or two characteristics and the white blood in other directions. For instance, the white blood has gone into the abundant long black hair and left the dark face and full features; in others the Negro blood has asserted itself particularly in the hair, leaving the light color and European features. In some others the hair has received the slight red tinge and the blending is more complete. In still others the Negro blood has moulded the features, leaving the light color and hair in ringlets. All this is instructive to the student of heredity as showing visibly many things which lie hidden from the eye in the blending of races of the same color and features."

Of type C, *Quadroon types,* he says: "They are colored people with more than one-half and less than seven-eighths of their blood white, so far as I can ascertain. They represent about three and eight-ninths per cent. of the American Negroes, if my other estimates are correct. Here again are examples of race-blending in large variety and with especial brilliancy of coloring. Sometimes the coloring is so prominent and assertive that one scarcely notices other features. Photographs, of course, fail to give any adequate idea of this group; the emphatic color may be velvet-brown in the face, or a brownish red in the hair. Again, the hair and features may both be yellow, or all brown or dark brown and yellow, or finally the skin may be strikingly white. These types I have grouped as the chromatic types.

"Again we may have the harmonious blending mentioned in the case of the mulattoes. The hair of the quadroons is of almost every conceivable variety and color; it may be black and straight, or black and wavy, or red-brown and waving, or crimped and brownish-red, or curly and fluffy, and so on in endless change."

Of type D, he says: "The octoroons and those with less than one-eighth of Negro blood pass so easily back and forth between the races that it is difficult to estimate their real number. In a single small city 100 colored families were estimated to have been listed as white in the census of 1890, because the octoroon wife went to the door and the census taker did not dare to ask her 'color.' A considerable proportion of these persons identify themselves altogether with the whites —probably several thousands in all. These form about one and two-thirds per cent. of the colored population. They are easily classified according to the European types they most resemble, either accidentally or because of real blood-relationship."

I ask the fair-minded reader to consider carefully the facts here submitted, to examine thoroughly the illustrations of this book, and finally to study without prejudice the form and features of the colored people he meets. I am sure he will find the evidence sufficient to support the contention that the *individual variation in the American Negro is so great that any other treatment than that based on individual merit is a monstrous injustice.*

The American colored man is not only reacting successfully to his North temperate environment in physical *appearance,* but in physical *stamina* also. He has developed no diseases peculiar to himself[8] and has, under normal conditions, a normal resistance. The assumption that he has racially deteriorated physically since emancipation is unwarranted. The Negro's physical vigor of ante-bellum days was the gift of nature—the common heritage of her savage children. His survival is due to the merciless and murderous selection of the slave-trade across the Atlantic. Only the toughest physically could withstand the rigors of the slave-ship and the brutality of the slave-trader. The absence of sickness was due to the well-known fact that the weak did not survive to become sick. Miscarriages precluded invalidism, and the graveyard excluded the hospital.

"If the population were divided as to social and economic condition the matter of race would be almost entirely eliminated.[9] Poverty's death rate in Russia shows a much greater divergence from the rate among the well-to-do than the difference between Negroes and whites in America. In England, according to Mulhall, the poor have a rate twice as high as the rich, and the well-to-do are between the two. The same is true in Sweden, Germany, and other countries. In Chicago the death rate among the whites of the stockyard district is higher than the Negroes of that city, and farther away from the death rate of the Hyde Park district of that city than the Negroes are from the whites of Philadelphia."

Conduct and condition, not race, are the determining factors in disease and death. Nature is impartial as well as inexorable.

"Over one hundred years ago Villenet made the statement before the Academy of Sciences in Paris,

[8] See page 45.
[9] See "Housing and Sanitation," *Southern Workman,* Sept., 1906.

that while among well-nourished rich people there occurred one death in fifty, among the very poor classes the deaths were one in four."

II.—An Unsuspected Factor.

One of the most striking discoveries in the study of the race question is a truth the existence of which will not be admitted by the average individual of either race, namely, *in many ways the races are very much alike,* especially in those things wherein they most accuse each other. In nothing is this resemblance more shown than in the mutual vehemence with which they each deny its existence. It would astonish some of the most rampant negrophobes to know with what utter contempt they are looked down upon as inferior beings by many of the ordinary colored people. A contempt that is often tinged with bitterness from the very prevalent belief that some of these agitators are not pure Caucasians in either blood or association.

It is surprising how prejudice and preconceived notions can blind intelligent people to obvious facts. There is no more elemental truism of ethnology than that people living in the same country, speaking the same language, professing the same religion, and reading the same literature will in a general way think the same thoughts and have the same ambitions.

Much needless friction arises in the South by ignoring this simple truth. In this particular the white man is the greater sinner. The colored man reads the white man's books and papers, but the average white person, male and female, North and South, by a sort of conspiracy of prejudice, will not read the colored man's books and papers.[10] As a result the

[10] An amusing incident illustrative of this foolish prejudice came under the author's notice some years ago. A colored man of some literary taste had a social function at his home. A feature of the

colored man knows a good deal more about what the white man is thinking and saying than the white man does about what the colored man is thinking or saying.

This is a source of dangerous irritation because it leads colored people to regard many assertions as willful misrepresentations or downright falsehoods when in reality they are only honest ignorance on the part of the white man. No human folly can surpass the conceit of ignorance.

The white man that never visits a colored lodge, nor school, nor church, nor home; never talks to intelligent colored people except to hector them; nor exercises the amenities of culture in the most casual business relations with colored people;[11] never reads the books nor papers written by them, yet says that he knows colored people and persistently makes state-

---

service was a beautiful Japanese napkin embossed with the following quotation from Dunbar:—

"An angel, robed in spotless white,
Bent down and kissed the sleeping Night.
Night woke to blush; the sprite was gone.
Men saw the blush and called it Dawn."

The printer that did this work liked the lines and put a copy in his scrapbook. A friend saw them, told his wife about them. Wife liked them. They were used at a party. Guests liked them, and the napkins with the quotation were carried home and put away as choice souvenirs. Quite incidentally some months later, the question arose as to the authorship of the lines. Wife asked husband, husband asked friend, friend asked printer, printer asked colored man. Colored man produced the book and consternation reigned. Every copy was destroyed except the printer's. He kept his, saying that he was glad to have such evidence of the advancement of the colored people. The lady became angry with the printer because he would not take the quotation from his scrapbook.

[11] The efforts to avoid the terms Mr., Mrs., Miss, in addressing colored people has nothing to do with the relative merits of the two races, but is simply an illustration of what Pope describes in the following lines:—

"Few to good breeding make just pretense,
A want of decency is a want of sense."

This custom of manifesting superiority of race by inferiority of manners has taken on new vitality under the lead of men who violate alike the traditions and culture of the South by seeking in assumed race superiority a basis for distinction that finds no warrant in personal qualifications. There are well-authenticated incidents to show that neither Washington nor Jefferson possessed any of this snobbishness so characteristic of these uncultured advocates of impoliteness in interracial relations. See also page 245.

Medical graduates.

ments that the most superficial examination of race literature would show to be false,—this type of man is a source of irritation in the racial situation. If the average Southern white man, especially of the working class, only did know and understand the colored man, the race problem would be in immediate process of solution. It is white ignorance of actual conditions that forms the most irreducible factor in the race situation.

III.—Intraracial Activities.

The colored man's mental and spiritual response to his American environment is as notable as his physical reaction thereto. The facts submitted in Chapter XII support this proposition. I will submit briefly some additional evidence.

A. PROFESSIONAL.

The colored people have evolved a creditable professional class: teachers, lawyers, preachers, and physicians.[12]

"There is no more pathetic chapter in the history of human struggle than the smothered and suppressed ambition of this race in its daring endeavor to meet the greatest social exigency to supply the professional demand of the masses. There was the suddenness, the swiftness of leap as when a quantity in mathematics changes signs, passing through zero or infinity. In an instant, in the twinkling of an eye, the plow-hand was changed into the priest, the barber into the bishop, the housemaid into the schoolmistress, the porter into the physician, and the day-laborer into the lawyer. These high places of intellectual and moral authority into which they found themselves thrust by the stress

[12] See Appendix F, "The Negro Doctor."

of social necessity had to be filled with at least some semblance of conformity with the standards which had been established by the Europeans through the traditions of the ages. The high places in society occupied by the choicest members of the white race after years of preliminary preparation had to be assumed by men without personal or formal fitness. The stronger and more aggressive natures pushed themselves to the high callings by sheer force of untutored energy and uncontrolled ambition. That there would be much grotesqueness, maladjustment, and failure goes without saying. But after making full allowance for human imperfections, the fifty thousand Negroes who fill the professional places among their race represent a remarkable body of men and indicate the potency and promise of the race."[13]

From these professional workers there is evolving a genuinely intellectual class, whose attainments must eventually command the respect of mankind. (See plate, University Men.)

B. BUSINESS.

We are evolving a business class which the constructive genius of Booker T. Washington is welding into an effectual agency of racial advancement. The Negro Business League is not all banquets and speeches. Real advancement is being made toward supplying the demands and commercial needs of the race. Auburn Avenue in Atlanta, Georgia, and Cedar Street in Nashville, Tennessee, are striking illustrations of the race's growing business acumen and their leading spirits (B. J. Davis of Atlanta and A. N. Johnson of Nashville) are splendid evidence of the race's ability to "see large" and constructively in busi-

[13] Kelly Miller, "Out of the House of Bondage."

ness matters. Statistics on this line are not within the scope of this book. Ample evidence of this character will be found in the "Annual Reports of the Negro Business League," "Census Bulletin 129," "Negroes in the United States," and the files of the *Crisis,* a monthly magazine published in the interest of the colored peoples. We will therefore content ourselves by saying there are few avenues of business endeavor, from bootblacking to banking, that the Negro has not somewhere touched successfully. In every calling of civilized activity in this country some colored people somewhere are making good. As a race, the Afro-Americans are becoming self-sufficient. We have "first-bale cotton planters" in the South, "potato kings" in the West, and prize-winning students in the great colleges of the North.

C. EDUCATIONAL AND RELIGIOUS.

"The Negro is the most religious race in the world, and it is a great mistake to assume that he is now, or will be in the future, satisfied with any form of religious emotion that will feed his superstition. This may be true of the very ignorant, though I do not believe that anybody has sufficiently tested the matter to assert such as a fact. But I do know there is a large element increasing among the race who read and think, and who are satisfied with nothing short of the best that approves itself to their God-given reason and religious faculty."[14]

In school matters the colored man is making strenuous efforts to supplement the unfair distribution of the public-school funds.[15] Mr. Charles L. Coon,

[14] Bishop Theodore D. Bratton, of Jackson, Miss., before the Southern Sociological Congress, Memphis, Tenn., May, 1914.

[15] See Introduction, page 7, and Appendix G.

Superintendent of Schools, Wilson, N. C., makes a statistical investigation of the question, "Is the Negro Public School in the South a Burden on the White Taxpayer, and, if so, to What Extent?" Here is a fair summary of his conclusions:—

"The significance of these figures is that, while the Negro race has, at least, 40 per cent. of the children to educate, not quite 15 per cent. of the money expended on public education is devoted to their schools. . . .

"It is generally assumed in the discussion of the cost of the Negro public schools, that the white race bears all the cost or nearly all; that the Negroes of the South are truly the white man's burden when it comes to paying the bills for the public education. Much of this unseasoned talk reminds me of the North Carolina farmer who was in the habit of asserting on all occasions that he could live and get along so much better if it were not for his large and oppressive doctor bills. But the doctor declared at the next term of the court, on oath, that this chronic complainer had not paid him a cent in fifteen years, and that he was the only doctor in the community. . . .

"A somewhat careful study of this question for several years leads me to the conclusion that the Negro school of the South is no serious burden on the white taxpayer. . . .

"Such facts give us a glimpse of the economic importance of the Negro and abundantly justify us in hoping that the senseless race prejudice which has for its object the intellectual enslavement of Negro children will soon pass away." (See also what Mr. Barton says, page 234.)

"The Negro Church has furnished the Negro the best opportunity that the race has had in the United States to demonstrate its ability to govern itself. Scores of years before the great Civil War of 1861-

1865, Negroes in America were permitted, in many places in the North and West and also in a few places in the South, to have their own meeting-houses, and under a certain overseership were permitted to conduct their own meetings.[16] And since the War, or, that is to say, during the past fifty years, the Negroes have found in the church the chief opportunity to show to the world that they could organize in large numbers and conduct great business and religious enterprises.

"The leading denominations among the Negroes are the African Methodist Episcopal Church, the African Methodist Episcopal Zion Church, the Colored Methodist Episcopal Church, and the Missionary Baptist Church. We have some Presbyterians, Congregationalists, Episcopalians and Roman Catholics, and we have several thousand communicants in the Methodist Episcopal Church, which we usually call the Northern Methodist Church to distinguish it from the Methodist Episcopal Church South. As a matter of fact, nevertheless, these denominations last named are fewer in numbers than those named in the first list given, and, even if their numbers were larger, the last-named churches are so mixed up with the white denominations of the same names, officially and otherwise, that they do not furnish as bright examples of the possibilities of the Negro race as the Methodists and Baptists do. . . .

"The Negro Church has been a remarkable success. Considering the environment of the Negro race in this country, I doubt if the Negro Church could have more nobly filled its huge and multiform task. . . .

"I confess that among colored disciples, as among white disciples, there are doubtless many erring ones; yet, on the whole, I am sure that it is fair to say that

---

[16] See Payne's History of A. M. E. Church.

the influence of the Negro Church has been helpful and not hurtful, constructive and not destructive, good and not bad. It is true that every now and then some colored church-member will steal a chicken or a ham; but our friends should be charitable with us in this matter because every now and then I read in the newspapers where some white church-member has confiscated a railroad or a bank."[17]

The highest privileges of citizenship belong to those who are worthy of them. Beyond all controversy, the American colored man has proved himself *individually worthy* of all the rights and immunities of full citizenship. *This individual merit should remove the bar against the civil and political rights of the race.*

The attitude of the colored man toward the white man is well illustrated by the conduct of a little boy on a dusty and shadeless lane one hot summer day. A rather stout lady with a wide hat on was walking briskly along the road. She chanced to look down and noticed a boy walking close beside her.

"What do you want?" she asked.

"Nothing," said the boy, "I am just going to the store." Offering in no way to molest her, he still kept very close to her.

"Why do you keep so close to me?" asked the lady. "Go on about your business," commanded she.

"Please ma'am don't send me away," pleaded the boy. "I'll behave, I'm going the same way. I'll keep the dogs off you; and *you are the only shady spot on the road.*"

The same hard road leads from *slaveholder* to *freeholder* that leads from *freedman* to *freeman.* Fellow-travellers should not jostle each other. The white

---

[17] "The Negro Church as a Medium for Race Expression," C. T. Walker, D.D., Pastor Tabernacle Institutional Colored Baptist Church, Augusta, Ga.

man's culture can increase the colored man's speed, while the colored man's docility and patriotism can increase the white man's safety. The long journey from oligarchy to democracy will tax the endurance of both. They can make it only by co-operation.

"On every hand in this fair land,
Proud Ethiope's swarthy children stand
Beside their fairer neighbor;
The forests flee before their stroke,
Their hammers ring, their forges smoke,—
They stir in honest labor.

"No other race, or white or black,
When bound as thou wert, to the rack,
So seldom stooped to grieving;
No other race, when free again,
Forgot the past and proved them men
So noble in forgiving.

"Be proud, my Race, in mind and soul;
Thy name is writ on Glory's scroll
In characters of fire.
High 'mid the clouds of Fame's bright sky
Thy banner's blazoned folds now fly,
And truth shall lift them higher.

"Thou hast the right to noble pride,
Whose spotless robes were purified
By blood's severe baptism.
Upon thy brow the cross was laid,
And labor's painful sweat-beads made
A consecrating chrism.

"Go on and up! Our souls and eyes
Shall follow thy continuous rise;
Our ears shall list thy story
From bards who from thy root shall spring,
And proudly tune their lyres to sing
Of Ethiopia's Glory."

DUNBAR, "Lyrics of Lowly Life."

"He (the Negro) has remarkable and ungaugeable capabilities. It has been possible, over and over again, for individual Negroes to leap from a position of mental inferiority, such as the Caucasian's ancestors may have occupied fifty or even a hundred thousand years ago, to an equality in brain-power with some of the cleverest and ablest white men living at the present day. And it is always to be borne in mind (if we are not overrating the importance of the discovery of fossil negroids in Southern and Western France) that several branches of the Negro race may have known better days ten to forty thousand years ago, that the ancestors of the modern Negro in Africa may have pursued a downward course for many thousand years before their descendant was turned right-about-face by his Caucasian brother and compelled to take the ascending path which may lead him at some future period to a position of all-around equality with the white man."—Sir Harry Johnston, "The Negro in the New World."

Mixed-blood types.

CHAPTER XV.

RECAPITULATION.

THIS book is a *brief* and not a *credo;* primarily it is a summary and an analysis of the testimony of others and only incidentally an expression of my personal opinions and beliefs. I have appeared as an attorney for my people, not as a witness. I do, however, believe with my whole being the propositions herein sought to be established and have faith in the people I represent.

I have suppressed no testimony and have introduced no self-serving witnesses. I have sought to strengthen the judgment with facts rather than fire the imagination with prejudice.

The wail for liberty greets the dawn of history and the lash of the taskmaster is heard around the world. "A harsh, unrelenting tyranny of ancestral defect" seems to have inoculated the blood of mankind with the virus of oppression.

Injustice goes by greed and opportunity, and debauchery goes by weakness and passion. Color or race has little to do with either. The problems of Decatur Street in Atlanta, Ga., are the problems of City Roads in London, England; and so the world over. We are face to face with the age-long struggle man has made for liberty. In every age and every clime men have sung of liberty and preached of justice, but always with a circumscription that brought calamity.

It is our privilege to build upon the ruins of the past the civilizations of the future. Universality is the new light by which modern thought hopes to end man's age-long quest for justice.

When Frenchmen wrote with patriotic blood "Liberté, egalité, fraternité" on the escutcheon of France, its blessings were intended mainly for Frenchmen; when the Barons forced the Bill of Rights from King John at Runnymede they were defending the rights of a class. When the 54th Massachusetts unflinchingly faced death upon the bloody sands of Fort Wagner,

"The Old Flag never touched the ground,"

that the courage of a race might be vindicated. When Lincoln issued his famous Emancipation Proclamation, it was done to save a government. The religious liberty for which the Pilgrim Fathers broke up their homes and ventured across a chartless ocean, to reside in a trackless wilderness, was not broad enough to cover New England. Leonidas and his three hundred Lacedæmonians died at Thermopylæ in defense of Greece. Xenophen led the Retreat of the Ten Thousand for the same purpose. The Noble Six Hundred died for the martial glory of England, and Cæsar lived and died to glorify Rome. The "All Men" of the Declaration of Independence excluded the majority of mankind.

In all human history the spirit of slavery, or oppression, and the spirit of freedom, or democracy, have been struggling for the mastery.[1]

There is no phase of human thought more interest-

---

[1] "There is no difference between the white man and the colored man. Both will enslave their own blood. We are told that we have slaveholders now in our church. If we do not stop our members from slaveholding, our ministers will become slaveholders also. I say, again, every religious body is speaking out, and shall we not do the same? Shall we fear to speak out? I say today, being no prophet nor a prophet's son, if we allow our brethren to deal in this charitable slave-holding, in less than twenty years we shall have practical ones." (Debate in A. M. E. General Conference, 1856, M. P. Newsome speaking.) In the same debate G. Broadie, said: "The color of a man's skin does not change his disposition to apologise for slavery."

ing and instructive than the evolution of the slavery idea. The early writers before, and including Aristotle, take for granted its existence. Then there gradually creeps into the discussion the idea that a government *may* exist without slavery. This, however, is only a Utopian dream. But even dreamers never thought universal freedom compatible with difference of race.

So from the universal applicability of slavery, the idea gradually narrowed to its specific necessity. The men that established African slavery in America *believed in slavery,* and no ethnic classification was necessary to give it validity. *White men* and *red men* were just as acceptable as slaves as *black men.*

In 1538 the bull of excommunication against Henry VIII was published. "By that bull the king was deprived of his kingdom; his subjects were not only absolved from their oath of allegiance, but commanded to take arms against him and drive him from the throne; the whole kingdom was laid under interdict; all treaties of friendship, of commerce with him and his subjects were declared null; his kingdom was granted to any who should invade it, and all were allowed "to seize the effects of such of his subjects as adhere to him, and to enslave their persons."[2]

"The code for 1650" provided for the seizure of Indians "either to serve or be shipped out and exchanged for negars." The color of the African was only one of the last resorts of the oppressors, an inner fortification of the fortress of tyranny. The claim that the enslavement of the African was necessary to preserve the civilization of the world was the last agonizing shriek of a hoary old error "dying amid her worshippers." As the enslavement of the African in

[2] Fletcher, "Studies on Slavery," page 368.

America was simply another application of the old spirit of slavery, so the laws against him were but transplantations of old-world cruelties which Europeans had practised on Europeans.

The first fugitive-slave law originated not in the Congress of the United States at Washington in 1850, but in a Council of Bishops assembled in the city of Gangræ, Paphlagonia, about 325 A.D.:—

"Si quis docet servum, pietatis praetextu, dominum contemnere, et a ministerio recedere, et non cum benevolentia et omni honore domino suo inservire. Anathema sit."[3]

So the fugitive-slave law had its origin in the *system* of slavery, and not in the *race* of the slave.

About the year 442 A.D., the canonical law was established denying slaves or freedmen the right to testify in court. Some years earlier, possibly about 360 A.D., the right of the master to sanction, annul, or forbid the marriage of female slaves was canonically established.

Here we have two other cardinal injustices of American slavery of the African originating *not in the race of the slave, but in the system of slavery.*

The denial to the slave of the right to testify against the master was a bulwark of tyranny and laws of marriage were so interpreted and applied as to insure the concubinage or prostitution of the slave without blame to the master. The great mass of these slaves were of the same race and color as their masters. The principle of slavery is always the same. Britons raided Ireland for slaves and carried them home for sale among the Picts and Scots.[4]

---

[3] "If anyone, under the pretence of piety, teaches a slave to despise his master, and to withdraw his service, and not to serve his master with good-will and all respect, let him be anathema." (Fletcher, page 277.)

[4] See Eccles, "History of Ireland," vol. i, ch. iv.

"The savages of Africa may traffic with the Europeans for the Negroes whom they have seized by treachery or captured in open war; but the most savage conquerors of the Britons sold without scruple, to the merchants of the Continent, their countrymen and even their own children."[5]

The principle of slavery was held to be sound economics and universally applicable to all people. It was only when the rising tide of civilization condemned the principle of slavery that those interested sought in the features and disposition of the African a justification of its practice.[6]

The subjection of women was once just as firmly believed and stoutly argued on the ground of sex inferiority as the slavery of the African was defended upon the grounds of race inferiority. In fact, the inferiority doctrine is the oldest weapon in the arsenal of tyranny.

"In England," says Buckle (1822-1862), "wives are still occasionally led to the market by a halter round the neck, to be sold by the husband to the highest bidder." "The sale of a wife," remarks Borrow, "with a halter round her neck is still a legal transaction in England. The sale must be made *in the cattle market,* as if she were a mare, all women being considered as mares by old English law, and, indeed, *called mares* in certain counties where genuine old English law is still preserved." Wives were traded in this country.[7]

"Women," says Gage, "were taught by the Church and the State alike that the Feudal Lord or Seigneur had a right to them, not only against themselves, but as against any claim of husband or father. The law

---

[5] Fletcher.
[6] See Chapter X, on Mulattoes.
[7] See "Iron Furnace," by Aughey, ch. vii.

known as *Marchetta,* or *Marquette,* compelled newly married women to a most dishonorable servitude. They were regarded as the rightful prey of the Feudal Lord from one to three days after their marriage, and from this custom the eldest son of the serf was held as the serf of the lord, 'as perchance it was he who begat him.' From this nefarious degradation of women the custom of Borough English arose, in which the youngest son became the heir. . . . France, Germany, Prussia, England, Scotland, and *all the Christian countries* where feudalism existed, held to the enforcement of *Marquette.* The lord deemed this right as fully his as he did the claim to half the crops of the land, or to half the wool of the sheep."[8]

As the slave system found its last defense in the color and features of the African, so civic discrimination is hiding behind the assumption of unfitness for citizenship of the present generation of colored people. As the enslavement of all grades of mixed blood and even pure-white people destroyed slavery as a menace to the nation, so will the increasing general intelligence finally see that discrimination against any class of citizens will undermine the temple of justice. *There is not an argument now made against the full citizenship of the Negro that was not made against emancipation.*[9] In 1851 it was just as stoutly main-

[8] "Woman," vol. ii, page 343.

[9] Senator Vardaman is a worthy successor to Sen. A. G. Brown, of the same State. "A. G. Brown, United States Senator from Mississippi, to reconcile the poor whites to the peculiar institution, used the following argument in a speech at Iuka Springs, Miss. He stated that if the slaves were liberated, and suffered to remain in the country, the rich would have money to enable them to go to some other clime, and that the poor whites would be compelled to remain among the negroes, who would steal their property and destroy their lives; and if slavery were abolished, and the negroes removed and colonized, the rich would take the poor whites for slaves, in their stead, and reduce them to the condition of the Irish and Dutch in the North, whose condition he represented to be one of cruel bondage. These statements had some effect upon his auditors, who believed, from sad experience, that the

tained that the enfranchisement of women meant emancipation for the slaves as it is now maintained that votes for women mean "negro domination." Negro freedom ("abolitionism") was no more popular then than Negro rights are now.[10] Tyranny is always conservative and predicts disaster when freedom calls for progress. The inferiority and social equality arguments were worked overtime. Even the mob was resorted to freely and frequently, and not in the South only, but there were mobs all over the North wherever anti-slavery missionaries went. "July 4, 1834, there was a mob in New York when the house of Louis Tappan was searched. At the same time the schoolhouses and churches of colored people were attacked and damaged. August 13, in the same year, there was a terrible riot in Philadelphia, that continued for three nights. Forty-four houses of colored people were damaged and destroyed. Many colored people were beaten and cruelly injured, and some were killed.

"In the year 1835 Rev. Samuel J. May was mobbed five times in Vermont. If there ever was a man, at the same time perfectly courageous and straightforward, and also sweet-tempered and fair to his opponents, it was Samuel Joseph May. One would have supposed him to be the last man to be mobbed. October 21, 1835, there was a riot in Utica, and another on the same day in the city of Boston, when the meeting of the Woman's Anti-slavery Society was broken up, and Garrison was carried through the street with a rope round his body. He was protected by Major Lyman, and put in jail for safety. On the

---

rich could oppress the poor as they chose, and might, in the contingency specified, reduce them to slavery." ("Slavery and Secession," by Rev. John H. Aughey.)

[10] See Sojourner Truth's "Book of Life."

same day, a convention of delegates met at Utica and formed an anti-slavery society. They were shut out of the courthouse by a mob; then they went to a meeting house, but the assembly was broken up, and they were driven away with much violence. On the 17th of May, 1838, Penn Hall, built by the friends of free discussion at a cost of forty thousand dollars, and dedicated on May 14th, was burned by a mob. Colored orphan asylums and churches were, at the same time, attacked and damaged."[11]

Yet freedom came; for the arguments against freeing the colored man were but repetitions of the arguments that had been made against freeing the white man. "All the charms that a Divine eloquence and a felicitous diction could throw around a bad cause" once defended the slave system. It is, however, dead, and there is not a mourner in all the broad land. So will it be with the new serfdom so eloquently defended in the high places today.[12] It may obstruct but cannot stop the onward march of this country to real democracy.

Time has a wonderful power of metamorphosis. Slavery was first introduced in the South, but first defended in the North. Massachusetts objected to

---

[11] Clarke, "Anti-slavery Days."

[12] *Ready's Mirror*, a white paper of St. Louis, in a recent issue says: "Out upon the proposal now industriously pushed for the segregation of Negroes in this city! Segregation is a punishment. The community can only punish for crime. It is no crime to be born black. And there is no way by which we can deprive a Negro of his property, wherever located, without due process of law. The cry that Negroes ruin neighborhoods is a false one. Neighborhoods are ruined, generally speaking, before Negroes enter them. They are ruined by real-estate speculation luring residents to newer regions and by the refusal of landlords to keep property in such repair as will hold white tenants. We can't begin segregating Negroes without starting in a course that will end in our segregating 'poor whites.' We can't segregate Negroes without packing them into regions where they will be subjected to the exaction of higher rents. Back of segregation there's graft, but back of that is the desire of some mighty sorry specimens of people to have somebody they can look down upon."

Random types.

Negro soldiers in the Revolutionary War, and the vote of Massachusetts in the Constitutional Convention opened the door for slavery's entrance to the Union. Yet Massachusetts led the fight that expelled it and raised and officered the first Negro soldiers in the Civil War. The North sought secession to get rid of slavery. The South called it treason and resisted, yet the South fired the first shot in favor of secession and the North answered with an irresistible army for the Union. Pro-slavery and anti-Negro mobs began in the North, and now the North points the finger of scorn at the South. The South may yet become the real champion of the Negro's citizenship rights and the leaders of the world's civilization. Southerners are, and have ever been, a courageous and outspoken people. Once thoroughly convinced and aroused, there is no hesitancy or evasion.

The North is apathetic on the race discussion now, as it was for so long a time on the slavery question. The sections take turns at being interested. When they get aroused simultaneously, something generally happens. The South should lead. The facts of religion, science, and history all point the same way.

"We need not more facts, valuable as these are, but more faith; not more statistics and academic studies, but more religion, more genuine religion—more faith in the brotherhood of man and the Fatherhood of God—actually to believe in it, as we believe that the earth revolves around the sun; and not merely subscribe to it perfunctorily on Sundays. It is good science, as well as good religion, and we need to take it seriously. Let us confess it; we need more love and sympathy and charity and the milk of human kindness when we deal with people who are different and less fortunate than ourselves; more *noblesse oblige* with those handicapped in life's struggle. And these things are not to be had on the presentation of a few facts. They need to be cultivated and developed by constant preaching and teaching from press and pulpit and platform, in the schools and colleges and on the stump. We need missionary work and a company of fearless missionaries who will have the high courage to teach unpopular truths to their own people and in their own communities.

"I say these things, not as one who brings an indictment against his people. Far from it. I know we are a generous folk, warm-hearted, chivalric, and sympathetic; we have noble impulses and worthy ideals; we cultivate the virtues as well as the graces of enlightened society, and no people is quicker to respond to human appeals than we are. Had the slaves been taken originally to Germany, Russia, Turkey, or other foreign countries, I am sure that the most active and eloquent champions of their 'God-given and inalienable rights and privileges as human beings' would have come from our own Southern States. For we instinctively hate oppression and tyranny in whatever shape or form. And yet we do not altogether live up to this characterization in our treatment of the Negro. How shall we explain the inconsistency?

"To answer this adequately would require an extended psychological analysis of race prejudice, many elements of which are older than the human race, and not without their positive value in the evolution of the species. There is one element, however, which plays a very important rôle, but which has not as yet received its due recognition. I refer to the *power which ideas and beliefs have over conduct.* When Descartes persuaded his contemporaries that animals are mere automata, without intelligence or feeling, even the tender-hearted Malebranche could without hurt to his feelings kick the dog that was fawning on him. When belief in demoniacal possession was prevalent, excellent, God-fearing men helped to burn, stone, and drown the possessed. The belief that their ancestors were much wiser and better than they could ever hope to become had much to do with arresting development of the Chinese for more than two thousand years. And so the illustrations could be multiplied!

"I fear the attitude of many of our people toward the Negro has been determined to a considerable extent by equally erroneous ideas. They have been persuaded by a generation of short-sighted, uneducated, and unscrupulous demagogues that the development of the Negro is somehow incompatible with the best interests of the white man; that prosperity for the black man spells ruin for the white man; that what is good for the one is bad for the other; that what is true for one is false for the other. And so this strange state of affairs has come to pass: that those traits and things we admire when possessed by ourselves and all the white world, we dislike when they appear in the Negro; our virtues, when cultivated and practised by the black man, become by some strange alchemy transformed into vices. Thus we recognize that education is a good thing, and those who strive for it are deserving of approbation and even praise. Likewise, manliness and self-respect are commendable; and ambition and thrift and the pursuit of happiness are not to be condemned. And yet there are too many who prefer the ignorant, lazy, diseased, immoral Negro—even the vicious and criminal one—to the self-respecting, progressive, property-owning, educated one.

"Now, it is evident that this condition cannot long continue without endangering the very foundations of our civilization. Double-dealing of this sort is bound ultimately to bring bankruptcy and ruin. Hence the urgent need, as I see it, of courage, patriotism, and zeal to be spent in popular educational efforts which shall seek to bring about a change in the prevailing attitude toward the Negro similar to that Rousseau wrought, single-handed, in the field of education proper, and later in the realm of government."[13]

"To bring any public question fairly into the open field of literary debate is always a long step toward its final adjustment. It is across that field that the question must go to be so purged of its irrelevancies, misinterpretations, and misuses, personal, partisan, or illogical, and so clarified and simplified as to make it easy for the popular mind to take practical and final action on it and settle it once for all by settling it right.

"It is in this field that the Negro problem still forces itself to the front as a living and urgent national question." (Cable.)

Free speech is the salvation of freedom. A government must be free to be just, and must be just to be pure. But neither purity nor justice will come without freedom, nor stay when it is gone. Again I quote the forceful words of Mr. Murphy:—

"Dark, indeed, must be the fate of any land if compelled to approach the solution of any significant problem of its life with its lips sealed and its reason bound."

Tyranny does not always crush; it sometimes rebounds and explodes. Thus came the American Revolution. Thus came the French Revolution. Overeagerness to defend slavery brought on the Civil War and emancipation.

Slavery is dead, but its spirit lives[14] and modern

[13] Prof. Josiah Morse, Ph.D., University of South Carolina.

[14] How like ante-bellum philippics of Toombs reads Smith's Color-line!

Random types.

democracy is trembling at the apparition. The light of free discussion will banish the ghost. Let us wake up and shake off the nightmare of the past. Liberty is not dangerous. Only the belief that liberty is dangerous is a danger to freedom.

"We are too much inclined to underrate the power of moral influence. Nothing but freedom, justice, and truth is of any permanent advantage to the mass of mankind. This is 'an age when the accumulated common sense of the people outweighs the greatest statesman or the most influential individual.' You may build your Capitol of granite, and pile it high as the Rocky Mountains, if it is founded on or mixed up with iniquity, the pulse of a girl will beat it down.

"The gem forms unseen. The granite increases and crumbles, and you can hardly mark either process. The great change in a nation's opinion is the same. The accumulated intellect of the masses is greater than the heaviest brain God ever gave a single man."[15]

Let it be remembered that man can receive but one thing in exchange for liberty, and that is slavery; and no man can be wholly free while his neighbor is partly slave (segregated). The taint of involuntary servitude affects us all.[16]

The entire race question may be comprehended in a few words:—

I.

Is there anything in the blood, beliefs, conduct, or history of the colored American to disqualify him for full citizenship in this country?

My answer is, *No!* The facts impartially considered prove exactly the opposite.

---

[15] Wendell Phillips, "Public Opinion."

[16] Mosby, "Causes and Cures of Crime," page 166.

II.

Will the granting this full citizenship to the colored American in any way endanger the integrity of either race?

My answer is, *No!* It will, on the other hand, strengthen racial lines. The comity of races will encourage a friendly rivalry that will increase race pride while killing race prejudice.

III.

Is it not possible for the Afro-American and the Euro-American to co-operate peaceably and constructively in politics and economics and wisely leave the personal and social matters to settle themselves as all wise people have done throughout the world?

I answer, *Yes!* The more intelligent and reasonable each race becomes, and the better acquainted each race becomes with the other, the more clearly will they each see the folly of confusing public duty with private choice.

IV.

As the evidence submitted establishes the soundness of all three of the above-mentioned propositions, what is the best method of race adjustment now available to the people of the South under present conditions?

Science, religion, common sense, history, and experience all tell us the same thing:—

Start from where you are. Build on these propositions and the gates of hell shall not prevail against you!

At heart the American people believe in fair play. "Visioning the fruitage of the coming golden day," I am willing to accept the majority judgment of the American people; yea, of the Southern people, *if they will examine the facts, and hear the arguments of both sides.* This has not been done. In many sections only one side has been heard. Prejudice has arraigned the Negro in the Court of Civilization; I present a brief for the Defendant. I have impartially summarized the evidence for the convenience of the honorable court, *Public Opinion,* and pray judgment in accordance with the facts.

"Ruler of Nations, judge our cause!
If we have kept Thy holy laws,
The sons of Belial curse in vain
The day that rends the captive's chain."

At heart the American people believe in fair play. Welcoming the heritage of the coming golden days, I am willing to accept the majority judgment of the American people, and of the Southern people, if they will examine the facts and hear the arguments of both sides. This has not been done. In many sections only one side has been heard. Prejudice has sentenced the Negro in the court of Civilization. I present a brief for the Defendant. I have impartially summarized the evidence [illegible] the good conduct of the [illegible] and pray judgment in accordance with the facts.

> "[illegible] nations, make our cause!
> If we have kept Thy holy laws,
> The sons of Belial curse in vain
> The day that rends the captive's chain."

APPENDIX A.

THE COLOR-LINE PROBLEM IN THE UNITED STATES.

JUST after finishing the discussion of the mulatto in Chapter X I received the following letter, which contains a great many facts that should be known to all who would understand the race question. Without prepossession, prejudice, or comment, I submit the facts. Let each reader interpret them for himself:—

"In South Carolina we recognize the octoroons as white people."[1] These were the exact words of Senator B. R. Tillman, February 23, 1903, in the U. S. Senate in answer to Senator Spooner on the Indianola, Miss., postoffice case, where a mob in the form of a mass-meeting demanded the resignation of Mrs. Minnie Cox because she was not white. Among all the Southern senators present, none questioned the correctness of this classification by Senator Tillman, everybody seemingly agreeing that octoroons shall be classified as white; nor has anyone from any quarter since protested or disputed the South Carolinian's dictum. It is not my purpose now to call it in question, but rather to inquire why the color-line should stop at equal division, or mulatto? This whole color-line problem seems thoroughly inconsistent when tested by logic. In the very forefront we may ask, Who can explain why a mulatto is not a white man with Negro blood in him, rather than a Negro with white blood in him? If this is perplexing, what of the quadroon? By what law of ethnology is he classed with his African ancestors rather than his Caucasian? We know through Stroud and Blake how it came about, but who can tell why it is continued? Senator Tillman should next attack it. The quadroon should have been included as a matter of exact justice. This absorption and authoritative admission of the

[1] The Supreme Court of Georgia, in the case of R. W. White *vs.* W. J. Clements, 1872, upheld this view, and in effect said, everyone having more than one-half Caucasian blood was entitled to be classed as such. This was rendered in the contest for the clerkship of the Supreme Court of Chatham County, White being a quadroon.

octoroon on the white side of the line indicates a lowering of the former standard held to be correct in the South before the War, when the octoroons were sold as ruthlessly as were the blacks and, in the case of a female, brought fabulous prices; in a few cases as high as $25,000. In Boucicault's drama and Miss Braddon's novel of the "Octoroon," the practice in the South to sell octoroons for immoral purposes are fully set forth, and both authors are sustained by a hundred narratives on the subject. It cannot be safely affirmed that this phase of slavery, coupled as it was in many instances by human depravity almost beyond belief, in that fathers unblushingly sold their children, products of their intercourse with their female slaves, for gain, the prospective profit being the animating cause in begetting them. This did more, I may safely say, to determine the Christian people of the country to do all in their power to destroy such an iniquitous system, a system that made such a monstrous thing possible, than any other phase of slavery depicted in Mrs. Stowe's book, and really caused its overthrow. I recall reading of a particularly brutal exhibition of this kind that occurred in New Orleans. It seems a young man from the North who had studied medicine, on graduating went to New Orleans to practise. It was his custom in the early evening to take a stroll in the public park, where the mothers and nurses were gathered with the children. In this way he became acquainted with an attractive young girl, which continuing for some time, he offered his hand, was accepted, and the two were married. They set up housekeeping and were getting along nicely, he being very devoted to her and she equally loving. They had been married not more than seven months when a gentleman called one evening and asked to speak privately with the doctor, and then revealed the fact that the doctor's wife was his slave, and further said, unless he was given thirty-five hundred dollars immediately, she would be advertised and sold. The doctor loved his wife and, to save her, was obliged to agree to the harsh terms. He then gently upbraided his wife for not telling him her situation when he offered to marry her, whereupon she burst into tears and fell into his arms saying: "I could not, though I wanted to, because my heart was enlisted, and, further, I felt that the gentleman who called just now would not have disturbed me when he saw me so happily situated, *since he is my father!*" This shows very conclusively the folly of making color a test of character. Southern born as I am, I have no hesitation in saying, and I believe every decent man will agree with me, I would ten times rather admit to all the amenities of my home, a black gentleman, than this inhuman brute who demanded the price of his daughter under the threat of selling her. Could any decent man hesitate in his choice under such circumstances? Yet there are those who would make color a test of character.

So I say, this authoritative decision to include all octoroons in the white column is a distinct gain in Southern civilization. In Jamacia the children of octoroons are classed as white. It is very important, since now Alexander Poushkin, Robt. Browning, Empress Josephine, Lady Nelson (Lord Nelson's wife), Judah P. Benjamin, Alex. Hamilton, and Henry Timrod (this last is the recognized poet of the South; there is a monument to his memory in Charleston and numerous Timrod Societies do honor to his name) need not longer share their glory with those of the African race. Another step, absorbing quadroons, and the race will lose its share in the Alex. Dumas, Diego Silva de Velasquez, Chevalier St. Georges, Robert de Cabane, Cagliostro, General Rigaud, General Paez, and Alexander de Medici, 1st Duke of Florence, and many other world-famous characters.

How Christophe, King of Haiti, Settled the Color-line.

The same question, as to the social status of the different colors that now perplex the people of the United States, raged with no less fierceness in Haiti and the West Indies up to about 1812 than it does today in the Southland. All through the Santo Domingo Revolution, in addition to the hostility of the French under Leclerc and Rochambeau, there was constantly present in the councils of the natives the struggles between the colors and their relations to each other. In the French colonies there was no mulatto or mixed-blood slavery; every child followed the Roman law or the condition of the father, hence there were three classes,—whites, composites, and blacks. It is interesting to note that while African slavery began in June, 1619, mulatto or mixed-blood slavery in the United States did not begin until 1661, and thus early only in Virginia, the other States not adopting it until a much later period. There were a large number of mixed breeds, but they were the legitimate children of legitimate marriage between the races. So the mulattoes did not have their origin, as some in their ignorance believe, in the illicit relations of the two colors. The whole is set forth in detail in Blake's "History of Slavery," and in the first chapter of Straud's "Laws of Slavery."

As previously mentioned, Haiti and San Domingo were torn with civil dissensions between the colors, the blacks, mulattoes, and whites, and for more than ten years after the French invaders had been expelled from the islands did this question of caste vex and divide the people. Christophe, to end the matter, promulgated his famous rule in which he declared that, everybody who in color came up to a certain standard, which he fixed, should be accounted and classed as white, and all who fell below should be classed as black; and as King Christophe[2] was himself black, this rule was accepted by the blacks, who were the most numerous element in the islands, with undisguised equanimity. This solution as made by Christophe of the vexatious color-line has continued until today in the West India Islands.

Before the War of 1861-5, in many of the large Southern cities, a similar division among the colors, blacks and composites, existed; notably was this so in New Orleans, Charleston, Savannah, Lynchburg, and Mobile, and a little less in other places.

Pure Caucasian Children Raised as Slaves.

The fact that octoroons could be held as slaves led to the enslavement of a large number of pure Caucasians. In many instances scandal was suppressed in wealthy families by turning over the unwelcome child to a bright-colored slave to be reared as her own. The grandfather, when financially pressed,

[2] Christophe was an officer with Rigaud, of Haiti, and assisted the Americans at the siege of Savannah in 1777.

would sell the child with as little remorse as was occasioned by selling a hog, after which its identity was usually lost. The writer has been told of numerous such cases, a notable one occurring in North Carolina in 1835. In the narrative of Chas. Ball, he tells how the instinct of maternal affection overcame shame and caused a white mother to acknowledge the maternity of a boy who was being reared as a quadroon slave in the neighborhood. It seems that her father had been left a widower when she was not more than 10 years of age. On the plantation was a mulatto woman for whom her father had shown no little partiality during his wife's life. This woman had several children, one a very handsome boy, her master's son, and at the time of the wife's death, about 12 years old. The widower sent his daughter to a boarding-school, where she remained until she was grown. Returning, she installed herself mistress of her father's house. In about a year there was a hasty family council to devise means to avoid a terrible scandal, since evidence of her intimacy with her half-brother could no longer be concealed. Says Ball, "At this meeting it was proposed to send the girl to one of the Northern cities until after her accouchement, that the child should be provided for in some way, and the mother free of scandal return home after the restoration of her health. This proposition was acceded to by all except the paternal uncle, who said that he would agree to nothing but the exposure of one who had brought such infamy upon the reputation of the family, and if she was sent away and secreted he would himself divulge the whole to the world, lest it should be imagined that he, who was himself the father of several daughters, had given any countenance to so base an attempt to impose upon the public. It seems that this gentleman assigned as an excuse for his cruelty to the poor girl, a tenderness of the good name of his own family, but it was said by many that the hope of ruining his niece and forcing her father to disinherit her in favor of his own children was not without weight in his mind. Be this as it may, the girl was kept in the house until after the birth of her child, which she was not permitted to nurse, it being taken from her and sent to the kitchen to be nurtured by its paternal grandmother, the mulatto head-servant. The mother was degraded from her rank in society, and when the child was 8 years old it was sold by its grandfather, together with the mulatto woman and all her children." "It seems," says Ball, "that the father of the girl was induced to this course by reason of his desire to marry a wealthy widow in the neighborhood, who discouraged his suit, and pointed to the bad state of affairs existing in his domestic arrangements; consequently he sought to improve them and make himself more acceptable. He never got the widow, but was soon after murdered by one of his slaves, a negro woman, in revenge for having sold her husband. . . . The murderess accomplished her object by secreting herself in his chamber and cutting his throat with a carving knife as he lay asleep in a room, through the window of which the moon shone, which gave sufficient light to enable her to complete her purpose. By his death, his whole estate, which was said to be of great value, descended to his daughter, who now became the mistress of the entire property. She immediately took measures to trace out the identity and residence of her son," to claim whom "she journeyed to the plantation where Ball was working. He saw her when she, accompanied by the master, got the boy and witnessed the frantic joy she exhibited as she hugged and kissed him after the long separation."

So it is clear that octoroons were not always classed as white, since had such been the case we would have been spared the recital of the brutal cases mentioned.

The Composite.

The decision of the Missouri Court in 1900, that a mulatto is not a Nego, is quite appropriate to quote in this connection. It seems that a white man, who died intestate in Missouri about three years before, left considerable property to which a mulatto man laid claim as the son of the deceased. Other relatives contested his right on the grounds that the plaintiff was a Negro and that it was inconsistent for a Negro to claim to be the son of a white man. The court overruled this contention and said: "The plaintiff is not a Negro nor is he a white man, but a *composite*. He represented the beginning of a new race, since all *new races* are formed by the union of a male and female of opposite races. The diversity of races came about in this way and only the most grossly ignorant would hold that there was a separate creation." The mulatto lost the case because he could not prove that the deceased was his father. He testified that his mother had always told him so. The court ruled that her testimony unsupported was not conclusive. Had the deceased during his life acknowledged his paternity or done anything, such as supporting him, to give color to the claim, he would have unhesitatingly given him the property.

The old idea that deterioration followed amalgamation is not now urged by any ethnologist of standing, since the contrary is true. That the Indian and the Jew, who are singularly pure in their blood, are deteriorating or standing still must be admitted by every truthful investigator. There are some strong reasons to justify the statement that there are fewer Jews in the world now than there were in the time of Christ, nineteen hundred years ago. The mulatto or composite race now numbers in the United States about two million; there were one million, one hundred thousand and three hundred by the census of 1890, the growth of amalgamation in less than two hundred and fifty years from the parent stock unreinforced by emigration. The Indians have stood still; certainly they have not increased to any appreciable extent. Years ago, it was generally believed, the responsibility for such belief resting upon desire and ignorance, that the mulatto was a hybrid and was of weak physique and doomed to die out; and some in their zeal were able to picture the thoughts and reflections of the last one, like Macaulay's New Zealander sitting on a broken arch of London Bridge contemplating the decay of centuries. But they are not dying out; indeed, they have greater stamina, larger families; more prolific in sexual union, greater mental power, and a larger percentage of increase than either the white man or the black man. But why were not these facts known before? There are two reasons,—first, prejudice against all the Negroes and all his kindred, prejudice which has been defined by one, "as opinions received without examination. A second ignorance engrafted on our natural ignorance. A person armed with old views or opinions which without examination he opposes to the new. The necessity of weak minds, the art of false ones." Secondly, lack of time for observation and testing of theories. It was fortunate for the composite race that these false ideas gained currency, otherwise the growth of the race would have been greatly retarded. No one it seems bothered himself about its growth, believing it would cure itself and die out.

The Law on the Subject.

A patient and exhaustive search of the statutes concerning the races in the Southland shows that there was ever a differentiation in legal language between Negro and mulatto; every decision being held that a mulatto could not be held amenable under a statute that applied only to Negroes, and to meet such cases the word mulatto was invariably inserted so as to make such amenable. The most authoritative was the decision by the Supreme Court of Louisiana, April 29, 1910, declaring that a mulatto was not a Negro. The Fourteenth Amendment prohibits any State from using such a designation in its laws. The Constitution of South Carolina, 1896, in the 34th section reads:

"The marriage of white persons with a Negro or a mulatto, or person who shall have one-eighth of Negro blood, shall be unlawful and void."

To this provision, while under consideration in the Constitutional Convention, Robt. Smalls, a man of mixed blood, proposed an amendment adding "Any white person who lives or cohabits with a Negro or mulatto, or person who shall have one-eighth or more of Negro blood, shall be disqualified from holding any office of emolument or trust in this State." . . . This amendment was voted down by a larger vote than was cast on any other proposition brought before the Convention. Mr. Smalls, in the course of a speech on his amendment, made the following sharp retort: "If a Negro should improperly approach a white woman his body riddled with bullets would be hanging on the nearest tree before the next morning, but if my amendment should prevail and all white men who cohabit with Negro women be disqualified, this Convention would have to be adjourned *sine die* for lack of a quorum." A member called Smalls to order, saying that he had cast a reflection on the Convention. To this Smalls replied: "I do not wish to reflect on the Convention but to say, if the gentleman has clean hands he will keep his seat. I do not mean to reflect on any man who objects to cohabiting with a Negro or mulatto woman."

SOCIAL EQUALITY.

Having unusual opportunities to talk with most cultured colored people from every part of the United States, I find this sentiment unanimous. All social associations must be mutually agreeable and cannot in the nature of things transcend this line. When it is agreeable to all concerned there can be no legitimate grounds of offense to anyone. A man who has nothing else to recommend him save his color would not be an acceptable guest at any gentleman's table, and one who has everything else should not be excluded. General George Washington slept in bed with Primus Hall, a young mulatto valet of Col. Pickering (see "Godey's Lady's Book," 1849); Thos. Jefferson had Mr. Julius Melbourn at dinner in 1815; his other guests were James Monroe (afterward President); Wm. Wirt, John Randolph, Mr. Edmund Pendleton, who introduced Mr. Melbourn, whose status was sympathetically discussed during the dinner party.

It may not be wholly profitless, though not strictly pertinent to this inquiry, to refer to some conditions existing in the States in the early part of the century: From the Hon. Thomas E. Millner, of South Carolina, I learn that in the Southern States, in the early days of the 19th century,[3] every man having less than one-eighth of African blood, provided that eighth came from the father, was entitled to all the privileges of citizenship accorded to the most favored, including the right to vote, and that this rule continued until 1831, the year of the Nat Turner insurrection. A more liberal rule obtained in North Carolina and Maryland. In New York all free colored men were entitled to vote without other qualifications, but after New York abolished slavery, which it did on July 4, 1827, and thereby largely increased the number of its

[3] Judge McCay, of the Supreme Court of Georgia, said: "There never has been in this State, at any period of its history, any denial in terms of the right to vote and hold office to colored persons as such."

free inhabitants, it was urged by Mr. Van Buren, and ultimately adopted, that some restriction should be placed on the suffrage of colored men, and after that period a property qualification of $250 was required, and all colored men having said qualification were able to vote in New York State up to the adoption of the Fifteenth Amendment, when such qualification was not longer required. When the property qualification of Van Buren was established the Hon. Gerritt Smith bought fifty thousand acres of land in New York and gave to each colored family, selected by a committee, fifty acres to enable them to qualify under the law. In Ohio in 1860, by a decision of its Supreme Court in Anderson's case, every man having less than one-half African blood was declared entitled to all and every privilege accorded white men and not subject to any other pains and penalties.

In Rhode Island a property qualification was required of all save free colored citizens, and under this law a large number of whites voted, not otherwise qualified, by claiming to be of African descent, and so flagrant were the frauds practised through white men to enable them to vote, claiming to be octoroons, that the legislature was petitioned and repealed the exception in favor of colored men. These historical facts in regard to the suffrage are quite pertinent at this time, as showing the attitude of the South and North in former times in dealing with this color-line, and should be remembered, since they cannot but have an important bearing when the subject of Negro suffrage is under consideration in any form.

DANIEL MURRAY,
Washington, D. C.

April 20, 1915.

APPENDIX B.

PARALLELISMS AND DISPARITIES IN THE CONDITION OF THE ANCIENT HEBREW IN EGYPT AND THE MODERN NEGRO IN AMERICA.

It is more than an idle fancy that compares the colored people in the United States with the Children of Israel in Egypt. There are many resemblances, but more differences. The untrained mind, however, dwells more readily upon resemblances than differences, and most minds are untrained; therefore the similarities of situations have received more attention than the differences.

Let us examine critically this oft-quoted, but superficial and misunderstood similitude:—

1. The Israelites were voluntary immigrants into Egypt. They enjoyed not only freedom but privilege and honor. They were finally reduced to a form of slavery through ethnic jealousy and national proscription.

2. Deliverance came through the efforts of an educated, trained, and consecrated leader of their own blood.

3. They left the land of their degradation and the presence of their oppressors.

4. They started for a definite place with a definite object in view, namely, to realize the promise that they were to become a great and numerous people.

5. They had no desire to be like anybody else, but gloried in the fact that they were to be a peculiar people.

6. The Israelites were not chattel slaves in Egypt as were the Negroes in America, and did not live with the Egyptians as servants.

The district of Goshen (frontier), also called the land of Rameses (Gen. 47:2), where the Israelites were settled during the period of their sojourn in the land of the Pharaohs, was the most easterly border-land of Egypt. It was scarcely included in the boundaries of Egypt proper, and was inhabited by a mixed population of Egyptians and foreigners. (Exod. 12:38.)

They were a pastoral people, independent and prosperous, whose growing strength in the minds of Egyptian statesmen became a menance to the supremacy of the Pharaohs.

On the other hand,—

1. The Negroes were involuntary captives brought to this country by force and were compelled from the start to labor without reward under the eye and lash of the master whose absolute property they were. No segregation then.

2. Manumission came through extraneous sources, changing ideals and conditions of the masters rather than struggles of the slaves—yet the fugitive slave from the South helped produce the abolitionist of the North.

3. The Negro remained with his former owner and faced at close range the horrors of reconstruction.

4. The Negro had an intense longing for freedom, but no definite object in view.

5. At Emancipation the Negro had lost whatever of racial consciousness he had brought with him into captivity. A puerile and disastrous desire to be "like de white folks" had completely displaced the tribal ego.

6. The forty years in the Wilderness under Moses welded the heterogeneous horde of fugitives into a compact nation, but after fifty years there is no Negro Race in the United States today—only a similarly conditioned people of varied but cognate physical contour.

These are great and fundamental differences that must be considered in drawing conclusions if our findings are to be of any value.

There are, however, some undoubted and striking similarities:—

1. Their numbers increased the prejudice against them.

2. Their prosperity and industry brought on opposition and discrimination; in fact, decency and aspiration were more resented than ignorance and criminality. (To illustrate,—white people do not object to Negroes living in poor houses, etc. The great segregation move is against the Negroes seeking modern homes—Baltimore.)

3. The same excuse was made for injustice practised

against them. The Egyptian equivalent of "Nigger Domination" was worked for all it was worth.

4. They learned the virtues and vices of their oppressors. Their intellectual horizon was widened and their moral strength weakened by this contact. (The only crime for which organized society has been willing to risk its existence by condoning lynching is a vice of civilization unknown alike to the red savages of America and the black savages of Africa.)

5. They "increased and multiplied" despite oppression.

6. Their lot was made harder by internal strife and treachery. It was not Egyptian injustice and oppression, but Hebrew ingratitude and treachery that made Moses a fugitive. The petty jealousies and tale-bearings of fellow-slaves were often more burdensome and galling than the lash of the master during those "agonizing, cruel slavery days."

Tales of "nigger risings," with all their attendant horrors and barbarities, usually had such incipiency. Unfortunately for us, this tribe is not yet extinct; for we have no "secret orders" nor "sacred conclaves." One may find out on the streets any day the doings of any Negro lodge the previous night.

7. Their progress was hindered by their tendency to take the advice of the ignorant rather than that of the wise among them. While Moses was up in the mountain his followers made a golden calf. The Negro has had a hard time to overcome his fondness for the counsel of ignorant preachers, hoodoo doctors, and barber-shop lawyers. Less than three years ago I had an apparently intelligent colored man reject my advice in the treatment of a sore eye and accept that of a blacksmith.

The "mixed multitude" was a disturbing factor. How much better it would have been for the freedmen had the carpet bagger not been born! (This opprobrious epithet applies not to the religious missionaries who came in the wake of the Union Army with a spelling book in one hand and a Bible in the other. Their feet were shod with "the preparation of the Gospel of peace." This holy band, comparable only to the ante-bellum Southern abolitionists, is now almost gone.)

APPENDIX C.

Cruelty is not choice of victims, and slavery comes by power and opportunity and not by color.

In the year 1852 there was published "for the author," in the city of Philadelphia, by Crissy and Markley, a book, "The North and South, or Slavery and Its Contrasts," in which it was claimed that "Mrs. Stowe's book is an unjust and unfaithful picture of Southern life and characters." Warning the "wonder-working abolitionists that justice, as well as charity, begins at home," and upbraiding them for failure to "sympathize with the slavery of the North," the author asks:—

"Do we have no cruel whippings, no torture, no forcing the poor overburdened frame to labor beyond its capabilities? In a word, oh! free and happy citizens of the North, have you no slaves in your midst?"

He continues:—

"I should like to draw upon the memory of the public a little, and see if they can recall one case which a short time ago appeared in most of our Northen papers, where a so-called lady whipped severely a little bound girl she had living with her, and then, after the whipping, shut her up in a room at the top of the house for many days without food, and when at last she was released with life just remaining in her, she died in a few hours of starvation. What was this but murder, and yet the monster who perpetrated it was never brought to justice. The story was hushed up, and the rich lady is at liberty to commit as many more murders as suits her convenience."

Further along he quotes an editorial correspondent to show: "The deplorable effects of ill-timed and ill-advised emancipation in Jamacia, Antigua, and the Mauritius Islands, was such, the Earl of Derby himself declares, that the blacks were rapidly relapsing into a state of barbarism. Were our mock philanthropists here to have their own way, what a wretched condition would they eventually sink our black population to!"

The following story is one of his illustrations of the fierce cruelty of the bond slavery of the North.

"You remember that I was sent to the country to learn farming. I was bound to Mr. Hardgripe till I was of age, and you were no doubt satisfied that I was in comfortable quarters. I had not forgotten, my dear mother, our happy home in New York, and all the endearing recollections of my boyhood. If I had never known them it would have been better for me, for I would then perhaps have learned to submit to indignities that galled my proud nature. As to hard work, I did not mind that; I liked to be busy about something, and I cared little what, but I did dislike the cruel taunts I received about eating the bread of charity, and about my family, who were starving for bread in the city. I was forced to put up with every kind of insult, and was, indeed, the scapegoat of the family. Each one felt entitled to give me a kick or blow, and no one ever thought of giving me a kind word. Thus it was that a disposition, naturally buoyant and merry, became moody and sensitive, and when I sat in the chimney corner in the kitchen, looking into the blaze, and trying to figure out my future life, somebody would be sure to kick me out, and tell me to go split wood or fetch water, or do something besides looking into the fire so sulky. No doubt I seemed to them to be in the sulks, but I was not, mother. I was only trying to feel happy within myself, you know. Mr. Hardgripe has a daughter just my own age; a very pretty girl, but a very proud and selfish one. From the very first hour that I went beneath their roof, this young girl took every opportunity to make me feel the difference in our positions. She ordered me about in the most dictatorial manner, and if I did not move quickly enough to please her, she would slap me or kick me as if I had been a dog, and woe be to me if I dared to complain, or say one word in my own defense; the whole house would rise up against me; the father would appear with a cow-hide, the mother with the tongs, and the brother with a heavy walking stick, and I would be fairly chased out of the house, and forced to take up my quarters in the stable.

"While the warm weather lasted, and I had work to do in the open fields, I was comparatively happy, for I worked so hard there was no time to quarrel with me, till I went home to my supper, which was never made up of anything beyond salt meat and brown bread. However, I had a good appetite, and relished it, simple as it was. When I had performed all that was required of me about the house, I retired to bed in the garret, and slept as soundly, I am sure, as did my mistress or her pretty daughter.

"But as I grew older the kicks and cuffs I received began to awaken in my mind feelings of revenge and retaliation. My spirit rebelled against the indignity with which I was treated, and I not infrequently spoke freely in my own defense, but, alas! I soon found I was riveting my own chains. However, the spirit of opposition was aroused within me, and I determined to fight it out to the end.

"A constant warfare was the consequence of my resolution to assert my rights, and the very first time that I received a kick from Miss Jane, I kicked back. She ran screaming to her mother, and I made good my retreat, and ran out the back way, and across the fields till I reached a patch of woods, about a half-mile distant from the house. There Mr. Hardgripe and two of his men found me. He seized me by the hand and led me away to the open field, muttering as he went, and grinding his teeth together; I could hear him say, 'What shall I do with this little wretch, that kicked my daughter? How shall I punish him; how shall I hurt him enough?'

"Mr. Hardgripe led me with long strides to the foot of a tree. He ordered me to undress. I did so. He told the men to tie me up to a limb of the tree with some strong cords they had brought with them. This they soon accomplished, and then I felt the hard, heavy blows of the cow-hide, cutting and bruising my flesh, and seeming to be grinding my bones to powder. I held out as long as I could, but at last I begged for mercy. I implored his pity; but still the blows descended, and at each repetition laid open the quivering flesh. In the midst of this agony, consciousness forsook me, and I knew not what happened for hours afterward.

When, however, I at last opened my eyes, I found I was laid in my own garret, but there was no one near me. I felt an intense burning thirst. There was no water at hand. I tried to rise from the bed, but my bruised and mangled body would not permit. I writhed in agony, and in that hour I remembered the prayer you had taught me,—oh, my mother! I remembered that you had told me there was a God who was a friend to the friendless and the destitute, and was I not friendless indeed? I called upon His name so long forgotten, and prayed that He would help me in this hour of sore distress. But my help was not yet. I heard a noise on the stairs, of a heavy step ascending. The next moment Mr. Hardgripe entered the room. He held a lemon in his hand, cut in two. For what purpose he had brought it, I soon learned. He turned me over on my side and, with a malicious leer on his face, he squeezed the juice into the open cuts on my back. Oh, God! Oh, my mother, can you imagine the torture he inflicted upon me? I felt the cold shivering of agonized despair run over me. I implored him to have mercy upon me, as he hoped for mercy from God; but, no, he pursued his purpose till he had satisfied himself, and then left me, deaf to my cries for water, deaf to everything but the cruel promptings of his iron-like heart.

"Hours rolled by: *such long, such weary hours.* I thought of you and my sweet sister Gazella, and thought how glad you would have been to dress my wounds, and allay my maddening thirst. The peaked roof of the garret only threw back the echo of my own voice. Night came on, and still the fever burned in my veins, and my body increased in soreness. At last the men came up to bed. I implored them to get me some water. They brought it, and I drank a long, refreshing draught. It cooled me and brought me comparative ease, but I was still suffering too much to sleep. I laid awake till near daylight, looking through the little dormer window at the beautiful stars, and the soft, bright moon, that lit every portion of my garret. Hope awoke within me. I knew that the world was wide; that all men were not tyrants. I resolved to run away and, while planning the how and the when, I fell asleep."

APPENDIX D.

THAT the feeling which leads the Negro to protest against the misrepresentation of his people in literature and the drama is not limited to the Negro, is shown by the following editorial:

SHYLOCK AND CHILDHOOD.

In the current issue of the Nashville *Young Men's Hebrew Association News* an article appears urging that "The Merchant of Venice" be not included in the course of study in the High School. Admittedly one of Shakespeare's masterpieces from a literary standpoint, the argument is made that its reading produces in the mind of the young child a deep-seated prejudice against his Jewish classmate, Shylock being accepted as the type of all Jews. The Jewish child, the article continues, "sits in his class embarrassed and cowed, his cheeks tingling with the blush of humiliation and shame, powerless to say or do aught for his own relief."

All of us know that a desire to take human blood in lieu of money due is not characteristic of the Jews. In "The Merchant of Venice" the money-lender is what the persecutions and the heartlessness of his Christian neighbors have made him. He demands his pound of flesh not because he is a Jew, but because he is a human being who has suffered and seeks revenge. "The Merchant of Venice" is not less an indictment against the uncharity of a community professedly Christian than against avarice. "But," says the article in the *Young Men's Hebrew Association News,* "the unformed and untrained mind of the child does not see these things and cannot overcome the impression which this play produces."

We would be inclined to think that the teacher, if she explained the play as the class read it, might obviate these evils. There must always be the danger, however, of having children fall into the hands of teachers who might not have the tact to explain properly. There is the possibility, as mentioned in the article, that nothing the teacher could say would weigh with the child against what he conceives Shakespeare to mean.

Certainly the Jewish child should not be humiliated in the schools. Certainly the Gentile child should not be given a false impression. Possibly "The Merchant of Venice" does not produce so much of an evil effect as some are disposed to think it does, but if the Jewish people think it does there is justification for eliminating it from the course of study. "If meat maketh my brother to offend, I will eat no meat," declared the Christian, Paul. That is good Christianity now.

Anyway there are enough of the great Shakespearean plays adapted to use in High Schools that no injury would be done the literary balance of things by eliminating "The Merchant of Venice." (Editorial, *Tennessean and American,* April 8, 1915.)

APPENDIX E.

THE growing liberality of the Southern press is indicated by the appearance of the following communication in a recent issue of the leading morning paper of Middle Tennessee, under the general heading, "Editorials by Our Readers":—

THE PSYCHOLOGY OF CRIME: AN APPEAL.

To the Editor of the Tennessean and American:—

The problem of democracy is to preserve and promote the general welfare with the least possible curtailment of the liberty of the individual. This ideal can be realized only when the individual is self-governing. Anything therefore that tends to make the individual considerate, fair-minded, and just is a direct contribution to the welfare of our country. On the other hand, anything that tends to personal irresponsibility and individual injustice is against the general welfare. The soul of democracy is surrendered when the ignorant or vicious gain control.

America is the most criminal of civilized nations, and the colored people contribute much more than their share to this awful record. It is the duty of every citizen to promote the general welfare by lessening crime. Even-handed justice is the surest road to this desirable goal. A sense of injustice is an incentive to crime, and suggestion plays an important part in our criminal record. Here is where the "liberty of an unlicensed press" becomes a factor in the psychology of crime.

Two items in Sunday's edition of your paper will illustrate my meaning.

One reported the death penalty for a brutal crime, but was so worded that force and brevity were both sacrificed to give the item a racial tinge.

The other reported a case of highway robbery and mentioned the word "Negro" (with a small "n") nine times in an article nine inches long. This type of journalism increases crime in three ways:—

1. Along the borderline of crime and respectability, it enables the criminally inclined Negro to bully his law-abiding neighbor by showing the latter that he gets no credit for his goodness.

2. It makes the Negro criminal believe there is little danger of punishment if he but confine his crimes to his own race.

3. The white criminal is given letters of marque against the Negro race.

On behalf of the respectable, law-abiding Negroes of this city, I appeal to the great morning paper of the Athens of the South to set the noble and democratic example of not mentioning the race or religion of a criminal in giving criminal news.

C. V. ROMAN,
1303 Church St.

January 22, 1915.

APPENDIX F.

THESE articles from *The Medical World* show several things, among which we call attention to the following: (*a*) There is a class of people who desire "to keep down" the colored people. (*b*) This class is not any more liberally endowed intellectually than morally. (*c*) The sentiment of "keeping down" is not unanimous. (*d*) A colored physician's views.

WANTS TO KEEP NEGRO PHYSICIANS DOWN!

Dr. C. F. Taylor, Ed. of The Med. World.

DEAR SIR:—What is the negro physician doing as a whole through out the country as a physician and surgeon? What are they doing financialy? How do they compare with the white aplicants in State examinations through out the country? I notice in some places they seams to be makeing more money then the white physicians. What is the best thing we can do to keep him down? Please let me here from you in the nex No. of the *World* Yours Truly,—. —. ———.

[The above comes from a Southern State, but we venture the opinion that it does not voice the sentiment of Southern medical men. We print the above letter exactly as received. It does not show high literary attainments. In some States there are Negro State medical associations, and there is a "National Medical Association," composed of Negro physicians, and this National Association publishes a very creditable journal at 1303 Church St., Nashhville, Tenn. It is entirely proper that there should be Negro physicians, educated to care for their race. We understand that they are making very commendable progress. We congratulate them, and bid them godspeed. If we have any Negro subscribers, and we suppose we have, we invite them to give a more full reply to the above letter than we can do offhand—for example, statistics concerning numbers, the degree of prosperity which they achieve, what record they have made before State examining boards, etc.—ED.]

[*The Medical World,* February, 1914.]

Status of the Negro in Medicine.

Editor Medical World:—As a reader of your valuable journal I wish to say something of the letter in the February *World* about the Negro physician and surgeon.

1. The writer asks how is the Negro physician and surgeon succeeding professionally; that is, is he curing his patients?

2. What is the Negro doctor doing financially?

3. How do the Negro applicants for medical license before the various State boards compare with white applicants?

4. "I notice," says the writer, "in some places they seams to be makeing more money than the white physicians." This he regards as a menace and asks you to tell him in "the nex No. of the *World* what is the best thing we can do to keep him down?"

Ignoring the spirit displayed under heading IV, which would exclude the inquirer from the information sought on the ground of impure motives, I will attempt to answer in detail his inquiries:—

I.

Professionally, the Negro doctor is a success. He has a reasonable grasp on the principles of medicine and surgery and is able to apply those principles to the healing of the sick and the prevention of disease.

Comparative statistics show that the mortality rate in hospitals conducted by Negro physicians is not excessively high, and the percentage of cures is up to the average. I am familiar with the workings of two large colored hospitals, the George W. Hubbard Hospital, in Nashville, and Andrew Memorial, in Tuskegee. I have known long series of major operations in these hospitals without a death. I have reliable information that the same is true of the Frederick Douglass and Mercy Hospitals in Philadelphia; Freedman's Hospital, Washington, D. C.; Lincoln Hospital, Durham, N. C.; Fair Haven Infirmary, Atlanta, Ga., and Leonard Hospital, in Raleigh, N. C., to say nothing of the numerous private hospitals and infirmaries run by colored men.

The colored physicians are liked by their clientele and are usually on good terms with each other and with the white physicians.

There are State societies in New England, New Jersey, Pennsylvania, Ohio, Virginia, West Virginia, North Carolina, South Carolina, Georgia, Florida, Alabama, Mississippi, Tennessee, Kentucky, Missouri, Arkansas, Texas, Louisiana, and Oklahoma.

There is a Tristate Society, including Georgia, Florida and Alabama. There were more than twenty States represented in the last annual session of the National Medical Association. There are local societies in all the cities and large towns of the country that have a numerous population—Baltimore, Md.; Washington, D. C.; Philadelphia, New York City, Boston, Chicago, Kansas City, Mo.; Dallas, Tex.; Nashville, Tenn., etc. The ability displayed in some of these society meetings I am sure would astound some people who claim to "know all about the Negro" and yet never attend his lodges, churches, or societies. On the rosters of these societies you will find alumni of the best medical colleges of this country.

There have been fifteen presidents of the National Medical Association. In addition to the leading Negro medical colleges —Meharry, Howard, and Leonard—Harvard, Yale, Long Island, Western Reserve, University of Pennsylvania, and Ann Arbor are represented in this brief list. Some of these men have had the advantage of foreign travel and study.

Emphatically, and without exaggeration, the Negro doctor has made good professionally; good for his people, his country, and himself.

II.

When the rewards become the dominating object of professional pursuits, degeneration sets in and a calling becomes a trade. Nevertheless, the permanent welfare of a profession demands that those who honestly and efficiently perform its duties should be able to answer without embarrassment the elemental but insistent questions: "What shall I eat? And what shall I drink? And wherewithal shall I be clothed?" In this country, continued extreme poverty in any vocation must be accepted as an indication of incapacity. The converse is also true. A man that accumulates wealth must be conceded a measure of capacity—a capacity that must not be overvalued, however; for no virtue more easily becomes a vice than the power to accumulate wealth.

The colored doctor has met the financial test. The average income among us is up to or a little above the general average; we are seldom represented in the extremes either up or down. The humblest usually make a living, and eventually gather a modest competence, while the more fortunate and able occasionally become comparatively wealthy. Among us there is no exception to a lamentable fact of civilization, viz., the brainiest and most useful often remain poor, because of their kindnesses and sacrifices, while the less able but more selfish frequently grow rich. I beg to assure your correspondent that there is no danger of the Negro doctor's cornering the wealth of the nation.

III.

How do the colored and white applicants for medical license compare? This is a difficult and dangerous question to answer, for from time immemorial comparisons have been odious. Prejudice takes some queer turns, and life reveals some unexpected compensations. Nature is hard to cheat and meanness seldom proves a permanently valuable asset to an individual or race. The writer, while a post-graduate student in a great American city, joined with three of his fellow-students [white, we suppose] to make a class of four to employ a special demonstrator for certain operations. A consciousness of superiority led them to form a secret compact by which he should come last, which was really the best place, for he had the advantage of the teacher's repeated demonstrations and of their errors. He good-naturedly accepted the place assigned him, but inwardly resolved to make the best of it. This he did, being the only one of the four to do the operation successfully at the first trial. They were kind enough and blind enough to attribute it to his superior ability. This happily broke up further snobbishness in the class.

The State boards have not been guilty of any culpable

leniency to Negro applicants; consequently, if there be any pronounced difference in the qualification of the applicants, it fails to appear in the accepted product. The licensed Negro doctors have met the same test as licensed white doctors, and things being equal to the same thing equal each other. The average Negro doctor is certainly as efficient with his people as the average white doctor is with his.

IV.

Your correspondent asks "What is the best thing we can do to keep him down?" As I said at the start, the spirit of this interrogatory would properly exclude the inquirer from the information sought, on the ground of impure motives. But envy and malice are but perversions of the virtue of self-preservation. I therefore ignore the manifest unkindness and seek to give my neighbor light.

Creed is greater than color, and brain is more potent than brawn. The real differences in races and individuals are intellectual rather than physical. The ignorant and vicious white man is close kin to the ignorant and vicious Negro; and all who love the truth and seek the right, regardless of kindred, tribe, or tongue, shall eventually be numbered with the elect, both here and hereafter. So it was in the beginning, is now and ever shall be, Amen. So have believed the great and wise of every age and every clime. Liberty is for all or for none. Civilization will never triumph until all men desire freedom for all men. In the words of Burns—

> Then let us pray that come it may,—
> As come it will for a' that;
> That truth and worth o'er a' the earth
> Shall bear the gree and a' that.

C. V. Roman, M.D.,
1303 Church St., Nashville, Tenn.

[*The Medical World,* April, 1914.]

APPENDIX G.

THE APPORTIONMENT OF PUBLIC-SCHOOL FUNDS IN THE SOUTH.

THE city of Jacksonville, Fla., recently voted a million-dollar-bond issue for the erection of new school buildings. The school board has completed its program and has decided to expend for white schools the sum of $850,000, and for colored schools the sum of $115,000. These figures are not secret, but have been published in the Jacksonville daily papers; which fact goes to prove either that the school board is not conscious of any unfairness in such a division or that it is not ashamed to be unfair.

According to the census of 1910, the colored population of Jacksonville amounted to 50.8 per cent. of the total population; that is, a little more than half. There are now, perhaps, 35,000 colored people living in that city; and it is safe to say that there is not a community in the South that has a more industrious, enterprising, progressive, and law-abiding Negro element than Jacksonville. That this is not a mere assertion is proved by the fact that the Florida metropolis is one of the fastest-growing and most prosperous cities, not only of the South, but of the whole country; and if more than one-half of its population was backward and shiftless and lawless it could not make such progress. No matter how energetic the white people might be, they could not carry that amount of dead weight.

The colored people of Jacksonville are engaged in every kind of business, from peanut vending to banking. (It is needless to mention how much support they give to white business enterprises.) They work at all the mechanical trades, from mending shoes to building skyscrapers and steamships. They do all of the hard labor. Many of them are home owners, and pay a fair share of taxes. In fact, they are essential contributors to the wealth and prosperity of their city.

On the other hand, what do they get? They get no such returns as come from holding office and municipal jobs. They benefit only to a small degree from the funds appropriated for public improvements. They have no share in the money spent for public recreation. The only direct return they get is the pittance spent upon the education of their children.

This being the fact, is it not just and right and righteous that they should receive a fairer share of the public-school fund than is now contemplated by the Board of Education?

We cite this case because it applies in a general way to nearly every city in the South.

Look at the figures given below. They are from the "Negro Year-Book" for 1914-1915, and show the amount expended per child of school age in the following eight Southern States:—

Virginia	for whites, $10.92;	for colored, $3.43.
Florida	for whites, 14.75;	for colored, 3.10.
North Carolina	for whites, 6.69;	for colored, 2.50.
Louisiana	for whites, 16.60;	for colored, 1.59.
Mississippi	for whites, 8.20;	for colored, 1.53.
Alabama	for whites, 8.50;	for colored, 1.49.
Georgia	for whites, 9.18;	for colored, 1.42.
South Carolina	for whites, 9.65;	for colored, 1.09.

By way of comparison, look at the following figures prepared for the "World Almanac" of 1915, and showing the amount expended per child of school age in eight Northern States:—

New Jersey	$58.51.
New York	49.73.
Massachusetts	49.13.
Pennsylvania	40.09.
Connecticut	39.92.
Rhode Island	37.06.
New Hampshire	36.88.
Vermont	34.80.

A glance at these two tables brings up the problem in higher arithmetic often propounded by Dr. Booker T. Washington, "If it costs $49.13 a year to educate a white child in Massachusetts, how much education can a black child in South Carolina get for $1.09?"

We cannot complain because South Carolina does not spend as much as Massachusetts for education, for the simple reason that she has not got it to spend; but we are justified in complaining of the fact that South Carolina pays out $9.65 a year on the education of each white child, and only $1.09 on each colored child.

Going back to the case of Jacksonville, the statement made above that the colored people of that city pay their fair share of the taxes has nothing to do with the merits of the question. The theory of political economy which recognizes the landowner as the one who really pays the taxes is not tenable. It is obsolete, and the school boards of Jacksonville and of every other Southern city know it.

The 35,000 colored people in Jacksonville live in houses either their own or belonging to somebody else, and they pay either taxes or rent; in either case, they pay taxes. Besides, they contribute their *pro rata* of all indirect taxes, and no reduction is made for them in fines and licenses. So, for the white citizens, because their names are in the majority on the tax books, to claim that they have to stand the cost of educating the Negro children of the community is as absurd as it would be for the relatively few landowners of New York City to complain that they have to stand the financial burden of educating the thousands and thousands of children whose parents pay rent for tenements and flats.

The South often makes the boast that it has spent hundreds of millions for Negro education, and that it has of its own free will shouldered this awful burden. It seems forgetful of the fact that all of this money has been taken from the public tax funds for education. Let the millions of producing and consuming Negroes be taken out of the South, and it would very quickly be seen how much less of public funds there would be to appropriate for education or any other purpose.

As the conditions set forth above are general and concern the whole race, let us consider what we are going to do about the matter. To narrow it down to the case before us, What are the colored people of Jacksonville going to do about it? I can almost hear some reader answer, "Nothing."

But something should be done. The matter should at first be laid before the school board in a comprehensive, direct, and intelligent manner. If this step should fail, the question should be appealed to the white citizens at large. It is difficult to believe that there are not enough fair-minded white people in Jacksonville to influence such a case as this.

If there are not enough so fair-minded as to be able to see the justice of a more equable, if not equal, division, there ought at least to be enough who from an economic point of view could see the advantages of it. They evidently want their city to continue to develop and prosper; well, it can't if more than half the population is kept back and down. It can't if eight times as much is spent upon a white child in order to give him a chance to become a good citizen as is spent upon a colored child. It would be common sense and good business to reverse the figures.

If neither of these steps succeed there is only one left, and that is for the colored citizens to raise sufficient money to legally oppose the spending of the proceeds of the bonds in the manner designated by the school board. Let them raise a sufficient amount to take the case, if necessary, to the Supreme Court of the United States.

JAMES W. JOHNSON,

[*The New York Age,* March 11, 1915.]

GLOSSARY.

Aborigines. First inhabitants of a country; literally "from the beginning."
Abortive. Happening out of time; used in medicine to refer to a child born before time, *i.e.*, before it is fully developed. Hence the word means, happening before time.
Abrogate. Abolish, repeal, annul.
Achromatic. Without color.
Adipose. Fatty.
Adjudication. The passing of judgment.
Adolescent. Approaching manhood or womanhood; youthful.
Agenesic. Without the power of reproduction.
Alchemy. The doctrine of early chemists; hence any magical or mysterious power or process of transmuting or transforming.
Alibi. A form of defense by which the accused, in order to establish his innocence, undertakes to show that he was elsewhere when the crime was committed.
Alienism. Estrangement; alienage.
Altruism. Literally "otherism"; opposed to egoism or selfishness; unselfish kindness.
Anaphylaxis. Inability to resist disease; susceptibility.
Anarchy. Without government; lawless.
Anatomization. Minute examination; analyses of anatomical structure.
Anthropology. Science of Man.
Anthropometry. That department of Anthropology which relates to the proportions of the human body.
Antonym. A word directly opposed to another in meaning; a counter word. The opposite to synonym.
Apodictic. Defined on page 5.
A posteriori. Reasoning from experience; empirical; opposed to *à priori* reasoning.
A priori. A method of reasoning opposed to *à posteriori.*
Architectonic. Defined on page 329.
Assertory. Defined on page 5.
Atrophy. A drying up or withering away, or to dry up or wither away; a medical term.
Autocentric. Self-centered.
Avatar. A champion or embodiment of a doctrine; literally, an incarnation.
Averments. Statements; assertions.

Bastardize. To beget out of wedlock; to render mongrel or hybrid.
Biology. Science of life.
Blancoid. Defined on page 266.
Blanco-Negro. Defined on page 246.
Brachycephalic. Defined on page 167.
Burke. Defined on page 128.

Caliber. Size (fig.); capacity or compass of mind.
Canon. A law or rule, especially ecclesiastical.

Canonical. Pertaining to a canon or ecclesiastical law.
Carcinoma. Form of cancer.
Casuistry. Science or doctrine of cases of conscience; or of determining the lawfulness or unlawfulness of what one may do by rules and principles drawn from the Scriptures.
Catalytic. Some bodies have the power of inducing or causing by their presence chemical changes in other bodies without themselves undergoing any change. This power is called catalysis or catalytic action. In sociology, then, a group of people might be said to have a catalytic value when their presence influences the composition of the social fabric.
Caucasian. Term invented by Blumenbach to describe the white variety of mankind.
Cellular. Pertaining to or composed of cells; cell, the unit of physiology.
Cephalometry. Defined on page 329.
Chaotic. Confused; disordered.
Chromatopsia. Disordered color-vision. A disorder of vision in which color-impressions arise subjectively. It may be due to disturbance of the optic centers, or to drugs.
Climacteric. A critical period. In medicine, the menopause.
Coeval. Born at the same time, or existing together.
Cohorts. A band or body of warriors.
Complementary. Completing; supplying a deficiency; supplementary.
Composite. Made up of parts. A mixed blood; used as equivalent to the general term mulatto.
Congeners. Born together. A thing of the same genus; a thing allied in kind or nature.
Congenital. Existing from birth.
Consanguineous. Of same blood; related by birth; descended from same parent or ancestor.
Constituent. One who establishes, determines, or constructs. One who assists to appoint or elect a representative to an office or employment.
Contingent. Not existing or occurring through necessity; conditional.
Contravention. The act or state of being in conflict with something.
Corollary. A deduction from previous propositions.
Coup d'etat. An unexpected stroke of policy; a bold or brilliant piece of statesmanship; generally unconstitutional, executed suddenly, and often accompanied by violence.
Craniometry. Measurements of the skull.
Crucial. Critical; very important; severe; trying or searching.
Cryptogram. Secret characters; cipher.
Cultural unity. Tending to promote refinement or education; hence, "cultural unity" means a group of people having similar ethical and economic standards.
Cupidity. Inordinate desire to possess something; covetousness; lust.
Cystoma. Form of tumor or swelling containing fluid.

Delinquency. Failure or omission of duty or obligation; a shortcoming.
Detriment. Injury; mischief; harm.
Diapason. The entire compass of a voice or of an instrument.
Diatribe. Bitter or violent criticism; a strain of invective.

Dicteria. Plural of dicterion; schools of prostitution.
Dicteriades. A class of prostitutes among the Greeks.
Dicterion. School of prostitution.
Differentiation. Formation of differences or the discrimination of varieties; specialization.
Disputant. One who disputes. Disputing or debating.
Disputation. A reasoning or argumentation in opposition to something.
Doctrinaire. Theoretical; impractical.
Dolichocephalic. Defined on page 167.
Dysgenesic. Reproducing with difficulty.

Ebullition. Boiling; effervescence which is occasioned by fermentation; outward display of feeling or agitation.
Elephantiasis. A tropical disease characterized by an enormous enlargement of the affected part.
Embryological. The development of the embryo and fetus of animals; pertaining to anything in its first rudiments or undeveloped state.
Emmenagogue. A medical term used to designatė a medicine or agent to stimulate menstrual flow.
Emmet. An ant.
Empirical. Depending upon experience and observation without due regard to science or theory.
En masse. A French phrase meaning all together; in a body.
Envisage. To look in the face of; to apprehend by a direct or immediate act; to know by intuition.
Epithelioma. A kind of cancer.
Equivalent. That which is equal in value, weight, dignity, or force.
Ethnical. Racial.
Ethnology. The science which treats of the divisions of man into races, their origin and relations, and the differences which characterize them.
Etiolation. Defined on page 351.
Eugenesic. Easily reproducing.
Eurignathic. Defined on page 328.
Execration. Cursing or abusing; detestation; imprecation of evil; utter detestation expressed.

Facial angle. Defined on page 331.
Fatuous. Feeble in mind; weak; silly; stupid.
Fecundation. Fertilizing or making fruitful.
Fibroma. A form of tumor or enlargement.
Finesse. Delicate skill; refinement; subtlety of contrivance; cunning; strategy.
Flagellation. Whipping; flogging; discipline with the scourge.

Gamut. Figuratively, the whole scale, range, or compass of a thing.
Ganglionic. A cluster or nodule of nerve-cells.
Genitalia. The sexual organs.
Genito-urinary. Pertaining to the bladder, kidneys, and the sexual organs.
Ghetto. Jews' quarter in Rome. A segregated district.
Glandular. Pertaining to glands.
Glottologist. A philologist; one versed in or engaged in study of languages.
Gregariously. Having the habit of living in a flock or herd; not habitually solitary or living alone.

Gullible. Easily deceived; tricked; cheated or defrauded.
Gynecology. The medical study that treats of women and the diseases peculiar to the female sex.

Hegemony. Leadership; preponderant influence of authority; usually applied to government.
Heterosexual. That natural affinity occurring between opposite sex.
Hexiology. Defined on page 228.
Hierarch. One who rules or has authority in sacred things.
Histological. Pertaining to the tissues. That branch of biology that treats of the structure of tissues of organized bodies.
Hominidæ. A zoölogical classification designating man as distinct from other living creatures.
Homogeneous. Sameness of kind or nature; uniformity of structure, elements alike.
Homosexual. When persons of the same sex are attracted to each other sexually, the affinity is said to be homosexual; an abnormality.

Iconoclastic. Breaker or destroyer of images or idols; exposer of impositions.
Ideomotor. Thought-rule, or governed by ideas rather than feeling. The opposite of sensorimotor.
Idyl. Literally a little form or image. A short poem; properly a pastoral poem.
Immanent. Indwelling; inherent; remaining within.
Immiscibles. Not capable of being mixed.
Immunity. Freedom from obligation; exemption from any charge, duty, office tax, or imposition; a particular privilege.
Impregnable. State or quality of being invincible; that cannot be taken by assault. In biology, capable of being impregnated.
Inadequacy. State or quality of being insufficient or unequal to a requirement.
Inalienable. Incapable of being put off or transferred to another.
Inanity. Void space; emptiness; frivolity.
Incarcerate. Imprison; to confine.
Incorrigible. Hopelessly depraved.
Increment. A growing bulk, number, quantity, value or amount; augmentation.
Infinitesimal. That which is extremely small; less than assignable quantity.
Inhere. To be fixed or permanently incorporated.
Insidious. Sly; treacherous; crafty; wily; designing.
Intermediary. That which lies between or is intermediate.
Iridescent. Having colors like the rainbow.
Iteration. Repetition.

Keloid. A peculiar kind of tumor or swelling that grows about scars. A keloid seems composed of scar-tissue.
Kinetic (Physics). Of, pertaining to, or due to motion; often contrasted with potential, as kinetic energy.

Lacedæmonian. Spartan.
Laissez faire. A French phrase abbreviated from a sentence meaning let alone, the world revolves of itself; hence, the expression means non-interference; doctrine of letting things alone; in economics, unrestricted competition.

Lascivious. Wanton; lewd; lustful.
Latent. Hidden; in secret or concealed manner.
Lecherous. Lewd; strong propensity to indulge sexual appetite.
Leiotrichi. Defined on page 328.
Leonidas. A king of Sparta famous for his courage; was killed at Thermopylæ.
Leptorrhinian. Thin-nosed; used to describe certain classes of people.
Lugubrious. Sad; mournful; indicating sorrow.

Marchette or Marchetta. A feudal custom by means of which the lord of the manor controlled the marital rights of the daughters of his tenants.
Martyrology. History of martyrs; a catalogue of martyrs.
Matrix. A mold.
Megasemes
Mesosemes } Defined on page 332.
Microsemes
Mesorhinians. Classes of people having certain bird-like noses; small-nosed.
Microcosm. A little world. A miniature institution. Hence man, supposed to be an epitome of the universe or great world.
Milieu. A French word meaning environment.
Mirabile dictu. Latin phrase meaning wonderful to tell.
Mirage. An optical illusion.
Misanthrope. A hater of mankind; one who harbors dislike or distrust of human character or motives in general.
Miscegenation. A mixing of races; amalgamation.
Miserere. One of the penitential psalms; a prayer or ejaculation for mercy.
Misology. Hatred of discussion or inquiry; aversion to enlightenment.
Monochrome. One color; as a painting with a single color.
Monogamy. Single marriage; principle which upholds marrying only one.
Monogenesis. Oneness of origin.
Monograph. A special treatise on a particular subject of limited range.
Monomaniac. Insane on some particular subject.
Monopoly. Exclusive control; command or possession.
Moral obliquity. Crookedness.
Morganatic. Pertaining to a kind of marriage, called also left-handed marriage, between man and woman of different ranks in which the one of inferior rank inherits no title or possession of the superior.
Morphology. That branch of biology that treats of the form and structure of animals and plants.

Nebulous. Having its parts mixed, confused, or blended; figuratively, not clear; hazy.
Negrophily. Love of the Negro.
Negrophobe. One unreasonably excited about the Negro.
Neoplasm. An abnormal growth.
Ne plus ultra. Nothing more beyond; a latin phrase.
Noblesse oblige. A French phrase meaning, literally, nobility obliges; noble birth or rank compels to noble acts. Hence the phrase means the obligation of noble conduct imposed upon those favored with high position or authority. The very posi-

tion of the white man in this country should make him kind and considerate in dealing with the colored man.

Nomenclature. A system of naming.

Norm. A rule or authoritative standard; a model; a type.

Nostalgia. Excessive longing for home or country; homesickness.

Nouveau riche. Newly rich; uncultured.

Nuance. A shade of difference in color; a slight degree of difference in anything perceptible to senses or mind.

Objectivity. The quality of being manifest; visible, or tangible.

Obsessed. Vexed or besieged by evil spirit.

Oligarchy. Class government.

Ontogeny. The history of the evolution of the individual; germ history.

Orgie. A wild or frantic revel; a nocturnal carousal; drunken revelry.

Orientation. Finding the east; locating the points of the compass; getting one's bearings. Defined on page 12.

Orthognathic. Defined on page 328.

Orthognathism. The condition of being orthognathic.

Palaver. A parley; a conference.

Paleontology. The science of the ancient life of the earth, or of fossils which are the remains of such life.

Pariah. Beggar; outcast; one rejected by society.

Pelvis. The open, bony structure at the lower extremity of the body, usually inclosing internal urinary and genital organs and always connecting posterior members with the spine.

Personnel. The body of persons employed in some public service, as the army or navy, as distinguished from the material.

Perspective. A view; a vista.

Phallic. Pertaining to the genitalia.

Philology. Study of languages.

Philtre. A potion to excite sexual love or desire; a love potion.

Phylogenetic. Appertaining to phylogeny.

Phylogeny. The evolution of the species as distinguished from ontogeny, the evolution of the individual.

Placental. A mammal having a placenta.

Platyrrhine. Wide- or broad- nosed; one of a group of monkeys having large, wide nostrils.

Poignant. Painful; severe; piercing; very painful or acute; sharp; penetrating.

Polychrome. Many-colored.

Polygenesis. From Greek words meaning many and origination; hence it means arising from many sources.

Polyp. A small animal of extremely simple construction.

Potential. Having latent power.

Precocious. A premature growth or development; early ripeness.

Predestination. Foreordaining events. Often the preassignment or allotment of men to eternal happiness or misery.

Prerequisite. Previously required or necessary to any proposed effect or end.

Primate. One of a group of mammals in the Linnæan system, including man and monkeys, sometimes only man.

Primordial. First in order; original; of very earliest origin.

Probity. Rectitude; uprightness; honesty.

Problematic. Questionable; uncertain; unsettled; disputable; doubtful.

Procreative. Reproductive; generative.
Progenitor. An ancestor in the direct line.
Progeny. Offspring; race; children.
Prognathism. Projection of the jaws forward. See Facial angle.
Prognathous. Defined on page 328.
Protoplasmic. Pertaining to the first formation of living bodies.
Pseudo-science. Pretended or counterfeit science.
Psychical. Of or pertaining to the human soul or mind.
Psychology. Science of the human soul; mental science; mental philosophy.
Pulsometer. A pumping device. Frequently spelled pulsimeter.

Reconnoiter. To make a preliminary survey or investigation.
Recrimination. To retort a charge; to charge back a fault or crime upon an accuser.
Reincarnate. Reclothe in flesh; embodying again; a manifestation; a personification.
Reiteration. Repetition; tautology.
Repertoire. A list of numbers, pieces, or the like, that a person or company is prepared to perform, and from which programs may be made up.
Res adjudicata. A Latin phrase meaning settled or adjudicated matter; a closed question.

Salient. Prominent; conspicuous.
Sarcoma. A tumor made up of embryonal connective tissue.
Satraps. Rulers; governors.
Savant. A person eminent for acquirements.
Sedentary. Inactive; motionless; sluggish; accustomed to sit much, or long.
Sensorimotor. Action controlled by sense impressions or feelings rather than reason. Defined on page 168.
Sensorium. A center for sensations, especially the part of the brain concerned in receiving and combining the impressions conveyed to the individual sensory centers.
Sentient. Having a faculty of sensation and perception; perceiving.
Seriatim. In regular order.
Simioid. Resembling a monkey; monkey-like.
Snobbishness. Pretentiousness; to pretend to be something better than one is.
Spurious. Not legitimate; bastard; false; counterfeit.
Steatopyga. Enormous fatness of the buttocks.
Stigmatize. To mark with a stigma or brand; to set a mark of disgrace on; to disgrace with reproach or infamy.
Strabismus. Squinting; the act or habit of looking asquint. An affection of the eye, or eyes, in which the optic axes cannot be directed to the same object.
Sub-brachycephaly. Defined on page 167.
Succedaneum. Substitute; that which is used for something else.
Synonymous. Identical; interchangeable.

Tablier. An apron; in anatomy, used to designate a peculiar formation of the female genitalia.
Tenet. An opinion, principle, dogma, or doctrine that a person holds or maintains to be true.
Tetrapod. A quadruped; four-footed.
Thermopylæ. Famous Grecian pass. Battlefield in B.C. 480.

Thews. Sinews or muscles, especially when well developed; hence, bodily strength or vigor.
Transcendentalism. In general the doctrine that the principles of reality are to be discovered by the study of the processes of thought; surpassing; excelling; superior or supreme.
Travesty. Burlesque; parody caricature.
Triplicate. Threefold, or to make threefold.
Trireme. A galley or vessel with three ranks of oars on each side, commanded by a trierarch and often manned by over 200 men.
Turpitude. Inherent baseness and vileness of principle, nature, or conduct; depravity.
Tyro. One in the very rudiments of any branch of study; a beginner in learning; a novitiate.

Ulotrichi. Defined on page 328.
Unsophisticated. Free from adulteration; free from artificiality; simple; artless; showing inexperience; verdant.

Vacillating. Swaying back and forth; wavering.
Venality. State or character of being venal or sordid; mercenariness; prostitution of talents, offices, or services for money or reward.
Venereal. Of or pertaining to venery or sexual intercourse.
Venery. Gratification of sexual desires.
Verisimilitude. Probability; likelihood; appearance of truth.
Vicarious. Acting or suffering for another; performed or suffered for another.
Vicinage. Neighborhood, vicinity; a village.
Vicissitude. Complete change; a revolution; mutation.
Vis-a-vis. In a position facing one another.
Vitiates. To make void; to impair; to spoil.
Votaries. Persons devoted, promised, consecrated, or engaged by a vow.

Yclept. Named; called.

Zygomatic. Of or pertaining to the zygoma, a bony arch placed in man upon the side of the head, back of the cheeks, and extending from the prominence of the cheeks to the ear.

INDEX.

90 0392194 0